Key Issues in Economics
Introduction to Regional and Urban Policy
in the United Kingdom

Key Issues in Economics

Series editors: Alan Griffiths, Keith Pye and Stuart Wall

Introduction to Regional and Urban Policy in the United Kingdom

Roger Prestwich and Peter Taylor

Longman
London and New York

Longman Group UK Limited,
Longman House, Burnt Mill, Harlow,
Essex CM20 2JE, England
and Associated Companies throughout the world.

*Published in the United States of America
by Longman Inc., New York*

First published 1990

British Library Cataloguing in Publication Data
Prestwich, Roger
   Introduction to regional and urban policy in the
   United Kingdom. – (Key issues in economics).
   1. Great Britain. Regional economic planning
   I. Title   II. Taylor, Peter, 1935–   III. Series
   338.941

   ISBN 0-582-29659-5

Library of Congress Cataloging in Publication Data
Prestwich, Roger, 1942–
   Introduction to urban and regional policy in the United Kingdom
by Roger Prestwich and Peter Taylor.
      p.   cm. – (Key issues in economics)
   Includes index.
   ISBN 0-582-29659-5: £9.95 (est.)
   1. Urban policy – Great Britain.   2. Great Britain – Economic
conditions – Regional disparities.   3. Regional planning – Great
Britain.   I. Taylor, Peter, B. A.   II. Title.   III. Series.
   HT133.P74   1990   89-12280
307.76′0941 – dc20   CIP

Set in Linotron 202 10/11pt Times Roman

Produced by Longman Group (FE) Limited
Printed in Hong Kong

Contents

PART TWO

List of figures

List of tables

Acknowledgements

We are grateful to the following for permission to reproduce copyright figures and tables:

Cambridge Information & Research Services Ltd. for fig. 7.6 (CIRS, 1986) © 1986 Cambridge Information & Research Services Ltd.; Cambridge University Press for fig. 2.4 (Cambridge Modern History Atlas, 1970); Centre for Urban & Regional Development Studies, University of Newcastle upon Tyne for fig. 12.2 (CURBS, 1983); Century Hutchinson Publishing Group Ltd. for table 3.4 (Goldsmith, 1980); Chatto & Windus and The Hogarth Press for fig. 5.1 (Mackintosh, 1968); David & Charles Publishers for figs. 7.1, 7.2, 7.3 & 9.1 (Law, 1980); Department of Trade & Industry for figs. 2.1 & 7.5 (Commission of the European Communities, 1978); Duckworth & Co. Ltd. for table 2.2 (Jones & Pool, 1940); The Ecologist and the author, B Waites for fig. 12.1 (Waites, 1984); Elsevier Science Publishers Ltd. for fig. 7.9 from "Development Agencies and the promotion of rural community development" ed. A. W. Gilg (Hudson & Williams, 1986); Gower Publishing Group Ltd. for table 9.2 (Slowe, 1981); Her Majesty's Stationery Office for figs. 1.1, 4.1, 7.4, 7.8 (C.S.O., 1987a), 8.1, 8.2 (Moore *et al.*, 1986a), 9.2, 9.3 (Department of the Environment, 1986), 10.1 from fig. 2, p. 10 in *Inner City Programmes 1987/88 A Report on Achievement & Development* by Dept. of the Environment (The Planner, June 1987) and tables 4.1 (C.S.O., 1987b), 7.3, 7.5 (Government Expenditure Plans 1987–88 to 1989–90), 8.3, 8.4, 8.5 & 10.1 (Moore *et al.*, 1986b); Longman Group UK Ltd. for an Appendix figure from *Applied Economics* 3rd ed. by Griffiths & Wall, 1989, figs. 2.2, 2.8 & 6.1 (Cook & Stevenson, 1983), tables 3.2 (Cameron, 1980), 8.1 (Prestwich & Griffiths, 1989); Methuen & Co. for figs. 3.1 from a figure on p. 234 of *The Changing Geography of the United Kingdom* by Johnston & Doornkamp 1st ed. 1982 (Cameron, 1980 & Hall *et al.*, 1976) and fig. 6.4 (Keeble, 1976); Royal Institute of British Architects for table 7.4 (RIBA Survey, 1985); Shelter for fig. 5.4 (Shelter, Report No. 1); Times Newspaper Ltd. for fig. 4.2 (The Times, 1985); Town & Country Planning Association for part of table 9.1 from a table in *Town & Country Planning* October, 1985 (Balchin & Bull, 1987); George Weidenfeld & Nicholson Ltd. for tables 3.3 (Briggs, 1983), 8.2 & part of table 9.1 (Lawton, 1982).

Whilst every effort has been made to trace the owners of copyright material, in a few cases this has proved impossible and we take this opportunity to offer our apologies to any copyright holders whose rights we may have unwittingly infringed.

In memory of my parents, EB and WP. Dedicated to LP, ATP and NKP.

Roger Prestwich

To Barbara, Matthew, Andrew, Giles and Jonathan

Peter Taylor

1 Introduction

The march on London of the unemployed from Jarrow (Tyne and Wear) in 1936 dramatically brought to national public and political attention the striking differences in economic well-being between Britain's regions. Since then we have seen over half a century of regional assistance, but we still retain the spatial imbalance of economic wealth and it remains a political issue of note as witnessed by the repeat march in 1986.

Jarrow was a case of localised high unemployment in an *urban* centre but was seen as representative of a *region's* malaise. Any specifically urban aspects of a region's economic difficulties were largely subsumed under the regional heading, and urban problems as such were not really identified until the mid-1960s. These two points raise the major issues that we wish to address in this book: first, that regional and urban problems are highly interrelated, both economically and spatially; and second, that the time periods over which regional and urban policy measures have operated are relatively short. The 'ups' and 'downs' of economic fortune are part of a continuous, long-term process – regional and urban inequalities in wealth have always existed in the past and will almost certainly continue to do so in the future. To these ends, the book is divided into two main parts, Part I being a broad-brush treatment of the nation's economic development, while Part II looks in detail at the regional and urban policy measures adopted by successive governments, and at their effects and effectiveness of such policies.

1.1 Geographical framework

What we need to do at the outset is to clarify what is meant by *region* and *urban*. Regions, when viewed from the 'top' down, are subdivisions of the nation's economic space; but, when viewed from the 'bottom' up, they are aggregations of urban and rural areas. Perhaps the best place to start is at the scale with which people are most familiar, the local scale. People in both urban and rural areas are very aware of their local environment and the differences that are apparent in terms of land use, type of industry or farming and the general landscape. They are also aware of the differences between their own, familiar areas and other less familiar areas some distance away. At the very local scale this means starting with an awareness of the street and neighbourhood, then shifting the awareness outwards to include other neighbourhoods, the town or city centre, the total built-up area and the surrounding rural farmland.

For purposes of comparative study, the socio-economic evaluation of urban centres, towns and cities needs to be more precisely defined in a consistent and geographically meaningful way. The definition of a town or city must include the built-up area, but the question is how far out into the surrounding countryside should the urban boundary be extended? All urban centres have hinterlands containing small towns, villages, hamlets and farms that are dependent upon, and therefore integrated with, the urban centre for such functions as jobs, shopping, entertainment, etc. There is, therefore, considerable logic in extending the area boundary of an urban centre to incorporate its surrounding territory, hence the *urban* or *city region*. Such a functional approach has been developed by the Centre for Urban and Regional Development Studies at Newcastle University. Using areas defined on the basis of 'patterns of commuting mileage to a set of centres which have been identified from employment and retailing statistics' (CURDS, 1983, 1) yields 228 *functional urban regions* containing 95 per cent of Britain's total population. These functional regions can be grouped together ('aggregated') into 20 *metropolitan regions* each with its dominant urban centre. If we add to these the 115 relatively self-contained 'freestanding' *urban regions* we end up with a subdivision of the national economic space into 135 regions (Fig. 12.2). The larger the urban centre, the larger its region which, in turn, will contain smaller centres with their smaller regions, in a hierarchical system of urban regions.

If we extend the scale of knowledge and familiarity that people have about their own urban region, we soon arrive at the *county* level of aggregation. With relatively minor boundary adjustments all the counties could be shown to be collections of contiguous urban regions. Counties have been basic administrative units for centuries, and most people are familiar with their own county and, to a lesser extent, with adjacent counties and those of historical significance in other parts of the country (e.g. Lancashire, Yorkshire, Cornwall, Kent). By aggregating contiguous counties we can then identify sections of the national space which form part of most people's general knowledge about the country as a whole – hence, Lancashire and Cheshire as the North West; Cornwall, Devon, Somerset and Dorset as the South West; Norfolk, Suffolk and Cambridgeshire as East Anglia. Further to these commonly perceived groupings of counties in England are the readily identifiable *countries* of Scotland and Wales and the *province* of Northern Ireland. These combinations of rural and urban areas within their county groupings can be described as 'regions' and indeed were formalised as such into 'Economic Planning Regions' in 1964 (Chapter 7).

Simply defined, a region is a portion of the earth's surface that possesses certain characteristics (physical, economic, political, etc.) which give it a measure of unity and differentiate it from surrounding areas, thus enabling us to draw boundaries around it. Britain's 'regionalising' of counties, while recognising certain economic criteria, has largely followed *administrative convenience*. The validity of current groupings of counties into *Standard Planning Regions* can be debated, and we will return to this point in Chapter 12, but given that they have formed the spatial framework of central government's regional and urban policy for the last quarter-century we will not query their value at this stage. Suffice it to say that these regions are *not* absolute, and neither are those of any sub-regional division. In fact, there

ELECTRICITY BOARD REGIONS

REGIONAL HEALTH AUTHORITY AREAS

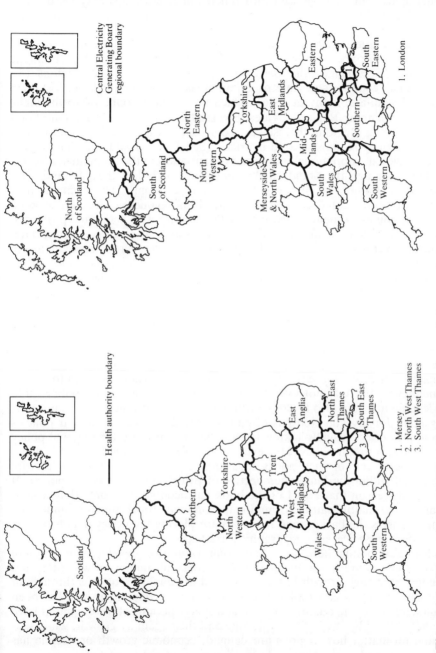

Figure 1.1 Regional boundaries vary with function and do not always coincide with county boundaries.
Source: Central Statistical Office (1987a, 158)

3

of any sub-regional division. In fact, there are numerous ways in which national space can be organised into functional regions – simply choose the desired criterion and draw the boundaries accordingly, e.g. health, gas, electricity, post office, water (Fig. 1.1).

The most crucial feature of the Standard Planning Regions and sub-regions is that they are now the units of classification for many official government statistics. In England, the basic area units are the 46 sub-regions (39 'traditional' counties and 7 metropolitan areas – although the latter lost their financial semi-autonomy in 1986), which are in turn grouped into the eight Standard Planning Regions. Wales, Scotland and Northern Ireland are Standard Planning Regions themselves, comprising respectively 8 counties, 12 local authority regions and 26 districts. (See Fig. 7.4 and the chart of the UK's regional, subregional and urban organisation in the Appendix.) Nevertheless, although the Standard Planning Regions reflect the past and form the spatial framework of present and future economic development, they have not been treated as such by political and economic decision makers. When it comes to identifying areas of the country with economic problems, and to providing them with whatever assistance is deemed appropriate, central government has invariably opted for the bureaucratic convenience of *established administrative districts*. Consequently, regional and urban problems have been treated separately despite their interrelatedness.

1.2 Time framework

Regional and urban problems cannot be considered in isolation from the longer-term economic development of the nation. There is an unfortunate tendency in the UK not only to examine regional and urban policy quite independently, but also to do so within a very limited time-frame. The starting point for investigation has often been the date when particular policies came into effect, usually taking 1934 as the starting date for regional policy and 1946 for urban policy. However, in order to understand fully the 'whys' and 'wherefores' of such policy measures, it is essential that they are appreciated within the longer perspective of British economic development. It is for this reason that Part I of the book has been written, providing a summary of the major features of national economic growth since pre-industrial times. This is the background necessary for placing the policy details of Part II in their historical and geographical contexts.

The key points here are: first, that economic development has *not* proceeded smoothly for the nation at a constant annual growth rate; and second, that such growth has *not* occurred in equal proportions throughout the nation and its geographical regions. In fact, economic growth has been characterised by inequalities of time and space: periods of development have been followed by stagnation or decline and then again by growth; while spatially, no matter how regions are defined, economic growth or decline has never occurred at the same rate in all regions at the same time.

Economic growth as we know it in the UK is directly associated with the process of industrialisation. Consequently, the nation's economic history is usually conveniently subdivided into major economic or political periods associated with that process – hence, the pre-industrial period up to about 1780; the 'Industrial Revolution' from 1780 to 1840; the railway era, from 1840 to 1914–18; the inter-war period from 1914–18 to 1939–45, and the post-war period since 1945 (perhaps a pre-OPEC period to 1973, the year of oil price rises, after which came a post-OPEC period of unknown length). Within each of these periods there have been times of rapid growth and of slump or recession, each with particular spatial implications. A key question is whether any *longer-term economic* patterns can be discerned over the last 200 years of industrial development.

In 1981, Peter Hall, an urban geographer, published a paper in which he suggested that economists and geographers, and indeed politicians, should look again at the idea that economic development since the onset of industrialisation has been characterised by a series of *Long Waves* or cycles, each associated with major *technological advances*. These Long Waves, each of about fifty years' duration, are named after Nikolai Kondratieff, a Soviet professor of economics writing in the 1920s. (Since he did not forecast the total collapse of the capitalist system, Kondratieff was imprisoned in 1931 in the Gulag Archipelago, where he later died in solitary confinement. His name and reputation were 'rehabilitated by the Soviet authorities early in 1988.) Although forming part of Marxist-Leninist economics literature since then, Kondratieff's Long Waves were given more prominence after they appeared in the translation of Mandel's book *Late Capitalism* (1975, 108–46).

Each Long Wave of capitalist economic development is supposedly associated with a sudden increase of investment in new industrial technology, which is followed by increased profit, employment and general prosperity. (The emphasis on innovative technological clusters in particular time periods, and their catalytic impact on economic growth, is also central to Schumpeter's discussion of Long Waves or cycles (1939).) After twenty or thirty years, however, as the market becomes saturated, growth slackens, profits fall, as does investment, and unemployment rises – in other words, we have a recession. Labour is laid off, and the profits that are still attainable are channelled into *new* technological developments which, once in place, start the next wave of growth in motion. At any point in time, therefore, the economic geography of the nation will display evidence in the landscape of all *preceding* waves (old mining areas, settlement patterns, transport types, industrial plants), some of which will have retained their importance while others will have become obsolete. (See Damesick, 1987; Johnston and Doornkamp, 1982.)

From a geographical standpoint, of course, some parts of the country will have locational advantages over others for industry, settlement and transport, so that they will enjoy the benefits of the investment and growth – but not for ever! Some cities and some regions will experience boom conditions in one Long Wave, or perhaps even in two or three consecutively, but it would seem unlikely that any one place could be constantly at 'centre-stage' in every growth period (although capital cities and/or centres containing business headquarters might be in with a chance!).

There is considerable dispute over the historical and economic validity of the Kondratieff model of Long Waves in economic growth (Rosenberg and Frischtak, 1983), but the model docs provide us with a time framework into which we can readily fit Britain's economic development. It also provides us with a set of mainly *economic* criteria for determining significant time slots, rather than those derived primarily from political history. The Long Waves are not smooth curves, however, since there is an uneven pattern of 'upswings' and 'downswings' and there are sharp temporary reversals of trend within each swing. What Kondratieff was able to identify was a series of erratic Long Waves in the movement of price levels, interest rates and money wages from about 1790 onwards. The key to understanding these Long Waves lies in the relative shortage or abundance of basic commodities (raw materials and fuels). Each Long Wave begins with increased investment in production on the basis of *new technology*, followed by an absolute or relative decline in the prices of basic commodities. Both factors contribute to the *upswing*. This is succeeded by the *downswing*, a period of relatively

Table 1.1 Kondratieff's Long Waves of economic development in the United Kingdom

Long Wave	Upswings/ Downswings		Characteristics
First: 1781–1841	Up	1781–1823	Expansive, rising rate of profit; spread of steam power in production
	Down	1824–41	Slackening, stagnant rate of profit; growth of towns on coalfields and other power sources
Second: 1842–94	Up	1842–73	Expansive profit; steam engine is dominant source of power *First technological revolution*
	Down	1843–94	Slackening profit; development of industrial cities
Third: 1895–1939	Up	1895–1913	Expansive profit; development of consumer-based industries *Second technological revolution*
	Down	1914–39	Slackening profit; footloose industry moving away from coalfields, beginnings of suburbanisation of industry and housing
Fourth: 1940–95?	Up	1940–66	Expansive profit; maturity of consumer-based industries *Third technological revolution*
	Down	1967–95?	Slackening profit; growth of service economy, large scale suburbanisation of industry

Sources: Derived from Mandel (1975, 130–2) and Short (1984, 103); (see also Marshall (1987, 99)).

high prices for commodities during which time there is a 'shift in the direction of investment toward the expansion of supplies of (or substitutes for) the commodities in short supply' (Rostow, 1983). How do these Long Wave 'upswings' and 'downswings' fit the economic development of the UK? Following Mandel and Hall, we can extend the Kondratieff Long Waves from 1781 to 1995, as outlined in Table 1.1.

In summary, the *First Wave* (1781–1841) covered the so-called 'Industrial Revolution', which saw Britain transformed from an agricultural country to a largely industrial one. It was characterised by investments in water and steam power, in large-scale iron smelting using coal, in textile manufacturing, and in transport by turnpike road and canal. In spatial terms, the areas having locational advantages, and therefore seeing the greatest urban and industrial expansion, were the exposed coalfields and the flanks of the southern Pennines. The *Second Wave* (1842–94) was a period of industrial maturity and consolidation based on steel, coal and the railways at home, and the raw materials and markets of the colonies overseas. The urban and regional 'boom areas' continued to be the coalfields along the upland fringes of the North and West. The *Third Wave* (1895–1939) saw the beginnings of a shift in spatial emphasis to the Midlands and the South East as industrial investment moved into vehicles, chemicals and the new, more mobile, power sources of electricity and oil.

The *Fourth Wave* (1940–95?) was forecast by Kondratieff on the basis of preceding Long Waves and this has been subsequently modified by other writers (although Rostow (1983) argues that globally we have been in the Fifth Wave 'upswing' since 1972). The key developments in the current Long Wave have been investment in aerospace, electronics and motorways, accompanied by yet greater concentration of growth in the South. Meanwhile, the North has struggled to adjust to the decline of its traditional industries, with the associated high unemployment, to the loss of the Empire and markets and, since the early 1970s, to the higher prices for basic commodities (especially fuel). So, as we live through the 'downswing' in the second half of the Fourth Wave, investment is shifting into the new technologies of micro-electronics, robotics, biotechnology, and so on. If the Kondratieff model has any validity, this should mean a *Fifth Wave* 'upswing' of twenty or so years, starting in the mid-1990s, as industrial production based on the new technology grows, probably with its spatial emphasis still in southern Britain, until about 2020 when we will enter another 'downswing', yet again ushering in painful human and regional adjustments. (See Hall and Preston, 1988.)

1.3 Organisation of this book

What we will endeavour to do in this book, therefore, is to review the economic history of the UK from the three major viewpoints of *place of work*, *home* and *leisure*, within the set of time-frames offered by Kondratieff Long Waves. To this end, we have reorganised the basic statistical information about the country's population characteristics into the Long Wave model periods and at each stage we have sought to place the principal features of economic development in their spatial framework. So, the three chapters of Part I should provide a background survey of the geography of Britain's economic development appropriate to an understanding of the detailed policy presentations of Part II. The broad-brush approach of Part I thus gives way to a much finer level of detail in Part II, which concentrates on the time period from the Third Wave 'downswing' onwards. Our underlying concern here is with the *spatial* aspects of disequilibrium, i.e. with the unequal impacts of national economic change on regional and urban development, and with government policy responses to this. Consequently, in terms of *practical policy* the emphasis has to shift from the Long Waves of fifty-year durations to the short-run periodic interplay of economic forces and changing government parties and policies.

The increasing role of the State in the economy at national, regional and urban levels has been a characteristic feature of Kondratieff's Third and Fourth Waves, particularly during and following the depression of the 1930s. Increased intervention came about largely as a result of central government beginning to appreciate the *political* significance of the distress caused by *geographical* disequilibrium, itself the result of *economic* forces being left unchecked. Part II of this book therefore starts by briefly surveying the theoretical bases for regional and urban policy making at government level. This is followed by two chapters on policy responses to socio-economic stimuli, covering the periods from the late nineteenth century up to 1963, and from 1964 to the present time. The reason for the break at 1963/4 is simply because it marked a major change in government policy as the Labour Party came to power after 15 years of Conservative rule. The *measureable effects* of government regional and urban policies are then covered in Chapters 8 and 9, followed by an evaluation of the *effectiveness* of policies to date in Chapter 10. We conclude by noting the spatial and labour impacts of emerging technologies and by suggesting some modifications to the geographical framework of regional and urban policy administration as we move towards the Fifth Long Wave of economic development in the United Kingdom.

PART I

PART I

2 Place of work

This chapter seeks to identify the why, when and where of employment in the United Kingdom: *why* the occupational structure of the nation developed the way that it did; *when* major changes in the long-term economic development occurred; and *where* in the country particular occupations became established. The pattern of where people work today, whether in fields, mines, factories, offices or shops, reflects both the structural and locational processes that have been operating since before the Industrial Revolution. In order to understand these processes we must delve, if relatively briefly, into Britain's economic history.

The single most significant influence on the location of jobs, and consequently of population concentrations, has been the *resource base* of the country. Ever since people first moved into these islands they have gravitated in the greatest numbers towards those locations particularly favoured in terms of the resources economically in demand and technologically available at the time. As time passed, technological developments meant that the *occupational structure* of the population changed as did the *locations* of people and their places of work, especially when new technology demanded new resources. After all, resources, be they good soils, forests, fuels or metals, are not distributed evenly throughout the national territory, but neither are they distributed randomly, in a totally haphazard manner. There is some order to the pattern, in the sense that a knowledge of the geographical character of the nation would reveal some natural logic in the arrangement of *better soils* in the lowlands to the south and east of a line drawn from the mouth of the Humber to that of the Exe. Again, *metals* like copper, gold, lead and tin are found in the uplands to the north and west and *coalfields* outcrop around the fringes of the upland areas (Fig. 2.1). This rather simplistic subdivision of the United Kingdom into two major physical regions is basic to an understanding of the general agricultural, industrial, urban and regional development of the country. What follows below is an outline of the changing occupational structure of Britain and its spatial connotations, from the pre-industrial era through the Kondratieff Long Waves of the industrialisation period up to what has been termed 'the post-industrial era' of the present time.

2.1 Pre-industrial to 1781

To set the scene for the changes wrought by the process of industrialisation it is necessary to determine the occupational structure and the locational distribution of employment on the eve of the Industrial Revolution. Unfortunately, statistics of the characteristics of the country's population have only

**Figure 2.1   United Kingdom: upland North and lowland South, using
the Humber–Exe line as a dividing boundary of convenience.**
Source: After Commission of the European Communities
(1978, 61)

© Crown copyright   Areas over 200 metres above sea level

Figure 2.2   The pyramid of English society 1688 (figures in thousands).
Source: Cook and Stevenson (1983, 144)

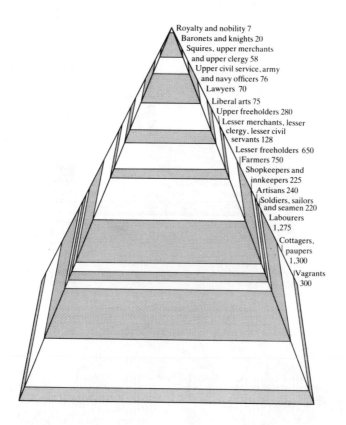

Royalty and nobility 7
Baronets and knights 20
Squires, upper merchants
  and upper clergy 58
Upper civil service, army
  and navy officers 76
Lawyers 70
Liberal arts 75
Upper freeholders 280
Lesser merchants, lesser
  clergy, lesser civil
  servants 128
Lesser freeholders 650
Farmers 750
Shopkeepers and
  innkeepers 225
Artisans 240
Soldiers, sailors
  and seamen 220
Labourers
  1,275
Cottagers,
  paupers
  1,300
Vagrants
  300

been collected systematically since 1801, and not reliably so until the census
of 1841. So, prior to 1800 any figures are estimates and we cannot vouch
for their accuracy, but they do give us some idea about the structure and
pattern of population.

Figure 2.2 is just such an estimate of the social and occupational character
of the population of England in 1688 and the map (Fig. 2.3) presents its
total distribution on a county basis in 1700. In order to provide some com-
parability between periods, it is necessary to regroup the statistics presented
in Fig. 2.2 into the standard occupational classes of primary, secondary, tertiary and quaternary (see Fig. 2.10). Although the figures refer, strictly
speaking, to social divisions, they can be viewed as representative of the
occupational breakdown and as such yield a structure similar to that of pre-
industrial societies today – hence 70 per cent were employed in primary
activities, just 4 per cent in secondary, 14 per cent in tertiary, 7 per cent in
quaternary (4 per cent in the armed forces) and 5 per cent (at least) were
unemployed (vagrants!).

About two-thirds or even three-quarters of the secondary, tertiary and
quaternary groups, together with most of the vagrants, were town dwellers,

13

Figure 2.3   United Kingdom: county population densities in 1700

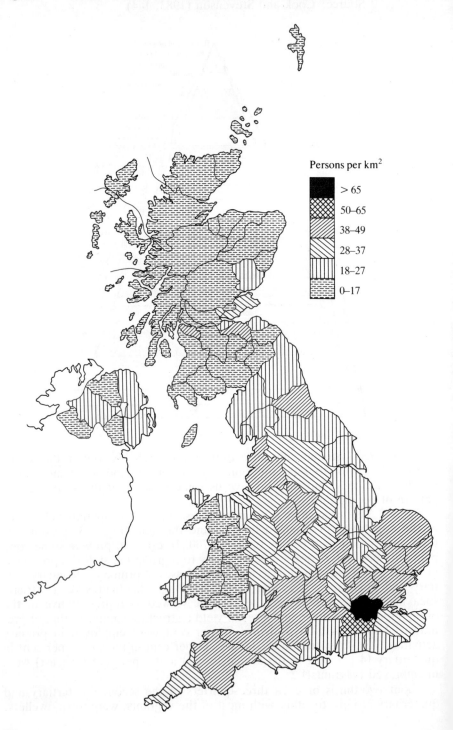

Persons per km²

> 65

50–65

38–49

28–37

18–27

0–17

as indeed were some of those in the primary group. However, a large majority of the latter lived and worked in the rural areas, and their predominant numbers meant that 72.5 per cent of England's population could be classified as rural and 27.5 per cent as urban, proportions that would probably also hold true for Scotland and Wales (Dury, 1961, 68). Of those in primary occupations a few thousand gained a livelihood as river or inshore fishermen and smaller numbers worked as foresters and miners, but agriculture dominated the economy. The physique and climate of upland Britain had offered little agricultural potential to the forebears of seventeenth-century farmers, so it is not surprising to see the highest population densities in 1700 on the better soils of the drier eastern and southern counties. Figure 2.3 shows this 'belt' of higher population density stretching from East Anglia to the South West, with the peak being reached in Middlesex.

Although not contributing greatly to the population densities of the counties in which they were located, miners were employed in the iron-stone workings of the Weald of Sussex and Kent, the Forest of Dean (Gloucestershire) and the iron ore workings of the Cleveland Hills (north Yorkshire). Miners were also employed in *non-ferrous metal* mining in the uplands of Britain – lead and silver in the Pennines of Derbyshire, Yorkshire and Durham, in Cumberland and in North and South Wales, tin in Cornwall, and copper in Devonshire, Cumberland and Wales. More important in terms of the numbers employed was *coal* mining around the flanks of the upland areas, mainly in the valley of the River Tyne (390,000 t shipped to London in 1680), south Nottinghamshire, the West Riding of Yorkshire, South Wales, and around the Forth estuary, especially Fifeshire, in Central Scotland. The industry was very rural, however, with many of the miners farming the land during planting, tending and harvesting times.

Also on the edge of the Pennines was the working of clay for pottery making, particularly in north Staffordshire, which had the advantage of coal for fuel and lead for glazing nearby. Potteries were otherwise urban-orientated, using local materials (clay and timber), with sizeable factories in Lambeth, Chelsea, Bristol, Worcester, Liverpool and other towns. Other mining and quarrying activities principally involved the extraction of building materials like clay and stone, which were generally worked as close to the point of consumption as possible in order to minimise transportation costs.

The true number of people engaged in the mining industry at the end of the seventeenth century is difficult to gauge, and it is equally difficult to ascertain the proportions of people truly rural and those truly urban. This is also the case with the *manufacturing* industries, since not all were necessarily located in towns, as we have seen with respect to potteries. Indeed, although the manufacturing of food, drink, clothing, household furnishings and some building materials took place in all towns according to the size of their population, the production of textiles was largely a rural household occupation. The textile industry was located with respect to its raw material – sheep. The result was a woollen cloth industry which had identifiable regions, each specialising in particular cloth types: broad-cloths (fine woollens) in Wiltshire, Gloucestershire and west Somerset: worsteds in East Anglia, the West Country and west Yorkshire; medium woollens in west Yorkshire and south-east Lancashire, and coarse woollens (low-grade cloth) in west Yorkshire (around Leeds), Merionethshire and Carmarthenshire in

15

Figure 2.4   England, Wales and southern Scotland: some economic distributions in the eighteenth century.
Source: Cambridge Modern History Atlas (CUP 1970, 97)

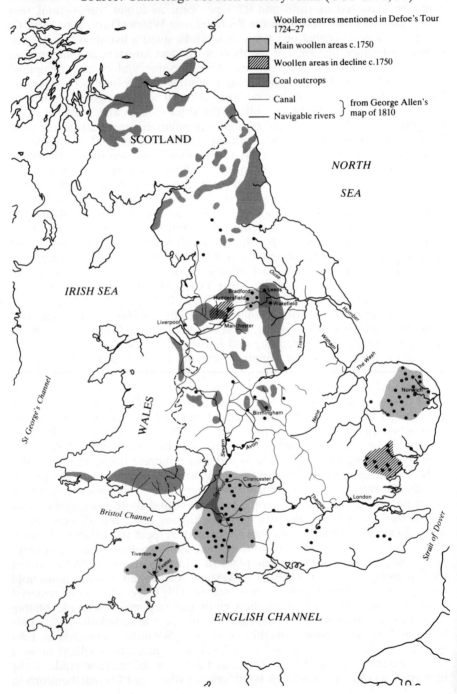

Wales, and several towns in Scotland, among them Dundee, Alloa, Kilmarnock, Galashiels and Hawick. The woollen industry accounted for about one-third of Britain's industrial output in the mid-eighteenth century.

Almost all the textile workers were handloom weavers working at home on their smallholdings or in small villages, so that, as with the miners, they could be classified as rural dwellers. Yet towns of an industrial rather than a rural-market character were developing by 1700. London, with a population of half a million, was the primate city, with functions not only of government but also of manufacturing (especially shipbuilding, naval stores and clothing) and trading. The occupational structure of the capital ranged through the secondary, tertiary and quaternary sectors, with wholesale/retail trades and house-servants particularly well represented. Towns with populations of over 10,000 included regional market towns like Norwich (35,000), Brecon, York and Edinburgh, ports like Yarmouth, Colchester, Bristol (35,000) and Exeter, and growing manufacturing centres like Birmingham (15,000), Manchester (10,000), Newcastle and Glasgow. But these urban centres only contained one in four of the nation's population (9 million in 1700) so that Britain was still predominantly a rural, agricultural society, even if fair numbers of farmers were part-time miners and textile workers. The occupational structure and the spatial distribution of the country's population were about to shift, however, from agricultural pursuits in lowland Britain to manufacturing pursuits in upland Britain.

The precise figures are difficult to determine, but there is no doubt that agricultural enclosure in the eighteenth century caused hardship to cottagers, smallholders and squatters, thousands of whom became landless farm labourers if they were fortunate, paupers or vagrants if they were not so fortunate. Rural society was divided into farmers and labourers and the proportion of the workforce directly involved in agriculture declined during the course of the century, probably to about 50 per cent by 1750. To survive, the unemployed and underemployed landless labourers had three choices: either to eke out an existence on marginal land and hope for some work during harvest-time; or to go as domestic servants in the 'big' country houses; or to migrate, either to the newly industrialising towns or overseas to the colonies. Internal migration was over relatively short distances owing to the difficulties and expense of travel. As a result, London drew mainly from the home counties and East Anglia, the East Midlands from the western part of East Anglia, and the West Midlands from the Welsh border counties. Similarly, South Wales drew mainly from western and central Wales and the West Country, Lancashire from North Wales and Cumbria, West Yorkshire from Lincolnshire and Humberside, Newcastle from Northumberland, Cumbria and North Yorkshire, and Glasgow, Edinburgh and Fife from the Southern Uplands and the Highlands. This shift in the spatial emphasis of Britain's population, which, in the main, was reflecting hoped-for employment opportunities, is discernible in Fig. 2.5. The labouring class, created by enclosure, was rearranging itself *locationally* by moving from rural to urban areas and *occupationally* by becoming labourers in the homes of the wealthy, in industry and in shops instead of in the fields.

Figure 2.5 United Kingdom: county population densities in 1780

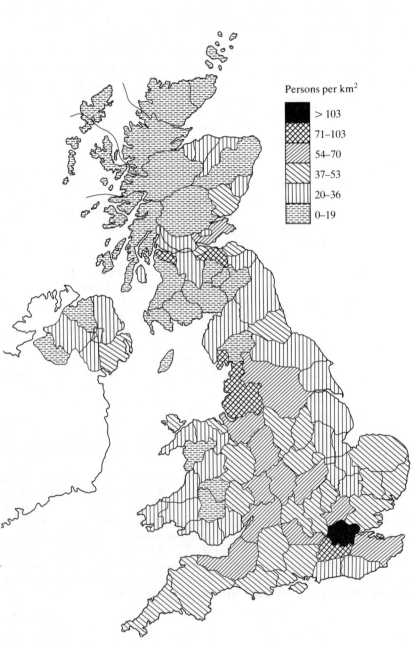

Persons per km²

> 103

71–103

54–70

37–53

20–36

0–19

2.2   1781–1841: iron, coal, textiles and canals

The chief characteristics of the *First* Kondratieff Long Wave were new investments in the production technology that enabled iron ore to be smelted with coal on a large scale, and in the water- and steam-powered machinery that caused textile manufacturing to move from home to factory. Other new investments included the canals and turnpike roads that improved the efficiency of transportation. The centralisation process quickened, with industry and people increasingly concentrated in London and in towns around the fringes of upland Britain.

The occupational structure of the country at the end of the eighteenth century showed a marked contrast with that of a hundred years previously – 30 per cent were employed in primary activities, 30 per cent in secondary, 20 per cent in tertiary, 9 per cent in quaternary (6 per cent in the armed forces) and 11 per cent were classified as paupers and vagrants (Fig. 2.10). The spatial concentration of the agricultural workforce in the better farming areas of eastern and southern Britain remained throughout the nineteenth century (and remains even up to the present day), but the number and proportion of people employed on farms declined continuously (this decline was especially intense during the major periods of enclosure: 1760–80 and 1793–1815). This is reflected in the occupational structure of the working population of Britain at the end of the First Kondratieff Wave, when primary activities had declined to about 24 per cent (20 per cent in agriculture), whereas secondary had increased to over 33 per cent, tertiary to almost 24 per cent while quaternary held at 9 per cent and 9 per cent were unemployed (Fig. 2.10). With many of the secondary, tertiary and quarternary occupations town-based, it is not surprising that by the census of 1841, 46 per cent of Britains's population could be classified as urban, compared with the 30 per cent so classed in 1790.

Many of the mining and manufacturing communities were still rural-based, however, and did not yet possess the service functions and other characteristics of urban centres. Such was the case in the metal and coal mining areas of upland Britain. Between 1785 and 1842 tin and copper mining in Cornwall and Devon expanded rapidly, output of tin metal rose from around 2,500 t in 1800 to around 5,000 t in 1840, and copper metal from 5,000 t to 11,500 t over the same period. Given the demand factor, much of the increase in output can be attributed to the improvements in 1765 by Watt to Newcomen's steam pump for draining mines, which enabled miners to go deeper. Also, the improved efficiency reduced coal requirements per horse power per hour from 11.4 kg to 4.5 kg and increased mine profitability. New copper mines were opened (e.g. Parys Mountain in Anglesey in the 1780s) and lead production increased from mines in the north Pennines, Derbyshire, North Wales and Somerset. Iron ore output grew rapidly after Neilson's hot blast technique for smelting iron was patented in 1828. This enabled the Black Band (Carboniferous) iron-stones of Central Scotland, Sheffield and the Midlands to be used, and the haematites from Furness and Cumberland, a development reflected in the growth of pig-iron output from 70,000 t in 1788 to 1,400,000 t by 1840. Throughout the eighteenth century Darby's technical breakthrough (1709), which enabled coke to be used instead of charcoal for the smelting of iron ore, had meant that the iron

Table 2.1 Mills versus cottages: cotton textile employees in England and Wales, 1805–45

Year	Mill workers	Handloom weavers
1805	90,000	184,000
1810	100,000	200,000
1815	114,000	220,000
1820	126,000	240,000
1825	175,000	240,000
1830	185,000	240,000
1835	220,000	188,000
1840	262,000	123,000
1845	273,000	60,000

Source: Cook and Stevenson (1983, 42)

industry was increasingly attracted to coalfield sites, and by 1800 the Weald and Forest of Dean had almost disappeared as iron producers of any significance.

Once steam engines had been modified by Watt to drive machinery, their popularity among manufacturers increased and coal became the 'power king'. The output of coal increased dramatically from about 5 million t in 1765 to almost 40 million t by 1840. Boulton and Watt's steam engine factory in Birmingham installed 178 engines in England between 1775 and 1800 (Cook and Stevenson, 1983, 38) and apart from the 21 in Cornish tin mines all the rest were around the fringes of the uplands where they were in direct competition with water power. Lancashire in particular, with 54 engines, dominated, reflecting the speed with which cotton textile manufacturing was being concentrated in mills, whether water-powered in the Pennine valleys or steam-powered on or near the coalfields. Manchester, for example, had just two mills in 1780 but by 1821 had 66 employing 30 per cent of the city's workforce. This is not to imply, however, that people were deserting their villages in droves and moving to towns to work in the mills. Indeed, the number of handloom weavers initially increased as rapidly as workers in mills, as Table 2.1 shows.

Gradually, however, the competitive edge of the mills made itself felt and the domestic side of the cotton industry was soon to disappear. The same was true of water power in its competition with steam power. By the mid-1830s there were over 2,000 steam engines in operation, most of them in the textile industry (supplying 80 per cent of cotton's power in Lancashire and 75 per cent of woollen's power in the West Riding of Yorkshire) but also in the iron industry, mines, potteries and other types of factories. Water power was set to follow horse power into obsolescence as steam engines demonstrated their superiority in industrial applications.

Given the advantages to manufacturer of applying inanimate power to the production process, and the profitability of steam over water power, the concentration of industry on or near the source of power – coal – was inevitable. Moving the coal to the steam engine, however, was expensive, with a journey by horse and cart or pack-horse over 5 km doubling the pit-head price. Movement by water was much cheaper, but navigable rivers around the upland edges and in the coalfields were few. The answer was to build canals,

Figure 2.6   Great Britain: the First Kondratieff Wave (1781–1841), annual rate of population change per county.

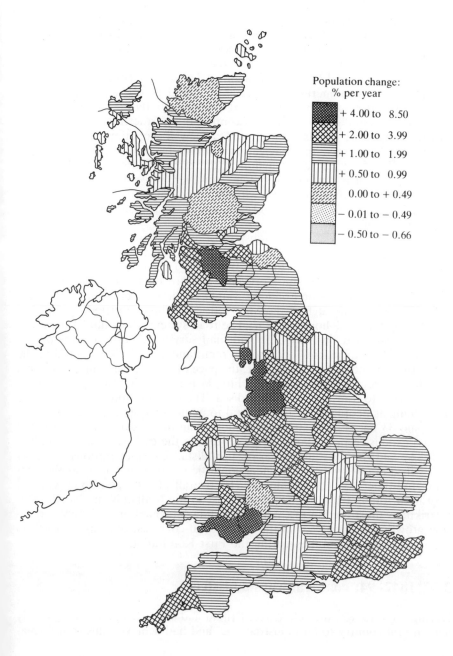

and the first, which opened in 1761 and was financed by the Duke of Bridgewater, linked the coal mines of Worsley with Manchester. The cost of coal transport was reduced by half, and the canal was extended to Runcorn by 1767.

Ten years later the Grand Trunk Canal was opened, connecting the Mersey with the Trent via the Cheshire salt-mining area and the Staffordshire potteries. The 1790s were the peak years for canal building and a network gradually emerged, so that by the early nineteenth century the claim could be made that south of Durham no place was more than 24 km from water transport of some kind. By 1830, in addition to the 1290 km of navigable rivers there were about 3200 km of canal and over 2090 km of improved rivers in England and Wales, plus another 322 km in Scotland. The cost of transporting coal, minerals, grain, manufactured goods, and even people, overland was dramatically reduced and thus contributed to the prosperity of the growing manufacturing towns of central and northern Britain. The construction phase of canals also created a 'new' occupational class of civil engineering labourers, the 'navigators' (navvies) whose experience was to prove invaluable in the construction of the railways after 1830. The canal network was not a continuous system, however, since it had been built in fits and starts by different people with different standards, so that there was no uniformity of width, depth and lock design, with resultant difficulties of interregional shipments.

While the capacity for cheap transport of bulky commodities was provided by canals, speed of conveyance was provided by coach and horses on a steadily improving turnpike (toll road) system. This owed much to the skills of Metcalf in Lancashire and Yorkshire, Telford on the London/Holyhead road and Macadam on the London turnpikes. The London–Manchester run, which had taken about four days in 1760, could be completed by the mail coach in less than 18 hours in 1837. The road system which linked the growing towns speeded up passenger and mail service, thereby improving the efficiency of order placing and money remittances, and also ushered in the era of the commercial traveller. But, the pace of change was still quickening, and the last decade of Kondratieff's First Wave witnessed the application of steam power to transport on land and sea. The urbanisation process was also quickening as people moved from rural to manufacturing areas seeking jobs that paid 33 per cent to 50 per cent more than in agriculture. This was not a mass exodus from the countryside (except in the case of Ireland's famines of 1782/3 and 1821/3), but a series of short distance step-migrations or simply reclassification of split-time farmers/domestic weavers or miners as they became full-time weavers or miners. The overall effect was a long wave of migration rolling from the South and East to the Midlands and North. This is strikingly illustrated in Fig. 2.6, which shows stagnant or very slow population growth rates per year in the agricultural counties, but rapid growth in the industrialising counties during the First Kondratieff.

2.3 1842–94: coal, railways and steel

During the First Kondratieff Wave, Britain had been changed from a largely agricultural country to an industrial one, and had achieved this transformation ahead of any other nation. The *Second* Kondratieff Wave saw Britain consolidate both its industrial and imperial pre-eminence, although the former supremacy began to succumb to foreign competition by the late 1870s. Domestically, economic growth continued to be spatially well-defined. The coalfield towns around the fringes of the Pennines experienced their most rapid growth during this period, and Central Scotland, South Wales, the Midlands and London also underwent rapid urban growth. About half the population of England and Wales were urban dwellers in 1842 and this proportion had exceeded 70 per cent by 1881. Enclosure of agricultural land, which mainly affected the better farming areas of lowland Britain, was effectively completed by the mid-nineteenth century.

Although enclosure could lead to more jobs on the land, the yeoman farmer who was forced to sell his small farm and become a landless labourer often chose to migrate either to the industrial towns or overseas. The Irish, forced to flee from another potato famine in the 1840s, had the same options, and many chose to move to Glasgow, Liverpool and Manchester, thus swelling their populations. These industrial 'boom towns' were death-traps, however, with mortality rates as high as 1 in 50 and infant mortality (under one year old) of 500 per 1000, figures not dissimilar from some less developed countries today. Birth rates remained high, nevertheless, so that population grew by 11–14 per cent per decade, but emigration meant that Britain suffered (or benefited) from a net loss of over one million people during the nineteenth century. Between 1840 and 1890, 9.6 million people emigrated from the UK, of whom 5.8 million went to the USA – 3.2 million from Ireland and 2.6 million from Great Britain.

Migration to town or port was increasingly facilitated by the mode of transport that dominated the Second Wave of Kondratieff – the railway. Coupling the railway to the coal industry meant that coal could be transported relatively cheaply over considerable distances at speeds and in quantities far in excess of those offered by the canal barges. In turn, this meant that steam engines could be used over a wider area and utilised in almost all branches of industry, including agriculture, especially after the compound engine was introduced in 1865. This engine reduced the amount of coal needed to raise 1 hp/hour from 4.5 kg to 1.1 kg and the amount was reduced again to 0.5 kg in 1884 with Parson's turbine. The combination of railway, steam engine and coal affected the demand for iron and steel (after 1856), which in turn facilitated further developments of the three major industrial sectors – coal, steel and engineering.

After the Stockton and Darlington railway was opened in 1825, and Stephenson's 'Rocket' won the Rainhill trials in 1829, the railway network began to expand, and by the beginning of the Second Kondratieff Wave Some 3220 km of track had been laid. By 1850 over 10,460 km were open, by 1860 over 14,500 km, by 1870 over 21,720 km and by the end of the century over 29,000 km. The building of this system was herculean in proportion, especially in terms of the number of 'navvies' employed, the kilometres of iron (weighing 400,000 t in 1847 alone), and later steel, track laid, the millions of bricks used in tunnels and cuttings, the cubic kilometres of earth moved, and so on. Its pattern, as with that of the canals, focused principally on the northern industrial towns with linkages to the capital and to ports. Some 'new' towns were developed as centres of railway engineering, e.g.

Crewe, Swindon, Derby. Steam power was also applied to coastal and ocean-going shipping, which was a significant development not only because of the dramatic increase in employment in shipbuilding that it brought about in Scotland, the North East and the North West, but also because the ships increased the possibilities of importing raw materials at prices competitive with those produced domestically.

Iron was essential to virtually all industries and it is not without reason that a large iron and steel capacity is often seen as the hallmark of a nation's economic power. The ore was still found in adequate quantities in upland Britain in 1850, when 9.6 million t were produced from the haematites of Furness, Cumberland and Glamorgan and the iron-stones of Lanarkshire, the Cleveland Hills, the Sheffield area and the West Midlands. However, the 11,000 t imported in 1850, mainly from Spain, were a portend of change. By 1875 domestic production had increased to 16 million t and imports had risen to 0.5 million t, but in 1900, while domestic output had slipped to 14 million t, imports had climbed to 6 million t. These figures are reflected in pig-iron production, which rose from 2 million t in 1850 (with iron exports of 142,000 t) to 9 million t in 1900 (iron exports of 1.2 million t).

Refining the iron to make steel was expensive until Bessemer introduced his converter in 1856, which reduced steel prices by 80 per cent thanks to fuel savings. Further developments followed, with Siemens' open-hearth in 1869 and the Thomas-Gilchrist process for using phosphoric ores in 1879. Cheapness and quantity meant that the superior tensile strength of steel over iron could be exploited in a vast range of uses, and production grew rapidly from just 300,000 t in 1870 to 5 million t by 1900 (20 per cent of which was exported).

In shipbuilding especially, the effect was dramatic: more sailing ships were still being built in 1850 than iron-clad steamers, but after steel-plate became available in 1870 the transformation of the industry was such that by 1890 9 out of every 10 ships registered at Lloyd's were made of steel. This meant the decline of wooden shipbuilding on the Thames, Solent and Severn and its concentration in those areas with the advantage of proximity to the steel suppliers – Clydeside, Tyneside, Furness and Merseyside.

The non-ferrous mining industry was contributing to the industrial growth of the 1841–94 period, but at a declining rate after 1850. Production of tin and copper in Devon and Cornwall peaked in 1850, with 10,300 t of tin ore and 150,000 t of copper ore, most of which was shipped to the Midlands and South Wales where the metal industries were growing, but by 1900 tin ore production had fallen to 6,800 t and copper ore production had collapsed to a mere 5,000 t. There were other producing areas, like the copper mines of Parys Mountain in Anglesey, but by 1900 output had declined to such an extent that *net* ore and metal imports of 15,000 t of tin and 220,000 t of copper were necessary for domestic demand. Similarly, lead mining in the Pennines peaked at 65,000 t of metal in 1850 and had decreased to 24,000 t by 1900, while net imports had climbed to over 50,000 t even by 1875. Most of these mining sites were in relatively isolated upland areas and operated on a small scale in difficult conditions, so that, as the better ores were worked out and high grade foreign ores could be imported cheaply into the metal-working districts, the domestic miners were unable to compete. By the 1890s, therefore, these areas were beginning to experience depopulation as miners moved to find work in the towns or emigrated to the Americas, Australia or South Africa.

Alternatively, some metal miners undoubtedly transferred their skills to the coalfields, which were not far distant from their home areas and offered growing employment possibilities as production expanded. There were about 175,000 miners producing 44 million t of coal in 1846; by 1891 there were 517,000 miners producing 185 million t (15 per cent of which was exported). Thanks to Davy's safety lamp and application of the steam engine to winding and ventilation, mines had gone into areas previously inaccessible because of gas and had driven deeper than ever before – from 425 m maximum in 1840 to·880 m by 1890. The main coal-producing areas were the Northumberland and Durham field, followed by Lancashire, South Wales and Yorkshire, areas of increasing population concentration. The iron industry stayed tied to coal production in the 1840–60 period in South Wales, Staffordshire and Scotland. After 1860 the spatial emphasis of steel manufacturing shifted, following the introduction of the Bessemer converter and open-hearth furnace, to the North East and North West, followed by Scotland and South Wales, but it was still coal-orientated.

Throughout the period of Kondratieff's Second Wave, the upland industrial towns located on and near the coalfields grew, many reaching their peak populations in the 1881–91 decade. On a county basis, the overall trend is illustrated in Fig. 2.7. The most rapidly growing counties (over 75 per cent, 1841–91) were: Dumbartonshire, Lanarkshire, Renfrewshire, Selkirk and Wigtown in Scotland; Glamorgan and Monmouthshire in Wales; Durham, Lancashire, Northumberland and the West Riding of Yorkshire in northern England; Staffordshire and Warwickshire in the Midlands; and the London area in the South East. Areas of decline were the Scottish Highlands and Islands, central and west Wales, Somerset and Cornwall, while very slow growth took place in southern Scotland, East Anglia (except Essex) and the belt of high-density rural counties of the south Midlands and the West Country (compare with Fig. 2.5). Migration was still partially the short-distance move that had characterised the 1785–1842 period, but the considerable improvements in transport after the 1830s meant that people were drawn from further afield: from the South West to South Wales, Lancashire and London; from East Anglia to London and Yorkshire; from the Scottish Highlands to Clydeside and northern England, and from Ireland to Lancashire and London (Ordnance Survey, 1982, 157).

The textile industry continued to attract migrants to work in the mills. Handloom weavers survived in considerable numbers – there were still 123,000 in 1840 – but by 1860 they totalled only 10,000 and by 1890 they had all but disappeared. Factory workers in cotton mills, meanwhile, were increasing from 262,000 in 1840 to 427,000 20 years later. In the West Riding of Yorkshire, however, the majority of piece-working weavers of woollens remained outside the factories as late as 1858 (Jones and Pool, 1940, 88), although by 1850 the area had already established itself as the principal woollen manufacturing district of the country with 40 per cent of the workforce in woollens and almost all of those in worsteds. In terms of numbers employed and output the textile industry had become highly concentrated by 1890. Ninety per cent of cottons were produced in Lancashire, and the remainder in the East Midlands and in Paisley, Scotland, while 75 per cent

Figure 2.7   Great Britain: the Second Kondratieff Wave (1842–94), annual rate of population change per county.

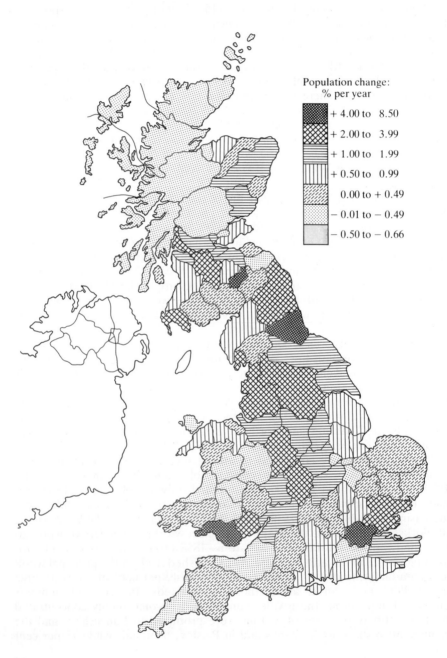

Population change:
% per year

+ 4.00 to   8.50
+ 2.00 to   3.99
+ 1.00 to   1.99
+ 0.50 to   0.99
  0.00 to + 0.49
− 0.01 to − 0.49
− 0.50 to − 0.66

of woollens were produced in Yorkshire, with specialist centres surviving in Norfolk (worsteds), the Cotswolds (blankets), the Leicester-Nottingham area (hosiery), the West Country (serge) and the Tweed Valley (tweeds). Other textile specialisms with notable concentrations of employment were linens in Belfast, Scotland (Dundee) and Lancashire/Yorkshire, silks mainly in Cheshire, Lancashire and Derbyshire and jute (for sacks) in Dundee.

The Second Kondratieff Wave, as the First, was not one of unmitigated growth and prosperity – there were periods of recession, even depression. The repeal of the Corn Laws (1849) meant that British farmers were open to competition from imports. This was not a problem during the 1850s, while transport charges on grain shipments from North America were relatively high, nor during the 1860s when the Americans were engaged in their Civil War. But prices were beginning to decline in Britain from the mid-1860s, and by the mid-1870s low prices produced a notable agricultural depression which lasted until the 1890s. The results were many bankruptcies among farmers, especially in eastern England, and a decline in the number of agricultural labourers from over 1 million in 1871 to 600,000 in 1901. The American Civil War also restricted raw cotton exports from Southern States, causing a 'cotton famine' in Lancashire. This resulted in much short-time working and unemployment, but once raw cotton shipments were resumed in full after 1865 the industry quickly recovered. The so-called 'Great Depression' of 1873–96 was a period that saw industrial productivity fall, mainly in association with slumps in the trade cycles, especially in the years 1879, 1884–87 and 1893. Unemployment in industry averaged 5.5 per cent and was particularly severe in those industries associated with agricultural equipment and with the 'traditional' textiles, metals and shipbuilding. The newer industries of steel, chemicals and electrical engineering were growing, however, as were some staples like woollens, brewing, food processing and construction.

2.4   1895–1939: vehicles, chemicals, electricity and oil

As the Second Kondratieff Wave went out with a recession, the *Third* Kondratieff Wave came in with improving trade and an upward movement of prices. There were downturns, however, in 1901–04 and 1907–09, when unemployment among trade unionists reached 6.0 per cent and 6.3 per cent respectively, but industry quickly recovered and even the staple industries were enjoying rising prices and prosperous conditions up to the outbreak of the First World War.

The occupational structure of Britain at the turn of the century had continued its swing away from agriculture and towards manufacturing and services. Primary activities had declined from 24 to 15 per cent of employment (8 per cent in agriculture, forestry and fishing, 7 per cent in mining) since 1842, secondary activities had increased from 33 to 37 per cent while the tertiary sector had grown from 24 to 32 per cent (15 per cent in domestic service) and quaternary from 9 to 11 per cent (Fig. 2.10). The distribution of population had achieved the pattern with which we are familiar today, with 77 per cent of the population urbanised, living in the towns and cities

27

of Central Scotland, South Wales, Durham, Lancashire, West Yorkshire, the West Midlands and the South East. The rural belt stretching from East Anglia to the South West had moderate densities of population but was still in the process of losing people to the industrial areas, the most severely affected regions in terms of rural depopulation being the Scottish Highlands and Southern Uplands, central Wales and East Anglia (Fig. 2.9).

The pattern of industrial, and therefore occupational, distribution in Britain was about to change, however, as new industries developed which were not so closely tied to coalfield locations as the traditional industries. This was largely because of the development of electricity, which transformed coal into an easily transportable power source for both industry and the home, the first public supply being in Godalming, Surrey in 1881. The new industries of alloy steels (e.g. stainless steel was developed in 1913), aluminium, rubber, chemicals, synthetic fibres (rayon, nylon), motor vehicles and electrical engineering started to grow before the end of the nineteenth century, but their true significance was masked up to 1914 while the traditional industries enjoyed a boom period. Hence, pig-iron production and iron exports achieved new levels, even though domestic output of iron ore declined, steel passing the 7.6 million t mark with exports of over 1 million t and coal output climbing to a remarkable 292 million t on the eve of the War, one-third of which was exported. The coal mining industry operated over 3,000 pits and employed over 1 million men by 1914, and continued to employ such numbers until the depression of the 1930s. The cotton textile industry employed over 650,000 and produced 8 billion m² of cloth, 87 per cent of which was exported, while the other textile sectors employed over 400,000. Employment figures of the same order of magnitude were attained in engineering and shipbuilding (over 850,000), iron and steel (over 200,000) and the railways (over 500,000). In the latter instance, it is interesting to note that the peak length of the railways, 32,682 km, was not reached until 1920.

Spatially, the vast majority of people employed in these traditional industries were located in the coalescing cities, towns and villages ('conurbations') of upland Britain, plus the London area. But the structure of British industry was changing. The new industries were not locationally tied to the coalfields, so as the industrial structure changed so did the regional distribution of industry and, therefore, of employment opportunities. A drift of people from the North to the South had already been noticed between 1897 and 1914 and this was a feature of population redistribution that was to become more pronounced after the 1914–18 War.

The War itself was largely fought on the basis of traditional industrial supplies, and it dramatically increased the number of women employed in engineering (800,000), even if only temporarily. This was significant in that it meant women gained factory experience beyond just that of textiles, clothing and office work, and this was to be of direct value to the labour requirements of the new light engineering developments during the inter-war period. Technological developments during the War in aircraft manufacturing, motor vehicles, chemicals, radio-telegraphy and so on, contributed directly to the structural shift in emphasis between 1918 and 1940.

The industries that expanded during the second half of Kondratieff's Third Wave fall into three groups:

1. old-established trades that grew primarily in response to population increase – food processing, brewing, tailoring;
2. newer industries producing 'consumer durables' – car and aircraft engineering, chemicals (pharmaceuticals and synthetic fibres especially), electrical goods (e.g. home appliances, electric motors);
3. old industries growing in response to increasing affluence – the distributive trades (wholesaling and retailing), building and allied trades, road and transport, entertainments.

To the list of 'old industries' could be added the quaternary sector of professional services and government, which grew substantially during this period. Some idea of the scale of these changes between 1923 and 1938 may be gained from the examples in Table 2.2 of percentage increase or decrease in employment.

In general, the contracting industries were those located in the older established manufacturing regions of upland Britain (except for agriculture), which had depended on exports for their prosperity during the Second Wave, while the expanding ones were in the Midlands and South East regions of lowland Britain and depended on emerging domestic demands. In fact, whereas in 1923 the Midlands and South East provided only 47 per cent of

Table 2.2 United Kingdom: expanding and declining employment sectors, 1923–38

		%
Expanding	Entertainments, sports, etc.	+151
	Electrical manufacturing	+129
	Motor and aircraft engineering	+109
	Road transport	+ 73
	Hotels, restaurants, etc.	+ 72
	Distributive trades	+ 65
	Building and contracting	+ 63
	Professional services	+ 62
	Furniture making	+ 57
	Local government service	+ 50
	Utilities	+ 34
	Printing and publishing	+ 28
	General engineering	+ 17
	Food processing	+ 16
Contracting	Shipbuilding	− 5
	Footwear	− 12
	Railways	− 14
	Agriculture	− 15
	Iron and steel	− 18
	Woollens	− 32
	Coal mining	− 42
	Cotton	− 43

Source: Jones and Pool, 1940, 281

29

the total employment of the UK, by 1938 their share had risen to 54 per cent. As Jones and Pool (1940, 294) observed, 'Britain's industrial centre of gravity has thus been persistently moving Southwards'.

This spatial rearrangement of Britain's economic landscape was facilitated by the development of electric power, which the National Grid (established in 1926) steadily extended across the country (consumption of electricity increased from 6 billion to 20 billion units, 1920–40). Manufacturers wishing to locate near markets could now do so, since they were no longer constrained by access to coal, and the growth in demand was emanating from the increasingly affluent consumers working in the growing industries of the Midlands and the London area. The car industry, for example, concentrated in Coventry, Birmingham, Luton, Oxford and London was located towards the south-eastern end of Britain's axial belt of industry running from London to Lancashire. The number of moter vehicles produced rose from just 10,500 in 1908 to 95,000 by 1923 and to 445,000 by 1938. Road transport went through a revolution during this period, the car/bus and lorry competing strongly with the railways for passenger and freight traffic respectively. Over longer distances, even the infant airlines were beginning to compete with ocean liners and trains, the number of passengers carried increasing from just 970 in 1919 to over 244,000 in 1937, but it was the Fourth Kondratieff Wave that was to see air transport come to maturity.

The last decade of the Third Kondratieff Wave saw another Great Depression which was to exceed in its severity that of 1873–96, but this time agriculture was not so badly affected. The worst affected industries were those that had already shown contraction before 1930 – coal mining, heavy iron and steel manufacture, shipbuilding and cotton textiles. These were the nineteenth-century industries that had saturated the domestic market and become dependent upon exports before the First World War, but the war years had been sufficient time to enable foreign competition to take over many of their previous markets and these could not be recovered in the 1920s. Hence, when the trade cycle slumped between 1929 and 1938 the areas of traditional industry were particularly badly hit, losing over 1 million workers during those ten years. The worst affected areas were South Wales, Durham and Northumberland, West Cumberland and south-west Scotland, as shown for 1934 on Fig. 2.8. The Midlands and the South East, however, where most of the new, expanding industries were located, exhibited much lower unemployment rates. The southern area with the highest unemployment rate was East Ham in London with 24 per cent, but even that figure was well below those of many northern areas. Indeed, even after rearmament began in 1937, which increased the demand for munitions and therefore prompted an expansion of heavy industries, unemployment in the North remained at higher levels and lasted much longer than in the South, with contracting industries having rates almost exactly twice those of expanding industries.

The downswing of the Third Kondratieff Long Wave gave way to the upswing of the *Fourth* Long Wave with unemployment falling as Britain prepared for another major war. The occupational structure had changed, of course, both on a sectoral basis and within sectors. Thus by 1940, if we try to discount the effects of wartime, employment in the primary sector had fallen to about 10 per cent (agriculture 6 per cent, mining 4 per cent), the

Figure 2.8 Great Britain: unemployment in 'distressed' and 'prosperous' areas, 1934.
Source: Cook and Stevenson (1983, 70)

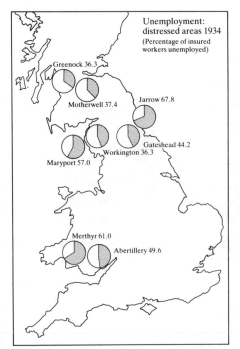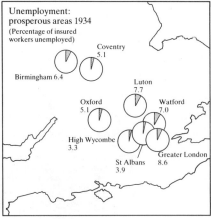

secondary sector had increased to 41 per cent (with a redistribution sectorally and locationally from contracting to expanding industries), the tertiary sector had fallen to 23 per cent (mainly because of a drastic decline in domestic service numbers) and the quaternary sector had increased to about 17 per cent (Fig. 2.10). Locationally, the spatial emphasis of employment opportunities was shifting southwards, not only because of the establishment in the Midlands and South East of the new industries, but also because the increase in the quaternary sector (particularly in London) was contributing to the region's growth – directly in terms of increased numbers employed and, together with the secondary expansion, indirectly because their rising affluence was creating the demand for growth in the number of jobs in shops, offices, transportation, entertainment, publishing, restaurants, construction, utilities, home furnishings and other consumer durables.

This shift is indicated in Fig. 2.9. The dramatic slowdown in the rate of population growth in traditional industrial counties and the speeding up in the growth of counties around London during the Third Kondratieff Wave is strikingly obvious. The upland counties of the North and West continued their depopulation or very slow growth, as did the rural counties of East Anglia, and London (Middlesex) itself began to lose population to its 'suburban' ring of counties.

31

Figure 2.9   Great Britain: the Third Kondratieff Wave (1895–1939), annual rate of population change per county.

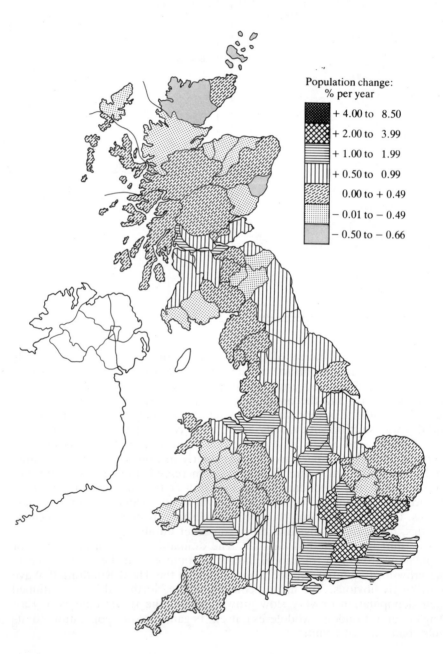

Population change:
% per year

■	+ 4.00 to 8.50
▧	+ 2.00 to 3.99
▤	+ 1.00 to 1.99
▥	+ 0.50 to 0.99
▨	0.00 to + 0.49
⋮	− 0.01 to − 0.49
▨	− 0.50 to − 0.66

2.5 1940–95?: aerospace, electronics and motorways

As with the First World War, the Second World War saw a temporary uplift in the fortunes of some older, contracting industries while the newer, expanding industries received extra impetus because of wartime demands. Coal, iron and steel, shipbuilding and textiles benefited from the increased domestic demand, but, more significantly, there were numerous technological developments in electronics and aircraft which were going to have a marked impact on the structure of British industry during the *Fourth* Kondratieff Wave.

Agricultural employment fell from over 800,000 in 1945 to about 200,000 in 1988, a mere 1.7 per cent of the total workforce. The capitalisation of the remaining workforce, however, has meant that it can produce as much food now as three times its number could in the 1930s. The major areas of rural depopulation continue to be in Scotland and Wales (see Fig. 2.11). Farm mechanisation has swollen the numbers of migrants from both the marginal and even the more prosperous farming areas of England as well, so that over a million people (farm workers and their dependants) have left the land since 1945 to seek employment, not so much in the older industrial areas but rather in the Birmingham–London area. The other parts of the primary sector, fishing, forestry and mining, have lost even more workers in total, especially the latter which has declined from around 1.8 million in the 1940s to little more than 100,000 now.

The production of iron ore experienced a mini-boom during the War years when output reached 20 million t. The old iron-stone workings in the coalfields were exhausted by 1950 and the haematites of Furness and Cumberland declined from over 1 million t in 1940 to 500,000 t by 1960 and to less than 100,000 t by 1985. The major expansion of iron ore was in the Lias and Jurassic fields of Lincolnshire and Northamptonshire, which increased output from just over 3 million t during the War to over 15 million t by 1965, but it had declined to less than 300,000 t gross by 1987. The Northamptonshire field closed in the late 1970s and Corby, which had been built (1935) as a steel town to utilise local ores, became a depressed area in the otherwise prosperous lowland Britain. The iron and steel industry expanded substantially during and after the War, with production of pig-iron climbing from 12 million t in 1950 to over 18 million t in 1970, and steel from 16 million t to 26 million t over the same period. However, lack of adequate investment in new technology early enough meant that by the 1970s Britain's steel industry could not compete with imports. In an effort to improve the competitiveness of the industry, therefore, the annual capacity for steel making was reduced from 30 million t to 17 million t (40 per cent exported) and the workforce from 208,000 to 52,000 with the closure of 10 plants between 1977 and 1987. With the exception of Corby, these closures took place in the traditional industrial areas of upland Britain (e.g. Shotton in Cheshire, Consett in Tyne and Wear).

Other metal mining has experienced mixed fortunes. Lead output (metal content) rose from 74,000 t in 1950 to 125,000 t in 1970, but fell back to only 5,000 t in 1979, then rose again to 14,000 t by 1983 thanks to new developments in the Pennines (Derbyshire, Cumbria and Durham), but declined to 3,600 t in 1987. Similarly, tin mining in Cornwall saw an increase in output from only about 1,000 t per year 1950–70 to about 3,000 t per year in the early 1980s (50 per cent of Britain's requirements), mainly because higher prices brought marginal deposits into the 'economically viable' category, but these prices collapsed in 1986 and so did the industry. Cornish mines also produce zinc and tungsten, together with small amounts of silver and copper which, in turn, are also mined in the Pennines, Wales and Scotland. Total output of all non-ferrous metals amounts to only about 22,000 t per year, however, and its mining employs about 45,000 people, so it is not a major industry, but significantly it is almost entirely located in upland Britain.

The same is true locationally of the coalfields (except Kent) but their output and employment are on rather a different scale. During the war years coal output continued the decline that had started in the Depression years, after a slight increase in the 1937–41 period (to 240 million t), so that by 1947 production had slumped to 175 million t. Following nationalisation of the coal industry in the latter year production increased fairly steadily to over 200 million t by 1960, gained with just over half the workforce (600,000) from two-thirds the number of mines (*c.* 700) compared with 1947. However, as oil became increasingly competitive as a fuel the demand for coal slackened, and this was mirrored in the decline in production to 165 million t by 1970 and to 107 million t in 1987, with only 2 per cent being exported. The associated decrease in the number of pits from 300 in 1970 to 109 in 1987, was inevitably accompanied by a further decline in the workforce from 290,000 in 1970 to just over 100,000 in 1987, with prospects of further cutbacks over the remaining years of the current Kondratieff Wave to 60,000–70,000 by 1992. Locationally, of course, this loss of 900,000 mining industry jobs since 1945 has taken place almost entirely within the traditional industrial areas, especially in the high-cost coalfields of Scotland, Durham, Cumbria, Lancashire and South Wales (the latter region losing 14 of its 28 pits between 1985 and 1987).

As far as Britain's energy requirements were concerned, coal's decline was matched by a rise in the importance of natural gas and oil, initially imported and then produced from the North Sea after 1967 (gas) and 1975 (oil), and by the emergence of nuclear power and hydro-electric power (HEP). Neither hydrocarbons nor atoms offered jobs on a scale to compensate for the decline in coal, however, nor were they located in coalfield areas. Nuclear power and HEP stations are sited at remote coastal and mountainous locations respectively, gas terminals in Norfolk, Humberside and Grampian and oil terminals in Cleveland, Grampian, Orkney and Shetland. The new power sources intermeshed with the patterns that had been emerging pre-1960, with nuclear power and HEP feeding directly into an expanding electricity grid system, oil replacing or complementing coal in thermal power stations and natural gas replacing coal gas (manufactured) in an already established distribution network to homes and industry. In addition, of course, oil contributed directly to the continuing transportation revolution as well as enabling Britain to become a net exporter of fossil fuels again on a substantial scale (1985–86 net exports of over 30 million t of oil and almost 4 million t of coal). Feeding these 'new' energy sources into the electricity grid, which by the 1970s was virtually ubiquitous, has enabled manufacturing industry to continue its locational dispersal away from the coalfields, while the expansion in road transport has made this means of moving people and freight around the country almost ubiquitous as well.

The number of vehicles on the roads increased from 3 million in 1945 to 10 million by 1960 and 20 million in 1987, carrying 92 per cent of all passenger traffic (up from 70 per cent in 1945) and over 75 per cent of inland freight tonnage (up from 40 per cent in 1945). The total length of roads only increased from 288,000 km in 1900 to just over 350,000 km in 1980 and essentially retained a medieval pattern, but improvements have been made to almost every kilometre and since 1955 over 2400 km of motorway have been constructed, which has further facilitated the rise to dominance of road transport. Railways, by contrast, have shrunk to a skeleton of their former grandeur. In 1945 there were still over 30,000 km of track in use, and even in 1960 about 24,000 km remained after some rationalisation, but following acceptance of the Beeching Report in 1963 this track length was further reduced to 18,000 km by 1980. This action was necessitated by the railway's loss of revenue both before and after the War as passengers switched to buses and cars (numbers using rail transport declined by 40 per cent 1920–38 and by 40 per cent again 1938–68), so that the railways now carry only about 7 per cent of total passenger traffic. Similarly, as freight switched to lorries, the railways experienced a decline in their proportion of freight carried, from 60 per cent in 1945 to 15 per cent in 1980, although this latter percentage is of a much larger total volume of freight than the former. Further freight competition for the railways has come from pipelines, which now transport much of the oil that used to be carried by rail (8 per cent total freight), while coastal shipping has seen its freight transfer to roads, especially since the building of the motorway system, and the remaining 550 km of commercial waterways (rivers and canals) handle less than 1 per cent of inland freight. Domestic air travel, although handling a mere 1 per cent of passengers, has seen its numbers carried increase from the 400,000 in the late 1940s to over 7 million in the early 1980s.

So, the Fourth Kondratieff Long Wave has witnessed the demise of coastal shipping (a feature of domestic transport since before the First Wave) and the canal (from the First Wave), the dramatic decline of the railway (from the Second Wave) and the disappearance of the steam engine from the rails (by 1968), and the rise to pre-eminence of the internal combustion engine (from the Third Wave) domestically and the jet engine (a Fourth Wave phenomenon) internationally. Similarly, in industry, each Wave's technological developments continue to be in evidence in succeeding Waves: some sectors suffer decline because of outmoded structure, organisation and lack of competitiveness (coal, iron and steel, shipbuilding, textiles); some survive by adopting new techniques (construction, utilities, food processing, mechanical engineering); and some emerge as new technology develops (motor vehicles, aerospace, chemicals, electrical engineering).

The most striking features of the Fourth Wave to date are the dramatic decline in secondary occupations, especially marked in traditional manufacturing industries, and a more rapid decline in primary occupations than at any time since 1800, but a substantial, although only partially compensatory, increase in tertiary and quaternary occupations (Fig. 2.10). Britain's proportion of total employment in manufacturing industry reached its highest ever, 48 per cent, in 1955, just over half way through the *upswing* of the Fourth Wave (Rowthorn, 1986, 3–4). In terms of absolute numbers, however, the

Table 2.3 United Kingdom: regional distribution of employment in manufacturing* 1952, 1965, 1979 and 1986

Standard Planning Region	1952 Nos. (000s)	%	1965 Nos. (000s)	%	1979 Nos. (000s)	%	1986 Nos. (000s)	%	1965–86 % change
South East	2,259	27	2,389	28	1,876	26	1,404	26	−41
North West	1,414	17	1,252	15	971	13	638	12	−49
West Midlands	1,119	14	1,185	14	986	14	709	13	−40
Yorkshire/Humberside	863	10	860	10	708	10	470	9	−45
Scotland	760	9	725	9	605	8	524	10	−28
East Midlands	534	6	620	7	606	8	491	9	−21
North	409	5	459	5	411	6	265	5	−42
South West	331	4	422	5	441	6	380	7	−10
Wales	268	3	311	4	315	4	206	4	−34
Northern Ireland	186	2	171	2	145	2	97	2	−43
East Anglia	138	2	167	2	206	3	188	3	+13
United Kingdom	8,281	100	8,561	100	7,270	100	5,372	100	−37

* Excluding construction and utilities.

Sources: Department of Employment *Gazette* (various years); Central Statistical Office, *Regional Trends* (various years)

peak employment of 8.9 million in manufacturing (over 38 per cent of the total workforce) was attained in 1966, the year marking the end of the upswing and ushering in the beginning of the *downswing* (Table 1.1). By 1976, manufacturing employment was down to less than 7.5 million (about 33 per cent of the total workforce) and by 1986 to less than 5.4 million (about 25 per cent of the total workforce), a fact mirrored in the decline of manufacturing's contribution to the GDP from 32 per cent in 1960 to only about 20 per cent in 1986. Some of the manufacturing and other secondary job losses were 'made up' by gains in the service sector (tertiary and quaternary) which grew from about 12 million in 1966 to over 14 million by 1986, but the 'gap' of 1.5 million in the 1980s contributed substantially to the 3 million or so unemployed, with the balance being derived from lay-offs in almost all other occupational sectors. These gross national figures do not, however, reveal the regional disparities in job gains and losses, nor do they show the urban-rural differences.

The major job losses occurred in traditional industries and, as we have seen in our brief review of Britain's economic history, these industries are predominantly located in the northern and western parts of the country – the upland areas. Table 2.3 shows the manufacturing employment changes by region, 1952–86. We have already noted the post-war loss of 900,000 jobs in the coal mining industry, and to that figure should be added over 600,000 losses in textiles – over half of them in the North West. Major job losses in the other traditional industries mainly occurred during the 1974–86 recession – over 180,000 in iron and steel, over 50,000 in shipbuilding and losses of similar magnitude in engineering. Even that stalwart 'boom' industry of the 1950s and 1960s, car assembly, which had been a magnet for thousands of workers from upland Britain, shrank from its peak production of 2 million cars and over 500,000 employees in 1972 to fewer than 900,000 cars and 130,000 employees by 1984. Nevertheless, during its growth phase, the car industry was instrumental in accelerating the drift of population from upland to lowland Britain, a phenomenon in evidence throughout the Third Kondratieff Wave, which intensified in the upswing of the Fourth Wave and which will undoubtedly continue for at least the remainder of the current downswing.

One result of this employment redistribution has been that lowland Britain increased its national share of employees in employment from about 53 per cent in 1936 to over 60 per cent in 1986. These figures include all types of employment, not just manufacturing, and strongly reflect the gains made by the South in service sector employment growth – in fact there seems to be a 2 to 1 ratio of service job generation in the South compared with the rest of the country. This is particularly so with the fastest growing job sectors of insurance, banking, finance and business services (14 per cent increase 1979–84, a sector with 63 per cent of the national total already in the South and almost 37 per cent in London alone), medical services (10 per cent) and the hotel trade (8 per cent). The service sector employment gains of 1983–86 are reflected in Table 2.4; they show little compensation for manufacturing job losses in the regions of the North compared with those of the South. The result has been continuing high unemployment rates in the North while the major job-gain benefits since 1983 have been for the South in general and for the South East (outside London) in particular.

Table 2.4 Great Britain: regional job losses and gains, 1979–86

Standard Planning Region	Net job loss (–) or gain (+), June 1979–83	Net job loss (–) or gain (+), June 1983–86
Scotland	– 204,000	– 12,000
North	– 191,000	+ 20,000
North West	– 374,000	– 41,000
Yorkshire/Humberside	– 240,000	+ 5,000
Wales	– 145,000	– 30,000
West Midlands	– 298,000	+ 78,000
East Midlands	– 132,000	+ 91,000
South West	– 84,000	+ 54,000
East Anglia	– 15,000	+ 74,000
South East	– 391,000	+269,000
Great Britain	–2,071,000	+500,000

Source: Department of Employment (January, 1987)

Within the regions, employment losses and gains have been highly variable. At the county level, over the years 1971–81 the only gains in manufacturing jobs were in The Highlands (57 per cent), Dumfries and Galloway (10 per cent), Powys (9 per cent), Cambridgeshire (5 per cent), West Sussex (3 per cent), Northumberland (1 per cent) and Dorset (0.2 per cent), while all the metropolitan counties lost by over 30 per cent as did South Glamorgan (–40 per cent), West Glamorgan (–38 per cent) and Cleveland (–35 per cent) (Keeble, 1984, 2).

The First and Second Kondratieff Waves were characterised by rural out-migration and population concentration in the industrial cities, the Third Wave continued this trend but at a reduced rate, while the Fourth Wave has witnessed dramatic population losses from all the major conurbations and free-standing cities, in turn reflecting the demise of manufacturing industry in the inner city. Between 1966 and 1986, London lost about 800,000 manufacturing jobs, Birmingham lost over 300,000, Manchester lost almost 300,000, Clydeside almost 200,000, Leeds/Bradford over 100,000, and so on. Hence, the 3 million-plus job losses in manufacturing from the mid-1960s to the mid-1980s was very largely an inner city phenomenon – the small towns held their own and the rural areas actually increased by around 25 per cent, compared with the urban losses of around 40 per cent on average. The occupational distribution of these job losses was in engineering (23 per cent), clothing (20 per cent), food and drink (9 per cent), textiles (8 per cent), motor vehicles and aerospace (8 per cent), timber and furniture (7 per cent), and paper and printing (7 per cent) – an interesting mixture of traditional and 'leading-edge' industries of yesteryear. (Fothergill and Vincent, 1985, 34)

Structural and locational changes in occupations have been, and will continue to be, permanent features of national economic development. The structural changes are illustrated in Fig. 2.10 (see also Fig. 9.1). The latest available figures for the mid-1980s show a continued decline in the primary sector to 2.9 per cent (agriculture, etc., to 1.6 per cent, mining to 1.3 per

Figure 2.10   United Kingdom: changes in occupational structure, 1700 to 2000 (projected).

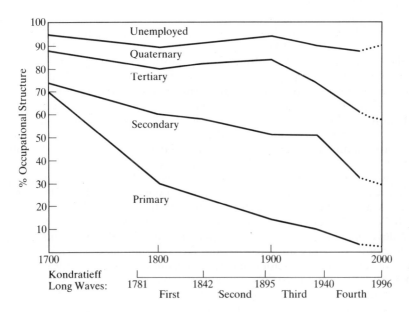

Primary: agriculture, forestry, fishing, mining and quarrying
Secondary: manufacturing, construction, utilities
Tertiary: transport, communications, wholesale, retail, banking, insurance, finance
Quaternary : government, armed forces, education, R & D, health, recreation, welfare, personal services
Unemployed: includes 'paupers and vagrants' before 1900

cent), a decline for the first time in the secondary sector to about 29 per cent (manufacturing down to less than 24 per cent), but increases in the tertiary sector to 30 per cent and in the quaternary sector also to 30 per cent (see Appendix for regional differences). The dominance of the primary and secondary sectors in Britain's employment structure ended around 1940, coincidentally the transition time from Kondratieff's Third to his Fourth Long Wave, and since then the service sector has risen to dominate the employment picture. The absolute numbers of people employed during the Fourth Wave climbed from about 18 million in 1945 of peak at 23 million in the mid-1960s and then declined to 21 million in the early to mid-1980s. During the remaining years of the Fourth Wave, it is expected that total full-time employment will continue to decline by around 200,000–300,000 until about 1990 and then possibly show a net gain to the mid-1990s. Between 1985–90 job *losses* are likely to be 100,000 in the primary sector and almost 550,000 in the secondary sector (250,000 from engineering-related occupations and 170,000 from light industries), but with some *gains* in the service sector: over 300,000 new tertiary jobs (380,000 in the distributive trades, finance and business services, but with a loss of 75,000 transport and communications jobs), and over 230,000 quaternary sector jobs (almost

39

300,000 new jobs in leisure and other services, but a loss of about 60,000 public service jobs) (Institute for Manpower Studies/Occupations Study Group, 1986).

The locational significance of these structural changes will be to maintain the regional emphasis on lowland Britain, particularly the South East outside London plus parts of East Anglia and the South West, as the 'core' of employment opportunities. In fact, the South East, with just over 30 per cent of the nation's population, already has 34 per cent of all industrial employees, 35 per cent of distributive trades and of administration employment, 42 per cent of transport and communications jobs, almost 50 per cent of banking and other financial services jobs and, especially significantly, over 40 per cent of the jobs in electrical engineering and electronics. If, indeed, the latter industrial sector provides the impetus for substantive economic growth in the *upswing* of the *Fifth* Long Wave, then lowland Britain already has 'more than its fair share' in place. However, this assumes that the speed of innovations and their introduction into product processing and the market place, which have increased during the Fourth Wave, will continue in the Fifth Wave. In turn, this necessitates higher and higher levels of research and development expenditure as a percentage of GDP, since this is critical to economic recovery and growth but takes time to make the transition from the laboratory to the factory and the consumer. Unfortunately for Britain, while all its major industrial competitors have steadily increased their R & D spending since 1979, this country's spending did increase to 1981 but then declined to 1983, and such figures have not been kept since then, but we are almost certainly lagging behind the competition. (See also Section 10.1.1, page 224–5.

Nevertheless, if we assume that current economic recovery trends continue over the short to intermediate run, there is little doubt that upland Britain to the north and west of the Humber–Exe line (Fig. 2.1) will suffer disproportionately from the forecast job losses outlined above, while lowland Britain will benefit disproportionately from the job gains. It has been estimated that over the decade 1985 to 1995, something like 900,000 new jobs will be created, many of them in the loosely defined 'high tech' category. Of the total, about 415,000 would be in the South East, 105,000 in London and 310,000 in the rest of the South East (ROSE), with the following distribution by county (percentage employment gain in parentheses): Essex 53,000 (8.3 per cent); Hampshire 51,000 (7.9 per cent); Buckinghamshire 38,000 (14.5 per cent); Kent 36,000 (5.9 per cent); Berkshire 31,000 (9.5 per cent); West Sussex 26,000 (9.5 per cent); Hertfordshire 21,000 (6.8 per cent); Bedfordshire 19,000 (8.4 per cent) (Moore, 1986).

Regional differences in real and perceived job opportunities have always been major influences on the decision by people to migrate from one part of the country to another, and there is no reason to assume that this process will change. Consequently, it would seem reasonable to suggest that the regional pattern of county and sub-county population growth and decline, as illustrated in Fig. 2.11, will continue for the remainder of the Fourth Wave and quite probably into the Fifth Wave. Hence, the drift of population from upland to lowland Britain that gained momentum during the *upswing* of the Fourth Wave thanks to such growth industries in the Midlands and South East as car assembly, aerospace and electrical engineering, will con-

Figure 2.11 Great Britain: the Fourth Kondratieff Wave (1940–95), annual rate of population change per county. (pre-1974 boundaries used for ease of comparison with Figs. 2.3, 2.5, 2.6, 2.7 and 2.9).

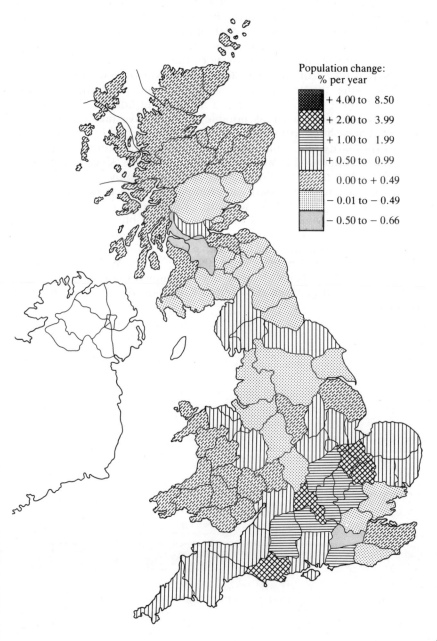

Population change:
% per year

+ 4.00 to 8.50
+ 2.00 to 3.99
+ 1.00 to 1.99
+ 0.50 to 0.99
  0.00 to + 0.49
− 0.01 to − 0.49
− 0.50 to − 0.66

tinue in the *downswing* to 1995. However, there will be a shift in spatial emphasis away from the Midlands and towards East Anglia, the South East outside the City of London, and the eastern parts of the South West, which contain those industries that will be the leading edge of economic development and employment opportunities in the upswing of the Fifth Wave. (See Hall *et al.*, 1987; Hall and Preston, 1988).

Ironically, many of the counties which had the fastest population growth in 1971–81 and 1981–86, and whose densities are therefore also rapidly increasing, are the counties that had the highest densities in the pre-industrial era (Fig. 2.5). These counties (e.g. Cambridgeshire, Huntingdonshire, Oxfordshire and Dorset) provided so many of the migrants who moved into the resource-based manufacturing towns of the North and West during the industrialisation phase of the First and Second Kondratieff Waves. Figure 2.11 also shows that the 'traditional' areas of rural depopulation, the Scottish Highlands and most of Wales, have just managed to hold their own during the Fourth Kondratieff, whereas notable declines have taken place in the North East, Lancashire/Yorkshire, the West Midlands and even parts of the South East (primarily reflecting outmigration from conurbations). The reversal of the earlier migration flows has serious implications, since not everyone can be expected to move southwards in search of employment, so it is not surprising that the growing disparity in economic fortunes between the North and the South during the Third and Fourth Kondratieff Waves (i.e. 1895 to 1995) should have given rise not only to economic but also to social and political concerns. It is increased awareness of this regional disequilibrium of Britain's spatial economy that has been a catalyst for various government attempts at 'rebalancing' policies since the late 1920s. We will return to a discussion of specific policies after we have examined the other related features of working and living in the United Kingdom, the place of the home and of leisure.

3 Place of home

Home is both a location and an environment. In this chapter the changes in location of the population since the advent of the Industrial Revolution will be considered and also their changing home environment as they became more affluent, more demanding in their environmental needs, and more able to achieve such needs.

Why people move is a complex question but no doubt the place of work will strongly influence where they live, and any transformation of employment and its location will lead to changes in the distribution of the population. Such changes are not part of a single cause and effect – people do not immediately move their homes because employment declines or disappears. Their homes are part of their lives and the decision to move may be a difficult one to take. Nevertheless, changing work patterns lead to changes in residential patterns, as this chapter will show.

3.1 Pre-industrial to 1781

Before the nineteenth century population growth had been slow, hampered by disease and poor diet. Most people lived in villages or resided in small market towns scattered across the countryside. Detailed statistics were absent before 1801 when the first census of population was undertaken, but there are some indications that although the population was still largely rural, there were signs of growth within the urban centres. Despite this, it was the rural scene and the changes in agricultural practice which were of most concern in the eighteenth century as the process of enclosure continued. Wealth was created, and agricultural practice improved, but at considerable cost. In Leicestershire, for example, the population of Wigston Magna tripled between 1524 and 1765, and a generally prosperous village community existed. In 1765, enclosure changed all this. The small owner-occupiers (two-thirds of the population owned less than 50 acres) virtually disappeared as a group within 60 to 70 years to join the swelling ranks of rural labourers and paupers.

Alongside the stark contrast between the increasing wealth of the large landowners and the despair of much of the rural community, there were signs of new urban employment in the last two decades of the eighteenth century as industrial activity gained momentum. As yet though, the geographical and psychological gap between the rural environment and the industrial town seemed too great to cross for the majority of the population. The time-lag effect mentioned earlier was evident here. When the first census was published signs of a surge in urban growth were hardly discernible, for at this count there were only 15 towns with a population of over 20,000; and yet by 1850 over one-half of Britain's population was urban. If each of the Kondratieff cycles is associated with an industrial transformation, then the period from 1785 to 1842 also witnessed the rapid expansion of our cities, which was to continue unabated throughout the nineteenth century.

3.2 1781–1841: urban take-off

The census statistics for the period make fascinating reading. It is almost impossible to believe that such a transformation took place, for not only were there spectacular increases in the population of both old and new towns, but a settlement pattern emerged which, although influenced by the pre-existing network of market towns, administrative centres and commercial cities (Herbert, 1982), nevertheless was new. It was a response to the changing economic conditions of the industrial revolution which created new industrial areas, greatly improved means of inter-urban travel, and generated rapid expansion of trade and commerce.

The proportions of this rapid growth can be seen in three different types of city: the old towns, those over 20,000 population, which in 1801 contained 7.21 per cent of the population of England and Wales; the new industrial towns; and the small residential towns which were largely associated with the sea and the growth in recreation which occurred later in the century (see Table 3.1).

Away from the residential towns, much of the spectacular growth which Table 3.1 reveals was closely linked to the rise of the factory system and the need for industrial workers on a scale not known before. This was the age

Table 3.1 Growth in three types of city 1801–91

	1801	1851	1891
Old towns			
London	864,845	1,873,676	4,232,118
Manchester	90,399	296,183	505,368
Birmingham	73,670	182,922	478,113
New industrial towns			
Bradford	6,393	34,560	216,361
Cardiff	1,870	10,077	128,915
Middlesbrough	25	5,709	75,532
Residential towns			
Brighton	7,339	46,661	115,873
Southport			
(appears as North Meols in 1801)	2,096	3,346	41,406
Torquay	—	4,085	25,534

Sources: 1801 Census, 171, 427, 438, 481, 503; 1851 Census, South East Division Population Tables, 42–3; 1891 Census, West Midland Counties Population Tables, 6.

of 'gigantism' in industry, as the new technology of the innovative period from 1780–1860 was applied to the productive process.The coal resources so vital for heavy industry and the steam engine acted as magnets for industry, and as a consequence the growth of manufacturing towns. This growth was most rapid between 1820 and 1830, although there were variations between towns. Manchester, for example, doubled its size in the first 30 years of the nineteenth century, whereas Sheffield and Birmingham increased by 40 per cent between 1820 and 1830.

In contrast with this, the older towns which largely escaped the industrial surge grew more slowly. For instance, between 1801 and 1851 Winchester only grew from 8,171 to 13,706. The settlement pattern which this differential growth engendered showed a heavy bias towards the coalfields and away from the old centres of population in the South and East Anglia. By 1851 Lancashire had the largest single built-up area in the country, stretching from Manchester to Oldham with a population of 400,000, whilst the rural areas of mid-Wales, Scotland, and to a lesser extent England, experienced population decline.

Urban growth at this unprecedented rate presented the Victorians with an enormous problem of building cities in a hurry, and without a reservoir of knowledge as to how this should be done. It is not surprising, therefore, that 'factories were built on any available site to meet the expediency of the moment, housing was run up for the workers as closely related to the factories as might be; crude, ill planned, and ill constructed, paying no regard to spacial conditions of amenity, and inhuman in the last degree'. (Briggs, 1983.)

In this age of *laissez-faire,* consideration of the living conditions for a large majority of the growing urban population was subservient to the drive for economic gain and industrial progress – did not the Mayor of Middlesbrough say in 1821, 'If there is one thing Middlesbrough can be proud of, it is its smoke.' Smoke signified industrial activity, employment, but also pollution. It was a symbol of both industrial progress and urban degradation, and even as late as the 1840s the former seemed to take precendence over the latter. *Laissez-faire* in terms of urban development allowed slum landlords and jerry-builders to crowd families into single rooms or thrust them underground into cellars, saving money by using cheap or poor building materials and providing no drains. In the 1801 census 2,306 people were recorded as living in cellars, By the 1841 census out of 175,000 belonging to the 'labouring classes' all living in slum conditions, 38,000 were accommodated in cellars.

The conditions in cities were further worsened by the arrival of the railway, which cut a sward of destruction through the poorer areas. Railways may be described as 'England's gift to the world' (Trevelyan, 1964), but to the poor they meant either the loss of their homes without compensation or the provision of alternative accommodation, or the dissection of their neighbourhoods, as the railway embankment isolated them from friends and neighbours. The railway embankment became a symbol of the ruthless exploitation of the mid-Victorian city, striding past working class houses at roof level, increasing the degree of overcrowding and compressing the city.

The lack of general concern for the social costs engendered by this rapid industrial and urban development could not continue without some reaction

45

from those with power to bring about change and improvement. If they remained blind to the appalling conditions, they could not fail to appreciate the possible consequences of social unrest which could result, nor the outbreak of cholera in 1848 which was no respecter of persons. The voices for change were growing and change had to come.

3.3   1842–94: urban consolidation

The magnetic force of the cities to the rural population was not lessened by the living conditions within them. By 1891 London's population had more than doubled from its 1841 figure of just under 2 million and Liverpool, Manchester and Birmingham were now all over half a million. The delicate balance between rural and urban population which the 1851 census recorded was destroyed by 1880, when 70 per cent of the population were categorised as urban.

This was a period of spectacular growth for the new industrial towns which took off in the 1840s, and one which saw the emergence of rather specialised towns which owed their establishment largely to the railways, either as railway towns like Swindon, Crewe or Wolverton, or seaside resorts which became increasingly accessible to the growing number of urbanites as the railway opened up the coast.

The new industrial towns can best be exemplified by Middlesbrough, which Victorians considered to be the 'outcome of present century enterprise and discovery' and a town 'which had won a name without history, an importance without antiquity'. Such claims would be difficult to refute, for in 1801 Middlesborough was not more than four houses with 25 inhabitants. Yet by the census of 1841 there were 5,709 people and by 1891 75,532 people resided in the town. What was interesting about this relentless increase in population was its points of origin. In 1861 73.2 per cent of its inhabitants came from Yorkshire, supporting the view expressed earlier that migration from rural to urban areas was over short distances. By 1871 the picture had radically altered, for iron workers had now arrived from as far afield as Durham, South Wales, Staffordshire, Scotland and even Ireland. Such moves could largely be explained by the growth in the rail system, which by 1900 had become a national network.

The railways not only facilitated movement, they could also create towns almost from nothing. Crewe, a railway engineering town, was absent from the census returns before 1851, when it recorded a population of 4,491. By 1891 Crewe's population had increased sixfold. Wolverton, another such engineering town, was more modest in its growth. Nevertheless, this 'first specimen of a railway town built on a plan to order' (Simmons, 1986) grew from a mere hamlet of 417 souls in 1831 to a population of 9,200 by the turn of the century. Both towns were a reflection of the growing importance of the railway, which was now reaching out towards the coastline to convert quiet fishing villages to vibrant holiday resorts. Blackpool, before the railway arrived in 1846, was described as a 'sweet little village by the sea'.

The railways also began to influence the place where people lived within the city. The main physical impact of the railways on the heart of the Victorian city was over by the 1860s and attention now turned to the suburbs, although it was not until the last two decades of the century that the railway companies showed real interest in developing commuter services. In most large cities, with the exception of Glasgow, the development of the suburbs preceded the railway by 10 years or more because the competition of bus and tram services was too strong over relatively short distances. Only London was sufficiently large to make a suburban railway viable, and yet even here it was very late coming. In the mid-1850s only 27,000 rail commuters entered London each day, whereas 244,000 arrived on foot or by omnibus.

At this time railway companies did not believe it their role to provide urban transport but only to provide efficient inter-urban services for goods and people. For the most part, they left urban transport to trams and buses. There were, however, exceptions. The Great Eastern Railway in London was early in introducing cheap rail fares, which without doubt assisted and sustained the enormous growth of suburban population in Edmonton and Walthamstow, where a 10-fold increase in population took place between 1861 and 1901.

If the railway's commuter role was as yet uncertain, the framework for such a service was gradually being installed. The opening of Victoria Station in London in 1860 'pointed resolutely to the commuter age' (Briggs, 1983), and the development of the underground railway from 1863 encouraged whole new housing areas in the south of London and in Metroland (areas served by the Metropolitan line), heralding the arrival of the rush hour.

A transformation in the social and economic environments was also necessary to match the change in transport technology if people were to move from the inner cities to the suburbs. The suburbs had always been a privileged place for the wealthy. The *Quarterly Review* in 1850 noted that 'nothing has so much contributed to drive away the opulent from the dwellings of the poor as the dread of their unwholesomeness and dirt'. Now with increasing wages (average income per capita doubled between 1800 and 1860), and a growing middle class, more people aspired to reach these residential areas of status and quality. To make this possible required capital, land, and a building industry capable of house construction at a sufficient pace to satisfy demand.

The need for capital for house buying was met by the building societies, which, although established in 1775, increased in number and influence during the nineteenth century. By 1850 there were already 2,000 fairly equally distributed throughout the country.

Land for residential building became available as a result of changes in the law on land tenure, which, from the 1840s onwards, increased the number of land owners who could grant building leases relating to settled estates, to church and ecclesiastical land. This new growth in demand for housing could only be achieved through a restructuring of the building industry. The model for change was provided by Thomas Cubbitt, who in 1822 removed the delays caused by subcontracting for skilled workers, by encompassing all the necessary skills for building within his own firm. This resulted in a larger but more efficient company. In the census of 1851 his influence was already clear, for nine firms were recorded each employing 200 or more men.

The second half of the nineteenth century, therefore, saw the foundation and initial growth of the transport technology, the financial institutions and the building industry which were essential not only for nineteenth-century urban expansion, but also for the boom in suburbia to come in the inter-war period of the twentieth century.

The figures for nineteenth-century suburban growth are impressive. London's outer ring of suburbs grew by about 50 per cent in each decade between 1861 and 1891. Birmingham witnessed the expansion in population in the district of Handsworth from 11,000 in 1861 to 70,000 in 1911, and Erdington from 2,600 in 1881 to 32,500 in 1911.

Such growth represented more than a desire for status, it emphasised a growing need for a better quality of life than that provided by the cities. For those who could afford this path all was well; for those who could not, the position, although grim, gradually improved as the technology of the In-dustrial Revolution reached the houses of even the poorest through the development of the 'underground city' of water and sewerage pipes and gas lines. The improving urban environment of the second half of the century owes much to the intervention of government into urban affairs. From the 1840s a long succession of legislation was passed through the Houses of Par-liament aimed at improving conditions in the cities. Initially, much of it was 'permissive' legislation requiring, not insisting, that local authorities should implement the measures of each Act. By the 1870s this had changed and the power of central government blew more strongly through the corridors of the town halls. New legislation covered everything from public health, the provision of parks, improvement of housing, to local government reform. No longer could the national government stand aside as cities developed. It had to guide and influence that development. The scene was now set for the twentieth-century growth in governmental power over where the nation's population lived and the quality of the environment in which they were to reside.

3.4 1895–1939: The growth of suburbia and the Garden Cities

The urban growth characteristics of the nineteenth century were sustained into the twentieth century as all the major conurbations continued to grow. There were, however, discernible shifts in population to match the growth of the new footloose consumer industries in the southern part of Britain. A north–south drift of population from the older industrial areas to the new was gathering momentum.

Greater London's population rose from 6.6 million in 1901 to 8.2 million by 1931, and 8.7 million by 1939 (Table 3.2). In the Midlands, Coventry, one of the fastest growing cities, increased by 20 per cent between 1931 and 1938 as against 3 per cent for the rest of the country. Such increases not only reflected high natural increase, but also a strong inflow of people from other parts of the country in search of work. Between 1923 and 1936 there was a population shift from the North and Wales to the South of about 1,160,000. In the three southern divisions of the Ministry of Labour there was an increase of 1,396,000, and in the Midlands 445,000, between 1923 and 1937. In comparison the insured population of the rest of Britain in-creased by only 576,000.

Table 3.2   Great Britain: population of the conurbations 1901–31 (millions)

Conurbation	1901	1911	1921	1931
Central Clydeside	1,374	1,498	1,618	1,688
Greater London	6,586	7,256	7,488	8,216
Merseyside	1,030	1,157	1,263	1,347
South East Lancashire	2,117	2,328	2,361	2,427
Tyneside	678	762	816	827
West Midlands	1,483	1,635	1,773	1,933
West Yorkshire	1,524	1,590	1,614	1,655
Total: 7 conurbations	14,792	16,226	16,933	18,093
Rest of Britain	22,208	24,605	25,836	26,702
Total: Britain	37,000	40,831	42,769	44,795

Sources: Cameron (1980, 15); Herbert (1982, 235)

Pressure of population upon our cities did not subside as the new century dawned, although the locational emphasis was changing. The problems of how and where the increasing national population should be housed remained. It was nevertheless a period of great promise, with changes in societal attitudes, exciting developments in transport technology, the emergence of modern town planning and an increasing awareness by government of a need to be more closely involved in housing.

In two particular respects the changing attitudes of society in the early twentieth century are important in understanding where people were to be housed. It had already become apparent before the end of the nineteenth century that the upper classes had shown a desire to reduce family size (Table 3.3). Their example was later followed by the middle and lower classes to the extent that between 1921 and 1931 class differences in fertility were considerably reduced with the average family now producing only two children. Such decline as this made it possible to house families in well-built small houses, usually of three bedrooms.

As the size of families was falling, the desire for amenity was rising. The second half of the nineteenth century had been a time for improving the quality of housing, introducing sewerage, water and gas to all classes of

Table 3.3   United Kingdom: family size 1890–1909 (average number of children)

	Couples married between	
	1890–99	1900–09
Professional family	2.80	2.05
White-collar worker's family	3.04	1.95
Skilled manual worker's family	4.85	3.24
Unskilled labourer	5.11	4.09

Source: Briggs (1983, 249) (figures taken from the text by arrangement with Weidenfeld & Nicolson)

home. Now the desire for amenity superseded the need for better sanitation. People not merely wished to live in better homes, but in pleasant environments corresponding in some degree to those enjoyed by the wealthier classes. Such environments would only be provided on the edge of the city in a suburban location.

To open up suburbia as a place to live required some fundamental changes in the financing of house building and in the organisation of the building industry. It was noted earlier that building societies had already emerged in the last century as providers of finance for house ownership. But their activities were on too small a scale to meet the latent demand for a suburban life style. As late as the 1920s only those who could afford a 25 per cent deposit were able to obtain mortgage finance. In the 1930s a remarkable transformation occurred as the building societies were seen as a secure place in which to invest money in a time of economic depression. Funds flowed in, enabling the societies to lend considerably more money than before and at lower rates of interest ($5–5\frac{1}{2}$ per cent). In financial terms this meant that the building societies grew from a situation in 1913 when their total assets were £65 million and they were advancing in that year £9 million to a situation in 1940 when the total amount outstanding on mortgages was £678 million and where one in eight of all families in Britain were mortgage holders.

One of the main barriers to home ownership before the 1930s was the size of the deposit – 25 per cent was too great for most families to find. To overcome this the 'Builders Pool' arrangement was negotiated between the societies and the house builders; under this arrangement a builder would pay a sum of money to a building society as a collateral security, and the society in return would advance up to 95 per cent of the purchase price of a new home. For the building industry to achieve such good financial terms required restructuring, for it was only the larger firms which could benefit from this new arrangement. In comparison with smaller firms they had superior credit-worthiness and could construct a larger number of houses at relatively low cost. It was possible, therefore, for a large builder to offer a house in the suburbs costing £800 for a deposit of only £25, with the builder paying the legal expenses. The example which Thomas Cubbitt had set in 1822 when he increased the size of his building firm to meet a growth in demand was now taken up by the building industry in order to satisfy demands for suburban housing of a semi-detached or detached kind, usually with three bedrooms. At the same time it achieved an agreement with the societies which would ensure the necessary capital to do so.

The inter-war suburbs could not have expanded so rapidly without significant developments in transport technology and in the establishment of a network of communications reaching far beyond the confines of the Victorian city. London, under increasing population pressure, developed the finest commuter system in the world through the expansion of the underground railway and its integration with the bus services which served the suburban stations. The underground was truly remarkable in the way it pushed out into the countryside to the north of London, opening up large areas of Middlesex to the commuter. In the north west of the county the Metropolitan line, the longest line in the system, was the main provider, whilst northern Middlesex was penetrated by several lines. In 1924 the

Northern Line was extended from Golders Green to Edgware. In 1932 a new line was laid to Stanmore, and by 1933 the Piccadilly line reached Cockfosters. To the south of the river the Southern Railway met the needs of the commuter through a fine mesh of lines and interchange points, together with the electrification of the whole system.

The year 1933 was also important for the creation of the London Passenger Transport Board. This brought some measure of unified control over passenger traffic in the London transport area. It took control over 170 railway, bus, tram, trolley bus and coach undertakings, so that it was now possible to integrate the suburban underground stations with bus feeder services and push the new suburban estates to locations away from the stations.

Further encouragement to the welling out of cities was given by motorised transport together with the growing number of arterial roads which swept through the suburbs. The car had, until 1914, retained a luxury image, but following the First World War the foundations of the car age were truly laid. Between 1919 and 1939 there was a 20-fold increase in the number of cars. The car industry through its improved assembly line production techniques and organisation was now able to offer cars at prices which a growing number of people could afford. In 1929 an Austin Seven could be purchased for £130, By 1935 Fords had produced their first £100 car, and four months before the Second World War the millionth car emerged from the Morris factory in Oxford. These 'wandering machines, travelling with an incredible rate of speed' (Liberal politician, 1909) brought an air of chaos to the fringes of the city. Villages were caught up in the fingers of ribbon development as housing spread out along the arterial roads, and good agricultural land was lost under the weight of bricks and mortar. The car and the railway unleashed a period of urban development unplanned and often out of control. The pressure was now on for government to restore order.

Government, at the turn of the century, had looked with favour on suburban growth, for it afforded a means of reducing population pressure on the inner city, whilst at the same time providing enhanced living conditions in a semi-rural atmosphere. John Burns, in introducing the first Town Planning Act in 1909, said, 'the Bill aims in broad outline at, and hopes to secure, the home healthy, the house beautiful, the town pleasant, the city dignified, and the suburb salubrious'. At the same time the government was also concerned at the way that: 'Every two and a half years there is a County of London converted into urban life from rural conditions and agricultural land. It represents an enormous amount of building land which we have no right to allow to go unregulated' (Parliamentary Debates on Housing, Town Planning Bill, May 1908; H. C. Debates, Vol. 188).

The Act of 1909 permitted local authorities to prepare town schemes. Unfortunately the legislation was vague and permissive in character, and although by March 1915 74 local authorities had been authorised to prepare 105 schemes, they did little to improve conditions in the cities or control suburban growth. If they failed, therefore, in this respect, it was nevertheless significant that town planning was recognised as a way of shaping and directing the physical growth of our cities. What was missing was the power to do it.

At this time one of the most influential figures in town planning was Ebenezer Howard. In 1898 he had set out his ideas on the form of future

51

cities in a book called *Tomorrow A Peaceful Path to Real Reform*, later revised in 1902 and entitled *Garden Cities of Tomorrow*. What was so remarkable about Howard was that he then proceeded to build two garden cities based upon the ideas in his book – Letchworth started in 1903, and Welwyn Garden City in 1919. In both these cities, which were planned to provide homes for about 30,000 people, he sought to intertwine the best of the countryside with the best of the town to form a garden city. The two cities contained within them a number of planning principles which were to influence future developments both in the inter-war garden suburbs, but more importantly in the New Towns built after the Second World War. These principles included:

(a) *Functional zoning*. The careful planning of land so that industrial uses were placed away from residential areas and an ordered pattern of land use was achieved which prevented the juxtaposition of conflicting uses.
(b) *Introduction of housing densities*. The garden city was to be a compact town of about 1,000 acres with a suggested population of 30,000, giving an overall density of 30 persons per acre. The housing densities were based upon an assumed family size of five and a half, and included access roads. This gave a density of 80 persons in about $14\frac{1}{4}$ houses per acre. When Raymond Unwin and Barry Parker were commissioned to design and build the first town at Letchworth, the densities varied from 6 to 12 houses per acre, and were part of the layout pattern informal in character, with ample private garden space at back and front, and a high degree of privacy.
(c) *Landscape*. The provision and planning of open space in the city was fundamental because it was an urban representation of the countryside. In Howard's diagrams of his city he provided a central park and a ring park 420 feet wide to contain the main schools with large playgrounds. In the actual design of the two cities the importance of large formal open space was maintained, if not in the exact form that Howard suggested. None the less, the formal gardens in Welwyn Garden City close to the shopping centre express what Howard was searching for. These fine gardens are just a part of the overall landscaping plan of the town which provided generous road verges planted with trees, grass verges and herbaceous borders. To prevent the removal of existing trees the roads were often planned around them so as to disturb the flora as little as possible.
(d) *Design control*. What Howard and his architects required was control over the design of all buildings, in particular houses where a multiplicity of design could destroy the overall quality of the urban landscape. In Letchworth this proved extremely difficult, since in a democracy the appearance of a house should, it was argued, be determined by the owner and his architect, not by an outside body. It therefore proved to be impossible to achieve this control, but in Welwyn Garden City, under the watchful eye of the town's architect, Louis Soissons, housing design was made to conform to an overall scheme for the town based upon the Hertfordshire Georgian style.

These two cities deserve close study because their influence on planning and urban design in the twentieth century has been so profound. They were the laboratories for testing urban ideas which were later applied to cities both here and abroad.

Ebenezer Howard and the Garden City Movement, together with such bodies as the National Housing Reform Council, pressurised the government into taking a more active role in the provision of housing, particularly for the poorer groups in society. The scale of the problem was such that a national policy on housing was required if residential conditions within existing towns were to be improved. Successive Housing Acts in 1851 and 1890 had empowered local authorities to build houses for the 'working classes', but the response had largely been ineffective. The need, therefore, for new initiatives was clear, although it required the First World War finally to convince the main political parties that state intervention was essential, and that 'homes for heroes' were necessary with the cessation of war.

In 1918 the *Tudor Walter's Report* was published, which provided standards of layout and design for proposed local authority estates. Many of the recommendations of this report were included in the *Housing and Town Planning Act* of 1919 (*The Addison Act*), which placed upon local authorities the responsibility for surveying their housing needs and submitting plans for house building, which would be subsidised by the State. It also gave guidance to local authorities on the development of council estates. This included:

(a) The recommendation that authorities purchased large lots of land surplus to immediate needs, on which up to 250 houses would be built.
(b) That semi-detached houses, usually of three bedrooms, should be provided since they commanded a higher rent, but at only a slightly higher construction cost than a terraced house.
(c) That sameness of design should be avoided and local materials used where possible.

Important though this Act was, its provision of housing subsidies was insufficient to persuade local authorities (several of whom thought the whole exercise no more than a temporary expedient) that public housing programmes were necessary. In the *Wheatley Act of 1924* a firmer foundation for the financing of public housing was introduced when the Treasury was enabled to provide a subsidy of £9 per house for 40 years on houses to let. Once this legislative framework had been provided a suburban housing programme was realised, with some local authorities developing new estates of considerable proportions. The London County Council, for example, built in 1925 the Downham Estate near Bromley for 32,000 people, and by 1934 had completed at Beacontree in Essex the largest estate in the world at the time, for over 100,000 people. These estates were used as a safety valve for the inner city, where the housing situation was often acute and the environment for living not much improved on that of the latter part of the nineteenth century. In fact, although this new public housing went some way to improving conditions for the poorer groups, it did not resolve the inner city problem.

The government, in response to this, passed in 1930 the *Greenwood Housing Act*, which provided subsidies for slum clearance. Then in 1933 they not only abolished the subsidies given under the Wheatley Act, but required local authorities to draw up programmes for slum clearance. Over a third of a million houses were demolished in clearance schemes begun in 1930. By

1938 these schemes were running at a rate of 90,000 houses demolished a year.

The State, which in the 1920s had built housing estates alongside private housing in the suburbs, turned back to the inner city just at the time when private house building was beginning to boom. Between 1930 and 1940 2,700,000 houses were built in England and Wales, the majority in suburban locations. Significantly, much of this growth was within the South and the Midlands, but more particularly in Greater London, where between 1919 and 1939 the population rose by 2 million, of which 1¼ million resulted from in-migration.

The inter-war period presented new problems of urbanisation, which to resolve required further government intervention. What form this should take emerged after the Second World War, which ironically provided, during a time of conflict and devastation, a check on urban growth and a moment of calm to consider what should be done next about the place where we live.

3.5   1940–95: Urban Sprawl and the North/South divide

The Third Kondratieff Wave ended with what has been described as the 'Devil's Decade', dominated by unemployment and ended by war. The immediate post-war period began with optimism and hope for the future with the new Labour Government taking power through the *New Towns Act of 1946* and more especially the *Town and Country Planning Act of 1947* to influence the use of the nation's land and concomitant with that, where people lived.

Two major issues required immediate attention. Firstly, the need to control the urban sprawl of the conurbations and large towns in order to prevent further removal of good agricultural land by urban development. Secondly, the need to reduce the economic imbalance between North and South which, during the inter-war period, had generated a population movement from the old industrial areas to the more affluent Midlands and South East. The long period of war had provided an opportunity for government to seek solutions to these problems. Far from being a time of inactivity, several important committees were constituted and their valuable work was to shape government thinking and legislation after the war.

The Barlow Commission, appointed in 1937, reported to government in the early months of the war its recommendations on the future distribution of the industrial population of Great Britain. It considered it 'not in the national interest, economically, socially or strategically, that a quarter or even a larger proportion of the population of Great Britain should be concentrated within 20 or 30 miles or so of Central London'. The Commission therefore suggested a policy of balanced distribution of industry and industrial population as far as possible throughout the different areas or regions in Great Britain. The implication of such a policy would have important ramifications on the places where people would live.

The Uthwatt Committee, set up in 1941, considered the difficult problems associated with the development of land. If governments were to control more closely the use of land, then a way had to be found to do this within a democratic framework. Nationalisation of land might be unacceptable, but control could be achieved, the committee suggested, by vesting the development rights in undeveloped land with the State. In effect, no one could develop their land for any purpose without first receiving permission. The Labour Government after the war accepted this view and incorporated it in the 1947 Town and Country Planning Act. This gave to the local authorities considerable power over where homes could be built, their character and their density.

The third committee which strongly influenced the way land was to be used was the Committee on Land Utilisation in Rural Areas, which produced the influential *Scott Report* in 1942. This stressed the need to protect the countryside, for the benefit of its inhabitants and for the agricultural industry, from the pressure created by the expanding urban areas. This protectionist vein within the report led to the recommendation of a 'green belt policy for the major towns and cities'. At the same time the Committee recognised the need to make the countryside more accessible to the urban population. To do this they suggested the introduction of national parks, a recommendation later implemented in the *1949 National Parks and Countryside Act*. The effects on population distribution would be far-reaching if the countryside was protected in this way, but with the recommendations of all three committees in tandem the changes would be profound.

Alongside, and to a large extent in sympathy with, the committee's views town and country planners were themselves exploring ways of directing future urban growth and revitalising the decaying and bomb-scarred cities once the War ended. The most important plan to emerge was Sir Patrick Abercrombie's plan for Greater London, published in 1944. In the plan it was suggested that:

(a) A green belt should be established around the capital to stop the physical growth of the city.
(b) That London should be developed at relatively low densities of population – 136 to the residential area over much of inner London, rising to 200 in a small area at the centre.
(c) That eight New Towns should be built beyond the green belt. This was necessary to provide housing and work for the 'overspill' population which inevitably would result from the implementation of the first two ideas.

The necessary legislation for this was contained in the New Towns Act of 1946, which provided for the setting up of development corporations to plan and create New Towns whenever the Minister was satisfied 'that it is expedient in the national interest' to do so. These corporations were given considerable power to 'acquire, hold, manage and dispose of land and property, to carry out building and other operations, to provide water, electricity, gas, sewerage and other services, to carry on any business or undertakings in or for the purpose of the New Town, and generally to do anything necessary or expedient for the purposes of the New Town or the purposes incidental thereto'.

55

The *1946 New Towns Act* was an indication of the wide powers government was prepared to take to control urban development and the use of land. The 1947 Town and Country Planning Act confirmed such an impression by recognising the need for town and country planning and providing wide powers for the new planning departments which would be established within the local authority structure. The Act provided that:

(a) The responsibility for town and country planning was to be vested in county councils and county boroughs.
(b) That almost all development was to be brought under control by making it subject to planning permission. No owner of land could normally be allowed to develop that land without permission from the local authority. Appeals against a local authority's decision lay with the Minister.
(c) Development plans were to be prepared for every area in the country and submitted to the Minister three years from 1 July 1948, thereafter to be revised every five years. These were to outline the way each area was to be developed, or preserved.
(d) The co-ordination of these plans was to be the responsibility of the new Minister of Town and Country Planning.
(e) Development rights in land were to be nationalised. All future land required for development would be compulsorily purchased at a value reflecting its existing use.

The measures within the Act were far-reaching. Ratcliffe (1981) commented that 'it is impossible to exaggerate the importance of the 1947 Act for it provided the most comprehensive and radical framework for the control of land use in the world'.

Planning for the reconstruction of our cities and the associated New Town strategy was conceived by planners and government within a belief that post-war population growth would be slight. The 1930s saw the birth rate fall, and there seemed nothing to suggest to the demographers that a major burst in the rate of natural increase could be expected. One view expressed at the time was that a fall in population was likely, and certainly Sir Patrick Abercrombie expected no increase for London. In 1949 a Royal Commission Report on the population of Great Britain rejected these views, but even its predictions fell short of what actually happened. It was officially forecast that the population of Great Britain, which had been 46.6 million in 1940, would only rise to 47.2 million in 1961, instead of an actual total of 51.2 million. This dramatic increase, of which the post-war marriage boom was a significant factor, led to anxiety that the population was rising too rapidly, and raised doubts about the country's ability to absorb all these people.

These fears proved unfounded when in 1966 the birth rate dropped dramatically from a maximum of 6.4 per 1,000 per annum during the decade 1956 to 1966 to a position between mid-1974 and 1978 when the population of the UK actually declined by 87,000, and another net fall was recorded in the year to mid-1982. Subsequently there has been a modest increase, but this cannot alter the fact that there is now a society of smaller families and delayed childbirth.

The post-war period has also witnessed changes in society which have affected the distribution of population and the morphologies of settlements.

In particular these have included:

(a) The restructuring of employment — the further decline of the basic industries (coal, steel, shipbuilding), the continuing growth of the
consumer industries, but most importantly the accelerating growth of
service industries, with in recent times the effects of new technology on
new forms of employment and location of work.
(b) The successive improvements in transport technology, which have
reduced the costs and to some degree the times of journeys to work,
with the result that urban residents can exercise a greater degree of
choice in their residential location.
(c) The growing concern for the quality of life, which has brought demands
for higher environmental standards both at home and in the work place.

All these factors, together with a growing range of regional and urban
policies, and widening planning powers over the use of land, have brought
changes to the place of home.

3.6 The evolving pattern of population distribution

The United Kingdom continued to increase its urban population (Table 3.4)
until the early 1970s in what Hall et al. (1973) described as 'megalopolitan'
England (Fig. 3.1), a functionally linked zone of city regions and high
population densities extending from the Channel coast to Lancashire and
Yorkshire.

Within these urban zones it was the suburban areas which accounted for
most of this growth, and in particular the small- and medium-sized towns
outside the green belts but within the urban hinterlands of the larger
cities. This growth underlined the continuing decentralisation process begun
during the inter-war years, which was now having serious effects in the inner
city areas of our larger cities, where slum clearance and large-scale
redevelopment schemes in the 1950s and 1960s created disillusionment
amongst the population, many of whom joined the stream of migrants
moving out to suburbia and beyond.

All the conurbations, with the exception of West Yorkshire, lost population between 1961 and 1971. This continued at a more rapid rate in the
following 10 years, when all lost a significant proportion of their inhabitants
(Table 3.5).

Table 3.4 Population in the United Kingdom 1951–71

	1951	1961	1966	1971
UK population (000s)	50,225.2	52,708.9	53,788.5	55,349.0
Population in megalopolitan England	30,489.2	32,241.9	32,864.5	33,839.3
Percentage of UK population	60.7	61.2	61.1	61.1

Source: Goldsmith (1980, 49)

Figure 3.1 Urban Britain.
Source: based on Cameron (1980, map 1); and Hall *et al.*
(1973, Fig. 6.3).

megalopolis England

● Cities over 200,000

Conurbations
1 Greater London
2 West Midlands (Birmingham)
3 S.E. Lancashire (Manchester)
4 Central Clydeside (Glasgow)
5 W. Yorkshire (Leeds)
6 Merseyside (Liverpool)
7 Tyneside (Newcastle)

SCOTLAND

Edinburgh

Sunderland

NORTHERN
IRELAND
Belfast

NORTH

YORKSHIRE AND
HUMBERSIDE

Teesside

Hull

NORTH WEST

Sheffield

EAST
MIDLANDS

Nottingham
Stoke
Derby

WEST
MIDLANDS

Leicester

EAST ANGLIA

Coventry

WALES

Cardiff
● Bristol

SOUTH EAST

SOUTH WEST

Southampton

Plymouth

Table 3.5 Great Britain: population of the conurbations 1951–81

	1951	1961	1971	1981	Percentage Inter-censal increase or decrease		
					1951–61	1961–71	1971–81
Central Clydeside	1,758,500	1,802,000	1,727,600	1,713,287	2.4	−4.3	− 0.8
Greater London	8,348,023	7,992,443	7,452,346	6,696,008	−4.2	−6.8	−10.1
Merseyside	1,382,443	1,384,381	1,266,723	1,127,080	+0.1	−8.5	−11.0
South-East Lancashire	2,422,650	2,427,807	2,392,993	2,244,859	+0.2	−1.4	− 6.2
Tyneside	835,533	855,555	805,434	738,156	+2.3	−5.9	− 8.4
West Midlands	2,237,095	2,378,005	2,371,565	2,243,726	+6.2	−0.3	− 5.4
West Yorkshire	1,692,687	1,703,678	1,728,251	1,681,879	+0.6	+1.4	− 2.7

Sources: 1981 census: Preliminary report for towns urban and rural population, England and Wales, 15; 1951 census: England, Wales. Report on Greater London and five other conurbations, 6, 81, 148, 213, 262, 313; 1971 census: Scotland, 3; 1981 census: Scotland, 3.
Note: There were small changes in conurbation boundaries between censuses but these are not generally significant.

Such falls in population are in one sense welcome because they reduce the pressure of population upon the older parts of our cities and give breathing space to restore and generate new life. Unfortunately the decline in population has been too much and at too fast a pace. Nowhere is this better illustrated than in London, where, for example, Islington lost 101,478 people or over 38.8 per cent of its population between 1961 and 1981, and Tower Hamlets, where the loss was and 62,707 (30.4 per cent) over the same period. This loss was the more serious because of its selective nature, removing the most able, skilled working or middle class people within the 25–44 year old band, and leaving behind the unskilled and the elderly. In Liverpool in 1981, one in five of the population was over 60.

The loss to the cities was to the gain of the towns and villages within their urban hinterlands, to the New Towns, and to the Developing or Expanded towns.

3.7 Towns and villages

The increasing affluence of the majority of the population, together with increasing car ownership, enabled people to live further from their place of work, in a new type of suburbia within towns and villages outside the physical confines of the city. Thus around all our major cities during the 1950s and 1960s these settlements increased their share of the urban population, whether they were such towns as Macclesfield or Wilmslow around Manchester or Weybridge, Watford or Reading around London.

3.7.1 New Towns

The emerging pattern of New Towns, begun by Stevenage in 1946, provided a quality of living and working environments which could not be matched in the inner city areas. For the most part people came to these towns to live and work, not to use them as dormitories while they continued to travel to the large cities for work. Ebenezer Howard's belief that towns could be largely self-contained and yet be within close proximity of cities was born out by the experience of the New Towns.

The New Towns have not been without their critics but they do represent a 'triumphant success' (Hall, 1966) in their main aim of acting as counter-magnets to the cities for industry and people as well as providing a new environment of quality for their residents. In recent times they have come into disfavour with government, as the problems of the cities have increased and the population growth on which New Towns depended has fallen away.

In *1978* Peter Shore, the Secretary of the Department of Environment, initiated the *Inner Urban Areas Act*, which provided for a switch of resources from New Towns and suburban growth back to the inner city through partnership arrangements between central and local government. This brought to an end the New Town programme, though not New Town growth, which in 1981 was still increasing despite the overall stabilisation of the population.

3.7.2 Developing Towns

The Labour Government, which introduced the New Towns after the war, had by 1950 established eight New Towns for London, two in Durham, one in the Midlands, one in South Wales and two in Scotland, and yet its support for this policy was lukewarm. The Conservatives who took office in 1951 seemed of a similar opinion, for they strongly favoured 'town development' by local authorities rather than New Towns. In *1951* they passed through Parliament the *Town Development Act*, which enabled small towns to expand by entering into agreements with cities wishing to export surplus population. Most of the larger schemes were related to London and towns within an average distance of 123 km from the metropolis. East Anglia was one region which saw this as an opportunity to revitalise its stagnating market towns through the input of new people and industry, Suffolk alone agreed six schemes with London, and Norfolk attempted to expand the town of East Dereham by importing the overspill population from Birmingham. This in fact failed, but it did not discourage towns like King's Lynn and Thetford from drawing up similar agreements with London.

The town development programme was criticised for being little more than a simple housing arrangement in towns where the population was too small to support the range of services or variety of jobs found in the New Towns. By the end of the decade attention turned again to the New Towns programme, which received fresh impetus as political sympathies changed. Nevertheless, the Developing Towns continued to play a role in the decentralisation process alongside the expanding outer suburbs and New Towns until the Greater London Council withdrew its support because London was losing too many skilled and affluent workers to these overspill towns.

With the fall in the birth rate and the run-down of the New Town and town development progammes in the 1970s, the results of the 1981 census were awaited with great interest. The initial analysis which subsequently took place has revealed some interesting trends in the population distribution of the country:

(a) The population of the UK saw only a slight rise over the decade of 280,711. Where there was a significant increase in any part of the country it could only be explained by migration, for the rate of natural increase was so low. In fact, from the beginning of 1976 to the end of the first quarter of 1978 more deaths than births were recorded, which was the first time this had occurred since civil registration began in 1837.

(b) The areas which gained population were:
   (i) the villages and towns at the end of localised decentralisation movements which, because they were within the commuter fields of the cities, maintained their growth;
   (ii) the New Towns and Expanded Towns, although the early New Towns either lost population or experienced low rates of growth;
   (iii) the districts in the rural peripheral areas of East Anglia, the South West, mid-Wales and many parts of Yorkshire, areas which in the 1960s were often losing population.

This last trend is particularly interesting, although its significance should not be exaggerated since the number of people involved is small. Nevertheless, it has prompted analysts to suggest, as Vining and Kontuly (1978) have for other countries where similar trends have been detected, that such movements from the high population core regions to the periphery represent a 'clean break' between the two. This view is not supported by Hamnett and Randolph (1982) in their analysis of the UK results. Rather it is suggested that this is a continuing part of the long-term evolution of population distribution. It represents the removal of the industrial pattern of population and the emergence of a post-industrial pattern where those that can afford it are seeking a higher quality of life in the more rural areas.

(c) The places which lost population were the conurbations and towns of over 100,000. The decline of the inner city areas has continued, but, as might be expected, the rate of decline has slowed largely because the mobile sector of the population has already left. There are also the beginnings of a re-evaluation of the inner city by the middle classes and a movement back into it as part of the process of gentrification. In Islington and Fulham, for example, the middle class are displacing working class people from homes close to the very centre of London which are structurally sound but where rehabilitation is required. Often, like Barnsbury in Islington, these were former areas of the middle class in the last century.

(d) The movement of population from the North to the South has continued. The long-term adjustment of population to the decline of the old industrial areas, and the re-emergence of the pre-industrial dominance of southern Britain is still present.

The South of Britain is now the technological leader, with the majority of the 'high tech' industries located there. It is also perceived to offer a better quality of life, perhaps because the climatic conditions of the south seem less extreme, and the towns appear unscarred by the Industrial Revolution.

The reasons for this drift may be complex, but more recent figures issued by the Office of Population Censuses and Surveys indicate it is still continuing. Between 1981 and 1985 Scotland's population fell by 43,700, that of the North West 73,200, and of Yorkshire and Humberside by 15,800. The gainers were the South East with 181,000, the South West with 119,000 and East Anglia with 70,000. This at a time when the birth rate was more or less stable.

The population movements since the Second World War suggest that government attempts to redistribute population away from the large urban areas have succeeded. British cities, which were for so long the destination for migrants from the countryside, no longer have the pulling power they once had. Many have shed population, as people have moved away to commuter villages and New Towns. This decentralisation process, already evident before the War, was stimulated further by governments in the post-war years through the constraining policy of the green belts and the counter-magnet New Town and Developing Town programmes. Where government has not been so successful is in stemming the movement of population from North to South. The more even spread of economic activity suggested by the Barlow Commission has not been achieved: the pull of the South remains.

The desire of people to move away from the cities is to some degree a result of their urban environments, which were designed and built during the 1950s and 1960s when the need for housing was acute. At this time 4 million people were still living in slums or largely unmodernised nineteenth-century housing. This prompted the post-war Labour Government to set an annual target of 247,000 new houses a year, which it never achieved, and the succeeding Conservative Government 300,000 houses a year. Sir Harold Macmillan, who was then Minister of Housing and Local Government, managed to achieve this high total by supporting the New Towns programme, by introducing the Town Development Act in 1952, and by in-itiating large-scale redevelopment schemes within existing cities.

Numbers are not everything. The quality of housing and housing layouts within the New Towns and Expanded Towns brought for the most part an improved environment to many people. In the major cities, however, the story was often very different. Here there seemed to be an obsession with 'bigness' and high density. Redevelopment schemes were large in concep-tion, requiring the destruction not only of decaying houses but also those of sound structure, over extensive areas of the inner city. Such comprehensive policies led to the disruption of the social fabric of these areas and to the redistribution of families to other parts of the cities. Little attempt was made to protect and maintain the communities that existed.

The obsession with density and also cost resulted in the high-rise blocks of flats, or the long horizontal blocks which can be seen in many of our cities. These new housing units were encouraged by government through housing grants and some 2 million people were rehoused in high-rise blocks in the 1960s. This continued until 1968, when the Ronan Point disaster in Newham, East London, brought the collapse of a 22-story block of flats and the death of five people.

If high-rise blocks fell from grace, the long horizontal blocks of flats did not. People with no tradition of flat living were still expected to raise children within environments at odds with family living.

The growing disillusionment with high-rise living and comprehensive redevelopment schemes coincided with a down turn in the economic fortunes of the country. Resources for urban renewal were cut back and a reassess-ment of housing policy became essential if the nation's housing stock was to be both improved and increased. In 1969 a total of nearly 73,000 houses were demolished; 10 years later the annual figure was only 30,000.

In the *1969 Housing Act*, grants which had first become available for home improvement in 1949 were raised in an attempt to persuade both local authorities and house owners to improve their properties, and to ensure that they contained the three basic facilities: a bath, a lavatory, and hot and cold running water. Local authorities, New Towns and Housing Associations now became eligible for aid in acquiring houses for conversion and improvement. Perhaps of more significance was the introduction of General Improvement Areas (GIAs) and Housing Action Areas (HAAs).

3.7.3 General Improvement Areas

The general improvement area was to be a residential area of 300–500 houses, although most are smaller, which local authorities were free to declare. The houses themselves were to have at least 30 years of life for improvement to be worth while. Initially grants for rehabilitation were no different from anywhere else, and owners were not compelled to improve their properties. It was not surprising, therefore, that take-up was slow. Furthermore, the small grants available to improve the environmental conditions by pedestrianising streets, providing play areas and landscaping, provided little incentive for real improvement.

By 1973 it was clear that the GIA was not satisfactory in its present form, and the government in the 1974 Housing Act clarified the GIA concept more precisely and gave a preferential rate for grants within these areas, increasing it from 50 per cent of the agreed cost to 60 per cent. The GIAs would now consist of fundamentally sound houses providing good living conditions for many years and under no threat of redevelopment programmes. The area would offer scope for creating a better environment and contain stable communities which were largely free from housing stress. The voluntary nature of the rehabilitation process was retained and for this reason predominantly rented accommodation was considered largely unsuitable.

3.7.4 Housing Action Areas

The *1974 Housing Act* also contained a new housing area, the Housing Action Area (HAA), which was designed to deal with housing stress. The emphasis was placed upon action and so these areas, where housing was judged unsatisfactory, would have to be effectively upgraded within five years. The aims were to improve:

(a) the housing accommodation in the area as a whole;
(b) the well-being of the persons for the time being residing in the area; and
(c) the proper and effective management and use of that accommodation.

The characteristics of the areas which could be declared HAAs were interesting because they included both social and physical factors. There now appeared to be concern about the *people* living in these areas and not the houses alone, which had in the past provided the criteria for grant aid. HAAs can be declared in areas with the following characteristics:

(a) large dwellings but small households — this would indicate multiple occupation and shared amenities;
(b) physical conditions which point to clearance but to do so would cause social disruption because no alternative housing is available;
(c) a predominance of private rented accommodation;
(d) unattractive surroundings with evidence of abandonment.

Such areas, which are mainly terraced and built between 1870 and 1910, are still a feature of inner cities, and although the suggested size of the HAA was to be between 300 and 400 houses, many, particularly in London and the West Midlands, are over 500, with some over 1,000 houses.

The hand of the local authorities in rehabilitating areas they designated was strengthened by giving them compulsory purchase powers, although it was envisaged that voluntary improvement and persuasion were of more importance. To some degree it was hoped that the grants, which were higher than the GIAs (government contribution 75 per cent of agreed cost and 90 per cent in hardship cases), would encourage house owners to improve their property, but this was difficult to achieve because the Fair Rent Act was considered to suppress rents and the house owner found it difficult to recoup his portion of the outlay because of this. Another problem which emerged was that grants were going to relatively high-quality improvements, and a government review of housing policy suggested that the 'work on the renovation of older houses should be directed more at bringing larger numbers of houses up to a decent basic standard rather than on higher standard improvements of a smaller number of houses'. (Housing Policy: Consultative Document, 1977.)

In the *1980 Housing Act* this suggestion was incorporated into a legislative framework which emphasised the need for a more flexible system which would direct resources to the houses most in need of them. To this end the grants system was restructed to provide three main grants:

Improvement grants — at the discretion of the local authority.
Intermediate grants — for standard amenities. These can be claimed as of right.
Repair grants — for pre-1919 houses.

In assessing the amount of grant available the local authority had for the first time to consider not only the property but its occupants, who should either be elderly or on low income and therefore least able to improve their property.

This system is now to be superseded by a much simplified grant structure with a single form of mandatory grant available to bring property up to a new standard of fitness. Above this standard, grant assistance will be at the discretion of local authorities (*Housing: The Government's Proposals*, 1987). Along with this simplified structure has come a cut in improvements grants from 75 per cent to 20 per cent of the total cost of the work undertaken (*Housing Act 1988*). The Government argues that as the Act allows landlords to charge higher rents, for the new 'assured tenancies', which are for a fixed period, or on a weekly, monthly or yearly basis, it is no longer appropriate to pay out large grants.

Since the 1950s successive governments have injected considerable resources into creating better houses and living environments for the poorer groups in society. More powers for action have been given to the local authorities and the introduction of town and country planning and its controlling governmental body, the Department of the Environment, should have brought a sensitive and flexible system to the provision of housing. Unfortunately, the Utopian ideas which were present during and after the Second World War do not appear to have been realised in the older housing areas of the larger cities. In some ways it is difficult to comprehend that in the New Towns, the development corporations were building houses with gardens for rent whilst in the cities local authorities, with government direction, were building high-rise blocks of flats for similar young families when there existed no tradition for such housing. In a detailed study of the post-war inner city housing estates, which covered over 4,000 blocks of flats with accommodation for some quarter of a million people, Coleman (1985) and her researchers highlighted the inhuman design of the tall blocks (the taller, the more lavish the governmental subsidy), with the resulting vandalism and crime which has now brought local authorities to the point where they are destroying them. This was accommodation which 'embraced the Utopian ideal of housing planned by a paternalistic authority, which offered hopes of improving standards, but also ran the risk of trapping people in dwellings not of their choosing'.

Fortunately since 1968, when government subsidy for high-rise blocks ended, these housing areas have no longer been built. In their place has come housing of lower level but still high density, a half-way house between the individual house and the high-rise block, a building compromise which still does not meet the desires of the occupants, who wish to live in individual homes. To Alice Coleman the inter-war semi-detached house, built when people were left free to secure the best accommodation they could, provides the ideal house and garden to satisfy people's housing needs.

The achievements in the private sector have been more secure where the requirements of the buyer have to be seriously considered. Nevertheless, the 1950s and 1960s saw housing of poor design and inferior materials being built throughout the country. At that time capital for housing was available, the demand was high and the need to achieve high building standards was not paramount. Conversely in the 1970s as depression set in, the building industry had to improve if it was to sell.

Today, the Government is concerned to increase house ownership. In 1951 there were 4 million home owners, in 1983 13 million, which represented an increase in private housing ownership of from 20 to 60 per cent of the housing stock. In mid-1987 this had risen further to over 63 per cent, with the possibility of reaching 72 per cent by the year 2000 according to the Building Societies Association. House ownership is popular and there are good reasons for encouraging it, since it offers a considerable degree of individual control over the environment and more mobility within an area than any other tenure. Despite this, it does present some disturbing features. The disparity between housing prices in the South of England and parts of East Anglia, and those in the rest of the country causes concern. In 1986 the North-South divide in property prices widened sharply. While house prices in the North of England increased by less than 10 per cent, they rose by more than 20 per cent in Greater London and the South East. Such a situation reduces labour mobility from areas of high unemployment to the relatively secure areas in the South. It also makes it extremely difficult for people to afford to buy without making an enormous financial commitment which may become difficult to maintain.

What is particularly disturbing about such a inflationary spiral in house prices in the South is that little is being done to stop or to limit its rise. Rather than releasing land for building and encouraging the building industry to provide more housing, the main effort appears to be to evolve more ways of borrowing money. A headline to an advertisement in *The Times* (26 August 1986) encapsulates this trend: 'Runaway house prices. Three new ways to catch up'. These three ways are new types of mortgage for people wanting £50,000 (or a great deal more). If housing is a basic need, who gains from this form of market economy in housing? One might conclude that it is the money lender rather than the house buyer.

For young couples it has meant buying houses at the lower end of the range, which usually means nineteenth-century, terraced properties, if they can afford to buy them. This generates in certain areas the process of gentrification as the young middle classes occupy housing formerly built for the working classes. The mechanics of this change are either part of the normal buying and selling of houses as particularly elderly owners die or move away, or as the result of landlords selling their properties and removing the sitting tenants. In the 1970s when this process of social change was noted in Barnsbury in Islington, sitting tenants were harassed if they refused to move by owners who wished to sell. It can be argued that gentrification leads to an upgrading of housing as the more affluent modernise these properties. It also increases the rate return to local authorities in the inner city, but it can also lead to a loss of housing to those in most need: the poor.

There is no doubt that British people are better housed then ever before, but there still remains a crisis situation in the inner cities and outer estates. It should not be forgotten that the number of homeless has risen steadily each year from 53,000 in 1978 (families accepted as homeless under the terms of the *Housing (Homeless Persons) Act of 1977*) to 83,000 in 1984, 93,000 in 1985 and in 1986 to 100,000. There are also at least 160,000 people living in board and lodging accommodation, 4 million homes are substandard and, at the present slum-clearing rate a house built today will have to last for 1,000 years.

Much has still to be done before all British people are well housed, so it is essential that housing forms a major priority in the plans of any government. The Archbishop of Canterbury's Commission Report (1986) underlined this when it concluded that 'the right to decent secure housing should take its place beside the right to adequate education, to appropriate health care, to food and clothing'.

4 Place of leisure

'The industrialised world is entering an important new era in which the dominant role traditionally given to work is being challenged by an altogether different human experience; the reality of leisure' (Pigram, 1983).

The importance with which leisure and recreation occupy our thinking in the latter part of the twentieth century reflects the torment felt by many in society who believe that the post-industrial age we have now entered will lead to fewer and fewer people working, to increasing levels of unemployment and therefore more people with a need to find other ways of filling time. The need, in effect, to switch from a life centred on work to one centred on leisure.

Michael Dower (1965) recognised this when (in 1965) he wrote about the impact which leisure was going to have on Britain. He placed his remarks within the Kondratieff sequence by pointing out that Britain had experienced three great Waves since 1800: the first, the sudden growth of industrial towns; the second the onset of railways and the effect on urban growth; and the third the sprawl of the car-based suburb. Now Britain was to experience the fourth, and in his view the most powerful, the Wave of leisure.

This chapter considers the importance of recreation and leisure in people's lives, and the impact that this has on policy decisions about the need for recreational provision both in the town, in the countryside and at the coast. However, the increasing importance of leisure must be seen within a historical context because the surge of the leisure Wave has come as a result of the generation of forces occurring during the nineteenth century. In fact, it is not out of place to suggest that the evolution of leisure can be set within the Kondratieff sequence.

But what is leisure? A simple working definition would be to suggest that leisure is closely associated with uncommitted time when the disciplines of work, sleep and other basic needs have been met. This is not completely satisfactory because leisure can overlap into work.

The weekend family shop may be a pleasurable time away from the demands of work, but for mother, at least, it can be considered as just another part of her working week. To go out to dinner is satisfying a basic need to eat but it is also a pleasurable occasion which takes place after the work of the day is finished. To define leisure is therefore difficult, for as Patmore (1983) suggests, 'Leisure is more readily experienced than defined.' Nevertheless, the concept of uncommitted time being closely related to leisure is valid.

There is often confusion over the meaning of the terms recreation and leisure, with the result that they are indiscriminately used. Though they are closely related, a distinction can be drawn between them, for recreation is concerned with activity and leisure with time. It is recreational activities which bring pleasure and satisfaction during the time laid aside for leisure. The increasing usage of these words within everyday speech is some indication of the growing importance of leisure time in people's lives, and an awareness of the Fourth Wave which seems increasingly to occupy an important part of social life. Where, then, does it begin?

4.1   Before 1781: Leisure and the élite

The discovery of leisure in society is of particular interest because it reveals changing attitudes, from a period when leisure was for a rich élite, to one where the majority have leisure time. Before the Industrial Revolution the population was concerned with survival, and any time in which recreational activities occured was closely associated with work. The majority of the population lived in rural areas where the rhythm of the seasons largely shaped the form of everyday life. Time for recreation could only be found when the demands of the land lessened, so, for example, holidays occured during the 12 days of Christmas, a week at both Easter and Whitsuntide, and other individual days such as Whitsun, May Day and Midsummer Day. To the medieval villager holidays were numerous, but they were not considered as separate from work, rather they were integrated with it. They were a part of life, a hard life which required some respite for feasts and ales, for song, music and dancing.

The aristocrats were a small élite who had a great deal of leisure time and were able to spend months enjoying themselves at expensive inland spas such as those at Bath and Tunbridge Wells, which were isolated either by distance (Matlock, Buxton) or price (Tunbridge Wells) from the middle or lower classes, Epsom's place in the aristocrats' list of leisure resorts was short-lived because it was 'cluttered with Company . . . being so near to London' (Morris (ed.) 1949, *Journeys of Celia Fiennes*. The eighteenth century marked the great age of the spa, when, for a few, much time was devoted to the pursuit of pleasure. There were, though, signs of a new order and new attitudes as the Industrial Revolution took hold, and to be industrious became a praiseworthy characteristic.

4.2   1781–1841: Leisure and the Industrial Revolution

This was a period which brought about fundamental changes in society's attitudes towards leisure. The aristocrats soon were unable to maintain their privileged position in the spa towns, which became increasingly invaded by the growing middle classes. By 1806, guide books pointed to a changing situation, commenting, for example, 'that Scarborough was now a resort of persons of inferior quality, but the coast was for a time a place where the élite could still find respite'. The Sussex coast became a great attraction during the summer months largely due to the publication of Dr Richard Russell's dissertation in 1750 concerning the 'Use of Sea Water in the Diseases of the Glands', and also due to the realisation by another learned doctor, Dr Relham, of the purity of sea air.

The rich, with further impetus of royal patronage, turned to the south coast, particularly Brighton, which by 1830 had surpassed Bath as the principal resort, or to Worthing, Hastings and Eastbourne. But resorts so close to London even for horse-drawn carriages, which could reach Brighton in five hours, could not maintain their isolation. With the coming of the railways not only the south coast but also those resorts in close proximity to the industrial towns became sources of pleasure to a growing variety of people.

Changes of this nature were cosmetic when viewed against structural changes which were to shape thinking and actions up until the present time. Alan Patmore (1983) suggested two such changes: the first concerned the changed organisation of work; and the second, the emergence of pervasive puritanism.

The Industrial Revolution of the nineteenth century was instrumental in setting totally new work practices on a population who previously had maintained themselves in small rural communities dependent upon work either on the nearby farms or in cottage industries of a few workers. The new industries brought a new scale of employment, of 'gigantism' where the size of both the living and working unit far surpassed anything that had gone before. Norwich, during the heyday of the East Anglian woollen industry, had never exceeded a population of 21,000. It was, up until the 1800s, the largest provincial town in England, and yet some new industrial towns by the 1850s were already reaching over a half a million.

Now a level of organisation had to be imposed upon the workforce of the new industrial towns which was to involve long hours of work throughout the year, to be paid for by a money wage. The result was fewer holidays, because, unlike agricultural labour, periods of work were not controlled by seasons. Factories could continue their relentless production throughout the year. The industrial workers, including women and children, toiled for long hours, until Lord Althorp's *Factory Act of 1833* set legal limits to the working hours of children and young people, with enforcement through the appointment of factory inspectors with powers to enter factories. *The Ten Hours Act of 1847* limited the daily work of women and youths in textile mills, and as a result compelled the stoppage of all work after 10 hours each day. Nevertheless, in the 1850s the average working week was 60 hours or more spread over six days, and this, with a severe reduction of periodic holidays, left little time for recreation for the working classes.

Paralleling this oppressive work structure, with the need to earn to be able to buy basic requirements, was the belief in work as a praiseworthy activity. Victorian society thought little of leisure, which filled a subordinate, even inferior, role to work. Gone also was recreation in the community, which had been a part of village life. In the city it was an individual or family activity when it was possible to pursue it; a welcome relief from work, rather that an integral part of it.

If the formative years of the Industrial Revolution saw the powerful emergence of the work ethic, they also witnessed the growing distinction between work and leisure time. This inevitably meant that as improvements in working conditions and working hours were achieved, so more time was available for leisure. This increasingly became a time for personal enjoyment and fulfilment, particularly as wages began to rise, giving some surplus income available to use beyond the provision of basic needs. As yet, though, this was still to come as society reacted to the evils of industrial towns and as the new-found technology of the railways gradually opened up new opportunities for working people to travel away from their homes.

4.3   1842–94: Leisure and the Victorian Economy

Despite the improvement in working hours, the working classes still spent most of their waking hours working. The people with time and money for recreation were the middle classes, who took advantage of the growing railway network to follow the fashion, initiated by the aristocracy, of going to the sea. Between 1801 and 1851 the coastal resorts were the fastest growing towns in Britain, mainly situated in the South East within reach of the middle classes, who could afford the high fares set by the railway companies. These were the 'excursion' trains for the proletariat, which, whilst fostering the growth of the southern resorts, had little impact in the north where as late as 1871 Scarborough's population was less than 20,000 and Blackpool's was only 6,000.

The influence of the railways could not be contained within one social stratum nor to one set of locations along our coasts. In 1841 Thomas Cook, who founded the travel agency, called for railways for the millions, and was instrumental in persuading railway companies to issue cheap tickets for daily excursions. The railway companies themselves gradually realised the potential for transporting people on daily visits to countryside and coast. The first excursion trains to Brighton ran in 1844, and in 1862 132,000 people were carried to the resort on Easter Monday, thus destroying the exclusive image which that town had enjoyed earlier in the century.

Urban destinations also begin to feature in the programme of excursion trains. In 1851 the Great Exhibition in London gave an opportunity for the railways to provide excursion trains from a wide area of the country to London. The journey from the West Riding to the Capital cost as little as 5*s*. Liverpool, Manchester, Birmingham, Derby and Nottingham were also among the major urban areas to receive these daily holidaymakers, but it must be said that such excursions were not always welcome. The Vice-Chancellor of the University of Cambridge certainly did not approve:

'The Vice-Chancellor of the University of Cambridge presents his compliments to the Directors of the Eastern Counties Railway and begs to inform them that he has learnt with regret that it is the intention of the Directors of the Eastern Counties Railway to run excursion trains to Cambridge on the Lord's Day, with the object of attracting foreigners and undesirable characters to the University of Cambridge on that day. The Vice-Chancellor of the University wishes to point out to the Directors of the Eastern Counties Railway that such a proceeding would be as displeasing to Almighty God as it is to the Vice-Chancellor of the University of Cambridge.'

Such opposition was not likely to stop the increasing desire to travel by train, which was given added impetus by a fall in the working week to 54 hours in the 1870s, and the introduction to Parliament in *1871* of Sir John

71

Lubbock's *Bank Holiday Act.* This gave working people four official holidays a year and 'ensured not only crowded trains but crowded beaches' (Briggs, 1983), for it was the railways which were now shaping the holiday geography of Britain and in so doing encouraging the growth of holiday resorts all around our coasts.

As leisure time gradually increased, the need for recreational opportunities within and near the home rose in importance. The countryside was no part of the industrial town, and for many it was impossible to reach without walking long distances. Urban green open space for recreational use had never been a consideration and when the first parks appeared in the cities it was for health rather than recreational needs. The provision of public parks was considered as one way of reversing not only the decline in urban living conditions, but also the increase in the death rate. Between 1831 and 1841 in the major cities the death rate rose dramatically from 20.69 people per thousand to 30.8. This, together with the mounting evidence of urban degradation, brought first a private, then public, response through the allocation of funding for parks within or on the periphery of urban areas. The first of these was the Derby Arboretum, constructed in 1839, as a gift from Joseph Strutt to the town. At first these parks were seen as places for walking, and as escapes from the monotony of the urban landscapes, but they later included areas for games. Birkenhead Park, opened in 1847, was one such example, containing not only the formal areas with lakes and gardens, but provision for less formal activities.

The parks, although an important first step towards the provision of open green space in cities, were criticised for often being in the wrong locations on peripheral sites away from the areas in greatest need. Many were later engulfed by the spread of housing, with the result that the emphasis had changed by 1880 to providing smaller open spaces, gardens and recreational grounds within the built environment. Provision of this kind became increasingly the concern of public authorities, as did the provision of museums, art galleries, libraries and swimming pools (closely associated with public health) in close proximity to working class areas. Such activities indicated the first stirrings of the government in recreational provision and the institutionalisation of leisure (Rapoport and Rapoport, 1975).

The 1870s and 1880s brought some release for many people from the unrelenting toil of work. The period saw the beginning of an improvement in the quality of life for the urban population, with more leisure time and rising wages to enable them to enjoy it. In the first and second quarters of the nineteenth century an average working week was 63 hours. During the last quarter it fell to 54 hours, accompanied by a rise of one-third in real wages. Many of the music halls originated from this time and most of the football teams, some of which, such as Aston Villa, Bolton Wanderers, Everton and Queens Park Rangers, had their origins in the social and sporting life associated with the increasing numbers of churches in the cities. The Saturday afternoon off introduced in the early 1870s became the time to follow the local football team.

In 1872 Disraeli had said that 'increased means and increased leisure are the two great civilisers of man'. A start in this direction had now been made.

4.4 1895–1939: Leisure, real income and mass mobility

To unlock the potential demand for leisure required further falls in working hours, more holiday time with pay, and improved wages. But to achieve this during a period encompassing a world war and deep economic recession might have seemed impossible. Yet enormous strides were made in these directions. By the end of the First World War the steepest decline in working hours had occurred, after which future gains were of modest proportions. For the manual workers a 48-hour week, just over eight hours per day, was normal, and by the 1930s the trade unions were pressing, but without success, for a 40-hour week. Furthermore, holidays became part of everyday vocabulary. In the 1920s 1.5 million wage-earners became entitled to a holiday with pay. The figure rose to 3 million in 1938 before the stimulus of the *1939 Holidays with Pay Act* pushed it up to 11 million. By 1945, 80 per cent of all workers had holidays with pay.

Releasing the workforce from its work place for longer periods each day and providing longer continuous stretches of time for holidays would be of little 'civilising' effect if the financial 'means' for enjoying this leisure time were not available. To the unemployed in the old industrial areas of the North, time they had in plenty, but work and wages were hard to find. Generally though, despite depression, wages rose. Between 1913 and 1938 real wages had increased by 50 per cent whilst the working week had decreased by 10–14 per cent. The allocation of the family budget showed some significant changes with expenditure on food falling from 60 per cent to 35 per cent and rent from 16 per cent to 9 per cent while other items of weekly expenditure of the average working class family increased. Money was now laid aside for trips to the cinema, theatre or football matches, and for holidays. Although such activities were of low priority set against such things as state insurance and medical fees, nevertheless they were becoming part of the family expenditure.

The inter-war period fostered the growth of mass mobility which, through improved transport technology, enabled holidays to be enjoyed over wider geographical areas. The importance of the railway continued but it was now joined by a more flexible mode of transportation, the bus, which was foremost in opening up the countryside to a wider range of people. Often the pattern was one of travelling by train to the coast for a holiday, and then using the charabanc to explore the country behind the resort. A common picture along the sea front was a row of coaches with blackboards propped near their doors advertising day or half-day visits to beauty spots or a 'mystery tour'. In 1926 there were 40,000 buses, and at their peak in 1964 82,000 were found travelling our roads.

The growing realisation that greater leisure time and mass mobility could constitute a problem emerged during the Great Depression of the 1930s. Ironically, at this period when several million people experienced enforced 'free-time', others were concerned with the possibility of a major social problem for large sections of the population as they acquired more leisure time and as their priorities shifted from a preoccupation with work to recreation. The full impact of the 'leisure revolution' was interrupted by the Second World War, but the seeds had been sown and the plant was already in growth when the War arrived.

4.5   1940–95?: Leisure during the Fourth Wave

The restoration of peace was followed by a period of economic and social recovery in which the government's major concern was to rebuild Britain's industrial strength and reconstruct its war-damaged and ageing cities. In this situation the pursuit of leisure and the planning of recreational facilities seemed out of place. Yet legislation was introduced which pointed the way ahead to greater government involvement in leisure and recreation and in the institutionalisation of recreational activities.

The groundwork for much of the post-war legislation occurred in the war-time committees, of which the Scott Committee was of particular influence. This Committee was formed to examine ways in which the countryside could be preserved and agriculture and rural amenities could be safeguarded. But their terms of reference went wider than this, enabling them to consider public rights of way and rights of access to open countryside, and the possible establishment of national parks and nature reserves. The Committee also in its deliberations examined the impact of recreational demand upon the countryside and the extent to which this could be encouraged and absorbed without damage. They came out strongly in favour of national parks as a way of providing access whilst maintaining the preservation of the countryside for agriculture.

The desirability of national parks set up within the framework of national land use planning was accepted in principle by government in the 1944 White Paper on 'The Control of Land Use', which referred to 'the preservation of land for national parks and forests, and the assurance to the people of enjoyment of the sea and countryside in times of leisure'.

What was of particular interest to emerge from the wartime period, was the evolving attitudes to the countryside and coast for recreational purposes. Clearly it was recognised that there existed a latent demand for recreation which would have to be satisfied following the war, but that this would be done within the framework of national land use planning which emphasised preserving the natural environment. People's desire to use their leisure time within the countryside was accepted, but not directly planned for. As Patmore (1983) has suggested, people's recreational activities would be absorbed, not accommodated, in the countryside. The élitist view of rural landscape, satisfying primarily the country lover with high aesthetic ideals and a desire to savour the countryside through physical endeavour, prevailed. Accommodation, which required positive planning for recreation, was not to emerge until the 1960s, when demand could no longer be absorbed.

It is also interesting to note that, as evidenced by the words quoted from the 1944 White Paper, recreational activity was considered very much in a rural and coastal location, not within the urban environment where the museum, art gallery and parks mentality born in the Industrial Revolution was still to the fore. The city as a resource for recreation had yet to be appreciated and positive thinking on urban recreation also awaited the 1960s.

The foregoing discussion suggests, therefore, that the post-war period should be considered in two parts: the first lasting until about 1965, when changes in society and technology quickly outstripped government thought and activity in recreational planning and provision; and the second starting post-1965 when, as Dower (1965) suggests, the Fourth Kondratieff Wave burst upon the country, and both public and private involvement in recreational provision escalated.

4.5.1   1945–65

This period is notable for a number of governmental initiatives which were of fundamental importance to recreational provision. At the end of the War the *1944 Education Bill* reached the statute book. This was significant not only because it brought full-time education to every child up to the age of 15, but also because through the teaching in schools children were made more aware both of their immediate environment and of more distant places within their own country as well as abroad. The desire of an increasing number of people to travel can be traced back to the activities and teaching in the schools, to the field trips, and the school holiday parties, which became a feature of school life once the nation's economy strengthened. The Education Act also imposed a duty on local authorities to acquire adequate facilities for recreation and physical education for all education establishments under their control. The new schools, with their surrounding playing fields, provided the early opportunities for sport which later were to occupy many people as 'sport for all' became more a reality.

Town and Country Planning Act 1947
The early years following the war saw the passing of two further acts which were to have a considerable bearing on the planning of recreation. The 1947 Town and Country Planning Act provided for the first time a means of controlling the nation's land through power given to county councils and county borough councils, who were required to prepare and submit for ministerial approval development plans for their areas within three years from 1 July 1948. These plans were to indicate how local authorities proposed to use land with the powers given to them through the nationalisation of the rights on land. In this situation no owner could develop his land without first obtaining planning permission. Such permission would only be granted if the type of development envisaged corresponded to the development plans. Under the powers given in this Act planners also had opportunity to initiate and encourage the provision of land for recreation. They also received powers to define and propose for the Minister's approval areas of great landscape, historical or scientific value.

National Parks and Access to the Countryside Act 1949
The introduction of national parks was a response to public pressure for greater access to the countryside which finds its roots in the early nineteenth century and the fight against enclosures. The Scott Report suggested the establishment of national parks and this recommendation was fully supported after the war by Dower, who in a personal report to the Minister of Town and County Planning (1945) defined a national park as 'an extensive area of beautiful and relatively wild country in which:

(a) the characteristic landscape beauty is strictly preserved;

(b) access and facilities for public open-air enjoyment are amply provided;
(c) wild life and buildings and places of architectural and historic interest are suitably protected; while
(d) established farming is effectively maintained.

This definition was accepted by government but the administrative organisation for the parks revealed a difference of opinion between the government and its advisory committees. The latter wanted commissions to establish and run the parks in the national interest. The government, on the other hand, was loathe to give these powers to a non-elected body and therefore vested control with the relevant local authorities. Nevertheless, the government appreciated the need for National Park Commissions, and created them as advisory bodies made up of members with particular skills and knowledge relevant to the needs of the parks.

One of the main tasks of the National Parks Commission was to determine, after consultation with local authorities, where national parks should be located. Between 1951 and 1957 10 national parks were designated in England and Wales, covering some 9 per cent of the total area with 9,502 km^2 in England and 4,098 km^2 in Wales out of a total of 151,096 km^2. They further received power to designate Areas of Outstanding Natural Beauty, and 33 were so designated in England and Wales (Fig. 4.1).

Scotland has no national parks, but powers were given through the Planning Act of 1947 to protect areas of natural beauty, in particular Loch Lomand/Trossachs, the Cairngorms and Ben Nevis/Glen Coe. In these areas all planning applications had to be referred to the Secretary of State for Scotland before any decision could be taken.

The Act also sought to overcome the difficulties involved with rights of way along country footpaths in order to give people greater opportunity of enjoying the countryside without fear of trespass. Under the Act county councils had to carry out a survey of rights of way and were expected to prepare footpath maps which could be used when disputes arose over rights of way. Draft maps were set to be published by December 1952. In fact it was to take much longer and they were still not complete in 1971.

This is not the place to consider the detailed provisions of this Act but it is important to emphasise that one of the driving forces behind the national parks movement was the need to open up the countryside for more and more people to enjoy during their leisure time. At that time no one envisaged the pressure that this was later to bring as the population became more mobile, more affluent, and with more time to give to recreational pursuits.

4.5.2 1966–1986

It was during the 1960s that the government grew increasingly aware that it required a more positive approach to the provision of facilities for recreation and sport. The Institute of Family and Environmental Research (1981) commented that the period 1965 to 1973 saw a burst of government involvement both at a national and local level in leisure facilities as it became clear that greater public provision was necessary. They pointed to a wide variety of government initiatives, which included increased spending on the

Figure 4.1   United Kingdom: designated areas of scenic beauty (national scenic areas in Scotland), 31 March 1986.
Source: Central Statistical Office (1987a, 73)

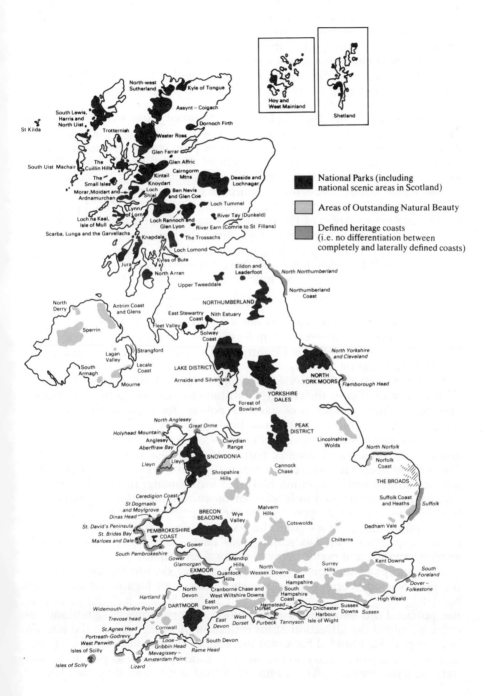

arts and adult education through wider powers given to local authorities in the *1972 Local Government Act*, and to the substantial increase in the budget of the Arts Council. In 1965 the government established the Sports Council to undertake surveys into the existing sports facilities and to improve the provision where they were inadequate. They were particularly successful in encouraging the substantial growth in local authority spending on sports halls, swimming pools, golf courses, etc.

The culmination of governmental activity came with the appointment of a Minister of State for Sports and Recreation within the Department of the Environment following the report of the House of Lords Select Committee on Sport and Leisure in 1973.

The Countryside Act 1968 replaced the National Parks Commission with the Countryside Commission. This was given a far wider brief, including the duty 'to review, encourage, assist, concert or promote the provision and improvement of facilities for the enjoyment of the countryside generally and to conserve and enhance the natural beauty and amenity of the countryside and to secure public access for the purpose of open air recreation'.

The Commission not only continued the work with the national parks and the designation of Areas of Outstanding Natural Beauty, but it was charged with the responsibility of making proposals to the Secretary of State (Department of the Environment) for long-distance footpaths and bridleways. Since 1968 eight such long-distance paths have been established in England and Wales: the Pennine Way, 250 miles (402 km); the Pembrokeshire Coast Path, 167 miles (269 km); South-West Peninsula Coast Path, 515 miles (825 km); Offa's Dyke Path, 168 miles (271 km); Cleveland Way, 93 miles (150 km); South Downs Way, 80 miles (129 km); North Downs Way, 141 miles (227 km) and Ridgeway, 85 miles (136 km). As yet these official paths, which are 'waymarked' by the Countryside Commission, have no equivalents in either Scotland or Ireland.

The setting up of Countryside Commissions in Scotland, England and Wales was a marker to the change in attitude to planning in the countryside and the gradual emergence of 'positive policies for recreational provision, linked to demand rather than to outstanding beauty'.

Another important provision within the Countryside Act was the support given to the creation of country parks. Prior to 1968 the Greater London Council had been keen to create a regional park in the Lea Valley, but until the Act no national recognition had been forthcoming. In the 1968 Act the country park was defined as a 'park or pleasure ground for the purpose of providing or improving opportunities for the enjoyment of the countryside by the public', and money from the Exchequer was made available for approved expenditure on landscaping, car parks, lavatories, litter removal, warden services, and major items of renewal and repair.

The concept of the country park owes a great deal to the aristocracy of the post Second World War years, who, faced with high death duties and escalating costs of maintenance on their stately homes, had to open up to the public. Lord Montague's contribution was particularly significant because he added the attraction of his collection of vintage cars to the interest in his estate. He founded his motor museum in 1952 in memory of his father and in so doing drew attention to the fine rural mansions as potential magnets for leisure seekers. This commercial trust was followed by the Duke of

Bedford and the Marquis of Bath, who planned parts of their estates for recreational purposes with the introduction of a range of activities, including the 'safari park'.

Where such commercialism has either not been possible or not welcomed the National Trust has in many cases come to the rescue. The Trust was founded in 1895 as a public company not trading for profit 'with powers to acquire and preserve beautiful and historic places' (National Trust, 1985). Its first property was not a building but 4½ acres of cliffland in North Wales. This early association with the coast has become of much more significance in recent times, as recreational pressures have endangered parts of the most beautiful stretches of our coastline.

An Act of Parliament in 1907 gave the Trust the responsibility of promoting 'the permanent preservation for the benefit of the nation of land and tenements (including buildings) of beauty or historic interest'. Their powers were widened in 1937 by a further Act of Parliament which enabled them to hold country houses and their contents as well as land and buildings. This Act was passed in response to the Trust's concern that many fine country houses and their surrounding estates were likely to disappear through heavy taxation.

The work of the Trust since 1945 has expanded to care for a most impressive range of properties. At this time it 'protects by ownership some 540,000 acres of countryside of outstanding natural beauty and protects by covenants (a legal agreement with the owners) a further 75,000 acres. It owns 87 large historic houses, more than 100 other buildings and gardens open to the public, as well as 1,181 farms and 15,000 cottages and agricultural buildings' (National Trust, 1986). In 1965 the Trust initiated a campaign, 'Enterprise Neptune', to increase their protection to 700 miles of the finest upspoilt coastline, and as a result 8 million pounds has been raised and over 450 miles are now protected from development. In 1985 Enterprise Neptune was relaunched in order to raise further funds to protect another 450 miles.

Perhaps the National Trust's most laudable achievement has been to open all this property and land to the public and thereby become an important agent for recreation. Leslie Giddes-Brown reporting in the *Sunday Times* (26 May 1985) pointed to the boom in National Trust membership, which increased by 190,000 in 1984 to 1.2 million with almost 8 million visitors to its properties. In 1986 membership further rose by 100,000; with an exceptionally large number of new members, to 1.4 million. To some degree the growth in visitors is now at the expense of the private stately homes, who find safari parks and adventure playgrounds of declining attraction. It may be that a more sophisticated public seeks the glories of the house and gardens rather than high profile activities which are not a natural part of the country estate. Such attractions are better located in 'theme parks', which are the latest addition to the recreational landscape of the countryside.

The theme park is a leisure park based upon a single theme or with separate theme areas within a site (Fig. 4.2). Most operate a 'one ticket' system, which enables the visitor to enjoy all the rides and entertainments free once the ticket has been bought. Its origins lie in the USA, not with Disneyland but with Knott's Berry Farm in Anaheim, California where, to find a new source of income during the Depression of the 1930s, the Knotts began selling fruit preserves and cooking chicken dinners. The dinners

Figure 4.2 Theme parks in England.
Source: *The Times*, 10–16 August 1985, p. 11

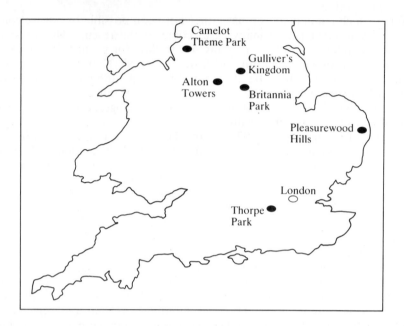

proved so popular that the owners Walter and Cordelia Knott created other amusements to occupy the crowds that came, including buildings used in the last Gold Rush. Such was the success that by the late 1960s the land was fenced and visitors were charged admission. The quality and variety of the attractions then required further improvement, as the park was now in direct competition with Disneyland. To do this the ghost town was given a mine and a train, and then in 1975 the first Corkscrew Roller Coaster was installed.

The theme park idea was first introduced into Britain in 1959, with the opening of Thorpe Park near London at Chertsey in Surrey. Now there are six, all, with the exception of Pleasure Wood Hills American Theme Park at Lowestoft, close to major urban areas with good access by road. To survive they need to attract a large clientele. So far the signs are encouraging, for of the 'top seven English attractions charging admission in 1987 Alton Towers and Thorpe Park occupied second and seventh places respectively (Table 4.1).

The growth in government involvement in recreation increased with the 1969 Development of Tourism Act, under which the British Tourist Authority and the four national tourist boards for England, Scotland, Ireland and Wales were established, each charged with the responsibility for encouraging people to visit and take holidays in their respective areas, and for encouraging the provision and improvement of tourist amenities and facilities. Each of the national boards created different structures for achieving their aims. In the case of England, 12 regional tourist boards ensure

Table 4.1 English tourist attractions

Attraction charging admission	Attendances at the most popular tourist attractions (millions)			
	1983	1984	1985	1987
Tower of London	2.2	2.3	2.4	2.3
Madame Tussaud's	2.0	2.1	2.3	2.4
Alton Towers	1.6	2.0	1.9	2.3
London Zoo	1.2	1.2	1.3	1.3
Kew Gardens	1.1	1.1	1.1	1.3
Thorpe Park	0.8	1.0	1.1	1.0
Blackpool Tower	—	1.0	1.1	1.5

Sources: English Tourist Board; Central Statistical Office, *Social Trends*, 1987b; *The Times*, 12 December 1988

effective co-ordination and co-operation of tourist matters at regional level with local authorities and commercial concerns.

The British Tourist Authority advises the government and the government is enabled to provide grants to assist tourist developments. This has included financial assistance in the Development Areas (northern England, Merseyside and the South West), which have so far been the only areas where such support has been permitted.

If recreational provision is seen as a responsibility of local authorities, the regional nature of the approach to tourism has brought a wider vision of the needs of, and ways of assisting, those local authorities which have been particularly hard-pressed.

The Water Boards have also been operating at a regional level. With the passing of the *1973 Water Act* they were required to realise the recreational potential of land and water in their charge. This provided the opportunity to release reservoirs for a variety of water sports which before were considered unsuitable in such environments. The pollution threat had been sufficient to persuade most water authorities to attempt to eliminate this at source by keeping the public out. The authorities found it increasingly difficult to sustain this position as modern treatment plants became available and pressure from various water users, particularly the yachting fraternity, increased. As a result of this Act most new reservoirs, as for example, Grafham Water in Cambridgeshire, make provisions for yachtsmen and fishermen to use the water area.

The 1970s also witnessed a growing concern with recreational provision in the urban areas. The deterioration of the inner cities could be measured not only by a lack of employment and poor housing, but also by an under-provision of recreational facilities. Denis Howell, the Minister for Sport and Recreation under the last Labour Government, commissioned a research project into 'Recreation and Deprivation in Inner Urban Areas', which was published in 1977. This was part of a new initiative by the government to revive the inner city and the aim of the study was to find ways in which this could be achieved for the disadvantaged population. The GLC in the introduction to its study of recreational disadvantaged areas pointed out that, 'in recreation, more than in other areas of social policy, individual opportunities are directly related to the distribution and location of specific facilities'. The study discovered that not only was the underprovision of sport and recreational facilities concentrated in inner London, but also that the socially poorer areas were likely to have the least provision. To a degree this imbalance resulted from policies which were designed to develop large prestigious sports centres and to concentrate resources, resulting in underprivileged areas being totally overlooked.

The multi-sport indoor centre is an interesting example of urban recreational provision. Before 1970 only Teeside possessed a reasonable number, but during the 1970s the picture radically changed. Between 1972 and 1981 the number of sports centres in England rose from 27 to 490 major and 280 lesser centres. Patmore (1983), commenting on the distribution of the centres, noted that 'the provision is still far from universal. Best served are the outer suburbs of cities and the free-standing towns of medium and large size.' In contrast to this the inner cities had a substantial deficit. Wandsworth, in London, with a population of 255,000 had none and Liverpool (510,000) and Oldham (220,000) one apiece.

These centres are expensive to build and to run, and the local authorities already hard pressed by government to contain their spending found it necessary to increase entry fees, often to a point where many poor people could not afford to attend. Accessibility to sports halls is therefore not just one of location but of cost – the costs of travel (for many depend on the car) and the cost of entry.

The inequality of recreational opportunities has not as yet been resolved, but this must not mask the fact that much has been achieved for the urban population in providing a wide range of facilities for formal and informal recreation: parks and gardens, canal and river walks, playing fields and golf courses, swimming pools and leisure centres. It is fortuitious that pressure on these facilities would be more intense were it not for the fact that much recreation takes place in and around the home.

Since the war home-based leisure activities have increased dramatically. This has occurred because the family has become more self-sufficient and the design of new housing areas at lower densities has brought increased private space at the expense of communal space. Further encouragement has come from the consumer industries, which have perceived a need and stimulated a demand. The electronics industry, in pursuing a course of miniaturisation, has developed a range of products ideally suited to the home environment. The General Household Survey (1986) showed that 98 per cent of householders had television, 17 per cent a home computer (data collected for the first time) and 38 per cent videos. The television's place in leisure time is considerable: in the first quarter of 1986 men watched on average 26 hours and 4 minutes, women 30 hours and 38 minutes, and those over 65 years, 30 hours a week.

More active pursuits have also found a place in the home. DIY is no longer considered a chore by many, but a creative and therefore pleasurable occupation. Many tasks have been eased by better products from the manufacturers, including such things as drip-dry paint, paint strippers, ready pasted wallpapers, and tools to make tasks easier. Outside the home, in the garden, activity has also increased with more people owning gardens and taking an interest in their cultivation. A relatively new feature in the landscape is the garden centre, which not only supplies the gardener's needs but is a recreational facility in its own right. The International Garden Centre Association estimates that in Britain there are over 600 of these centres, which they define as having an outdoor sales area for plants of at least 500 m², a covered area, and a shop of at least 100 m².

Such pleasurable occupations inside and outside the house demand space. Unfortunately in the inner areas of our cities individual space for homes and gardens has been reduced. High-rise or horizontal blocks contain flats with limited internal space and no private external space. The open space around the blocks is not part of the family's space, is not even recognised as communal space, but almost certainly as non-defensible space. As a result, in this space activities of a destructive kind, such as vandalism and mugging, have become common occurrences. The large-scale redevelopment schemes of the 1950s and 1960s did much to destroy the oldest play space in the world, the street. Some of the most interesting games are street games (Opie and Opie, 1969). But the streets provided, not only for children but for all ages, a place for enjoyment, an open space for street parties, for carnivals and markets. In the post-war rush to build, the streets were replaced by corridors and lifts, and the important social and recreational function of the street was forgotten. Today the need is to re-establish play streets and re-examine the organisation of space around the high-density housing areas of the cities in order to encourage its use for a whole range of community activities, of which sport is but one.

4.6 Reasons for the leisure revolution

It is not easy to point to a moment in time as the beginning of this revolution. A revolution can be a fairly instant occurrence or can develop over time. With the leisure revolution it is possible to suggest that the momentum of change has quickened over the last 20 years as part of a social revolution which now makes it possible for the majority of people to have and enjoy leisure time. What factors have accounted for such a revolution?

4.6.1 Use of time

The trend has been towards a reduction in working hours and an increasing holiday entitlement. In the 1960s the basic 40 hour week was introduced and since that time there has been a slow but continuous fall in average working hours. In April 1987 the average basic working time for men was 38.2 hours and for full-time women 36.7 (*Social Trends*, 1989). Though much of the reduction in working time from the 70 hours of the mid-nineteenth century occurred before the Second World War, the more recent reduction has enabled working time to be reorganised to reduce days spent at work. The four or four and a half day week is now a reality for some workers and the pressures are there for a 35-hour week with a three day weekend.

The reorganisation of time spent in work also affects holiday arrangements. The average holiday entitlement with pay has been increasing since the 1960s. In 1963 97 per cent of full-time manual employees had a basic holiday entitlement of only two weeks. By 1987 this had increased to four weeks or more for 99 per cent of the manual workforce.

Time without the resources to enjoy it creates frustration and not the freedom which is inherent in the recreational concept when people do what they wish to do. Thus increasing holiday time has become holidays with full pay. In Australia, for example, they have introduced holiday pay loading to enable workers to take better advantage of their vacation.

The decreasing time spent working provides the opportunity for 'leisure bunching' (Rodgers, 1969), in which the distinction between weekday and weekend could disappear. Again in Australia, they are introducing the 19-day month, or 9-day fortnight to provide longer periods of time for recreation. Such fundamental changes as these are not without their problems, and learning to live with so much leisure time is a challenge in itself. It is attractive to have freedom from work, but such unstructured time may be beyond the means of many to handle. A perpetual holiday was to Bernard Shaw 'a good working definition of hell'.

Demographic changes are also of importance in the discussion of time, for three reasons. Firstly, people are living longer. Today there are 10 million people over retirement age, two and a half times as many as in 1950, and for them recreation is a significant aspect of their lives. On average retired men have 93 hours per week of leisure time, women 80 hours. Furthermore, with an increasing number of people taking early retirement the period of time when older people are active participants in a wide range of leisure activities has increased. Secondly, at the other end of the spectrum, young people are staying at school longer, creating appreciable demands on recreational facilities during school holidays. The third and final change is the reduction in family size, which frees parents at a much earlier age to consider 'going out more' as the responsibility for the children throughout the day recedes. These factors, together with the recent rising population, all increase the latent or actual demand for recreation.

4.6.2 Increases in income

The point has already been made that leisure time without affluence may have little relevance. In fact, the 1960s and 1970s witnessed increasing affluence brought about; not only by increased incomes amongst males, but also by the growing practice of women entering either full- or part-time work. The resultant increase in family budgets provided more disposable income (money available after basic needs are met) to spend on leisure activities.

A proportion of this wealth was used for the purchase of cars. In 1961 31 per cent of households in Great Britain owned a car or van; in 1985 this had risen to 62 per cent with 17 per cent of households owning more than one. The implications of this for recreation are considerable, since the car gives flexibility of destination and time. No longer do the narrow corridors of train and bus limit destinations. At first sight this may appear advantageous because pressure on resources will be spread over a wide number of destinations and 'overload' will be avoided. To a degree this is true, but the habit of visiting the 'better-known' holiday areas, such as the West Country and certain coastal resorts, persists, with the result that ways have now to be found to reduce the flexibility which the car provides, by limiting car parking, increasing the use of double yellow lines and a host of other recreational management devices. The very freedom which the car now brings has, to a degree, to be eroded away if sensible management of recreational facilities is to be maintained.

The major problem, though, concerns the distinction between those who have cars and those who have not. There is a danger that, with more and more recreational facilities based upon the use of the car, the poor sections of the population will lose out. This inequality of opportunity presents a major challenge to society, at a time of high unemployment and a widening gap between rich and poor, which it cannot ignore.

4.6.3 Conclusion

In the last 20 years a culture based upon leisure has emerged. Attitudes have undergone a fundamental change so that for the majority of our society, leisure is no longer equated with 'frivolity and wasted time' (Pigram, 1983) but is seen in a positive light of enhancing people's life satisfaction. Much has been achieved in providing for the increasing demand which has come from 'lengthy segments of free time' (Pigram, 1983). Positive planning for recreation along the coasts and in the countryside has been paralleled with work of conservation to protect the areas of outstanding natural beauty and of scientific interest. In more recent times the recreational needs of the urban population have been recognised and the city townscape has absorbed new structures such as sports halls and floodlit all-weather playing surfaces.

The challenge of the Fourth Wave is far from over. Fears still exist of a 'collapse of work' as new technology becomes more pervasive (a subject for a later chapter), and there remains the pressing need to provide for the underprivileged sectors of society, those people living largely, though not exclusively, within the cities. Planning for recreation has increasingly become institutionalised and although commercial interest is to be encouraged it is the local authorities which can contribute most to redressing the imbalances in provision if the will is there and resources are available.

Part II

5   Theoretical input

The three chapters of Part I briefly reviewed the major empirical indicators of the United Kingdom's economic development throughout its process of industrialisation within the time-frame suggested by Kondratieff's Long Waves. Although apparently based on analyses of empirical data, Kondratieff's historical stages of economic 'boom' and 'bust' in capitalist economies in essence amount to a theoretical construct or model which seeks to explain and predict the phenomena of economic development through time. There is no evidence to indicate that this particular theory has had any influence upon political decision makers in the United Kingdom up to now, but there is the possibility that it might do so over the next few years. If so, this would mean that Kondratieff would have joined a 'select band' of economists whose theories certainly have had some impact on national policy making, although in his case with implicit rather than explicit regional and urban policy implications. Theories that attempt to explain economic development and its differential regional impact are largely products of the post-war era, and were originated by a 'new variety' of economists who 'appeared' in the 1950s. These were the regional economists, who wanted to know why the national economic policies espoused by scholars trained in classical economics sought neither to explain nor to offer solutions to the spatial disequilibrium substantially in evidence at the sub-national scale. Before moving on to examine the policy efforts of successive British governments to alleviate regional and urban imbalance, therefore, it is essential to place the political decision-making process in its theoretical context.

Generally speaking, regional and urban policies have been determined *after the fact* of problem identification — hence, most often a 'stimulus-response' to the symptoms of localised economic distress. In some respects, however, it is probably true to say that policy has run ahead of theory, since politicians do not have the reflective time available to academics — they must be seen by their constituents to respond quickly to the reality of a stressful economic situation. Nevertheless, whether determined by economic reality, economic theory or political expediency, or a mixture of all three, the action taken by any government must reflect the politico-economic philosophy of the party in office. Thus, any form of intervention in the national or regional economy, its form and its intensity, will exhibit a political perception of the problem as much as any economic one — we cannot separate economics from politics, or vice versa!

As we shall see in Chapters 6 to 9, the government, whatever its political colour, has intervened on the regional and urban level ever since 1928, with precedents even before that year. Given the perceived need to intervene by government, there are two basic questions that the policy maker has to ask before determining what policies to implement. Firstly, what is politically acceptable or unacceptable, both socially and economically, at the local scale and, secondly, what will be the impact on the efficiency and growth of the national economy of any measures to reduce or alter regional differentials? Answering these questions will depend to a considerable extent upon the *theory of economic growth* adhered to by the policy maker. In order to understand the 'whys' and 'wherefores' of British regional and urban policy measures over the years, and to appreciate more fully their effects and effectiveness, we must be well versed about ideas theoretical absorbed by policy makers. We should also recognise the interactive relationship between theory and policy, since theory influences policy and policy effects cause modifications to theory.

5.1 Regional development theories

Until the 1930s decision makers in government were largely unconcerned with spatial aspects of economic problems, assuming that the best course of action was simply to allow the economy to sort itself out. If there was a theoretical underpinning to this approach, it was probably that of nineteenth-century *mercantilism* with its principles of free trade abroad and *laissez-faire* at home. Economists at the time endeavoured to explain the regional problem by modifying classical *international trade theory* into a simple, or naïve, *spatial equilibrium theory* which predicted that, left to its own devices, the free-market system would be self-regulating.

5.1.1 Classical spatial equilibrium theory

This is a model of the *national* spatial economy which states that regional disparities in a dynamic economy must be short-run because, in time, market forces work toward equilising growth (in turn assumed to be constant, apart from trade-cycle hiccoughs) across all regions. Hence, while regional disequilibrium ('divergence' of one or more regions from the national norm) is recognised as an unavoidable problem arising naturally out of the process of economic development, the return to equilibrium ('convergence' of all regions towards the national norm) is seen equally as a natural counter-balancing process resulting from national economic growth gradually being transmitted to and encompassing all the regions.

Divergence is caused by changes in demand or supply in an economy and these changes will affect each region differently since each has its own particular industrial structure. A change in demand for a region's product could be triggered by new domestic and/or foreign market requirements or by cheaper sources of supply elsewhere in the country or overseas. If the demand increases for certain products or services, then the regions containing the producing industries will experience an increase in production, employment and income, whereas the opposite will be the case if demand falls. Prosperity levels will be higher, therefore, in those regions containing the appropriate industry of the moment and lower in regions possessing inappropriate (or inefficient) industry, so that regions will diverge one way or the other from the national norm.

Convergence will occur through the movement of firms (capital) into the high unemployment/low income regions because of the attractiveness of lower wage costs, while labour should migrate from the poorer to the more prosperous regions in search of employment and/or higher wages. Given the assumptions in classical theory that capital and labour are perfectly mobile and that no impediment to their inter-regional movement exists in a free-market economy, then it follows that regional differences should disappear as capital and labour are voluntarily redistributed between poorer and more prosperous regions. Hence, in poor regions unemployment will fall and wages rise as firms move in and some labour moves out, whereas in prosperous regions unemployment will rise and wages fall as firms move out and labour moves in. (More recent formalisations of this classical theory into a mathematical model has warranted use of the term *neo*-classical. See Richardson, 1984, 10–12.)

Given sufficient time, and no imperfections, the classical view of economic development suggests, therefore, that government need only concern itself with measures to support national economic growth since any regional aberrations are only temporary and do not require intervention. In practice, there are imperfections in the spatial economy and, as we noted in Chapter 2, the whole process of economic growth in Britain has been characterised by constant regional inequalities with some regions lagging behind the national norm for very long periods of time. Indeed, the persistence of regional growth differentials was recognised in the 1920s and prompted early attempts of government intervention (Chap. 6), but new theoretical approaches had to wait until the 1950s.

The intervention of government during the inter-war years essentially sought to enhance the workings of market mechanisms, and in particular to reduce the imperfections affecting labour and capital mobility. Obstacles to the true mobility of labour include lack of knowledge about opportunities in other regions, the cost of moving house, the breaking of social ties, the need for retraining, and so on. From the standpoint of the firm, obstacles to capital mobility would again include lack of knowledge about opportunities and also the cost of relocating plant and machinery, the quality of communications, the availability of social amenities and housing for the workforce, restrictions on the price of labour or capital (e.g. maximum or minimum wages, limits on dividend issues), level of unionisation or just plain lack of interest. As we discuss in the next chapter, government intervention to coax firms to move into more disadvantaged regions began in the 1930s, but did not really have impact until after the Second World War. By the end of the 1930s, however, it had become obvious to some in government, especially members of the Barlow Commission (see below, p. 119), that intervention in the national economy was essential not just to supplement market forces but to offset the persistent trends of divergence. The theorists also began to recognise the fact that spatially even development did not occur and, consequently, that *spatial disequilibrium* was a more normal situation than was *spatial equilibrium*, if indeed the latter was even attainable following the onset of industrialisation. Generally speaking, however, there was a lack of interest in spatial analysis by economists during the inter-war years, and this neglect was not really rectified by the Keynesian revolution, since '. . . with its stress on national aggregates the Keynesian model was, from the regional point of view, little more than a neo-classical wolf in sheep's clothing' (Parsons, 1986, 171).

In the post-war years some economists began to take a greater interest in regional disparities on the national scale ('regional economics') while others turned their attention to the international scale and examined the process of growth in different countries ('development economics'). The resultant theories of national and international development overlapped, so that it is possible to apply the models which were originally designed to explain the process of economic growth in non-industrial Third World countries to in-dustrialised developed countries like the UK. The earliest models were those suggested by Perroux (1950, translated from the French), Rostow (1955), North (1955), Myrdal (1957), Hirschman (1958) and Friedmann (1966).

5.1.2 Growth pole model

François Perroux is a French economist best known for his concept of *poles de croissance* (growth poles). The *growth pole* in a national economy is an industry (or a group of interrelated industries) which grows more quickly and to a larger size than other industries, and which, because of its strong linkages with other industries and sectors of the economy, has a propulsive impact on national growth. The concept is aspatial, Perroux having dismissed geographic space as 'banal', and is best visualised within an input-output matrix of the national economy, such that growth in the propulsive industry has an impact on other parts of the economy via the rows and columns of the matrix. Unfortunately, in subsequent literature the term 'growth pole' has been given spatial attributes (see Boudeville, 1966), which, although per-haps a semantic point, has led to some confusion in its use. (See Darwent, 1969.) This is not to say that a large growing industry does not have a spatial impact — of course it does — but to avoid confusion with Perroux's term it has been suggested that the terms 'growth centre' or 'growth point' be used whenever actual locations are being discussed. The growth point con-cept entered into regional planning policy in the UK in the 1960s with the identification of several in the Scottish and North East regions in 1963 (see below, p. 109).

When a particular industry is the growth pole of the national economy (e.g. textiles and shipbuilding in the nineteenth century, electronics and aerospace in the most recent quarter century), then its location is of consid-erable significance, because much of the prosperity that it generates will be spatially restricted so that its local region may grow more rapidly than sur-rounding regions. This returns us to the point made earlier about spatial disequilibrium as a normal result of the process of economic growth. It is probably true to say that the only time when spatial equilibrium is ap-proached in a national economy is when everyone is at the subsistence-agriculture level! Once agricultural or industrial development starts, then the area in which those changes occur will immediately become a growth region relative to other areas. Two types of theory have been sug-gested in attempts to explain the structure and pattern of such regional development — those of historical stages of growth and those of inter-regional income inequality.

5.1.3. Historical theories

Rostow's economic growth theory

Probably the best known theory of regional economic development is that expressed in the five-stages *economic growth model* proposed by the American economic historian Walter Rostow in 1955 (based on early ideas in 1951 and subsequently revised in 1959 and 1960). The idea that regions or countries move through a series of stages as they develop was not original to Rostow. Several German economists had suggested such sequential clas-sifications in the late nineteenth century, but Rostow formalised this thinking into a more sophisticated model.

The model assumes a traditional peasant society existing at a basic subsis-tence level, a stage of development which is indeterminate in its time of origin and therefore in its longevity. This first stage is characterised by limited technology, pre-Newtonian attitudes towards science and a static, hierarchical land-owning aristocracy which holds the political power over the agriculturists. For economic development to occur there has to be a change in the attitude of society from acceptance of the traditional *status quo* to a conviction that economic growth is essential if certain goals are to be at-tained, be they personal advancement, social welfare, national power or just higher material standards of living. If such an attitudinal change occurs in this second stage, the result should be an increase in the levels of productive investment, especially in agriculture and the extractive industries, which will lay the foundations of industrialisation — the 'pre-conditions for take-off'. This stage can last for up to a century, as in Britains's case from the mid-seventeenth to the mid-eighteenth centuries.

The new capital and technology which were developing in stage two sud-denly erupt in stage three, the 'take-off' which Rostow described as 'the great watershed in the life of modern societies'. This is the most distinctive feature of the model and is characterised by:

1. 'a rise in the rate of productive investment to over 10% of national income';
2. the 'development of one or more substantial manufacturing sectors, with a high rate of growth'; and
3. the emergence of a 'political, social and institutional framework' which encourages growth (Rostow, 1960, 39)

Although Rostow was concerned primarily with *national* growth, it is in stages 2 and 3 of his model that *regional* differentials occur, since this is when new leading sectors of industry become established (e.g. mining, iron and steel, textiles) and they have particular spatial characteristics because of the location of raw materials, energy, capital, labour or market. Consequent-ly, leading industrial sectors can readily give rise to leading industrial centres (towns and cities) and regions. As we saw in Chapter 1 and 2, Kondratieff also noted the association of industrial sector investment with periods of rapid economic growth, so that we can visualise not just one 'take-off' but a whole series through time, each one associated with new investment in technological developments resulting in rapid growth towards maturity and mass consumption of the new technology. However, such economic growth will not occur on an equal regional basis since successive leading-edge industries are not going to be continuously in the same cities and regions.

The fourth stage of Rostow's model, the 'drive to maturity', follows the 30 or so years of the 'take-off' period, and during this phase the impact of growth is transmitted to all parts of the economy. This is essentially the *convergence* phase of classical economic growth theory. The attitudinal transformation of society has been completed by this stage, farmers accept commercialisation and innovation, the infrastructure is fairly comprehensively developed and the secondary and tertiary sectors are numerous and wide-ranging, enabling the economy to produce almost anything it chooses. The 60 years of this stage are then followed by stage five, the 'age of high mass consumption'. The process of economic growth is now virtually complete, as sectoral leadership in industry shifts to mass production of consumer durables and has the capacity to cater for the total demand for goods and services, although that capacity can be turned by the State towards the pursuit of military power or social welfare rather than mass consumption by the individual. Rostow did not include a sixth stage in his model, but he did suggest the directions in which society could move following its achievement of high material standards — *either* heavy investment in new towns, urban renewal, environmental protection and higher education, and greater appreciation of such non-economic objectives as art and music, *or* what he terms 'secular spiritual stagnation' — the boredom and discontent arising from too much of 'the good life'.

Rostow's model is an historical description of the economic growth stages through which the UK, other Western European countries and the USA passed, rather than an exposition of economic laws. He himself argued that there is nothing automatic about the process and that variation between countries is inevitable, being dependent upon the resources available, size of population and the kind of society. From a regional development standpoint, the chief difficulty with the model is that it is aspatial so that its applicability at a sub-national scale has to be derived (Rostow recognised this failing in 1964). Other criticisms focus on the model as a model, with general acceptance of the variables singled out as the crucial ones, but with reservations about the identification and the separateness of successive stages in the real world, and about Rostow's failure to specify any mechanism linking the different stages. These critcisms cast doubt on the analytical and predictive qualities of Rostow's model, but the model certainly generated an enormous amount of research, both aspatially at national scales and spatially at sub-national scales.

North's 'export base' theory

The second variation of the stage model does attempt to suggest a mechanism for regional development. This is the *'export base' theory* propounded by another American economic historian, Douglass North, in 1955. North suggested that a region's exports play a key role in determining its rate of economic development. Usually, the process commences with the export of primary commodities (products of agriculture, forestry, fishing or mining), although the trigger could also be tourism or industry, but whatever the case a region is able to sell its products to other regions and to attract capital from them. This generates income which can be spent in the market, thus increasing demand for goods and services, and invested in the export base industry and in new industry to cater for the rising local demand. These new industrial enterprises can then expand their capacity in order to satisfy the wants not only of their local market but also of other markets outside the region. Since the natural and social endowments of regions will rarely be identical, the early exploitation by one region of its advantages will inevitably lead to spatial disequilibrium. However, any particular imbalance can only be temporary over the longer term since technological developments and changes in demand structure will mean that the competitive advantage, and therefore the positive balance, will shift to other regions. Hence, at the national scale the UK's shipbuilding industry, and its associated local prosperity, shifted from the Thames and the Seven to the Tyne and the Clyde during the nineteenth century, and at the international scale from the UK to Japan and South Korea during the twentieth century.

The export base model was suggested by North to apply to the development of a subsistence economy through five stages to a mature, diversified industrial economy, and he derived his ideas from American economic history. The theory has been criticised as being only a partial explanation of economic growth and not a good predictor, with too much emphasis on the role of exports (namely, external demand), and not enough on the local growth impulses. Furthermore, North neither provided satisfactory criteria for defining export industries precisely nor did he clarify why and how regional economic growth could or could not be sustained (Browett, 1977). Nevertheless, the theory does stress the facts that regional economies are open systems, nationally and internationally, and that their export capabilities are good indicators of their economic health (the greater their specialisation in the poroduction of goods in demand, the greater their wealth). Hoare (1983, 81) even notes that in Britain the value of exports per manufacturing employee varies inversely with the level of regional aid. The export base theory suggests that regional inequalities are a feature of economic growth, although it begs the question of convergence or divergence over time and does not identify any interventionist role for government, even if demand for a region's product declines. These points are partially dealt with by the concept of the regional multiplier and, more specifically, by the inter-regional income inequality models.

5.1.4 Inter-regional income inequality theories

The regional multiplier model

The *regional multiplier concept* is closely associated with economic base theory but places greater emphasis on the likely persistence of regional income inequalities. Simply expressed, the multiplier concept states that 'growth begets growth'. The concept has its origins in classical economic theory, modified by Keynes in the 1930s, but has received more attention regarding its relationship to export base theory. As a region's basic (exporting) industries expand they will create requirements for increased inputs, thus promoting new manufacturing industries to supply them, and as export earnings flow in, they will be spent on local goods and services, thus encouraging the latter's expansion. Not all the income generated will be spent by companies and individuals within the region, however, and some is bound to 'leak' into other regions. It is the ratio between the initial investment in new industry and the extra income generated by that investment, plus the total subsequent expenditure within a region, that is the *regional multiplier*, a kind of 'virtuous' circle of growth.

Regions vary in their ability to absorb the impact of industrial expansion and, therefore, to prevent 'leakages' of income to other regions, but generally speaking it would be true to say that the more diversified the economy of a region, the fewer the leakages and consequently the greater the multiplier effect. The effect itself can be measured at both regional and national scales by the use of input-output analysis, whereby the impact of increased demand for inputs in the growth industry can be seen in the total economy as increased outputs in related industries. Such analysis, however, is aspatial and akin to Perroux's approach, but in the 'real' world industrial growth or decline has strong spatial attributes. The first attempts to incorporate these considerations into regional development model building were made by Myrdal (1957), Hirschman (1958) and Friedmann (1966).

Centre-periphery models: Myrdal, Hirschman and Friedmann

Gunnar Myrdal is a Swedish economist whose concept of a *process of cumulative causation* and its associated regional inequality in economic development has been one of the most useful contributions to our understanding of spatial disequilibrium. Cumulative causation is a self-reinforcing process which ensures that once a region has emerged as a leader, it will strengthen and maintain its leadership over an indeterminate time period. The leading region may emerge because of local natural advantages or because a 'propulsive industry' has located there, but once started this 'growth region' will develop economies of scale and localisation which are cumulative, thus enabling it to achieve positive *divergence* from other regions.

The growth region will attract into it labour, capital and commodities from other regions, and its goods and services will out-compete the production in these other regions so that the latter slip even further behind. These are the *backwash effects* of Myrdal's model, and the fact that labour and capital flow in the same, rather than opposite, directions makes this model quite different from the classical version (Section 5.1.1 above). The result is a *dual economy*, with a rapidly growing region experiencing all the benefits of the multiplier effect and the in-migration of labour and capital, while the other regions decline or stagnate. Furthermore, these growth rate differentials not only may persist over time but can even become wider if the increasing returns-to-scale effect continues. The loss of capital from declining regions means that little is available for indigenous investment. The loss of labour is socially and politically as well as economically significant since it is highly selective, involving the younger, more mobile and adaptable component of the regional labour force. What is left behind is an older, less adaptable labour component which is less productive and less attractive to potential industrialists. The unattractiveness of such an old, declining industrial region to new investment may be compounded by high trade union membership, and associated wage rates, and by a deteriorating physical environment.

Myrdal suggests a three-stage development process, starting with a pre-industrial phase when regional disparities are minimal. This is followed by an industrialisation phase when one or several regions 'take off' and, through the process of cumulative causation, *diverge* from the stagnating regions. The third phase involves *convergence* of the growing and stagnating regions, as the growth process spreads throughout the national space economy. These centrifugal *spread effects* are achieved by the growth regions seeking cheap-labour locations for some industries in, by purchasing more raw materials from, and by developing the markets of, the stagnating regions. Myrdal initially assumes that governments do not intervene in the process, but he does accept that intervention may be necessary to enhance the spread effects in order to ensure that they overcome the backwash effects of the growth region and move the nation toward regional convergence.

The role of government in attempting to counteract the deleterious effects on the rest of the nation of regionally limited economic growth was emphasised rather more by Albert Hirschman (1958). Quite independently, Hirschman, an American economist, developed his own version of an inter-regional income inequality model, which is remarkably similar to that of Myrdal. In this model there is spatial interaction between the north (a growing region) and the south (a lagging region), with the north generating *polarisation effects* ('backwash') involving the 'pulling-in' of labour, capital and commodities from the south (to the south's detriment). This process results in regional divergence until the north's growth leads to *trickling down effects* ('spread') which promote regional convergence toward equilibrium. If the trickling down of economic growth is not strong enough to overcome the polarisation effects, and the south begins to have a braking effect on the north's growth, then Hirschman sees government intervention occurring. This could happen possibly even to stave off the threat of political action or revolution by the south, but it is a new element in the model and not merely an enhancement of the 'trickling down' effects. The other main structural difference between the two models is that Hirschman does not propose cumulative causation as the process leading to spatial disequilibrium. Instead, he argues that there is an *implicit geographical imbalance* in the economic growth process and that the inequality of regional development is reinforced by powerful forces of concentration and specialisation favouring those areas which emerge as leaders.

Probably the most striking feature of the models propounded by Myrdal and Hirschman is the emphasis on *long-lived spatial disequilibrium*, which almost inevitably appears to require some form of intervention by central government in order to achieve something approaching regional parity. The role of government regional policy as a 'natural' element in a country's endeavours to achieve spatial equilibrium is an accepted feature of the four-stage model suggested by the American regional economist Jony Friedmann in 1966. His model, is a partial reformulation and refinement of those of his predecessors but it is his terminology that has become widely accepted – for 'growing' or 'north' read centre or core and for 'stagnating' or 'south' read periphery. This *centre-periphery* or *core-periphery* model is also designed to identify the critical structural and locational factors involved in the economic growth of a less developed country, but a number of the basic principles are equally applicable to mature industrial economies.

Friedmann sees economic growth being instigated by the export-base industry of a region, followed by the development of residentiary industry which further enhances the advantages of the growing region, the *centre* or *core*. The rest of the country is *peripheral* to the core region, supplying it with capital, labour and raw materials and providing a market to be exploited. The consequent divergence of regional incomes can be overcome by transmitting economic growth from the core throughout the periphery so that the latter effectively disappears. Friedmann proposed that such convergence can be achieved via an initially simple *matrix of urban regions*, since urban centres already possess valuable localisation economies and are therefore favoured points of growth. Economic development on a national scale can thus be accomplished through a hierarchical system of cities and towns, their functional regions forming the building blocks upon which an increasingly complex economic superstructure will grow as the spatial economy becomes integrated and equilibrium is ultimately achieved.

Thus central place analysis, which has formed part of urban geography's methodology since its introduction by Walter Christaller in 1933 (translated in 1966), can be coupled with the growth centre idea and offered as the basis of a 'dynamic spatial theory of economic growth with direct applications in regional planning strategy' (Smith, 1971, 457). We will discuss this point further in Chapter 12.

The polarisation models developed by Myrdal, Hirschman and Friedmann can all be grouped under the general heading of centre-periphery models and as a group they have proved to be applicable to a broad spectrum of time periods and geographical scales. In particular, these models do have some predictive value regarding the divergence or convergence of regions when the national economy is in the centralising or early decentralising phases, but they cannot satisfactorily predict *what* will happen next, *when* and *where*. Testing the centre-periphery models has revealed that even when peripheral regions have economically converged and achieved partial equilibrium, inter-regional growth differentials can persist (Richardson, 1984, 13). Such a situation implies that, at some future date, the growth rate of one region could dramatically increase, resulting in a new centre-periphery spatial arrangement. Hence, we are dealing with a continual process whereby growth regions periodically emerge, either because of shifts in the trade cycle or because of new technological developments, and each has an associated change in resource requirements which, in turn, have particular spatial attributes. Centre-periphery models, therefore, add a spatial dimension to the Long Waves of sectoral technical innovation envisaged by Kondratieff (Chapters 1 and 2).

Innovations in technology require capital investment if they are to be beneficially exploited, but capital, although mobile, does tend to favour those regions which are capital generators. According to numerous post-Keynesian *demand models of inter-regional growth* the availability and level of capital investment in any region depends upon the initial distribution of capital stock, since capital generates income which allows savings which add to capital. In an open system, there will almost always be polarisation flows in favour of higher-income regions, so they will acquire a disproportionate share of capital, which will contribute to divergence. (See Richardson, 1973; Thirlwall, 1980.) Even if capital is not invested directly in the growth region it is often controlled there, especially if this region contains the nation's largest city with its financial and company headquarters (e.g. the South East contains 623 – London alone has 458 – of the UK's top 1,000 companies' headquarters).

One of the characteristics of industrial organisation that has emerged over the last two or three decades is the tendency of large multi-plant cooporations to separate their headquarters and productive functions, the former being located in or near the capital city while the latter are located according to contemporary 'cheap' sources of raw materials or labour. Since the less prosperous peripheral regions tend to have lower average income levels, they are the areas which receive branch plants seeking to tap low-wage labour, often non-union and/or female. (See Massey and Meegan, 1979; Susman, 1984.) Profits, of course, are channelled back via the corporate headquarters to shareholders, and although substantial proportions of earnings may be invested in the branch plants, the tendency is for the benefits to accrue to the region containing the headquarters. A further problem is that if a multi-plant corporation sees an opportunity for increasing its profitability by moving production capacity to cheaper labour sources in Third World countries, the branch plant in the peripheral region of an advanced economy will suffer closure, but profits from the new location will continue to be processed through the headquarters in the growth region. These points are stressed in Marxist, or radical, interpretations of regional economic development (Section 5.1.5 below).

Location of headquarters' functions in the capital city or other major metropolitan areas also increases the occupational disparity between centre and periphery, with greater proportions of the tertiary and quaternary employment sectors in the centre and of primary and secondary sectors in the periphery (Holland, 1976; Leigh and North, 1978). The influence of industrial organisation and re-organisation on regional economic performance has come under increasing academic scrutiny in the UK recently. This is especially because multinational corporations have received very substantial proportions of government regional aid, but have not hesitated to expand their production facilities overseas while closing branch plants in Assisted Areas and reducing employment domestically Regional Studies Association, 1983; Townsend, 1983; Cooke *et al.*, 1984; Gaffikin and Nickson, 1984; Massey, 1986).

5.1.5 Marxist uneven regional development theory

The models of spatial inequality that we have discussed so far have all been based on assumptions that we are dealing with variations in capitalist economies. An alternative, Marxist, view would claim that the real reason for such inequalities is not to be found in shortcomings like industrial structure but in the very nature of the capitalist system. The Marxist, or to be more correct the neo-Marxist, theory of *uneven regional development* proposes that differences in the growth rates of regions are not the result of uncontrollable market forces, but simply reflect the intentional actions of the capital-owning class. Richardson (1984, 16) notes five ways in which neo-Marxist theory explains the spatial manifestations of capitalism:

1. Urban centres (the homes of capitalists) exploit the surplus production of rural areas, thus providing cheap food and helping to minimise urban wages, while any rural savings are diverted to fuel capital accumulation in the cities.
2. The spatial concentration of production is not the result of market orientation (i.e. transport cost minimisation) or of the uneven spatial distribution of raw materials, but is explained by the centralisation of capital into large production units, especially in manufacturing.
3. The spatial penetration of capital is very uneven, because private profit rather than social benefit is the primary motive behind capitalist decisions. So there may be large areas of a country, region or city that are chronically deprived of investment.
4. Capital is highly mobile and thus offers many opportunities for exploitation (as noted earlier).
5. Regional policies will have only marginal impact in improving welfare because regional aid is essentially a subsidy to industrial capital in an attempt to improve its chances of survival at a time of a squeeze on profits.

So, according to Marxist theory, inequalities in spatial development are inevitable since they reflect the crises and instability that are characteristic of capitalism. From a regional policy standpoint, therefore, capitalist governments can only ever tinker with the symptoms of regional imbalance – they can never cure a condition which is endemic to the economic system of capitalism. Consequently, government assistance to declining regions is essentially a 'sop' to their political representation, while true political power lies with the capital-owning individuals and corporations. In turn, the latter are more than willing to move labour-intensive production facilities from the peripheral areas of advanced countries to Third World countries if this will mean greater profits. This is a process referred to as *devalorisation*, or reduction in the value of capital, and is most apparent during economic crises. Devalorisation is seen as part of a '. . . capital restructuring process in which the affected region is "re-adjusted" to better fit into the international division of labour' (Susman, 1984, 91). Hence, those regions in advanced economies with a high proportion of industries undergoing devalorisation (usually industries with obsolete production technology) will experience major changes in economic structure and in employment opportunities as the more unionised, higher skilled jobs are transferred to more profitable locations overseas by the multinational corporations. Meanwhile, if there is any alternative employment in the domestic regions, it will demand lower-skilled, unorganised workers. The control centres of the capital accumulation and disbursement of such overseas operations will remain in the metropolitan core regions, thereby contributing to the latter's growth (especially in the service sector) and maintaining or increasing the disparity between the growth region and peripheral regions. (See Holland, 1976; Fothergill and Vincent, 1985, 32–3.)

Neo-Marxist theory therefore sees spatial disequilibrium (*divergence*) as endemic to the capitalist system and consequently only a radical change in its politico-economic organisation can ever hope to bring about equilibrium (*convergence*). There is certainly some empirical evidence to support the descriptive aspects of the Marxist explanation, but this is more in terms of general features of national historical development and the behaviour of large corporations than specifically related to regional imbalance. Indeed, it has often been pointed out that even those countries run according to Marxist-Leninist principles have experienced notably persistent problems of regional imbalance (Sant, 1982, 23). From a theoretical standpoint, therefore, the Marxist model does not seem to explain regional disparities fully and rigorously, and from a policy standpoint it does not offer proven means of achieving regional balance. The political economy approach of uneven regional development theory does, however, focus our attention on the political aspect of decision making as it affects governmental regional policy or corporate locational policy.

5.2 Urban development theories

'Everyone knows what a city is "except the expert"', is a penetrating observation revealing the difficulty of understanding the complex nature of cities. The more one seeks to comprehend how they work the more complex they appear, and like all growing organisms this complexity is heightened because it is in a continual state of change. At one moment the focus of activity is in the central zone and at another in the suburban fringes. Areas once noted for their affluence become the territory of the poor. In such a situation, and with a pressing need to resolve a wide range of problems from employment and housing to roads and recreation, it is easy to support the view 'Hang the theory – What needs to be done?' (L. Allison, 1986). But if something is to be done it can only come from an understanding of the urban system, and to this end the formulation of theory may provide a way forward.

It has too often been the case that supposed solutions, even when backed by financial aid from government, have produced very little; such is the experience gained from the piecemeal measures taken in the 1960s and early 1970s in the inner city. The treatment for deprivation brought some relief of the symptoms, but no cure for the disease. It is prudent, therefore, to suggest that recourse to theory and its development may produce insight into the urban condition and may facilitate policy formulation which will provide a better environment and quality of life for those living in our cities.

5.2.1 Theories of settlement location and the internal structure of cities

Much of the early activity on understanding settlements was aimed at their spatial organisation. In 1933 Christaller presented his central place model, which he viewed as a 'general deductive theory', to explain the size, numbers and distribution of towns, believing that there was some ordering principal governing their distribution. He considered that towns and villages were not randomly distributed about the countryside but were part of a hierarchical system with a high degree of interrelationship. This he demonstrated through a hexagonal framework with each settlement at the centre of a hexagon or region which it served, nestling neatly into a hexagon of a more powerful place above it in the hierarchy. Such a rigid, regular lattice of hexagons may seem far from the reality of settlement patterns spread across Britain, but he did awaken interest in understanding the interrelationships between settlements, and in particular the relationship between a city and its region.

The city region concept was later given credence by Senior (1965), who, as part of the argument for a new structure for local government, demonstrated that the country could be divided into 42 such regions (Fig. 5.1). He argued that people look to the nearest large urban centre for many services, and so the best units for providing these services, for carrying out strategic economic plans, and for rallying a sense of local involvement and loyalty, are city regions. To achieve such a division he distinguished four kinds of region:

(a) the mature centre, with some 2 million people;
(b) the emergent, with a dependent population over 1 million;
(c) the embryonic, with hinterland populations between 300,000 and 800,000 people;
(d) the potential, where the population served was close to the 300,000 mark.

When local government reorganisation came in 1974 his proposals were not adopted by the government of the day, but the principles upon which Christaller and Senior worked could not be dismissed and in fact may be of greater relevance today.

Understanding the cities also requires the urban analyst to concentrate upon the cities themselves and their internal structure. In this respect the search for order has followed two channels of enquiry: firstly, the operation of the urban land market; and secondly, the structure of urban land use. In the former case it was suggested that an understanding of the pattern of land values would help in understanding the internal structure of cities. In the latter, attempts were made to demonstrate that a degree of order in the land use patterns of individual cities did exist, although there was disagreement about the nature of this order.

The explanation of the urban land market was propounded by Hurd (1903), Alonso (1960), and Wingo (1961) (see R J Chorley and P Haggett (eds) *Socio-Economic Models in Geography*, Chapter 9), who suggested that land use patterns resulted from a multitude of decisions made by individuals about location, with an outcome in which sites would be occupied by the 'highest and best uses' forming an orderly pattern of land uses. In this situation rents would be maximised and all activities optimally located. Further it was argued that the rent an occupier paid was based upon the logic that site rents represent a saving in transport costs in overcoming the 'friction of distance'. Each user of land is in effect trading savings in transport costs for extra rent repayments. Therefore, for the commercial activity seeking a high degree of accessibility a city centre location represents a saving in transport costs over less accessible sites, although demanding higher rent. On the other hand, suburban house dwellers are trading off the lower rentals or prices of property for higher transport costs, particularly if they work and shop in the city centre.

Such explanations provide some clarity to the operation of the land

Figure 5.1 The 'city regions' of Great Britain.
Source: Mackintosh (1968)

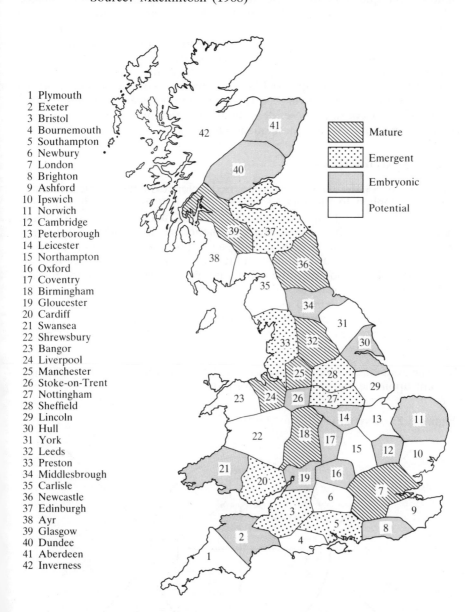

1 Plymouth
2 Exeter
3 Bristol
4 Bournemouth
5 Southampton
6 Newbury
7 London
8 Brighton
9 Ashford
10 Ipswich
11 Norwich
12 Cambridge
13 Peterborough
14 Leicester
15 Northampton
16 Oxford
17 Coventry
18 Birmingham
19 Gloucester
20 Cardiff
21 Swansea
22 Shrewsbury
23 Bangor
24 Liverpool
25 Manchester
26 Stoke-on-Trent
27 Nottingham
28 Sheffield
29 Lincoln
30 Hull
31 York
32 Leeds
33 Preston
34 Middlesbrough
35 Carlisle
36 Newcastle
37 Edinburgh
38 Ayr
39 Glasgow
40 Dundee
41 Aberdeen
42 Inverness

Mature
Emergent
Embryonic
Potential

market. They also raise a number of questions, particularly about the people and institutions which compete for sites or buildings of the city, and whether such competition will lead to an ordered and optimal system of land use.

The second channel of enquiry, into the land use structure, produced three models: the concentric zone model, the sector model and the multi-nuclei model. These models, which are well documented elsewhere, are more valuable for the questions they pose than for those they answer. Nevertheless, like the ideas about the distribution of settlements and the operation of the urban land market, they exposed, in the search for order, powerful sets of interrelationships which pointed to the adoption of a systems approach as a way forward to understanding the spatial character of the city. They also raised questions about the actors who take part in the drama of land allocation and how a situation approaching an optimal use of land can be achieved without conflict or, at the very least, competition between interested parties.

We will now consider these ideas, firstly by examining systems theory and then urban managers and the managerial thesis.

5.2.2 Systems theory

In recent times the concept of systems developed in the physical sciences has been applied to the social sciences. As it is a tool of analysis for unearthing the relationships of complex bodies of materials it has particular relevance to the urban milieu. Systems theory has limitations and it is not without its critics, but it does provide an important contribution to urban analysis. It is analytical thinking, an attempt to simplify or modify the real world in order to identify the most important variables and to indicate relationships between them.

A *system* can be defined as 'a set of objects with relationships between the objects and their attributes' (Haggett, 1965). It displays a range of elements which are integral to systems theory (Fig. 5.2). The relevant points about such a system are:

(a) The state of each object is constrained by, conditioned by, or is dependent upon the state of the other objects.

Figure 5.2   A system.

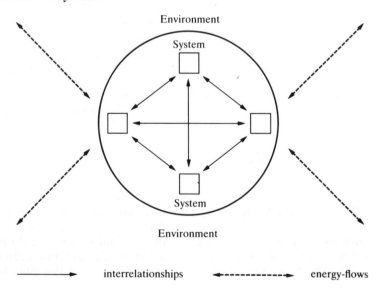

interrelationships   energy-flows

(b) The system has organisation in which the objects exist as a whole which is greater than the sum of the parts.
(c) Systems are open, except in rare instances, receiving energy from their environments. These are the inputs which are necessary for the system to remain in a steady state of dynamic equilibrium (homeostasis).
(d) Open systems are analytically closed for study. A boundary is drawn to separate the system from its environment. The environment is considered to be anything not included within the system.

To apply these ideas we could consider the housing situation within the city. (Fig. 5.3).

The objects are the housing providers – the local authority, the housing associations, the private sale and rented sector. Their attributes can be measured in terms of the quantity and type of housing they provide. Clearly they are interrelated, as for example in the way that in recent years the rented sector has shrunk as the private sector has grown. This is not an immediate cause and effect relationship, but a lagged one, with the decline in one gradually being offset by a rise in the other, or vice versa.

The environment is more difficult to define but it is possible to distinguish between the local environment and the wider system's environment, or between those which are pertinent to the local housing situation and those whose influence is indirect. The former category might include the social structure, demographic characteristics, the physical environment (climate and topographical features), the local economic environment (the local resource or tax base), and the attitude of the local authority towards housing provision. The wider system's environment would constitute the rest of the

Figure 5.3 An urban housing system.
Source: based on Goldsmith (1980, Fig. 2)

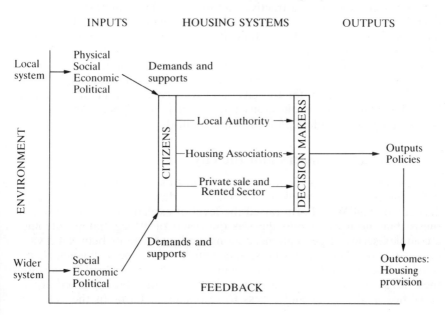

environment, in particular the state of national housing provision and the political and economic situation.

The environments provide the setting within which the city housing system works, giving both opportunities and constraints. The government, for example, can support and encourage local authorities in their efforts to provide accommodation through its legislative procedures and its allocation of resources. At the same time both the government and the local citizens can make demands for housing, in terms of numbers to be provided and the type and quality.

The housing system produces outputs which in this case will be policies which a local authority seeks to pursue over a given number of years. The outcomes could be the construction of new housing and the rehabilitation of old, or the decision to limit the expansion of a town by not releasing land for further development. Now this intended policy might lead to unintended results. In Cambridge, for example, strict controls on expansion were introduced in 1954 in order to retain its unique university town character. This seemed an appropriate course of action, which worked satisfactorily, but in so doing it created an environment which in the early 1980s was attractive to the new high technology industries, their workforce, and people seeking a higher quality of life. Housing demand was stimulated which could only be partially met, and an inflationary situation in the private sector of housing was created – an unintended outcome.

A final aspect is the concept of feedback, which is the process by which outputs and outcomes are fed back into the different environments, setting off a new series of changes to which the system responds. In the example mentioned above the feedback of information about the housing shortage could produce a change in policy direction leading to further releases of land which would reduce the inflationary pressures and return the system to a state of dynamic equilibrium.

Systems analysis is an attractive method of seeking understanding, but it is criticised because it is not an 'explanation theory' which tells us exactly how a system works, and it is difficult to test, particularly as the boundary between environment and system is empirically difficult to draw. Furthermore, in an area where scarce resources are a fact of life, systems analysis goes only some way to provide answers to such vital questions as who provides the resources for the city, and who controls their allocation and how. To address these questions requires a political perspective; putting politics back into explaining what happens in the city.

5.2.3 Urban managers and the city

In many of the models mentioned earlier in this chapter the distribution of the urban resources was taken as read. It was described but explanation was partial. In 1954 W H Form raised the level of explanation by proposing the thesis that the urban landscape was the result of a 'negotiated outcome of a complex series of perceptions, actions, and interactions between a variety of actors, including landowners, speculators, developers, financiers, planners, politicians and real estate agents. Ray Pahl (1969, 1979) developed these ideas further in his managerial thesis, in which he explained areal inequalities in the cities and access to resources in terms of the values and goals held by various urban managers of the urban system.

Those who administer the allocation systems he termed 'managers' and those who work for the managers were the 'gatekeepers'. From the point of view of the general public, it was the gatekeepers whom they were most aware of and who were seen as the source of power. The building society manager and the estate agent occupy this role, but they do not ultimately control and allocate resources. Such individuals or groups are found within organisations, whether public or private, which are part of the system of managerial bargaining which all advanced societies use to allocate their scarce resources.

To understand the resource allocation system of the city means to understand the values and goals held by the various urban managers. In the public sector, the colour of the government is a determinant factor. At present the Conservative Government seeks to encourage private sector initiatives in inner city areas. The Urban Development Corporations in the London Docklands and in Merseyside and the privatising of council housing are examples of this. Alternatively, a Labour government might be expected to require greater public sector involvement in urban revitalisation programmes.

Whatever the political colour of the government, their policies will contain a social awareness, a realisation that resources should be directed towards a common good. In the private sector the goals are likely to be different where managers have to perform well for their shareholders and where profit is a measure of performance. Resource decisions by the property companies in the late 1960s and early 1970s, for example, favoured the construction of offices and capital flowed from the banks, pension funds and insurance companies to sustain this because it was considered good investment policy. Thus the managers can profoundly affect the urban environment, for as L S Bourne (1975) stated, 'private developers are the prime initiators of structural change and they are the architects of urban spatial organisation in capitalist cities.

Figure 5.4 provides an indication of how the land development system works in this country. Resource decisions by the private sector institutions are taken at Switch 1, where investment can go into the Stock Exchange, the development industry or overseas, and at Switch 2, where the type of development is decided. Within this model the government is seen as having a modifying role on the outcome. In such a system conflict would seem inevitable as the various institutions jostle for position in order to gain the greatest return from their investment. In Pahl's view the types of urban environment which are produced are 'a result of conflicts between these institutions with different degrees of power in society'. A negotiated outcome (Form, 1954) or a system of 'managerial bargaining' (Pahl, 1979) are perhaps softer ways of expressing this, but the city's form is the result of a power struggle, which is continuing.

In reality it is unlikely that the various urban managers act in isolation, developing their own strategies which bring them into conflict with others. Conflict is reduced when strategies are closely interdependent, 'with each group acting as a major component of the decision environment of the others' (Ley, 1983). Where managerial coalitions occur, then the institutional power is increased and the investment strategies are attainable. It is

107

Figure 5.4   The land development system in the United Kingdom.
Source: Shelter, *Report No. 1*, London

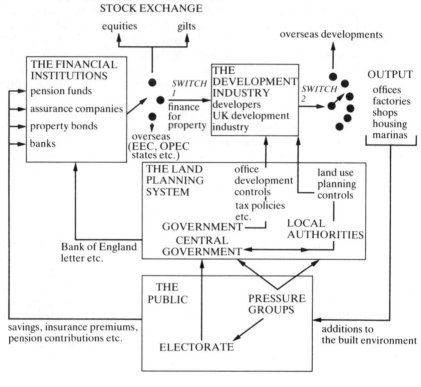

SWITCH 1
allocates institutional investment
between alternative outlets

SWITCH 2
allocates development effort between
alternative built forms

argued that the urban form is a conscious manipulation by an alliance of élite interests with social and economic power. Such a theoretical position can be supported by, for example, the way financial institutions and property developers work together to initiate city centre developments. At a lower level the housing coalition of solicitors, estate agents, building societies and insurance companies is a grouping which brings benefits to its members, but also to the house buyer in providing the financial and legal services which are necessary.

The economic and social power of large institutions can be considerable, and the pressure they bring upon the political institutions to get their own way in the city can be tremendous. In the late 1960s and early 1970s as one office block went up after another, it seemed that the institutions were manipulating the city for their own ends, and the government seemed powerless to prevent it. Increasingly conflict arose, not so much between the institutions, but between them, the government and the people, so although coalition between managerial groups brought common objectives, it did not necessarily follow that conflict was subdued. What is clear is that in situations like this the eventual outcomes will come from the resolution of these conflicts.

Theories of urban management, of managerial coalition and of a manipulated city are essential starting points in the search for an understanding of why our cities are what they are. They can provide only partial answers, but seen within a systematic frame (outlined early in the chapter) they form fertile soil for further research into the complex nature of our cities.

5.3 Theoretical input – real or imagined?

The foregoing overview of the major theories addressing national, regional and urban economic development raises a critical question in the context of British regional and urban policy – how much theoretical input has there actually been into the political decision-making process? Influences of theories and models have been both explicit and implicit: explicit in the sense that they have identifiably become part of actual policy; implicit in the sense that they have undoubtedly influenced the thinking patterns of politicians and their advisers, therefore making indefinable but none-the-less real contributions to policy.

It was noted at the beginning of this chapter that regional policy has tended to 'run ahead' of regional theory, but there are notable exceptions to that observation. For example, Perroux's growth pole concept, in its growth centre guise, became a key element in the 1963 *White Papers* on solutions to the regional problems of Scotland and the North East. Similarly, it could be argued that the new designation of 'Intermediate Areas' in 1969 for those parts of the country which had the potential of becoming depressed if left to their own devices, was a reaction to some theoretical input – although we could equally argue that it was simply a response to recognition of the empirical factors which would lead to regional decline if left unchecked. In our survey of the actual measures taken by successive British governments to alleviate regional problems (Chapters 6 and 7) such explicit influences of theory on policy will be readily apparent. It will also emerge quite clearly that the type and intensity of policy measures have varied according to both the prevailing economic conditions and the political philosophy of the party in power. The latter aspect, in particular, is probably more implicitly than explicitly influenced by theories.

Implicit theories are found in the background and training of the people in office and, probably more to the point, of their advisers. If the decision makers do not have the appropriate knowledge they may seek the advice of those who do – predominantly academic researchers and individuals or groups with previous experience. A recent example is that of the Conservative Government requesting such input in its review of regional policy in 1981–83, and receiving a notable memorandum from the Regional Studies Association (1983). Other papers and recommendations were also submitted, and all doubtless had some impact on the new policy outlined in the 1983 *White Paper on Regional Industrial Development*. The input primarily took the form of suggested steps that the government could, and should, take to modify current policy in order to enhance Britain's prospects for mitigating regional malaise and encouraging new development. There is no question that the recommendations were underlain and framed by the conceptual knowledge about and perceptions of regional and national economies held by the people involved.

What is said of regional policy is apposite for urban policy. In terms of actual application of theory to practice perhaps the New Towns stand out as a successful development. No large urban centres could have been planted in the closely packed settlement system in Britain without considerable damage to existing towns and villages, in terms of employment and retail provision, had not the interrelationships within the system been firmly understood. It is therefore to the credit of those who chose the locations of New Towns that no significant damage was done to existing settlements in close proximity to them.

This has not always been the case in the existing cities, where governments have reacted too quickly, often under pressure from opposition parties in parliament and/or sections of the general public. Government transport planning in the 1960s was indicative of this when, to provide for the growing tide of cars and lorries, urban motorways were introduced, existing roads widened and a plethora of traffic management devices introduced to ease traffic through existing streets. The result was to encourage still more people to travel in cars which brought physical and social damage to our cities. Little heed was paid to the relationships between various land uses and traffic generation, and no cognisance was taken of the damage to urban communities and to the built environment within which they lived.

In similar vein successive governments have failed to appreciate the need to see the inner city crisis as a problem of the urban system. Policies have been produced in piecemeal fashion in reaction to difficulties in education, social service provision, housing and employment. No overall policy framework has been established which would enable these different initiatives to work in harmony and simultaneously. The interrelationship concept contained within systems theory has not been fully understood, nor the interconnectivity which characterises a system. The resolution of multi-deprivation and the revitalisation of inner areas can only be achieved when it is recognised that the inner city is part of an urban system which operates in a national, even international, environment. The answers to the inner city problem can only partially be found within the inner city itself.

A comprehensive systems approach to policy formulation by government is essential, and in the present Government's 'Action for Cities' programme (see Chapter 10), which contains a range of policy initiative running across several government departments, there are signs that the theoretical underpinnings of the systems approach to urban development appear to be appreciated. Only time will tell whether this is true.

The contributions of information and opinion from academicians, public pressure groups and government commissions can make a difference to regional and urban policies, both directly on the specific policy measures adopted and indirectly in the more general influence on policy makers via published works and committee service. The relationship between theories and politics is in a state of constant flux, however, influenced by current economic conditions, recent practical experiences, empirical evaluations of past policy measures (e.g. the probable influence of the Moore *et al.* report (1986) on the policy changes of early 1988), and the pragmatism of political and economic realities. In turn, any or all of these influences, and the latter especially, will periodically shift the emphasis of any government programme. The dynamics of these relationships will be evident in our discussion of policies in Chapter 6 and 7, of their effects in Chapters 8 and 9, and of their effectiveness in Chapter 10.

6 Problems of place I: policy responses before 1964

So far in this book we have endeavoured to provide background information on the industrialisation of Britain sufficient for current regional and urban problems to be appreciated in their historical and theoretical contexts. The realisation that, regardless of whether current spatial disequilibrium problems are structurally and/or locationally caused, they are part of a process of continual change (as reflected in Kondratieff's Long Waves of economic development), is fundamental. We can now turn our attention to a presentation and discussion of government policy responses to the regional and urban problems wrought by the forces of economic change during the nineteenth and twentieth centuries.

Appreciation of the fact that industrial change causes social and economic distress in certain categories of employment and, therefore, in certain regional and urban locations, was not of particular significance until the Second Kondratieff Long Wave. It was during this Wave that the vote was extended to the urban working class, in 1867, and to rural labourers, in 1884. Universal adult male suffrage had to wait until 1918 and that of women until 1928, but meanwhile the Trades Union Congress had been founded in Manchester in 1868 and the Labour Party in 1900. Trade union membership rose from 250,000 in 1869 to over 4 million by 1914 and over 8 million by 1920, while the Labour Party saw its parliamentary members increase from 29 in 1906 to 142 by 1922. It is perhaps not too surprising that after 1900 the political parties increasingly saw fit to attempt to alleviate the poverty arising from economic dislocation, since such action could gain votes in the next election.

Awareness of poverty, and the enactment of remedial legislation to deal with it, however, are not purely twentieth-century phenomena. As we saw in Chapter 2, paupers, vagrants and the unemployed have been a feature of British society since pre-industrial times, and many people have lived a 'hand-to-mouth' existence because of illness, old age or low earnings due to irregular or poorly paid employment. During the First Kondratieff Wave poverty was very much a feature of the rural areas, as it had been since 1601 when the Poor Law Act was passed. In 1834 when the Poor Law Amendment Act was passed, the major recipient areas were in eastern and southern Britain, as shown in Fig. 6.1. The newly industrialising growth areas of upland Britain were noticeably lacking in Poor Law expenditures, but this is not to imply that the industrial towns were free of poverty. Indeed, as the Second Kondratieff Wave progressed, the rural poor were gradually overtaken in numbers by urban poor, and by 1892 London, for example, had about 30 per cent of its population in the poor (21 per cent) or very poor (8 per cent) economic classes, a proportion not very dissimilar from that in other large towns and cities (Booth 1902; Rowntree-York, 1902). The

Figure 6.1   United Kingdom: Poor Law expenditure, 1834.
Source: after Cook and Stevenson (1983, 141)

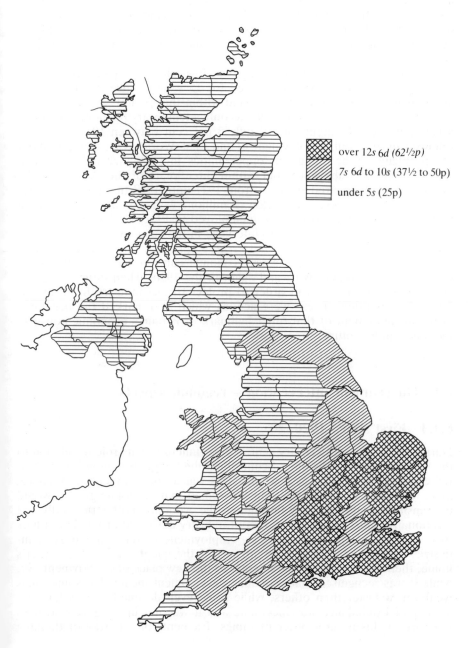

over 12s 6d (62½p)

7s 6d to 10s (37½ to 50p)

under 5s (25p)

workhouses, originally established in 1723, were not equipped to handle such numbers, especially when adverse terms of trade swelled the ranks of the unemployed, as in the mid-1880s (13.5 per cent unemployed), mid-1890s (6.5 per cent) and early 1900s (7.5 per cent). Realisation that these cyclical upsurges of unemployment were a feature of industrialised society that were not going to just 'disappear', coupled with the emerging political threat of a working-class-based Labour Party, prompted the ruling Liberal Party of 1906–14 to introduce major reforms. These included the establishment of Labour Exchanges ('Job Centres') in 1909, the introduction of old age pensions in the same year, and of National Insurance in 1911, to provide unemployment and sickness benefits.

The level of unemployment benefit was low relative to the average earnings of those in work and only lasted for 15 weeks, since it was felt that alternative employment could be found within that period, and in any case it was believed that unemployment was only a temporary phenomenon. With a national unemployment rate of only 3 per cent between 1911 and 1914, followed by the 'full' employment of the First World War, concern about the problems of declining job opportunities in particular industries and regions went into abeyance, but within three years of the War's end the problem had reappeared. In fact, from 1921 until 1939 the number of persons out of work never fell below 1 million, with a peak of 2.7 million (almost 1 in 4 of the workforce) unemployed in 1932. Understandably, the government finally felt obliged to intervene in the economy – an action contrary to the nineteenth-century *laissez-faire* approach. Such action was not without precedent, however, since economic controls had been necessary during the First World War, and again in the 1920s when duties were imposed on certain imports in order to protect British industry from 'unfair' foreign competition. These were actions which also marked the beginning of the abandonment of that other hallmark of Britain's economic power in the nineteenth century, 'free' trade.

6.1 Government intervention – regional aspects

6.1.1 First steps: 1920–40

During the nineteenth century central government saw its role in relation to the national economy as one of controlling the budget but allowing the spatial economy to develop as it would. This was a non-interventionist stance, as we discussed in Chapter 5, which assumed that economic growth would be transmitted automatically throughout the economy, both structurally and locationally. Thus, if certain sectors of industry advanced faster than others then workers would naturally seek employment therein, and if such industries were located in a different part of the country from the worker's home, then the workers would migrate to the new place of employment. So, while it was recognised that economic development meant that some areas would grow faster than others, while some even declined, it was felt that such spatial imbalance was inevitable and it was not up to government to interfere in this natural order of things. Elements of this way of thinking were still strongly in evidence in the late 1920s, even though the realisation had dawned that certain parts of the country which had suffered the hardships of higher than average unemployment before the First World War were still having more difficulties than other places.

Given the prevailing attitudes of the time, the reaction to persistent unemployment problems in certain areas was predictable – workers from declining industries should move to growth industries, wherever in the country the latter might be. The declining industries in the 1920s were coal-mining, iron and steel, shipbuilding and cotton textiles, mainly located in Central Scotland, South Wales, West Cumberland, County Durham and Lancashire, while the growth industries of chemicals, electrical engineering, motor vehicles, aircraft and the distributive trades were predominantly in the Midlands and the South East. Between 1921 and 1937 approximately 650,000 people (workers and their families) moved from the declining areas to the growth areas, especially London, a migration that was encouraged by the government with its setting up of the *Industrial Transference Board* in 1928. Through this Board the Ministry of Labour financially assisted those who were willing to move and also offered retraining schemes, especially to coal-miners. The Board selected migrants for support on the basis of age and skills needed in the growth areas. Thus, declining areas were actively encouraged by central government to 'lose' their younger, better trained workers! However, not all the migrants stayed in the growth areas, as many as 100,000 young adults returning to their areas of origin, but in total about 1.2 million people moved from upland to lowland Britain between the wars and almost half of them were assisted by the government. The Board's programme was not particularly well-received in the declining areas, nor were industrialists all that enthusiastic since the qualities of the workforce being encouraged to move by the government were precisely those that industry in the depressed areas would need once there was an upturn in the trade cycle.

Of more positive value, especially from the standpoint of a manufacturer thinking of locating in a depressed area, was the *De-Rating Act* of 1929. Prior to this Act the burden of finding the money to pay out unemployment benefits had fallen on local ratepayers, a hangover from the days of the Poor Law. This meant that areas suffering industrial decline, with the associated job losses, had to support increasing numbers of unemployed on a decreasing rateable base. Rates therefore had to be raised in order to find the money to pay out unemployment benefits, but high rates were discouraging to industrialists, whereas rates remained low in the more prosperous areas. The De-Rating Act was an attempt by government to remove this disparity so that, in effect, ratepayers countrywide would cover unemployment benefits – perhaps the first attempt by central government to redistribute spatially the costs and benefits of unequal economic development.

These early, tentative tinkerings with the economic problems of particular places in the country were largely overshadowed by the national economic decline of 1929–32, when unemployment increased from 8 per cent to 17 per cent of the total workforce and industrial production declined by over 16 per cent. The industrial decline was structurally and therefore locationally very biased, however, with major slumps in those industries producing export or capital goods (namely, mining, iron and steel, textiles, engineering, shipbuilding), whereas growth was experienced by industries producing consumer goods for the domestic market (namely, electrical goods, cars, furniture, food, etc). (See Table 2.2). The decline in employment in some places was so dramatic (to over 40 per cent unemployed – see Fig. 2.8) that the government commissioned studies of the worst hit areas, and with expenditure on welfare peaking at 39 per cent of government spending in 1930 there were both social and exchequer implications. The studies were published by the Ministry of Labour in 1934, and although their recommendations for government assistance to certain areas were seen as responses to a temporary economic situation, they nevertheless set in motion a sequence of government interventions in regional economics that has varied in intensity but has persisted to the present day.

The *Special Areas (Development and Improvement) Act* of 1934 was the first serious attempt by a British government to deal with the problem of persistent unemployment in particular regions. The Act implicitly recognised the fact that wholesale movements of people from declining to growing areas was not practical on the scale necessary to solve regional unemployment problems. Furthermore, there was also a realisation that the growth industries of the Midlands and the South could not be expected to absorb the enormous numbers of people who would need to be transferred without creating serious problems of congestion within the growing regions themselves. The Special Areas Act was therefore designed to encourage industrialists to locate their factories in places where there was a 'labour surplus' (i.e. high unemployment). Four Special Areas were designated (Fig. 6.2): Central Scotland, North East coast of England, West Cumberland and South Wales, plus Northern Ireland which had separate arrangements. The Act was criticised immediately on the grounds that certain areas that were just as depressed as those chosen, if not more so, were excluded (e.g. southeast Lancashire and Teesside), and that the major towns and cities within the Special Areas (e.g. Glasgow, Cardiff, Newport, Newcastle) were also excluded since it was thought that they should be able to take care of themselves.

Two unpaid Commissions were created to administer the £2 million made available by the government 'to facilitate the economic and social improvement' of the Special Areas, one to cover Scotland and the other England and Wales. Unfortunately, the powers of the Commissioners were at first very limited and they were not allowed to start or assist any private firms that were intended to be profit-making, nor any public-funded undertakings. Money was therefore spent on sewerage schemes (90 per cent of the funds in Scotland) and on settlements of labour on smallholdings, but the Commissioners were able to establish *industrial trading estate companies* for each of the Special Areas to meet the need for provision of modern industrial premises. Trading estates were set up at Treforest (Cardiff), Team Valley (Gateshead) and Hillington (Glasgow) in a bid to begin diversification of industry away from too narrow a reliance on traditional industries. Hoped for private investment in the wake of government spending in the Special Areas did not materialise, so further Acts were necessary.

In 1936 Parliament passed the *Special Areas Reconstruction (Agreement) Act*. This Act empowered the Bank of England to provide loans to small private firms in Special Areas which were perceived to have success potential

Figure 6.2   United Kingdom: Special Areas, 1934–45.

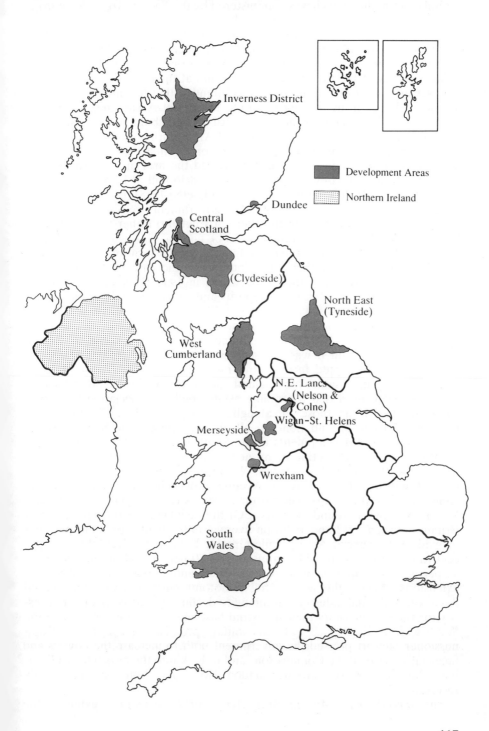

but were unable to raise the capital elsewhere. The Bank had a nominal capital of £1 million which was administered by the *Special Areas Reconstruction Association* (SARA), but since advances were limited to £10,000, and to small firms, the Act was quickly seen as inadequate to the principal task of reducing unemployment on a substantial scale in the Special Areas. Private financiers recognised the need for more capital to supplement that being made available by the government, and at the end of 1936 Lord Nuffield set up a trust of £2 million. It was intended that this money should be loaned to larger firms wishing to locate in Special Areas, and within one year most of the £2 million had been distributed to about 50 establishments.

In addition to small-scale help to Special Areas during the 1934–36 period, the government became directly involved for the first time in the location decisions of heavy industry when it pressured the firm of Richard Thomas to locate Britain's first-ever continuous steel strip mill at Ebbw Vale in the South Wales coalfield (announced 1935, completed 1938) instead of at Scunthorpe on the Jurassic iron ore field. The government's reasoning was social and political (with funds from the Bank of England) rather than economic, but problems of the latter nature were to be an issue throughout the 40-year lifespan of the plant. Government influence on the location of new heavy industry capacity was rather more indirect in the case of Corby, where Stewarts and Lloyds built their tube works in 1936. This was to take advantage of both the local iron ore deposits and an increased domestic market following the Steel Tariff Protection Act 1932, which had increased the expense of importing tube strip steel from Germany.

Private industry still totally dominated the economic scene in Britain during the 1930s, and it was the success of the private trading estates in particular that prompted further government action in 1937. Sir Malcolm Stewart, the Commissioner for England and Wales (appointed after the 1934 Act) had been impressed by trading estates built in association with local authorities, such as those at Slough, Welwyn Garden, Trafford Park (Manchester) and around London, all of them outside the Special Areas. Indeed, industrial developments in the South East were considerable, with London especially attracting many new firms to the recently built arterial roads (e.g. the Great West Road, Western Avenue, the North Circular, Great Cambridge Road, Eastern Avenue, Sidcup bypass, Purley Way and Kingston bypass) and associated trading estates (e.g. Acton, Perivale, Park Royal, Wembley) around its fringes. Of the new factories opening in Great Britain between 1932 and 1936, on average only about 2 per cent per year opened in the Special Areas, while Greater London received about 45 per cent (a deceptive figure which translates as 80 per cent of the net increase, 40 per cent of employment in new factories, and 35 per cent of all factory extensions). Seeing this new spatial dichotomy emerging, with the Special Areas of traditional industry continuing to decline and the consequent necessity for them to diversify their industrial base in order to develop, while the South was growing apace with concomitant problems of congestion, Commissioner Stewart pressed the government both to increase the powers and financial support of the Commissions and to look into the possibility of limiting industrial expansion around London. Both suggestions were favourably received.

The *Special Areas (Amendment) Act* of 1937 considerably extended the role of the Commissioners. The establishment of more trading estates was encouraged and the Commissioners, acting through the trading estate companies, could let factories to firms anywhere within the Special Areas. Furthermore, the Treasury allocated an initial budget of £2 million to a Special Area Loans Committee, which could lend money to larger firms than was the case under the 1936 Act, as well as contributing towards the rent, income tax or rates for up to five years of firms locating in Special Areas. In addition, under the 1937 *Finance Act* firms setting up in the Special Areas could be excused their national defence contribution of 5 per cent payable on their profits.

In total, the government had spent or committed almost £21 million on the Special Areas by 1938. About 60 per cent had gone into improvements in water and sewerage facilities, clearance of derelict sites, removal of slag-heaps, construction of parks, the building of hospitals, the provision of cheap milk for babies, and the 'creation' of smallholdings and allotments (Lee, 1980, 35). The other 40 per cent had been spent on factory sites and buildings, with their associated infrastructure. By 1939 some 12,000 workers were employed on the Special Area trading estates, and the national proportion of new factories opened in the Special Areas increased from the 2 per cent per year in 1932–36 to 4.4 per cent in 1937 and 14.7 per cent in 1938.

Coupled with the Ministry of Labour's encouragement of people to migrate out of the Special Areas during the 1930s, the actions of the Commissioners did help to lower the levels of unemployment. It must be remembered, however, that at the same time there was both an upturn of trade (industrial production increased by 48 per cent 1932–37) and a rearmament programme, which together had far more impact on increasing employment than did the trading estates! In fact, the four Special Areas still contained one in four of the nation's unemployed in 1938, but as Britain prepared for war, contracts for naval vessels were placed on Clydeside, Tyneside and in Barrow, many 'shadow' factories making armaments were located in the Special Areas, and orders for munitions and heavy equipment like tanks and artillery were placed with firms in these areas. Increasing demand for the products of traditional industries, together with full mobilisation of the population for the War, meant that Special Area unemployment dropped from 17 per cent in 1939 (compared with 11 per cent nationally) to about 4 per cent by 1945 (2 per cent nationally). The Second World War did not solve the problems of the Special Areas, however, it merely postponed them for a few years.

Commissioner Stewart's other suggestion, that industrial expansion in the Greater Londer area should be restricted, was instrumental in prompting the government to appoint a *Royal Commission on the Geographical Distribution of the Industrial Population*, under the chairmanship of Sir Montague Barlow, in 1938. The Royal Commission was set the task: 'to inquire into the causes which have influenced the present distribution of industrial population . . . to consider what social, economic or strategical disadvantages arise from the concentration of industries . . . and to report what remedial measures, if any, should be taken in the national interest' (Royal Commission, 1940, 1). The *Barlow Report*, as it became known, was published in 1940, when its strategic recommendations about the relocation of defence industries away from areas vulnerable to air attack received greatest attention. Technological developments in weapons delivery systems during the War rendered this aspect of the Report obsolete by 1945, but the other recommendations were far-reaching in their significance to post-war governments' urban and regional policies.

The Barlow Commission was the first to attempt to evaluate the socio-economic impact of allowing free-market forces to determine the locational pattern of industry and therefore of population in Britain. The Commission recognised that the continuing drift to the South East of the industrial population was having deleterious effects both on the areas of origin, which were losing their most skilled/educated and younger, adventurous people, and on the areas of receipt, which were experiencing increasing congestion in a strategically vulnerable part of the country. This was a noteworthy appreciation of the fact that localised areas of high unemployment in some parts of the country and rapid growth in others were not isolated economic features but were interrelated structural and locational elements of the national industrial space economy.

The Commission argued, therefore, for increased intervention by the government in industrial location decisions, and recommended a central authority that would endeavour to achieve balance in regional development by encouraging new industry to locate in depressed areas while restricting industrial developments in overcrowded growth areas. In addition, it was felt that while redevelopment and industrial diversification should take place in the larger cities, the best overall approach would be to decentralise industry and population, principally through the greater use of trading estates, garden cities and expanded rural and satellite towns. Implementation of a policy aimed at achieving these objectives was seen as essential to regionally balanced national growth with the 'proper distribution of industry' (i.e. industry located according to the existing distribution of population). In turn, this would lead to the rebuilding of employment in the Special Areas, whereas without such measures the high unemployment problems would simply return after the War. Interestingly, the Barlow Report noted the existence of centres within depressed areas which had the potential for rapid economic growth, thus anticipating the concept of growth centres which was to feature prominently in post-war regional planning in many countries, notably France.

The Barlow Commission's concern about a post-war return to the regionalised high unemployment levels of the 1930s was shared by the wartime coalition government. A *White Paper on Employment Policy* was published in 1944 in which the government declared its intention to encourage growth in depressed areas after the War, but warned that not every mining or manufacturing village could be saved. The White Paper continued,

Table 6.1   United Kingdom: political parties in office, state of 1945

Year	1945	'51	'58
Government	Labour	Conservative	
Economy	Reconstruction	Prosperous	Recessionary
Policy	Active	Passive	Transitional

at least implicitly, the policy of the Industrial Transference Board (1928–38) of encouraging worker mobility, structurally between occupations and locationally both within and between regions. This is not to say that the Barlow Report and the White Paper were at odds in their respective proposals regarding the achievement of full employment after the War, but in the former case the emphasis was on taking work to the workers whilst in the latter there was recognition that the movement of workers to places of work would also be necessary. Both approaches assumed the central role of government in the process of attaining regionally balanced national economic growth, an attitude reflecting the general acceptance of Keynesian economics during the 1930s, and quite different from the previous *laissez-faire*, non-interventionist approach.

Thanks partially to this change in the attitude of central government, and partially to the wartime emergency arrangements, the mechanisms necessary for implementing regional policy on a much larger scale than pre-war were already in place by 1945. The fear of a return to high and prolonged unemployment in areas of traditional industries, together with the realisation that reconstruction on a substantial scale after the War offered a remarkable opportunity to influence significantly the pattern of industrial location, prompted the government to act in 1945 on the recommendations of the Barlow Report and the White Paper by replacing the Special Areas legislation of the 1930s with a new *Distribution of Industry Act*.

Variations in regional assistance, 1945–63
During Kondratieff's Fourth Wave (1940–95), we have witnessed varying levels of government assistance for regional development. The intensity of support has fluctuated according to the state of the national economy and the political philosophy held by the party in power about the necessity for government intervention. The basic relationship between a party's terms of office, the strength of interventionist policy and the prevailing economic conditions can be shown in the simple line diagram of Table 6.1.

For the purposes of discussion, therefore, the post-war years can be conveniently subdivided into several time periods, and, given the direct relationship between government and policy, it seems as reasonable a framework as any to use the periods in office of the Labour and Conservative Parties.

6.1.2 Labour Government, 1945–51

The *1945 Distribution of Industry Act* replaced the Special Areas legislation of the 1930s and the Board of Trade took over administratively from the

the national economy and strength of regional policy since 1945

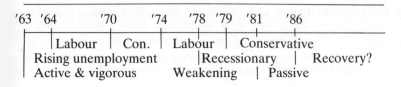

121

Special Areas Commissioners. This was not exactly what the Barlow Commission had in mind, especially since the Board of Trade had expressed misgivings about government direction of industry in its submission to Barlow, and had really wanted to see an entirely new National Board established, with research, advisory and regulatory functions concerning industrial location. However, the Labour Government considered that the experience gained during the war years by the Board of Trade's Factory Control Division warranted its continuation as the department responsible for implementing the new regional policy.

In order to create more 'compact regions' suitable for socio-economic development, the Board of Trade immediately modified the Special Areas, extending their boundaries and incorporating the urban centres that had been specifically excluded by the 1936 legislation. The resulting Development Areas (DAs), as they were renamed, now contained 6.5 million people compared with the 4 million in the Special Areas, and these were added to in 1946 (Wigan-St Helens, Lancashire, and Wrexham, Clwyd) and again in 1948 (Nelson-Colne, Lancashire, Merseyside, Dundee and the Inverness district of Scotland), as shown in Fig. 6.3. These changes increased the proportion of the national working population within Assisted Areas (AAs) from the 8.5 per cent of the 1930s to 13.5 per cent by 1945 and to 20 per cent by 1948. Northern Ireland, as a self-governing province, had its own arrangements for attracting new industry.

The aims of the 1945 Act were fourfold: to buy land and build factories; to lend money to industrial (previously 'trading') estate companies; to reclaim and improve derelict land; to provide the basic infrastructure (transport, utilities, housing, health service) necessary to attract industry. In addition, the Treasury had the power to give loans or grants to manufacturing firms in Development Areas which were having difficulty raising finance, subject to scrutiny by the Development Areas Treasury Advisory Committee (DATAC). Underlying the specified aims was the desire of government to establish and maintain 'full' employment (defined by Lord Beveridge in 1944 as 3 per cent unemployed), by encouraging traditional industries to improve their efficiency and become export-orientated again, whilst at the same time 'pushing' new industries to locate in DAs and thereby improve the diversification of the latter's industrial bases. The methods used to encourage manufacturers to locate in DAs were initially of the 'carrot' variety, with £9.3 million being spent annually on the measures noted above between 1946 and 1949, but the Government was also concerned with the increasing congestion in the growth areas of the Midlands and the South East.

Barlow had recommended that restrictions should be placed on new developments in the more prosperous regions in order to push firms towards the DAs, hence the 'stick' side of the policy. The method used by the Board of Trade derived from a building licence system introduced during the War. Any industrialist who wanted to build a factory with a floor space of 10,000 ft^2 (930 m^2) or more had to apply to the Board of Trade for a licence. If the factory was to be built in a DA, a licence was issued almost automatically, but if outside the DAs, the firm could wait a long time before a licence was issued. The Board of Trade could thus delay, but could not stop, further development in the South. The legislative power to accomplish the latter came with the *Town and Country Planning Act* of 1947.

Figure 6.3   United Kingdom: Development Areas, 1945–58.
Source: after Keeble (1976, 224).

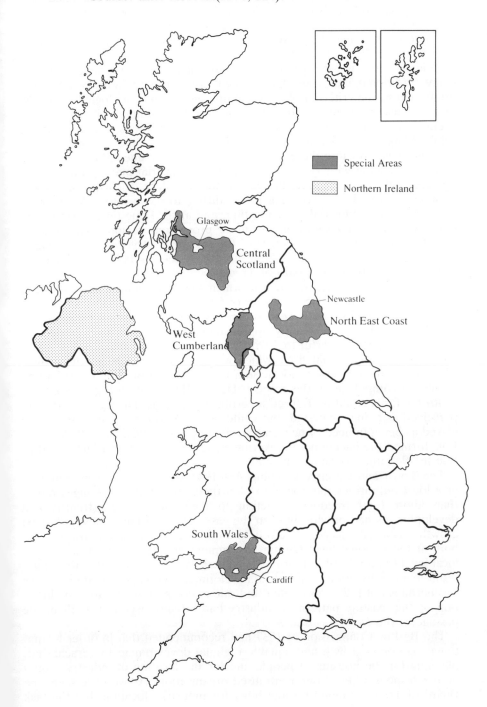

The intention of this Act was primarily to achieve a 'proper distribution of industry' nationally. Precisely what this meant was never defined, but there appears to have been an implicit assumption that the 'proper' place of heavy industry at least was in those locations where it had concentrated by the time of the First World War (namely, the upland fringes of the North and West). In this sense, consequently, the Act sought to maintain a pattern of industrial location irrespective of the spatial economic efficiency levels of many traditional industries. Government assistance to industry remained firmly tied to the criterion of high unemployment, and the logic behind the regional disbursement of aid was essentially quite simple – if higher than average unemployment occurred in the traditional industries (coal, steel, shipbuilding, textiles) which were, in turn, located in their 'proper' place, then aid must flow into these areas in order to reduce unemployment levels. Although dealing with *symptoms* of regional industrial malaise rather than fundamental *causes*, the Act did endeavour to reduce disparities in growth between regions by encouraging new industry to move into DAs, thereby improving their industrial diversification, and at the same time discouraging new industry from locating in the more prosperous regions. The method used to achieve the latter was that of the *Industrial Development Certificate* (IDC), which replaced the building licence system in 1948 but which was still administered by the Board of Trade.

An IDC was required by any firm which sought to build a new industrial structure with a floor space in excess of 5,000 ft ^{2} (465 m^2). This could be a single-storey building only 22 m square, which is very small by industrial standards, so it can be readily appreciated that the Board of Trade now possessed a quite powerful tool with which to influence industrial development. It was hoped that firms which were refused an IDC in the growth areas would then choose to locate in a DA, but the Board of Trade had no powers of compulsion in this respect. Hence, IDCs were a *negative form of control* – firms could be refused a certificate in areas that the Government perceived as being congested, but could not be forced to go into areas perceived as being in need of new employment opportunities. Nevertheless, the IDC formed the backbone of government regional policy from its introduction in 1948 until its demise in 1981.

The Town and Country Planning Act 1947 also introduced measures to give local authorities the power to plan their own land use changes rather than allow total freedom of action to land owners, industrialists and developers, as had previously been the case. The location of new industrial growth was to take place, therefore, in a more restrictive spatial framework, both at the national level (within government-designated DAs) and at the local level (within local-authority-designated areas). The risk that this might result in a continuation of industrial developments in inappropriate locations was perhaps not fully appreciated, but one major preliminary to a modification of the existing pattern of industry had already occurred in 1946, the passage of the *New Towns Act*.

The Barlow Commission of 1937 had recommended that in order for national economic growth and equable regional development to be achieved, planning for the housing of people and for the location of industry should be the responsibility of one centralised organisation. As we have seen, the Board of Trade assumed responsibility for industrial location, but the task of constructing the New Towns, as well as generally rehousing the urban population, was given to the newly created Ministry of Town and Country Planning. Since the New Towns were meant to be self-contained, balanced communities (homes, jobs, shopping, entertainment, etc.), they needed to attract industry in order to be viable. For those New Towns which were located in DAs (e.g. Cwmbrân in Gwent, Aycliff and Peterlee in Durham, Glenrothes in Fife) there was not, of course, any IDC requirement. But for the New Towns and Expanded Towns of the South East, which were intended to rationalise decentralisation from London, the fact that they were located in growth areas of full employment meant that strictly they were not eligible for IDCs.

For a short time after the war, therefore, we had a situation where one aspect of the Labour Government's policy, the provision of employment opportunities in new communities, was being actively pursued by one department, while another aspect of policy, the provision of employment opportunities in DAs, was being similarly pursued by another department, the latter effectively denying achievement of the former's goal. This apparent contradiction in the execution of policy was short-lived, however, because after the reconstruction years of 1945–47 Britain began to experience serious balance of payments difficulties. Government policy emphasis therefore switched from regional to national levels, with particular stress on the export market in order to earn US dollars. Industrialists were left increasingly free to expand on site or build new capacity where they pleased, as long as they pushed up output and exported as much as possible. The newer types of industry grew substantially in the Midlands and the South East, and even the traditional industries of the north and west benefited from this production drive, so that the regional problem faded into the background of policy, although it had not really disappeared.

Britain's economy enjoyed boom conditions from 1947 to 1950 as output expanded to take advantage of dollar-earning export markets. Balance of payments difficulties persisted, however, and in 1950 fears of a recession, coupled with an impending general election, prompted the Labour Government to pass its second *Distribution of Industry Act*. This 1950 Act had rather more positive measures that its predecessor, with increased financial assistance (subject to the Treasury's approval) available to industry in DAs. The Board of Trade was empowered to:

1. make higher grants and loans to firms locating in DAs;
2. assist financially with housing provision;
3. subsidise the costs of migration of key workers and their dependants; and
4. subsidise the costs of firms moving plant and equipment to new sites in DAs.

Although there was a mild recession in 1950, which significantly raised the levels of unemployment in certain DAs (especially Scotland, the North, and East Midlands/Yorkshire-Humberside) and was an ominous portend, events on the political front masked regional economic problems as the Conservatives won the 1951 election.

6.1.3 Conservative Government, 1951–64

The new Government continued the process, started by Labour in 1948, of relaxing controls on industrial location. Financial incentives were still available for companies that wished to locate in DAs, but in the export drive it was seen as more efficient to allow firms to expand where it was best for them rather than for the individual regions. Since so many of the growth industries were in the Midlands and South East, the Board of Trade eased the IDC restrictions there in order to encourage expansion of capacity. Regional policy effectively went into abeyance, therefore, as national growth received priority, and in turn this meant that lowland Britain was favoured relative to upland Britain. This was especially so with the introduction of the *Key Workers Scheme* in 1951, which was intended to assist the migration of those workers possessing the skills deemed to be in short supply in growth industries, many of which were in the Midlands and South East (cf. the Industrial Transference Board of 1928, Section 6.1.1 above). Regionally, however, the signs were there that all was not well, despite national economic growth. This was demonstrated in 1952 when unemployment increased to 2.0 per cent nationally (from 1.2 per cent in 1951) because of a fall in the terms of trade, with the North West rising from 1.2 to 3.7 per cent and Scotland from 2.5 to 3.3 per cent, while the South East rose from only 0.9 to 1.3 per cent.

Until the mid-1950s, Britain's economy as a whole continued to grow at a moderate rate, but then slowed down in 1955–57 as inflation rates started to increase, followed by balance of payments difficulties again. This time, however, the option of expanding production further and selling it overseas was not as readily available as in 1945–50. This was especially so for the products of traditional industries, since these were precisely the industries that foreign competitors had developed to cater both for their own domestic markets and for the international markets. Also, British industry was becoming less competitive, principally because of its penchant for simply taking on more labour in a trade cycle upturn in order to increase production rather than investing in new equipment, so that when a downturn came industry was no more efficient, was unable to compete with overseas producers, and therefore could only respond by laying off labour. The whole economy suffered from deflationary pressures, but the hardest hit areas were those dependent upon traditional industries – that is, the DAs. As recession loomed again, together with the prospect of a general election in 1959, the Government started to tighten its control over industrial developments: firstly by refusing to grant IDCs outside DAs, and then by passing the third *Distribution of Industry (Industrial Finance) Act* in 1958.

This Act extended the powers of the Treasury to make loans or grants to any business undertaking (not necessarily manufacturing) willing to locate in any area that was either actually, or in danger of, experiencing high levels of unemployment. By extending assistance to all businesses the hope was that jobs would be created in all the problem areas. Definition of the latter was made by the *Development Areas Treasury Advisory Committee* (DATAC), and as unemployment climbed from the 1.4 per cent of 1957 to 2.1 per cent in 1958 and 2.2 per cent in 1959, not only were the DAs expanded (and renamed Development Districts) but in addition a new list of

Figure 6.4   United Kingdom: Development Districts and DATAC areas, 1958–66.
Source: after Keeble (1976, 227)

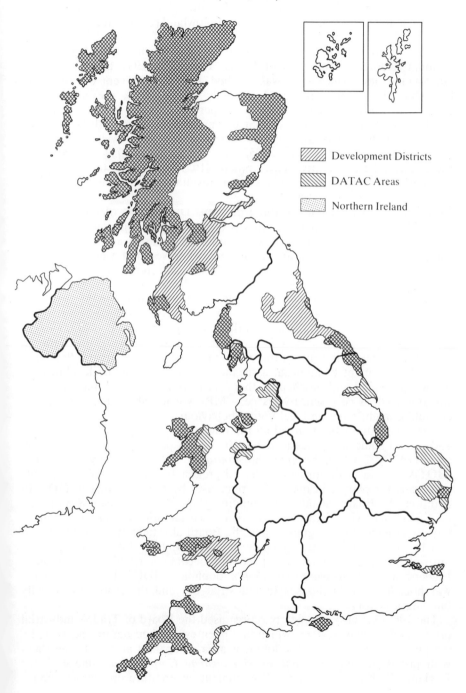

Development Districts

DATAC Areas

Northern Ireland

DATAC areas was proposed, some of which overlapped with existing DAs and some of which were completely new. Figure 6.4 maps these changes.

An interesting feature of the pattern of problem areas in Fig. 6.4 is the appearance of peripheral coastal localities throughout the country suffering from high and persistent unemployment. In lowland regions, their unemployment levels were masked by the economic health of the South as a whole, but this was not the case in the upland regions, which all had higher than national average unemployment levels. Hence, in 1959 the highest unemployment level since 1947 was reached, with 2.2 per cent out of work, but while the South East registered only 1.3 per cent, the North West climbed to 2.8 per cent, the North 3.3 per cent, Wales 3.8 per cent and Scotland 4.4 per cent. The fact that unemployment rates in these areas of traditional industries in the 1958–59 recession were over twice the national average, as had been the case in 1952 and even earlier in 1929–32, prompted the re-elected Conservative Government (1959) to review and attempt to rationalise existing regional policy, with resultant new legislation in 1960, the *Local Employment Act*.

This new Act repealed the three previous Distribution of Industry Acts and endeavoured to shift the emphasis of government regional policy away from providing for the 'proper' distribution of industry and more toward simply counteracting high unemployment wherever and whenever it occurred. The DAs were therefore abolished and replaced with smaller Development Districts (DDs) based on local Employment Exchange ('Job Centre') areas, but allowing rural areas to be designated for the first time (e.g. Highlands and Islands, north-west Wales). To be included on the DD list a locality had to have been suffering from, or to expect to suffer from, an unemployment rate of 4.5 per cent (i.e. about twice the national average). In theory this meant that the Board of Trade had greater flexibility in its disbursement of financial assistance and could schedule localities for aid when needed and deschedule them once they recovered, but the latter was politically a very sensitive issue – MPs worried about the impact descheduling might have on local voting behaviour!

The Board of Trade retained all the powers acquired in earlier legislation and gained some new ones in the 1960 Act. In particular, the Board took over DATAC, which became the *Board of Trade Advisory Committee* (BOTAC), and in the process received greater freedom to disburse grants and loans for plant and machinery purchases by firms locating in DDs. In addition, the Board introduced a building grant for those businesses moving into DDs that wished to construct their own factories rather than rent or buy government-built premises, and the Board also tightened up IDC usage and broadened its scope to include any industrial *use* rather than just industrial building. The latter aspect had become a problem in southern England where firms were exploiting a loophole in IDC rules by converting warehousing or even houses to industrial use and therefore not actually building a factory.

The 1960 Act also completely reorganised the Board of Trade's industrial estate management system, which had been established before the War, by scrapping the five major development area companies and replacing them with just three *Industrial Estates Management Corporations*, one each for England, Wales and Scotland. Government expenditure on regional policy (factory building, loans and grants) averaged £30 million per year 1961–64, a substantial increase over the £5 million per year average for 1953–60, even allowing for inflation! (See McCallum, 1979, 10–12.) The 1960s were emerging as a much more active period of regional policy, a feature emphasised in 1963 with the publication of two White Papers on regional problems, a new Local Employment Act and a Finance Act. Perhaps not insignificantly, these major policy developments occurred in the year prior to that of a general election.

The two *White Papers* of 1963 dealt with the economic problems, and their possible solutions, of central Scotland and North East England. These White Papers were similar to a report on the Northern region published earlier in 1963 by the National Economic Development Council (NEDC), which saw the duty of government as attempting to encourage the best use of any unemployed resources in a region in order to ensure growth in the regional, and therefore, national, GDP. How this might be achieved was discussed in detail, and the recommendation of all three documents was that government assistance should be concentrated in those parts of each region which possessed the greatest potential for growth, rather than scattering assistance thinly across all localised pockets of high unemployment.

This growth area approach to regional development was based on the ideas of the French economist François Perroux (see p. 92), originally published in 1948 and introduced into Britain as early as 1952 by the Scottish Council (Lee, 1980, 61), but not becoming part of policy until 1963. The growth areas selected for manufacturing development were, not surprisingly, based on old and new urban centres. In Central Scotland *growth centres* were selected within the urban regions of both Glasgow and Edinburgh, especially Cumbernauld, East Kilbride and Irvine in the former's case and Glenrothes, Livingston and Grangemouth-Falkirk in the latter's case. In North East England a single *growth area* was identified covering Tyneside, Teesside and Country Durham east of the A1, with the conurbations of Tyne-Tees and Darlington-Aycliff designated as the *growth centres*. These regions were to be administered by a new Regional Development Division of the Board of Trade, responsible for the preparation and implementation of regional plans and for advising on aspects of regional development, and as DDs the three regions remained eligible for standard regional assistance in addition to new public service investments (mainly infrastructural improvements).

With the prospect of a national election in the not-too-distant future, the Conservative Government introduced two new pieces of legislation affecting companies interested in a DD location. The *Local Employment Act* 1963 replaced the 1960 Act and sought to clarify the rather complex provisions of the latter regarding building grants to industrialists. These were raised from an average of 17 per cent to a straightforward 25 per cent grant towards the cost of factory building in DDs. In addition, for the first time the Board of Trade was given the power to make cash grants towards the cost of new plant machinery of up to 10 per cent. Both types of grant were conditional upon associated job creation in the DDs, but they were now available as a right from the Board rather than at an official's discretion. Further inducements to locate in DDs were made available to businesses by the tax provisions of the *Finance Act* 1963. In particular, this Act allowed a company to write-off its taxable profits against the full depreciation of new equipment at a rate and over a time period of the company's choosing, which meant that in effect no tax on profits needed to be paid until the debt on new machinery had been amortised. This interest-free loan from the Inland Revenue was very popular among the larger and more established companies, but it is debatable how much it helped new small businesses. These two Acts of 1963, while marking a change in approach to regional policy as the realisation dawned that the DDs were too small, too localised and offered little scope for real growth, proved to be just a prelude to the major changes embarked upon by the Labour Government following its return to power in 1964.

6.2 Government intervention – urban aspects

The response to the appalling conditions of the industrial towns was not a simple one. At the beginning of the nineteenth century the idea of state control in the interests of the working classes had little attraction for the rulers of Britain. This was a time of the doctrine of *laissez-faire* and so it remained for a large part of the century. Nevertheless, it was not in force in all directions at the same time. The House of Commons, which was responsible for the repeal of the Corn Laws in the name of *laissez-faire*, also passed the *Ten Hours Act of 1847* which gave powers to the government to control and inspect conditions of work in factories – an act of legislation which was in defiance of the doctrine.

Despite these flurries of government activity, it was clear that government did not relish an interventionalist role in either urban or industrial affairs unless the pressure was so great that it could not be avoided. Such pressure for change was often generated by the actions and writings of individuals who possessed a social conscience and were stirred not only by a desire to improve society, and in particular the lot of the working classes, but to create new environments in which to live. One such person was Robert Owen (1771–1858), who was first to grasp the modern doctrine that environment creates character and man controls that environment. He not only expressed his beliefs and ideas through his speeches and writings, but by practical application. In 1799 he took over a cotton mill and industrial village at New Lanark near Glasgow, where he followed the principle that good work could only be expected from workers who were 'well fed, well clothed and well educated' (Trevelyan, 1964). In the village he enlarged houses to relieve overcrowding, abolished child labour, set up a school and compelled attendance for employees' children up to the age of 10. He also built an institute for the formation of character, to be used by children during the day and adults in the evening.

His experience in New Lanark provided the kernel for his later ideas on the development of communities for 800–1,200 inhabitants, which he detailed in a publication entitled *Villages of Unity and Mutual Co-operation*, in which he envisaged a network of carefully planned factory villages, each built at an estimated cost of £96,000, spread across the countryside. Unfortunately none of these villages was ever built, but Owen demonstrated that factories need not be located in large towns, and that given the right kind of built environment not only would the working class be content, but greater profit would be forthcoming from industrial enterprises.

The paternalistic approach of Owen and the scale of his operation were later to influence a series of industrialists who, for various reasons, decided to build company villages or towns for their workforce. Amongst these was Bessbrook, begun in Northern Ireland in 1846 by John Grubb Richardson for his new linen mills. He built four-roomed cottages to let at 3*s* per week, and two-roomed cottages at 1*s* 6*d*, set within generous areas of open space in the form of village greens, playing fields and allotments. The care for the people living in the village which Owen had shown, was also present here in the provision of schools with evening classes, a community hall, dispensary and medical centre, several shops run on co-operative lines and a savings bank.

The most important project, or certainly the one which attracted most attention at the time, was Saltaire, built by Titus Salt, a self-made man, former mayor of Bradford and a woollen manufacturer. It had been his intention to retire at the age of 50 but the outbreak of cholera in Bradford during his term of office as mayor, and a damning report from the Royal Commision on the State of Towns in which one of the Commisioners described the town as 'the dirtiest, filthiest and worst regulated town in the Kingdom', persuaded him to create a new town. In this town the quality of housing and level of hygiene for his workers would be far superior to anything which was available in Bradford. He sought 'every improvement that modern art and science had brought to light, a town clear of smoke which would in this respect as in many others teach an important practical lesson to the mother town of Bradford'.

The town of Saltaire which emerged between 1851 and 1871 was, in many ways, unremarkable. It had more in common with the existing industrial towns than the factory villages of Owen and Richardson. Houses were arranged in terraces along a grid of straight streets and packed together at a high density of 32 houses and 170 persons per residential acre. There was no green belt to separate it from Bradford, nor much open space within the town itself. Nevertheless, it provided well-built homes, mostly of three bedrooms with a living room and kitchen, and a small yard with privy at the back. Where it did show considerable improvement was in the provision of facilities for the inhabitants. Salt, with his concern for the quality of life of his employees, paid for a number of public buildings, which included schools, public baths and washhouses, hospitals, almshouses and an institute building for the acquisition of culture, the learning of trades and the playing of non-gambling games.

The desire to improve the living conditions of working people was taken a stage further when, in the latter part of the nineteenth century, George Cadbury and W J Lever both built villages around new industrial premises on green field sites. Port Sunlight, started by Lever in 1888, and Bournville by Cadbury in 1893, were similar in that they broke away in their plans from the grid streets of the industrial cities and instead gathered their houses in informal groups at low density (Port Sunlight 5–8 houses per acre, and Bournville 7 houses per acre) along broad, tree-lined avenues.

W H Lever viewed his village as part of a profit-sharing scheme for his workforce, but to make it independent of any individual he called it 'prosperity-sharing', the aim being to use the profits created by the workforce to build houses and reduce rentals. George Cadbury's village was an experiment in community planning, for he never intended it to be an employees' village but one containing all classes of workers, many of whom would not work in the chocolate factory.

These two industrialists raised still further the standard of living conditions and added to the social experiments which began with Robert Owen. They were all part of an 'anti-urban' movement which saw the way forward as building afresh, away from the existing urban centres, and in this they encouraged the process of decentralization. They all held in common the aim of planning environments for the needs of the people who would live in them. People were more important than buildings. But these experiments were small fragments on a large canvas. Their achievements had amounted in practice to only a handful of villages housing a few people, but they did encourage an 'inspired advance in the practice of town and country planning by a great pioneer' (Burke, 1971). This was Ebenezer Howard, who in his garden city concept, brought together all the Utopian ideas of the nineteenth century and prepared for their application in the twentieth century as part of the New Towns movement.

The Utopians, philanthropists and industrialists of the nineteenth century demonstrated that new towns and villages could be built to quality standards barely discernible in existing cities. To a degree it was easier to build afresh, but this 'bypass' approach had little impact on the solution to the growing problems of existing cities. To resolve this would require not only private, but public action as well. But how could governments which supported the *laissez-faire* concept be compelled to intervene in urban affairs?

At the beginning of the nineteenth century this might have been considered highly improbable, but by the end it had been largely achieved. This change was evolutionary in character, passing through a number of distinct stages which could be described as:

(a) an awareness stage;
(b) commissions and reports stage;
(c) permissive legislation stage;
(d) positive legislation stage.

6.2.1   Awareness stage: 1800–1839

Governments often need to be made aware that a certain problem exists, because for the most part they only react to situations once they are understood. Very often, therefore, it is through the work of private individuals or groups that problems are highlighted and initially researched. In England in the early nineteenth century this was certainly the case. The tireless work of such campaigners as Edwin Chadwick and Lord Shaftesbury in exposing the evils of the day cannot be underestimated. With them lay the task of amassing evidence which might convince those in power of the enormity of the problems of the urban working class and stimulate them to some form of action to improve what was a potentially dangerous situation.

Sophisticated means of data collection were not available at that time – the first national census had been produced only in 1801 – and yet such data collection was necessary because of its objectivity and precision. The quality of the statistical information which was presented to, for example, the Select Committee on the Health of Towns in 1840 was impressive. A witness was able to illustrate the deterioration in conditions in Glasgow by statistics on the death rate which showed that in 1821 1 in 39 of the population had died, rising to 1 in 30 in 1831, 1 in 29 in 1835 and 1 in 26 in 1838, and that the mortality in children under the age of 10 had risen from 1 in 75 to 1 in 48 between 1821 and 1839.

Other statistics of a spatial character showed the variations in infant mortality between streets of differing physical condition. According to a medical report on Preston, 'the deaths of infants in Preston *under one year* were: in well-conditioned streets, 15 deaths to 100 births; in middling-conditioned streets 21 deaths to a 100 births; in ill-conditioned streets, 38 deaths to 100 births, and in worst-conditioned streets 44 deaths to 100 births'.

To a growing body of such data could be added the enormous qualitative evidence provided by responsible people in the community. For example, there was Gutter Alley in Belfast in 1837 with its nine houses of two rooms, each under 6 ft high, in which 174 people lived, or the 'filthy close and unwashed state of the houses in the East End of London, and the poisonous conditions of the localities in which the greater part of the houses were situated, from the total want of drainage, and the masses of putrifying matters of all sorts which are allowed to remain and accumulate indefinitely' (Southwold Smith in Ashworth, 1954). Clearly the pressure placed upon the national government to do something to improve conditions was considerable.

6.2.2   Commissions and reports stage: 1839–1845

The first step in governmental reaction was to set up commissions which would sift through the available evidence and then make recommendations which the government could consider. The Select Committee on the Health of Towns (1840) and the Royal Commission on the Stage of Large Towns and Popular Districts (1844–45) are two such examples. Both of these committees recommended that new legislation be introduced which would lay down general regulations about buildings and street widths, bring common lodging houses under public inspection and control, and give the central government power to inspect the execution of all general sanitary regulations in large towns. In effect, the foundations were being laid for government involvement in urban affairs.

Perhaps the final and most potent of pressures which made the government act was the outbreak of cholera in 1848, which provided the most alarming evidence of the state of the cities.

6.2.3   Permissive legislation stage: 1846–1860

There then followed a period of considerable government activity as legislation was quickly formulated and passed through Parliament. It included the *Towns Improvement Act of 1847*, the *Public Health Act of 1848*, and then in 1851, sponsored by Lord Shaftesbury, the *Common Lodging Houses Act* and the *Labouring Classes' Lodging Houses Act*. Yet for all these Acts, and many more, 'the same unwanted characteristics of towns that were exposed in the thirties and forties were still being illustrated from just as abundant contemporary experience twenty or thirty years later, that the same reasons for reform continued to be preached, that similar remedies continued to be urged and their non-application noted' (Ashworth, 1954). To a degree this was to be expected, for as the Royal Commission of 1845 concluded, no rapid improvement in the condition of the buildings in the most densely crowded districts could be achieved.

Yet more could have been done if the legislation had made it obligatory for local authorities to carry the measures out. But this was a period of per-missive legislation, when local authorities were not required to enforce the provisions within the Acts. To do this required further changes in the form of urban government, which at this stage was ill equipped to understand and overcome the problems besetting the city. The main concern appeared to be economy, with the Liberal press of the day calling for 'good, cheap and honest government'. Reform and improvement could not be done cheaply. If it did not pay, why do it at all? If local government was to be in step with development in the city, it needed reforming. Some attempt at this had oc-cured with the Municipal Corporations Act of 1835, which widened the franchise and reduced the level of corruption.

Unfortunately, this important reform did little to create effective urban government, and until this happened the implementation of measures of reform within the city were rarely possible. Clearly the task before central government was to formulate legislation with sufficient powers to bring real improvement which was enforceable at the local level.

6.2.4   Positive legislation stage: 1860–1940

The latter part of the nineteenth century saw those twin aims largely achieved. *The Reform Act of 1867* widened further the franchise to include artisans and small householders at national and local elections, thus placing, for the first time, the English franchise on a really democratic basis. Then the important *Public Health Act of 1875* laid down certain sanitary rules by which all householders had to abide. It amended and consolidated existing laws on public health; it covered sewage, water supply, nuisances and infec-tious diseases, and through the establishment of a Local Government Board set up in 1871, brought order into the national sanitary administration. This was now based upon urban and rural sanitary districts, each with its Medical Officer of Health.

Such was the reaction of central government that the prospects for town improvement increased appreciably. Much had yet to be done, but the force of *laissez-faire* was gradually being replaced by what might be called 'municipal socialism', with the public now able to influence change through its elected members.

The advent of the twentieth century saw the Utopians and those working for change within the existing cities coming closer together in their efforts to maintain the momentum of environmental improvement. The emphasis was changing from one of providing the sewerage, lighting and heating for largely rented housing, to one of improving the quality of the urban environment, as part of the desire for amenity. To do this, attention turned to suburbia, which with the improving transport network and the increase in personal incomes, was now a place where more people could live. Land values, which began to rise on the edge of cities, were still cheap enough to tempt the London County Council at the beginning of the century to build the first housing schemes at Tooting and Tottenham, although the growth and improving quality of suburbia in the early years of the twentieth century was largely a concern of the private sector. In this respect a number of societies were formed in the early 1900s with the aim of providing improved living conditions through suburban expansion, rather than new towns, which were more complex and expensive to establish.

The most significant of these suburbs was Hampstead Garden Suburb, established by Henrietta Barnett, who, with her husband, had done much for the poor in the East End of London. Her concern was to create improved housing in a pleasant environment for the working people of London. She secured a site of 256 acres, formed a trust in 1906 to preside over the building of the suburb, and then in May 1907 started construction. Amongst the aims of the scheme were:

(a) to provide for working people a cottage and garden at a moderate rent within easy reach of central London;
(b) to provide houses for wealthy people in order to bring a better understanding between different classes of society – this 'social engineering' was to prove impossible to achieve;
(c) to produce a plan for the suburb in which the presentation of the natural environment would be of considerable importance. Where possible houses and roads would fit around the trees and hedgerows and not vice versa.

The architects appointed to design the suburb, Raymond Unwin and Barry Parker, had already, in 1904, designed Letchworth Garden City, so there existed a link between Henrietta Barnett and the garden city movement. It was also significant that Henrietta Barnett was more in tune with the times in demonstrating that the design principles and ideas of the garden city movement could be best used in the existing cities rather than in new towns. Urban development for almost the first half of the twentieth century was about suburbia. Not until Sir Patrick Abercrombie's plan for Greater London (1944) did the dreams of Ebenezer Howard begin to be realised. Nevertheless, pressure for change generated by the reformists and the Garden City Association (founded by Howard in 1899), convinced the national government that new initiatives were required.

The Housing and Town Planning Act of 1909 could be seen as a response to these pressures, but it was also part of a process leading to the acceptance of the principle of town planning which could be traced back to legislation enacted in the last century. For example, the *Artisans and Labourers' Dwelling Improvement Act* 1875 was concerned with the reconstruction of insanitary areas, whilst the *London Building Act* of 1894 brought public control into the form and width of streets, the degree of open space around buildings and their height. As Ashworth (1954) commented, 'town planning was not altogether a leap in the dark, but could be represented as a logical

135

extension, in accordance with changing aims and conditions, of earlier legislation concerned with housing and public health'.

The 1909 Act enabled local authorities to prepare schemes for controlling the new housing development in suburbia which the improved urban transport networks were encouraging. Thus local authorities would be able, through town planning schemes, to secure 'proper sanitary conditions, amenity and convenience'. With little guide as to exactly how this was to be done, and with the requirement to consult all interested parties, it was not surprising that few schemes were completed. Nevertheless, the first steps towards the major Town Planning Act of 1947 were laid down.

The period following the First World War saw the introduction of local authority housing under the *Addison Act of 1919*, which further encouraged the process of suburbanisation. The government continued to believe that new development on the edge of cities would bring relief to the hard-pressed inner city. Unfortunately this was only partially so. There still remained the task of clearing many old slum dwellings and replacing them with new. By 1930 the government was forced to redirect funds from public sector housing in the suburbs to the inner city.

At the same time the government grappled unsuccessfully with the wave of new development taking place within the private sector, which was devouring land and creating a pattern of 'ribbon development' along major roads, which was considered undesirable. The *Town and Country Planning Act of 1932*, which extended powers of control over land whether built up or undeveloped, and the *Restriction of Ribbon Development Act of 1935* were too cumbersome to reduce the speed of development, so little was done. The need to control suburbia therefore remained, and was seen as one of the most pressing problems facing the government after the Second World War.

6.2.5   1945–1964 Stage

In a previous chapter (chapter 3) the plans of Sir Patrick Abercrombie were considered in some detail. They strongly influenced the post-war Labour Government towards a policy of New Town development in combination with a green belt policy. The twin aims were to control and shape population migration carefully away from cities, whilst at the same time halting the spread of cities themselves.

This decentralisation policy, together with the later *Town Development Act 1952*, have indeed achieved these aims. The New Towns, in particular, have been successful in attracting employment and in providing high-quality homes and residential environment. Even so, not everything has worked. Social experiments, like the neighbourhood areas and the creation of neighbourliness, have floundered, but Henrietta Barnett and Ebenezer Howard had already demonstrated that even with the highest intentions, social engineering did not work. People will do what they wish to do, not what the planners would like them to do. Despite this, for many people from the poor housing areas of the old cities, new houses have been provided and environments created of a standard they could never have expected.

Success is often at a price. In this case, the New Towns drew much of their lifeblood from the cities, attracting the more skilled and highly motivated young people, and drawing industrial firms from the congested city locations to the green field sites especially planned with their needs in mind.

At first this policy appeared to make sense, since it reduced pressure on the cities and gave them some breathing space to adjust to the needs of revitalising decaying and war-damaged environments. Unfortunately, not sufficient thought was given to the potentially damaging effects of decentralisation if it was not carefully controlled. As much needed employment was lost, the young, skilled population moved away and the proportion of old and unskilled people increased. The inner city problem had not disappeared; problems which were exposed in the nineteenth century were still to be found in the cities of the 1950s and 1960s. Yet again the government would have to turn from its successful decentralisation policies to seek ways of encouraging inner city regeneration.

The problems of the inner city were to be exacerbated still further by the housing policies followed after the War. The Government through the *1947 Town and County Planning Act* had taken unprecedented power to control development within the cities, with the expectation that they would provide new and improved environments, and that slums would become a thing of the past. Unfortunately this was not to be, for as was discussed in Chapter 3, successive governments strove with admirable endeavour to build 300,000 houses a year, but in so doing spawned a multitude of problems. Housing built on the cheap, in a hurry and without consultation with those who were to occupy it was bound to bring trouble. The poor, the old and the unskilled in our inner cities were trapped in housing they did not like and in areas from which employment was disappearing. This was the legacy of this period which later Governments would have to tackle.

7 Problems of place II: policy responses since 1964

The early 1960s were a transition period from the relatively passive regional policy years of the 1950s to the much more active years of the later 1960s. As we have seen, following the recession of 1958 the Conservative Government began to move towards greater intervention in the economy, with quite dramatic increases in spending in Assisted Areas (AAs), the publication of the two White Papers, the Local Employment Act 1963 and the Finance Act 1963. The rationale for this notable increase in the regional awareness of central government was undoubtedly the need to respond to a worsening economic situation, but the prospect of a general election in 1964 must have had some influence in Downing Street. Notwithstanding the flurry of expenditure and legislation (intended to be beneficial to the AAs) on the eve of an election, the nation's economic situation was worsening in 1963. Unemployment had reached a new post-war peak of 2.5 per cent, with the monotonous North-South differential of jobless rates much in evidence – only 1.6 per cent in the South East and 2.1 per cent in the West Midlands, but 3.1 per cent in the North West, 3.6 per cent in Wales, 4.8 per cent in Scotland and 5.0 per cent in the North. Actual, and fear of, unemployment must have had some bearing on the voting pattern in the election, and it is probably not too surprising that the older industrial areas and inner London went solidly for Labour. The new administration interpreted its victory as a mandate to introduce radical change to the whole field of regional policy; after all, many of the Labour voters were in actual or potential Assisted Areas.

7.1 Government intervention – regional aspects

7.1.1 Labour Governments, 1964–66 and 1966–70

The Labour Government immediately established a *Department of Economic Affairs* (DEA), which took over the regional policy and planning functions of the Board of Trade, and shortly afterwards presented to Parliament its plans for a national spatial framework of regions within which economic planning could take place. England was subdivided into eight planning regions, and Wales, Scotland and Northern Ireland were each accorded planning region status, bringing the total to eleven (see Fig. 7.1). Administration of each region was placed in the control of two separate planning bodies: a *Regional Economic Planning Council* and a *Regional Economic Planning Board*. The membership of each *Council* was chosen from people living and working in the region (from industry, local authorities, universities, etc.) who had the experience and knowledge appropriate to discuss 'objectively' the formulation and implementation of

Figure 7.1 United Kingdom: Standard Economic Planning Regions, 1964–74.
Source: Law (1980 p. 29)

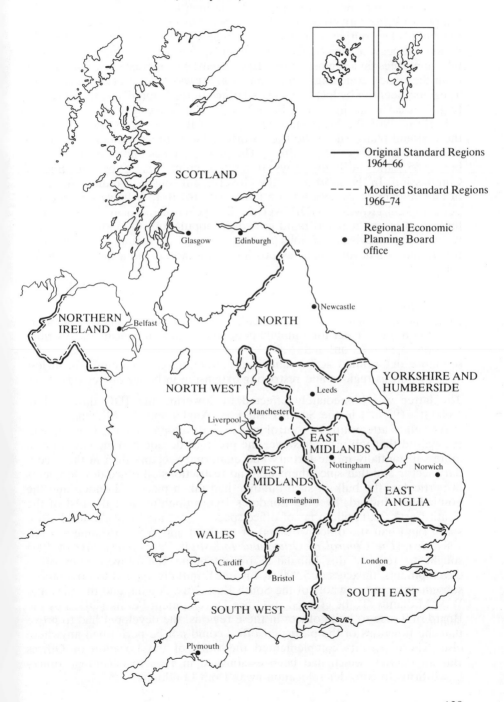

139

development plans for their own region. The Councils met in secret and were not accountable to the region but had direct access both to government information and to Ministers, so that they really acted as advisory committees whose recommendations, while influential, were not necessarily followed by the Government. The *Boards*, however, were concerned with the day-to-day routine of preparing the regional plans and co-ordinating the regional aspects of government departments, thus acting as inter-departmental committees on a regional basis. Each Board's membership was not always from the region concerned, but some attempt was made to give each Board a regional identity by locating its head office in the 'capital' city of the region (e.g. Newcastle in the North, Bristol in the South West).

Early in 1965 the DEA stated that one of its main tasks was '. . . to fit the regional plans within the framework of the national economic plan and secure the best order of priorities'. The plan itself was published in September 1965, and in many ways reiterated points made by the Barlow Commission. In the short term, the Government sought to reduce the levels of unemployment by speeding up industrial growth to achieve a target of 5 per cent real growth in GDP over the five years of the plan. In the longer term, with an anticipated rapid growth in population, the Government envisaged the provision of jobs and housing in as regionally balanced a programme of development as possible. This was to be achieved in three ways:

(a) public investment to improve infrastructure in poorer regions and congested larger cities;
(b) support for urban overspill schemes and better environmental planning of housing to cater for a mobile population, thus influencing the distribution of population; and
(c) more determined action aimed at stimulating economic growth in less prosperous regions and restricting expansion in better-off regions.

The latter was immediately effected by lowering the IDC threshold to 1,000 ft^2 (93 m^2) in the South East, East Anglia and the Midlands.

As well as attempting to control industrial developments, the Government recognised that job prospects over the previous decade had increased much more substantially in the tertiary and quaternary sectors than in the secondary sector and that since there were no restrictions on office developments in particular, the bulk of such building had taken place in London and the South East. Indeed, by 1965 London's 16.6 million m^2 and the rest of the South East's 22.0 million m^2 of office space represented half the total office space (and half the office workers) of England and Wales (Manners *et al.*, 1980, 26). *The Control of Office and Industrial Development Act* of 1965 sought to remedy this imbalance by extending IDC coverage to office developments in excess of 5,000 ft^2 (465 m^2), initially applied to London but subsequently to the whole of the South East, East Anglia, and the East and West Midlands. To be granted an Office Development Permit (ODP) by the Board of Trade to build offices in these regions, the developer had to prove that the functions of the particular office could not be performed anywhere else. These permits complemented the work of the Location of Offices Bureau (LOB), which had been established in 1963 to encourage office-based firms to consider relocation away from London.

Figure 7.2   United Kingdom: Assisted Areas, 1966–71.
Source: Law (1980)

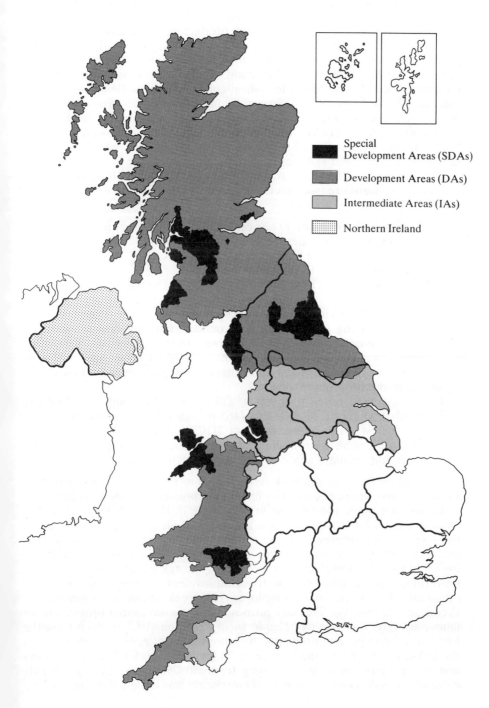

Special
Development Areas (SDAs)

Development Areas (DAs)

Intermediate Areas (IAs)

Northern Ireland

Balance of payments difficulties became acute during 1966 and unemployment started to climb again, so that it soon became apparent that the national plan could not possibly be achieved within the time-scale envisaged. It was therefore abandoned but the Regional Economic Planning Councils and Boards continued, charged with the production of regional development plans. Any future national plan would have to wait until all the regional plans had been produced, so the new Labour Government, which was returned to office after a 'snap' election in 1966 to increase its majority in Parliament, gave its attention to radical changes in the scale of regional assistance. The *Industrial Development Act* passed in August 1966 marked the first phase. The old Development Districts were replaced by much larger Development Areas (DAs), five new ones being created (Northern, South West, Wales, Merseyside, Scotland), which meant that much of upland Britain was now given DA status (Fig. 7.2).

The provisions of the 1966 Act were quite complex and have been dealt with in detail elsewhere (see especially Lee, 1980, 74–77), but its major points can be summarised as follows:

1. Investment cash grants of 40 per cent of equipment costs replaced the 10 per cent grant and free depreciation system in DAs (20 per cent outside DAs), while the 25 per cent cash grant for industrial buildings was extended from the DDs to the DAs.
2. DAs were determined by the Board of Trade on the basis of their employment, population change, migration and regional policy objectives rather than just unemployment levels, as with the DDs. The Board assisted firms by providing factories for rent or sale, building grants and other loans or grants; the Ministry of Labour covered the costs of training workers and of helping 'key workers' move to other areas; and the Treasury paid 85 per cent of local authorities' costs of derelict land clearance and infrastructural improvements.
3. IDC limits were raised to 3,000 ft^2 (279 m^2) in the South East and the Midlands and stayed at 5,000 ft^2 (465 m^2) in other areas outside DAs. The former was not a relaxation of IDC controls, however, since the definition of 'industrial building' was broadened to incorporate storage, research and ancillary space as well as production space.

The Labour Government took further steps in 1966 and 1967 to encourage firms to employ more people. The fear was expressed that the kinds of financial assistance made available to firms to date in DAs had been orientated towards capital-intensive developments and that this was inappropriate given the large labour surpluses of these areas. The *Selective Employment Payments Act* of 1966 started the process of subsidising labour in DAs by allowing employers in manufacturing to reclaim the tax which they paid to the Government per employee (Selective Employment Tax) and also to claim a premium of 37½p per male employee per week (Selective Employment Premium). In 1967 the Treasury proposed a more substantial programme of labour subsidy, the *Regional Employment Premium* (REP), which took the form of a direct payment towards the labour costs of *every* manufacturer in the DAs. The payments made were £1.50 for men, 75p for women and boys and 47½ for girls, in total amounting to about 7% of the average weekly earnings of male manual workers. The scheme was designed to run for five years (later raised to seven) and the intention was that the REP would enable manufacturers to take on more workers. The hope was that the wages of the workers would have a multiplier effect, thus increasing the local demand for goods and services. This would improve the profitablity of firms in DAs, enabling them to plough back profits into capital projects that woulds raise productivity and increase competitiveness, and fairly quickly erode regional differentials as national growth ensued – hence convergence would occur thanks to government intervention. The chief criticism of the REP was that it might be seen by the trade unions as a right, which would raise the wage-levels of workers in DAs and make them less competitive with their counterparts in other regions.

As was the case with so many regional assistance measures, however, national economic events were moving more quickly than the effects of the measures: 1967 saw unemployment climbing again to 2.4 per cent from the 1.5 per cent of 1966, with particularly high rates in Scotland (3.9 per cent), the North (4.0 per cent) and Wales (4.1 per cent). As with any set of macro-region figures, the unemployment rates for the three most peripheral planning regions masked considerable spatial diversity within them and particularly underemphasised micro-regions with acute unemployment problems, especially old coal-mining areas. These were highlighted in 1967 by their designation as *Special Development Areas* (SDAs) within the DAs (Fig. 7.2). Locating a factory in a SDA meant that the company not only received all the DA benefits but also had the factory building grant increased to 35 per cent plus low-interest loans for the balance, or could rent a government factory for five years without charge, and was eligible for a grant of 10 per cent of total annual operating costs for the first three years (minus building and investment grants). This legislation represented a return to the welfare approach of the DDs, with government assistance aimed at trying to reduce the distress caused by high unemployment rather than necessarily 'priming' an area for new growth.

The prospect of continuing unemployment at levels considered high by post-war standards, in turn reflecting a slowing down of national growth, had implications not only for the DAs but also for contiguous regions. The latter saw themselves as facing increasing competition for resources with stronger growth regions, while government assistance was firmly favouring their neighbouring DAs. These contiguous regions were suffering many of the same problems as the DAs, since they also contained a disproportionately large amount of traditional industries, but their unemployment rates in general were not yet high enough for them to qualify for assistance. Recognising that these regions might become the DAs of the future if left to their own devices, the Government appointed a Committee (chaired by Sir Joseph Hunt) in 1967 to study these 'grey' areas, as they became known, and make recommendations for action, which it did under the title of *The Intermediate Areas* (Cmnd 3998, HMSO) in 1969. The Hunt Report concluded that these Intermediate Areas (IAs) exhibited major structural economic problems, poor physical infrastructure, low labour activity rates and high net levels of out-migration, and therefore recommended a substantial increase in financial assistance. The Government could not afford the level of assistance required and consequently it was a modified set of the proposals which were enacted by Parliament in the 1970 *Local Employment Act*.

Seven small areas were designated to receive assistance under the 1970 Act – north-east Lancashire, the Yorkshire coalfield, north Humberside, the Nottinghamshire-Derbyshire coalfield, south-east Wales, Plymouth and Leith (Fig. 7.2). Industrial building grants of 25 per cent were made available in the IAs, plus grants for training, the provision of government-built factories and 75 per cent capital grants towards the cost of derelict land clearance for industrial developments. The anticipated £20 million cost was met by removing the Selective Employment Tax and Premium from manufacturing industries in the DAs (see p. 183). By 1970 the cost to the nation of regional assistance had risen to £270 million annually, most of it in cash grants and subsidies, a phenomenal increase over the £30 million of Labour's first year in office, and Britain probably had the most extensive range of regional assistance instruments of any country. Nevertheless, as unemployment rose to 2.6 per cent nationally, the country went to the polls, Labour was defeated and the Conservatives returned to power.

7.1.2 Conservative Government 1970–74

In keeping with party 'tradition' and economic philosophy the new administration initially sought to shift regional policy emphasis from the labour subsidy and investment grant approach to one of tax allowances for companies. To this end a White Paper on *Investment Incentives* was published in 1970 (Cmnd 4516). This proposed that:

- investment grants be replaced with 'free' depreciation on immobile plant and machinery in DAs, compared with only 60 per cent in the first year elsewhere;
- tax allowances on mobile plant and on service industries be introduced;
- building grants be raised from 25 to 35 per cent in DAs and from 35 to 45 per cent in SDAs;
- SDA operational grants be raised to 20 per cent in the first three years; and
- grants to local authorities for infrastructural improvements be increased.

Also in 1970, IDC controls were relaxed from 3,000 ft^2 (279 m^2) to 5,000 ft^2 (465 m^2) in the South East, East Anglia, and the East and West Midlands, and from 5,000 ft^2 to 10,000 ft^2 (930 m^2) in other areas outside the AAs. Similarly, office development limits were raised from 3,000 to 10,000 ft^2 in Greater London, putting the capital on a par with the rest of the South East, and restrictions were removed completely in the Midlands.

Rising unemployment in 1971 (3.6 per cent) and 1972 (3.7 per cent) prompted a change of policy, especially in respect of the hardest-hit regions of the North West (4.8 per cent), Wales (5.2 per cent), the North (6.3 per cent), Scotland (6.4 per cent) and Northern Ireland (8.0 per cent) (see Table 8.1). In 1971 the number and size of SDAs were increased, with Tyneside, Wearside, Merseyside and Clydeside being included, and their operational grants were increased to 30 per cent, while seven employment districts were given IA status – Edinburgh and Portobello (Lothian), Bridlington and Filey (Yorkshire), Oswestry (Shropshire), Okehampton and Tavistock (Devon).

Unemployment reached 1 million in the winter of 1971–2 for the first time since 1947, and as the country slipped into recession the Government was under increasing pressure to 'do something' at a time of growing financial stringency. The reaction was a major expansion in government training facilities (the *Training Opportunities Scheme* of 1972) and, much more importantly, a White Paper on *Industrial and Regional Development*, which was soon legislated as *The Industry Act 1972*. This Act represented a complete turnabout for a Conservative Government, since it abandoned the tax incentive approach and reverted to grant payments, but it was so wide-ranging that it formed the basis of regional policy for the rest of the decade.

The 1972 Act set new regional development grants for buildings, plant and machinery in the manufacturing sector at 22 per cent in the SDAs and 20 per cent in the DAs, with 20 per cent available for buildings only in the IAs. These new grants were provided regardless of employment creation and all new firms, whether spawned locally or having in-migrated to the AAs, were eligible. Also, derelict land clearance areas were allowed the 20 per cent buildings grant for two years. The recommendation of the Hunt Committee that IA status should be applied to the rest of the North West, Yorkshire and Humberside, and Wales outside DAs was put into practice, so that well over half the national territory now had AA status of some kind (Fig. 7.3.) Within SDAs and DAs, IDCs were abolished, while outside these areas the threshold was raised to 15,000 ft^2 (1,395 m^2) except in the South East where it was set at 10,000 ft^2 (930 m^2). Other measures in the 1972 Act included phasing out the REP by 1974, increased expenditure on training schemes and centres (especially retraining redundant workers), and separation and removal expenses for key workers moving to new jobs in AAs. To complement these incentives the Government introduced *Selective Financial Assistance* (SFA) for manufacturing and service industry sectors in AAs and this was also available for major projects in other parts of the country. In addition, both a 100 per cent depreciation allowance in the first year on all new investment in plant and machinery and a 40 per cent allowance on new industrial buildings were available countrywide. The intention of these measures was to encourage any developments which might contribute to national economic growth since it was believed that this, in turn, would have 'spread' or 'trickle down' benefits for the less prosperous regions.

Administration of the Act came under the auspicies of a new *Industrial Development Executive* within the Department of Trade and Industry, and a Minister for Industrial Development was appointed and given special responsibility for private industrial developments in the AAs. In addition, regional *Industrial Development Boards* were established to advise the Executive in the AA regions (Scotland, Wales, North, North West, Yorkshire and Humberside) and they had considerable independence in the allocation of SFA. The shift in emphasis of regional policy towards service activities, which had marked legislation by Labour in 1965, received a boost in 1973 with the establishment of the *Office and Service Industry Scheme* (OSIS). This provided a relocation grant for employers moving to AAs, a grant for job creation there, worker-training support, low-interest loans and rent relief.

As in previous years, however, government schemes for regional assistance were overtaken by events, and 1974 was particularly significant in this respect because of the quadrupling of oil prices between 1973 and 1974. The slight economic recovery from the unemployment high of 3.7 per cent in 1972 was abruptly halted at 2.6 per cent in 1973–74, and the long-term decline

Figure 7.3   United Kingdom: Assisted Areas, 1972–77.
Sources: Law (1980)

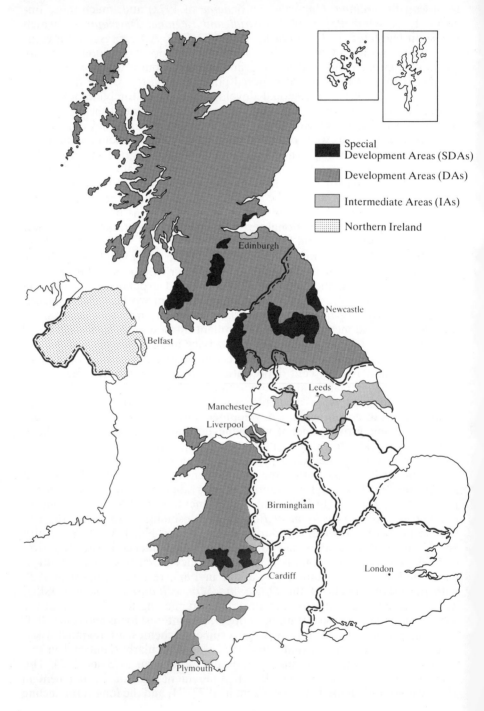

of Britain's manufacturing industry began to accelerate. When the people went to vote in the general election of 1974 they returned a Labour Government with a narrow majority over the Conservatives and dependent upon a pact with the Liberals in order to secure the passage of any legislation through Parliament.

7.1.3 Labour Government 1974–79

In general terms, the incoming Labour administration was content with the regional provisions of the 1972 Industry Act and was prepared to commit substantially increased financial assistance, raising the £310 million by of 1973/4 to £575 million by 1976/7 and to over £600 million by 1979/80. Immediate policy changes were fourfold:

- to reduce IDC thresholds to 5,000 ft^2 (465 m^2) in the South East, to 10,000 ft^2 (930 m^2) in other non-assisted regions, and to retain it at 15,000 ft^2 (1,395 m^2) in IAs;
- to extend DA status to Edinburgh and Cardiff, and SDA status to Merseyside and parts of north-west Wales (Fig. 7.3);
- to double the REP instead of phasing it out;
- to embark on a 'rolling programme' of small Advance Factory Construction schemes in AAs.

In 1974 the Standard Planning Region boundaries were slightly modified when county boundaries were 'rationalised' in the local government reforms (Fig. 7.4 – cf. Fig. 7.1).

The Budget of 1975 added cash (£100 million) to accelerate projects which had been shelved by the Conservatives and to help certain industries restructure and modernise, and additional funds were provided for industrial training of the unemployed (through the Training Services Agency) and for a new scheme, the *Temporary Employment Subsidy*. This TES was to be paid to companies willing to keep people employed rather than make them redundant (since if the latter occurred the Government would pay them unemployment benefits anyway), but there was a recognised risk that this could mean subsidies for inefficient firms just at a time when they should have been trying to improve their productivity per worker and become more competitive.

The national economic situation in 1975 did not lend itself to any reflationary measures designed to promote industrial output, as had been possible in previous recessions. Unemployment reached 4.1 per cent (the first of what was to be an annual post-war record level for the next decade), inflation was gaining momentum, sterling was beset with difficulties and the prospects looked even worse. Firms seeking financial help from the Industrial Development Boards did so for reasons of imminent collapse, not for expansion and job creation! The Government therefore sought to stimulate new development through several measures, the first of which in April 1975 was the *Accelerated Projects Scheme* (APS), intended to persuade companies to start planned investment programmes as soon as possible and not wait for recovery of the economy. Since labour-intensive projects in AAs were eligible for support from SFA funds, it was hoped that the APS would attract more capital-intensive projects. In September 1975 more money was made

Figure 7.4   United Kingdom: County and Standard Planning Region boundaries from 1974*
Source: Central Statistical Office (1987a, 157)

*See figure 2.1 for county names and appendix for details.

* See Fig 2.1 for County names and Appendix for details

available: for SFA investment (£80 million); for a job creation programme (£30 million via the Manpower Services Commission); for Advance Factory Construction (£20 million), and for upgrading industrial estates in AAs.

In November 1975 a new *Industry Act* was passed which aimed to enable the Government to enter into 'planning agreements' with major companies, to have access to company information about future plans and to try to prevent foreign take-overs of British firms where appropriate. There was a regional element in these measures in that the Government hoped to persuade firms to locate new capacity in AAs. However, national economic problems were increasingly coming to the fore of policy again. This was reflected in the Act's creation of the *National Enterprise Board* (NEB), whose functions were to lend investment capital to industry, to participate in the more profitable industrial sectors, to buy equity shares in companies which were having problems but had good potential, and even to help industrial 'lame ducks' if the Government wished (e.g. for employment reasons in AAs). Unemployment continued its apparently inexorable rise, however, breaking through the 1 million 'barrier' in 1976, with especially marked increases among school-leavers. The potential social unrest among the latter prompted several attempts to improve employment prospects, even if only temporarily. Among these were: the Youth Employment Subsidy (replacing the Recruitment Subsidy of April 1975); the Work Experience Programme; the Community Industry Project; and the Job-Release Scheme. Interestingly, of the 30,000 school-leavers who were found jobs between autumn 1975 and summer 1976, about half were employed in the service industries, one quarter in the distributive trades (mainly retailing) and a minority, therefore, in manufacturing, but 150,000 others remained unemployed in September 1976.

During 1976 financial assistance began to be available from the *EEC's Regional Development Fund* (ERDF), and Britain received 28 per cent of the total allocation for the period 1976–78. This money was meant to supplement national expenditure in AAs, going towards investment in industrial, handicraft and infrastructural developments, but the amount of £150 million made available over the three years was minor compared with Britain's total of £750 million spent in AAs in 1976 alone. But 1976 was the last year when sums of this magnitude were spent on regional policy – by the middle of the year, with high rates of inflation and unemployment still climbing, the Government was forced to start cutting public expenditure.

The REP, on which £213 million should have been spent in 1976/7, was reduced from mid-1976 and abolished early in 1977 (although in Northern Ireland a modified version continued). The one positive feature to emerge from 1976 was the creation of *Development Agencies for Scotland and Wales*, which were charged with the task of restructuring their regional economies in order to promote industrial expansion, to clear derelict land and to improve infrastructure. However, as the recession deepened and national unemployment levels reached 5.7 per cent in 1977 and 6.2 per cent in 1978, government policy reduced emphasis on the regions, since *any* growth in *any* region was considered to be better policy than restricting such growth to AAs, and the new 'high tech' industries were predominantly located in the South East. Perhaps somewhat disillusioned with Labour's apparent inability to improve the economic fortunes of the country, the voting public chose to return the Conservations to power in the 1979 general election.

7.1.4   Conservative Governments 1979–83, 1983–87, 1987–

When the new administration assumed office Assisted Areas covered about two-thirds of the national territory (Fig. 7.5), contained 43 per cent of the country's working population and were costing the Exchequer over £600 million per year. Continuing the policy of public expenditure cuts started in 1976 by Labour, the Conservative Government proposed to reduce gradually regional assistance by 38 per cent overall between 1979 and 1982/3 and to concentrate remaining aid on those areas with the highest unemployment. The latter were found, as in previous recessions, in areas of traditional industries (e. g. the iron and steel areas of Shotton and Corby received SDA and DA designation, respectively, in December 1979) and also in the inner city areas of the major conurbations, including London. Government assistance was becoming spatially more narrowly based as the Conservatives shifted the funding emphasis towards urban areas, local authority sources and private initiatives in distressed areas.

The process of change in the form and extent of government assistance to the regions and cities really got under way in 1980. At the *regional* level, RDGs were tightened up, with the 20 per cent building grant in IAs being withdrawn, and the 20 per cent grant for new factories, plant and machinery in DAs being reduced to 15 per cent but retained at 22 per cent in SDAs, thereby increasing the differentials between AAs. Also, office development permits were ended and the Location of Offices Bureau axed, as were the Regional Economic Planning Councils, and the IDC threshold was raised substantially throughout non-AAs to 50,000 ft^2 (4,650 m^2) and abandoned in the IAs. Assistance under the RSA scheme was also subjected to stricter criteria after 1979. From 1980, RSA financing was available only for projects which: '(a) had good prospects of viability, (b) created new jobs or safeguarded existing ones in the Assisted Areas, (c) strengthened the regional and national economy, and (d) needed assistance to make them go ahead . . . and then only up to the minimum necessary in order for the project to go ahead' (Moore *et al.*, 1986, 26).

At the *city* level, attempts to regenerate employment in inner city areas started in 1980 with the creation of *Urban Development Corporations* (UDCs) for the London and Liverpool Docklands. The UDCs were designed to undertake substantial programmes of land acquisition, with associated environmental and infrastructural improvements, and the intention was to involve private companies as much as possible in any development. UDCs were established under the *Local Government Planning and Land Act 1980*, as were the *Enterprise Zones* (EZs). In an effort to encourage manufacturing firms to locate in EZs, thus improving urban employment prospects, a number of incentives were offered for the first 10 years, including:

• exemption from local authority general rates, Development Land Tax, IDC controls and Industrial Training Board requirements;
• 100 per cent tax allowances on commercial or industrial buildings;
• fewer restrictions by the local planners.

Figure 7.5   United Kingdom: Assisted Areas, 1977–82.
Source: Commission of the European Communities (1978, 60)

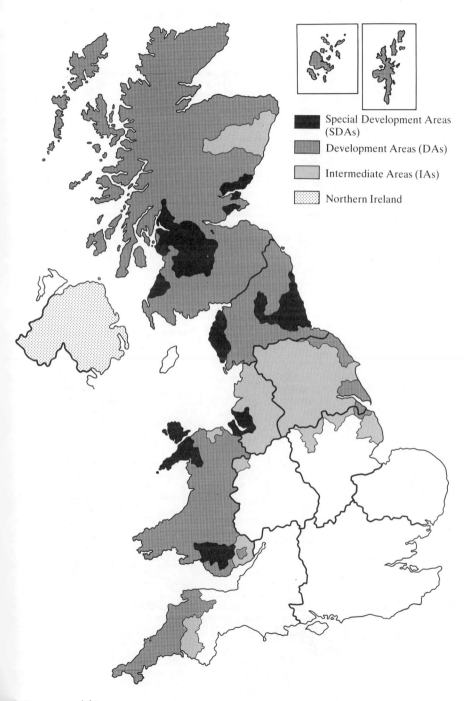

Special Development Areas (SDAs)

Development Areas (DAs)

Intermediate Areas (IAs)

Northern Ireland

**Figure 7.6   United Kingdom: New Towns, Urban Development
Corporations, Freeports, Enterprise Zones, and Steel Closure
areas.**
Source: Cambridge Information and Research Services (1986,
8)

Thirteen EZs, with an average size of 200 ha (mainly derelict land), were initially designated in 1981 and 14 more were added in 1983–84 (Fig. 7.6), followed by Inverclyde on 1988. Progress was slow in the early years, however, because of the necessity of dismantling existing planning procedures and of creating the legislation to allow the Exchequer to compensate local authorities for their loss of rate income from the nomination of an EZ within their boundaries.

During 1981, the Conservative Government carried out a preliminary review of the whole structure of regional assistance in Britain in the light of the policy intention to further reduce public expenditure. The results were abandonment of IDCs as a method of controlling industrial development and the drafting of a new map in 1982 which substantially reduced the areas eligible for regional aid (compare Fig. 7.7 with Fig. 7.5). The proportion of the national working population contained within AAs was reduced to 27 per cent and the pattern of assistance reverted to one not dissimilar from the early 1960s (cf. Fig. 6.4).

The cuts in assistance were not as substantial as the Government would have liked, however, since pruning on such a scale would have removed too many areas from an 'assisted ' status, thereby denying them the opportunity of applying for ERDF grants from the EEC. (The UK receives about 25 per cent of the ERDF grants, amounting in total to £587 million over the period 1975–88, with Scotland receiving 26 per cent, Northern Ireland 19 per cent, North 14 per cent, Wales 14 per cent and North West 9 per cent.) Indeed, following a further review of regional aid (see especially the submission by the Regional Studies Association, 1983), which resulted in the White Paper on *Regional Industrial Development* (Cmnd 9111), published in December 1983, the Government modified both the methods and areas of assistance. The revised scheme was presented to Parliament in November 1984 and became effective shortly thereafter.

For the first time certain service industry sectors could be assisted, a recognition of the fact that the main potential for job creation no longer lay with manufacturing industries. Coincidentally, 1983 was the year in which 'Britain became a *net importer* of manufactured goods . . . for the first time since the Industrial Revolution' (Morgan, 1986, 351), a sobering thought indeed for anyone who can recall the country's sometime claim to be 'the workshop of the world'! Spatially, new areas of the country were designated (namely, Greater Manchester, Sheffield, parts of the West Midlands) in order to ensure that they would qualify for ERDF grants. The main intent of the scheme was to save money, and the principal means of doing so was to restrict the RDG rate in the newly defined DAs to 15 per cent of new capital investment. A second ceiling on the grant was a limit of £10,000 per job created, or applicants could opt for a basic £3,000 per new full-time job instead of the capital grant – an option intended to favour labour-intensive projects. RSA was also reduced, but was available in IAs as well as DAs. The total cost of regional assistance to the Exchequer would consequently decrease from the £617 million of 1983 to less than £300 million per year in 1987–88 (instead of the £1 billion predicted for then if the 1978 policies had continued). From 1985, then, regional assistance concentrated on selective (RSA) rather than automatic (RDG) grants, and became available on a two-tier rather than a three-tier areal system. Hence, the 'old' SDA-DA-IA

153

Figure 7.7   United Kingdom: Assisted Areas, 1982–84.
Source: Department of Trade and Industry (1983)

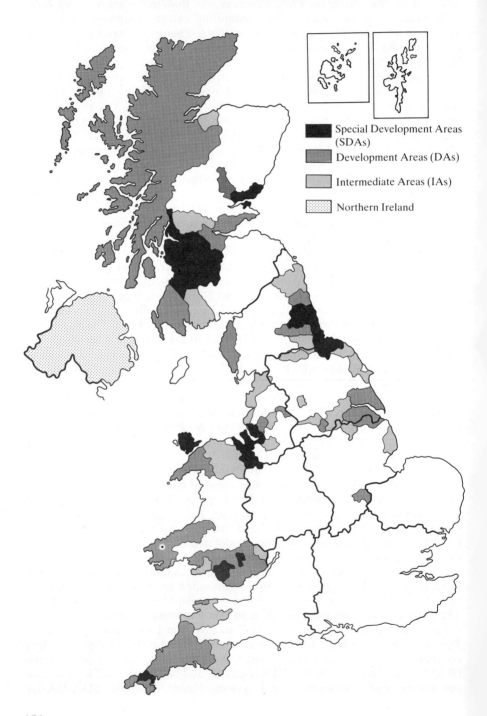

scheme was replaced by a simplified DA-IA scheme, with many of the 'old' SDAs becoming DAs, the 'old' DAs becoming IAs and the 'old' IAs almost disappearing, as shown on Fig. 7.8 (cf. Fig. 7.7).

The boundaries for assistance on the 'new' map of regional aid continued to be the travel-to-work areas used by the previous Labour Government. The proportion of the working population living in 'new' DAs decreased to 15 per cent compared with the 22 per cent in the 'old' SDAs and DAs combined, but the proportion in IAs increased dramatically from 5 per cent to 20 per cent, thanks in part to redesignation of areas but mainly to the inclusion of the Birmingham, Manchester and Sheffield conurbations. In total, therefore, the AAs accounted for 35 per cent of the nation's working population but for 50 per cent of the nation's unemployment in 1985, proportions that remain much the same currently. The addition of the West Midlands to the list of AAs marked a significant development in the national pattern of the industrial recession, since it had been classified as a growth region ever since the mid-1930s. This change in fortune reflected declines in the motor vehicle, engineering, metal working and chemical industries (1 in 3 jobs were lost between 1974 and 1982), the very industries which had been at the forefront of Kondratieff's Fourth Long Wave.

All the traditional industries continued to lose jobs during the recession years of 1979–86: textiles lost 180,000; iron and steel 132,000; coal mining 90,000; shipbuilding 26,500; railway engineering 17,000. The 'growth' industries of the Fourth Kondratieff also contracted markedly: motor vehicles lost 200,000; machine tools 30,000; instrument engineering 30,000; aerospace 25,000, and even electronics 15,000. In total, over 2 million manufacturing jobs were lost, and the gain of 340,000 service jobs was hardly sufficient to compensate. These job losses were reflected in the national unemployment rates of 13.9 per cent in 1985 and 13.5 per cent in 1986. Regionally the pattern was much the same as before, with higher levels of unemployment in areas of traditional industry, as indicated in the 1986 figures – Northern Ireland 21.0 per cent; North 18.9 per cent, Wales 16.9 per cent, North West 16.3 per cent, Scotland 15.6 per cent, West Midlands 15.5 per cent and Yorkshire/Humberside 15.1 per cent were all well above the national average, but well below were East Midlands at 12.7%, South West at 12.0 per cent, East Anglia at 10.7 per cent and South East at 9.9 per cent. These figures possibly marked the worst year of the recession, since they started to fall in the following year, as we will note below.

The collapse of Britain's old staple industries in this recession had a damaging impact on trade union membership, which declined drastically from 11.5 million in 1976 to 9.25 million in 1986, with a forecast total of only 7.75 million by 1996. This would be the lowest membership since 1920 (see Page 112) and has considerable political significance. The decline reflects not only the demise of traditional industries, but also shifts of public and workforce attitudes towards unions, as new 'growth' industries are non-union or single-union. As primary and secondary employment opportunities decrease while tertiary and quaternary ones increase, trade unions are being forced to reassess their political alignment in order to reflect the changing socio-economic structure of their membership. Similarly, as the 'working class' declines and becomes increasingly concentrated in the inner cities and as shrinking 'blue collar' unions lose their political clout to the growing

155

Figure 7.8   United Kingdom: Assisted Areas, 1984 onwards.
Source: Central Statistical Office (1987a)

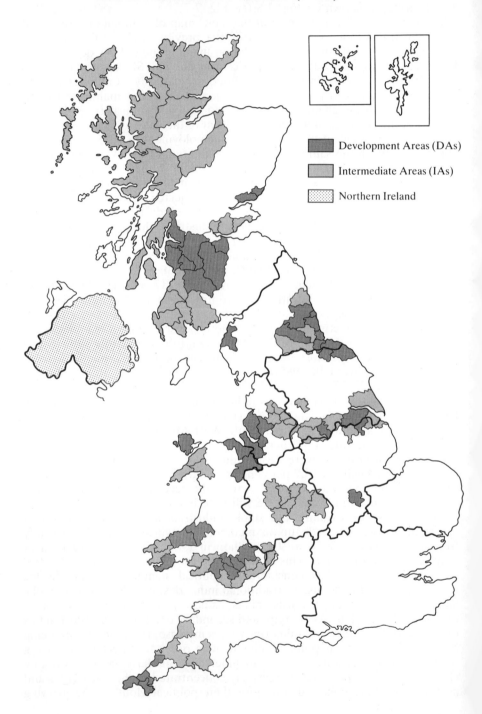

'white collar' unions, the Labour Party may have less and less chance of winning a national election. The 40 per cent of the voting population who are now classified as 'middle class' are predominantly non-union and cannot identify with Labour policies, but neither can many of them bring themselves to vote Conservative. This was the pattern in the election of 1987, when the inner London boroughs and the industrial conurbations of upland Britain went almost solidly for Labour, the suburbs, market towns and rural areas went almost solidly for the Conservatives, and the SDP-Liberal Alliance gained 25 per cent of the votes cast across the socio-economic spectrum, but kept coming in second! Since the number of parliamentary seats outside the inner cities and the coal, textile and steel towns is much larger than the number inside such electoral wards, the Conservatives won a third term in office in 1987.

In January 1988 the Conservative Government presented to Parliament a White Paper, *DTI – the Department for Enterprise*, which recommended an overhaul of the Department of Trade and Industry (DTI) in order to enable it to increase the competitiveness, encourage the innovation and improve the skills of individuals nationally, but especially in the AAs and inner cities. Regional grants, which totalled about £580 million in the fiscal year 1987/8, were seen by the Government as subsidies that were damaging industry's efficiency and were therefore detrimental to its ability to compete, especially given the 'open market' of the EEC after 1992. The kernel of the DTI's revamping is to switch its role from one of intervening in existing big industries to one of encouraging the formation of new companies. This continues the central objective of the 1983 revised policy on regional industrial development, which was to encourage the development of indigenous potential within the AAs with a long-term objective of self-generating growth in these areas. The Government believed that this objective would be achieved more effectively be changing the balance of regional policy.

The most striking feature of the new policy was the termination of RDGs in March 1988. A new scheme of incentives for smaller firms in DAs and Urban Programme Areas (UPAs) started in April 1988, which provided *investment grants* of 15 per cent towards the cost of fixed assests (£15,000 maximum) and *innovation grants* of 50 per cent to support product and process development (£25,000 maximum) for firms with fewer than 25 employees. A new range of business development initiatives was also introduced in 1988 (worth £50 million in 1988–89, rising to £80 million per year, 1989–92) covering computer-aided manufacturing, business planning, financial and information systems, and management consultancy for small-to medium-sized firms in both DAs and IAs. In total, these grants and initiatives in AAs and UPAs are expected to cost the Exchequer £254 million in 1990–91. A further £264 million will be spent per year by 1990–91 on Regional Selective Assistance, a substantial increase on the £79 million allocated for RSA in 1985–86. RSA remains a discretionary grant towards capital and training costs of projects which create or safeguard employment, but which would not be able to proceed in the AAs without government money. The changes brought about by the 1988 White Paper were not intended to reduce the planned level of spending on regional industrial measures but to re-allocate it, and the administration of RSA and the new incentives has continued within the framework of the 1984 regional map (Fig. 7.8).

157

The 1988 revisions to regional policy were predicated on a belief that continuous subsidy to industries in AAs was an inappropriate way for central government to encourage an attitude of self-help and a spirit of enterprise and competitiveness. Hence, if the regions are to experience convergence, much of the impetus will have to come from within the regions themselves, and government can only realistically facilitate this process – it cannot legislate for it nor make certain areas forever wards of the public purse. The policy revisions may also have been influenced by the fact that the national economy grew by 14.5 per cent between 1981 and 1987, and that unemployment showed a notable decrease in 1987 (although this was in part due to new definitions of unemployment). The regional dichotomy continued, however, with upland Britain above the national average of 11.3 per cent unemployed and lowland Britain predominantly below, thus: Northern Ireland 19.0 per cent, North 15.9 per cent, Scotland 14.5 per cent, North West 13.6 per cent, Yorkshire-Humberside 13.5 per cent, Wales 13.4 per cent, West Midlands 13.2 per cent, East Midlands 11.1 per cent, South West 10.2 per cent, East Anglia 8.9 per cent and South East 8.2 per cent. (See also Table 8.1.)

After more than 50 years of regional assistance, then, the basic upland-lowland division of Britain continues, with the older, traditional industrial areas of the North and West consistently registering above-average levels of unemployment, even in times of national prosperity. As we have seen in the last two chapters the type, intensity and areal coverage of the numerous measures aimed at achieving a reduction of the regional imbalances in economic prosperity have varied between governments and over time. All have conceded that some spatial redistribution of the national income is both socially and politically desirable, if not essential. The critical interrelationship between cities and the regions within which they are situated was not as fully appreciated in the planning process as might have been expected until the mid-1970s. This was possibly because of the ways in which parliamentary electoral boundaries were drawn, which resulted in MPs being 'urban' or 'rural' based, and biased, in their views of industrial developments and job creation. To some extent this is still evident in the spatial organisation of economic planning, with the DAs and IAs being predominantly urban-based (Fig. 7.8), as of course are the UDCs and EZs. Their rural-based counterparts are the Highlands and Islands Development Board, the Development Board for Rural Wales, and the Development Commission in rural England (and its agency, CoSIRA – Council for Small Industry in Rural Areas), whose spatial coverage is shown on Fig. 7.9. The budgets of these organisations, however, are miniscule (e.g. HIDB £30 million, DBRW £5 million in 1985–86) compared with regional assistance monies, which may help to explain their survival following the regional policy reviews of the early 1980s. (See Chisholm, 1984a, 1984b, and 1986.)

The reorganisation of the whole field of regional (urban and rural) assistance in Britain after 1979 occurred during a major recession, the worst since the early 1930s, and traditionally the kind of economic condition that has prompted increased government assistance rather than cutbacks. This radical policy review reflected a change of political-economic philosophy in Westminster not just because the Conservative Party had been returned to

Figure 7.9 Great Britain: Rural Development Agencies.
Source: Hudson and Williams (1986, 173)

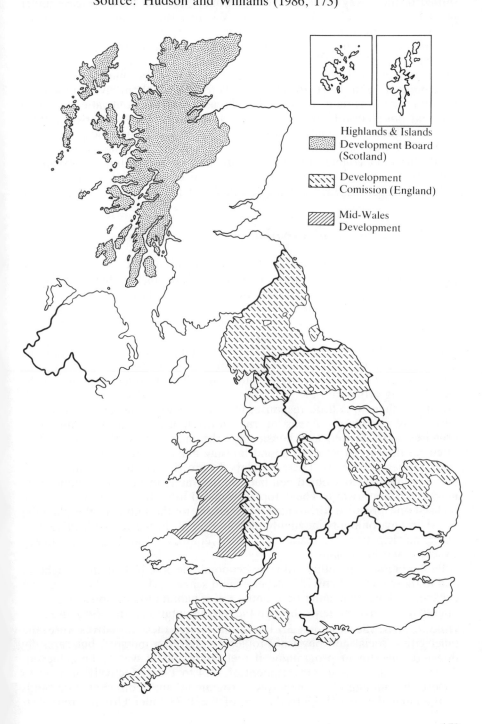

office, but also because under Thatcher's leadership the philosophy itself was shifted further away from intervention policy than had been the case under previous Conservative administrations. Whereas the Labour Party has been consistently interventionist in its policies, trying to ensure that industrial growth occurs equally in all regions, the Conservatives have stressed decreased intervention by central government and placed much more emphasis upon national economic growth within a more *laissez-faire* environment, with the regions left largely to fend for themselves in the competition for investment. (For a fuller discussion of the political economy of regional policy developments between 1979 and 1985, see Parsons, 1986, 239–80.) These two political approaches to regional economic policy raise both theoretical and empirical questions about the mechanisms of growth (or decline) in a country and its speed and pattern of distribution throughout the national space economy. The effects and effectiveness of intervention policies will be discussed in Chapters 8, 9 and 10.

7.2   Government intervention — urban aspects

The support and encouragement for the continuing decentralisation of people and employment to new and developing towns together with the application of green belt legislation was central to successive government's policy throughout the 1960s and 1970s. The aims were still to protect the countryside from urban development, and to reduce development pressures in the overcrowded cities. Unfortunately this was insufficient to resolve the multifaceted inner city problems where new employment and new housing were of paramount importance. The employment initiatives by governments were considered earlier in the chapter, but what of policy response to the deteriorating urban fabric?

Initially there was little response, for the policy of redevelopment of the 1950s was continued. Areas of run down housing and poor industrial premises were cleared and housing for the masses took their place. This often resulted in structurally sound housing being destroyed and close knit communities broken up. There developed a growing disillusionment with the urban planners who seemed hell bent on destruction whether for housing or new urban motorways. The Utopia promised after the war was not being realised and pressure for greater involvement by the public in the planning of urban environments inevitably increased until, in the *1968 Planning Act*, public participation was made a statutory requirement in the preparation of structure and local plans.

Public pressure together with the economic decline in Britain brought an end to these comprehensive redevelopment schemes. In their place came the cheaper and less damaging programmes of rehabilitation of housing and the upgrading of environments through the implementation of the *1969* and *1974 Housing Acts*. (See Chapter 3.) Important though these initiatives were, the inner cities' social and physical problems required a massive, but carefully directed, investment programme if real improvement was to be achieved. To this end the Labour Government of 1974 to 1979 effectively brought to a close the funding of the new town programme and redirected state funds to the cities through the introduction of the 1978 Inner Urban Areas Act.

This fundamental change in policy was taken a stage further in 1980 when the new Conservative Government embarked on a series of policy initiatives (see Chapter 10) designed to create climates of investment in the inner areas which would be attractive to the main financial institutions. In effect public funds would be used to improve the infrastructure in readiness for private development as is well illustrated by the formation of Urban Development Corporations.

This period shows then a significant change in emphasis from state funding to private funding in order to save the cities from a downward spiral of decay, but what has this all meant to those who live in these areas, what housing have these policy responses brought? The following pages contain a case study on urban housing.

7.2.1 The inner city inheritance

The history of housing since the early 1960s has largely been one of re-assessment as the building momentum generated after the War began to slow and the mistakes of building in a hurry became manifest. This was particularly so in the public housing sector, where the large, high-rise estates built from the late 1950s until the Ronan Point disaster were considered to mark the nadir of housing provision.

These 'towns in the sky' were the culmination of a sequence of housing estates first built before the War which form part of the inner city housing inheritance which we see today. In essence this inheritance contains three types of estates.

Pre-war estates – the first generation
The pre-war estates, although well-built, provided little space for the families they were designed for. In many cases they allowed on 4 m^2 per person, which included public space, and they were in no way compatible with modern family living.

Table 7.1 High-rise buildings in Glasgow

	Multi-storey blocks	Total multi-storey housing units	Multi-storey housing units as % of total housing stock
1960	3	219	0.20
1966	92	10,285	1.81
1969	178	18,283	12.84
1972	231	21,909	14.70

In 1972, of the multi-storey blocks:

%	No. of storeys
40.9	16–20
32.7	21–25
6.2	26–30
3.3	over 30

Source: Glasgow Housing Department

161

The second generation

The second generation, constructed in the late 1940s and 1950s, was of much lower density, about 350 people per hectare, but beyond this had little to commend it. This is the period of the housing drive, when the concern was to provide as many housing units as possible. In 1953 the local authorities achieved their highest number of dwellings completed at any time this century. Unfortunately, speed in production was not matched by care in design and construction, with the result that the flats, though fairly spacious, were inefficiently heated and lacked insulation.

Tower blocks – the third generation

The 1960s were the decade of the tower blocks. The introduction of these 'houses in the sky' arose from the coalescing of several factors: firstly, a belief that these estates represented an economical use of land (in cities where green belt legislation was introduced this was of particular significance); secondly, the view that costs of construction and building time would be reduced by the introduction of industrialised building systems which provided the ready-made facades, using prefabricated concrete, to pin on to the steel skeleton of each block; and thirdly, the conversion of British architects to 'modernist' architecture which sought new forms of building using steel, reinforced concrete and glass. One of its main contributors, Le Corbusier, had, in his Unité d'Habitation blocks of flats in Marseilles (1947) and Nantes (1952), introduced a new concept in housing which was followed and corrupted by successive architects, a number of whom were British. His conception of urban living was based upon the observation that 'we live in flats', which was largely true in France but not in Britain, where we accepted his ideas without questioning whether they provided an appropriate form of housing for the people.

There was therefore a certain rationale to the decision by government to encourage local authorities to build high-rise accommodation. The Conservative Government, in the *1954 Housing Act*, provided grants for local authorities to replace slum housing, with high-rise buildings. Unfortunately, in meeting the urgent need for housing, little attention was paid to the tenants who would occupy these new flats. Such accommodation was foreign to our tradition of building houses with some private space, and streets for communication and play areas for children. None of the working-class families who came to reside in these blocks had any experience of high-rise living, nor, its seem, did architects understand the needs of young families. All the more disgraceful, then, that the 1960s witnessed a second surge in public house building, much of it associated with these new tower blocks, and encouraged by government.

7.2.2 The fourth and fifth generations

The fourth and fifth generations of housing estates, which spanned the 1970s and early 1980s, contained a number of significant improvements. They were smaller in size, usually no more than three storeys, with each tenant possessing a separate entrance from the street and a garden. The quality of design and layout was improved, although the condition of some of these houses was substandard, with leaking roofs, cracking plaster and poor door fittings. Nevertheless, the local authority tenant was now beginning to receive accommodation comparable to the owner-occupier.

The 1970s also provided an opportunity to re-examine housing policies in the light of the mistakes that had already been made and of the prospect of declining resources as the economy became depressed. An increasing body of evidence pointed to the disruptive nature of large-scale redevelopment schemes, which resulted in not only the destruction of structurally sound houses, but also the fragmentation of communities at a high social cost.

It seemed wise, therefore, to change from these large-scale renewal schemes to the rehabilitation of existing housing and to general environmental improvement. This change of emphasis was introduced both in the *1969 Housing Act*, which contained the legislation for the General Improvement Areas, and the *1974 Housing Act* with provision for Housing Action Areas. Both of these strategies were discussed earlier (Chapter 3), and there is no doubt that the impact on the quality of the housing stock has been significant. Nevertheless, the extent to which this has helped the deprived groups in society is questionable, since such people either cannot afford to match a government grant with their own financial contribution, or because they do not reside in these older dwellings. For the majority who were caught up in the slum clearance programmes, their new destinations were the large housing estates with 'modern' housing conditions where improvements or repairs were not considered necessary. Yet it is these very estates where, because of bad design and/or poor building materials, the need for improvement now exists. It is ironic that estates built for former slum dwellers became slums within a decade, and now in an increasing number of cases have to be demolished.

7.2.3 Current problems and initiatives

It is encouraging to note that now there is an acute awareness of the growing gulf between the deprived of the inner cities and the rest of the nation's population, but whether there is the political will to do anything about this is not certain when the government has reduced expenditure in the housing sector by some 70 per cent in real terms since 1979. A Department of Environment (1985) report stated that council estates needed £20 billion for urgent repairs, a figure which, to independent consultants, may be an underestimate. It also suggested that to prevent further deterioration £600 million is the minimum required. And yet the Treasury was arguing for public spending cuts on housing in 1986/7 of the order of £200 million.

The present Government, in following an economic strategy designed to reduce inflation and severely control public spending, has attempted to concentrate its scarce resources in the most needy areas. The 1980 Housing Act provided the legislative framework for this. Its major objective was 'to secure a more flexible system that will get resources more effectively to the properties that most need improving, and to those persons who have most need of financial help to undertake improvements and essential repairs'. At the same time, the Government is revolutionising the ownership of residential property, as it concentrates on individual home ownership and the shedding of provision for rented accommodation from the local authorities

163

into the private sector. These changes are made clear in the Government Expenditure Plans for 1987/8, where their main housing aims are set out:

1. To give people a better choice through home ownership for those who want it, and the provision of a wider variety of rented housing for those who cannot afford or do not want to be home owners.
2. To concentrate resources increasingly on functions that cannot be carried out by the private sector, or on functions where public money can be used to attract private sector investment in areas which have until now relied wholly or mainly on public investment.
3. To encourage the provision of rented housing by agencies other than public bodies, using new forms of private finance to bring more variety and competition into the rented market.
4. To encourage local authorities to review their existing stock of housing to see whether satisfactory housing conditions could be produced by diversifying ownership and management and by including tenants more directly in the management of their estates.

In order to reduce the responsibility of the State to house those people who have the resources to buy their own homes, the government gives tax relief on the interest payable on mortgages, and has introduced a 'right to buy' policy which encourages local authorities, New Towns and Housing Associations to sell properties to sitting tenants at below market values. The discounts available under this scheme vary according to the type of accommodation and the length of time the tenant has resided in the property. Now that many of the houses have been sold these discounts are weighted to encourage the sale of flats, which are less popular (Table 7.2). So far the policy has been successful, although the initial impetus has fallen away as the better properties have been sold (Table 7.3).

If the encouragement to buy has largely been successful during the 1980s, the provision of rented accommodation has not, event though this is an es-

Table 7.2 Housing discount on market value of properties

Complete years of tenancy	House (%)	Flat (%)
2	32	42
15	45	70
30	60	—

Source: City of Cambridge Housing Department

Table 7.3 Sales of public sector dwellings in England

	1979/80	1980/1	1981/2	1982/3	1983/4
Local authority	53,500	68,200	128,200	181,200	122,000
New Towns	1,900	3,300	3,900	4,300	4,000
Housing Associations	—	200	9,300	19,100	18,100
Total	55,300	71,800	141,400	204,600	144,200

Source: Government Expenditure Plans 1987–88 to 1989–90 1988–89 to 1990–91.

sential part of housing provision. The decline of the rented sector can be explained to a large extent by the outfall of government policies, which have:

1. contained the rent levels under the Rent Act of 1965 to a point where it can be argued that it discourages landlords, who see little return from their investments;
2. encouraged the rise in house prices, which has made it more attractive to sell houses rather than rent them out;
3. reduced the number of council houses through the 'right to buy' legislation and virtually stopped all new council house building;
4. not, until recently, stimulated the rented sector through new policy initiatives.

In retrospect, it could be strongly argued that the thrust for home ownership should have been complemented by a more positive approach towards the provision of rented accommodation. As it is, the situation has reached such serious proportions, with increasing waiting lists for council property, growing demand for bed and breakfast accommodation, and rising homelessness, that some new initiatives are required.

The Government is now giving this serious consideration, not purely as an exercise in providing more rented property, but as part of a fundamental change in the way accommodation should be provided. At the close of 1987 the Government published its Housing Bill. In introducing this Bill to Parliament the Secretary of State for the Department of the Environment, Nicholas Ridley, pointed to the enormous task facing local councils as a result of the vast numbers of houses, flats and maisonettes which they control – some 4.5 million homes. To improve the situation, the Government is keen to allow housing trusts and other private bodies to take over the running of council estates where possible. To achieve this 'sensibly', rents would have to be charged which would be an incentive for the various agencies to take over these estates and also an encouragement for landlords and potential landlords in the private sector to increase their provision. To safeguard the poorer groups in the rented sector housing benefit would be available, but as the Secretary of State pointed out, it should not be used to allow landlords to inflate rents to excessive levels, or permit people receiving state benefits to occupy over-large or up-market homes.

These new initiatives are depicted as 'a cautious move towards the evolution of housing policy in the rented sector' (Nicholas Ridley), which suggests that the Government is developing housing policies similar to those found in the USA and France, where a system of subsidising the tenant or consumer, rather than the house, is followed (Howenstine, 1986). In effect this means that the Government would provide the difference between the rent

1984/5	1985/6	1986/7 (provisional)
91,400	82,300	85,700
3,900	2,300	2,600 (actual)
9,900	9,600	9,400 (actual)
105,200	94,200	

for a property in the private sector and the rent the tenant could afford to pay, rather than build housing themselves for rent through the local authorities. Clearly safeguards would be necessary to prevent landlords charging excessive rents, but it would take the burden of building and maintaining accommodation for the poorer groups in society off the shoulders of the State. This would then enable the Government to focus its resources in areas which cannot be dealt with effectively by the private sector. This relates particularly to the repair and renovation of public housing and to the encouragement of private owners to repair and improve their properties.

The renovation and restoration of older properties is part of an ongoing commitment by the Government, resulting from such findings as the Housing Condition Survey of 1981, which revealed some improvement in the overall condition of the housing stock, but still some 1.1 million dwellings unfit, 0.9 million lacking basic amenities and 1 million requiring repairs costing more than £7,000. These problems were further exacerbated by serious structural and other defects in public housing built before 1960 of prefabricated reinforced concrete. Further, in 1985 the Department of the Environment's stock condition enquiry showed local authority estimates that £18.8 billion of capital expenditure was needed on the renovation of 3.8 million local authority dwellings in England alone.

The task is of staggering proportions Table 7.4 and the Government considers this of such major significance that expenditure on repairs has been increased by 66 per cent from 1979 to 1986. Also, in June 1985, the Government set up an Urban Housing Renewal Unit to encourage local authorities to adopt new ways of tackling problems on run-down estates. These include intensive estate-based management for physical refurbishment and remodelling, closer involvement of tenants and, where possible, of private sector finance and expertise. It is forecast that during the period 1987–88, 150 schemes will be in progress, involving some 82,500 houses.

The improvement of private sector housing stock is an important objective of the Government and is encouraged through home improvement grants (Table 7.5). But this scheme has suffered a set-back in recent years as expenditure cuts have fallen upon this area of provision.

Table 7.4 Housing repair costs in 10 towns and cities, 1985

Town/City	Population	No. of council units	Repair costs at 1985 prices (£ million)
Bristol	400,000	42,500	76
Cardiff	280,000	23,500	69
Hartlepool	97,000	11,500	30
Hull	260,000	50,000	240
Leeds	750,000	98,000	459
Manchester	500,000	105,000	600
Norwich	122,000	24,000	95
Sheffield	560,000	58,000	500
Swansea	300,000	20,000	65
Tewkesbury	75,000	1,250	15

Source: Royal Institute of British Architects' Survey, 1985

Table 7.5 Home improvement grants

	1981/2	1982/3	1983/4	1984/5	1985/6	1986/7
Grants (£ million)	197	425	911	735	444[1]	444[3]
No. of grants	72,300	131,600	250,600	195,200	124,400	112,800

Source: Government Expenditure Plans 1987/8 to 1989/9   [1] provisional   [2] estimated.

A recent government aim is to stimulate the interest of the private sector in house building in problem areas like the inner cities. The first Urban Development Corporation in the London Docklands began this process by utilising government grants to provide infrastructure, such as roads, sewage, services, and the clearing of derelict sites, as a carrot to attract private investment in housing, and industrial and commercial activity. The objective of the Corporation was to match every £1 it spent with £5 from the private sector. In its annual report for 1988–89 the Corporation indicated that the ratio was now 1 to 12.5 and that in terms of housing more new homes were being built in Dockland than anywhere else in the country. Since the inception of the Corporation in 1981 13,500 houses had been built or were in the process of completion. Such revitalisation of the derelict docklands is clearly of considerable encouragement to the Government.

By similar means the Government aims to stimulate interest in inner city sites for housing and deflect the attention of private developers away from greenfield sites and the Green Belt. There is land available within the cities, much of which is owned by the State; which if released and prepared could form a magnet of attraction for housing provision. In Inner London alone a recent estimate by the London Dockland Development Corporation (1987) suggests that 5,000 acres of derelict land is waiting for development. The land which should become available under this form of stimulation will provide a further plank in the government's policy of increasing housing choice and more especially in expanding the range of rented accommodation, and with it real competition within this sector.

It is a major Government aim to achieve greater provision of rented housing using new forms of private finance. Already the Nationwide Anglia Building Society has announced its intention to earmark some 600 million pounds for the building of rented accommodation which, together with a relaxation on the level of rents to produce more sensible return to landlords, should help to foster a new and positive atmosphere in the private sector.

The favouring of private sector initiatives which permeates government thinking raises fundamental questions about the future housing role of the Local Authorities, and whether or not they actually have one. In the immediate future they will retain the management of a major housing resource, although some local authorities are already following the Government's wish to reduce this commitment. The Times (30th December 1987) reported that a number of local authorities are planning to rid themselves entirely of their housing stock. Rochford Council in Essex was about to decide to transfer all its 2,100 homes to a non-profit making housing association, and Westminster Council in London envisage the complete transfer of its 23,000 flats and houses to one or more housing associations. What is significant is that these initiatives are ahead of the Government Housing Bill which will allow local authority tenants the right to 'pick a landlord' with the

167

implication that agencies other than the Local Authority will find favour. In this respect the housing association's role in rented accommodation may increase, whereas up until now they have complemented the work of the local authorities by providing rented accommodation for single people, the retired and the physically handicapped. In October 1986 a new financial scheme was announced by the Government. Under this housing associations would be boosted by capital from the private sector as part of a financial scheme in which public and private money will be used to provide low-cost housing for rent for the homeless and those moving to find jobs. At present the Housing Associations, with grants from the Housing Corporation, build 15,000 houses a year and with the injection of private finance this could be tripled. Moreover, as more money is made available by the Government for the Corporation in 1989/90 this should go some way to reducing the number of homeless and those living in bed and breakfast hotels, as well as assisting young people who cannot afford to move to take up jobs to do so.

Every new government initiative brings with it a new set of problems. In the present situation, where new housing in the public sector is required, the cut-back in resources as part of the shift of housing responsibility from the public to the private sector is serious. For not only will the inner areas of cities suffer, but so also will those older suburban areas, a fact to which the Archbishop of Canturbury's Commission recently drew attention.

To attempt to overcome this resourcing problem the Government is increasingly turning to the private sector. It now intends introducing Urban Development Corporations to inner city areas along the lines of those for the London Docklands and Merseyside. In spring 1987 the Government launched four new English UDCs at Trafford Park (Greater Manchester), Teesside, the Black Country, and Tyne and Wear, and one in Wales at Cardiff. Then in December 1987 another three UDCs were announced for Bristol, Leeds and Manchester. These, with public finance, will create the infrastructure and initiate a new environment of hope and purpose which should encourage the private sector to invest in these deprived areas. Certainly the Urban Corporations should help to overcome the obstacles for private building firms wishing to construct houses in the inner city rather than in greenfield sites. Mr Roger Hamber, director of the House Builders Federation, indicated (*The Times*, 30 October 1986) that 'there has to be a more effective partnership between the public and private sectors, and there must be more public sector pump priming. Much of the work needed to revive the environment of the inner cities, such as providing infrastructure, is unprofitable and the house builder cannot do it.'

This shift to a property-owning society, however laudible it might be, brings with it the serious difficulty of attaining a balance between the supply and the demand for housing. If there is not sufficient housing available to meet demand, an inflationary situation is generated which, because of the complexity within the housing system, is difficult to readjust. Such a situation exists today in Britain, where in parts of the country prices of houses are soaring in the biggest seller's market since the 1970s. There are a number of factors behind this:

1. Easy money – institutions, from banks to building societies, are falling over themselves to lend money.

2. Supply and demand – the government is encouraging people to buy, but the housing stock only increases by 1 per cent each year.
3. Land scarcity – green belt legislation means that land for housing is hard to find and expensive to buy. In September 1986 George Wimpey, Britain's largest house builder, suspended purchases of land in South East England because of rapidly rising land prices.
4. Spending power – tax changes and the growth of real incomes give more people more surplus income.

These factors in combination account for the startling rise in property values, and their uneven application reflects and fuels still further the economic imbalance between the North and the South of the country. A wide chasm has opened between North and South in terms of house prices.

Houses in London and the South East are much more expensive than in the North and the trend is continuing. From July 1986 to 1987 house prices in the United Kingdom rose by 14.3 per cent. East Anglia had the highest level of house price inflation, 24.5 per cent. Greater London increased by 23.7 per cent and the South East by 22.9 per cent. In contrast, the North's average was only 7.4 per cent. This wide disparity does not make the North a more attractive place to live unless you have just retired in the South East and set up home in the Yorkshire Dales or the Lake District. For the employees who are moved north by their firms, there is the fear that at a future date it will be impossible to return south. Equally, workers from areas of high unemployment in the north seeking work in the south often find employment but cannot afford a place to live. This is significant when Professor Patrick Minford of Liverpool University has estimated that unemployment could be reduced by some 500,000 with improved labour mobility. The rocketing property prices in the South East and more recently in East Anglia are also making it extremely difficult for those living in these areas on low incomes and in the lower-paid professions. The latter category includes essential workers such as nurses and teachers, who find the rented accommodation and house prices so high that they either do not take up appointments or they move away particularly on marriage.

Without doubt the efforts by the Government to increase the number of property owners and to add a further 1 million over the next five years to 1991, has created areas of severe stress to a system which cannot be changed quickly. Housing takes time to build and rebuild, but government policies can be fashioned in a much shorter time-span. What we see in Britain at the moment is a period of transition as the new policies come into operation and the system adjusts to them. Unfortunately, at such times of disequilibrium some people suffer. In this case it is the poorer groups, those who wish to own homes but cannot afford it because of the high prices, and also that group of unfortunate people who have their properties repossessed because they are unable to maintain the considerable loan repayments that are required.

The majority of people in Britain are undoubtedly better housed now than at any other time since the War, but there still remains a significant proportion of families and single people whose needs are not met by either the private or the public sector. What is not certain, at the time of writing, is whether the new government initiatives will bring a fairer distribution of resources and a higher quality of housing to those in greatest need; but until this is attained the housing problem will not go away.

8 The effects of policy I: employment redistribution, subsidisation and retraining measures

In the previous two chapters we reviewed the patterns of government responses to regional and urban imbalance in Britain's economy. We now turn to the effects and effectiveness of these responses in terms of their impact on such variables as job creation and industrial redistribution. The *effects of policy* can be fairly readily determined by examining the facts and figures of government money actually spent, number of factories built or persuaded to move, number of jobs created, infrastructural improvements, and so on. The *effectiveness of policy* is rather more difficult to determine, since it involves judgements as to whether one policy approach is 'better' than another in achieving the economic (and political) objectives of the government. Any appraisal of policy effectiveness must consider what actually happened in the light of the aims of the policy. In this chapter, we will examine the effects of policies addressing labour mobility, factory mobility, payroll subsidies and labour retraining. In the next chapter we will consider the policy effects of measures to reduce congestion, especially in London, and to improve the industrial structure, locational accessibility and environmental quality of AA regions. The question of policy effectiveness will then be discussed in Chapter 10.

As we have already noted, the aims of any government's regional or urban policy are couched in terms consistent with the economic philosophy of the political party in power. There have always been striking differences between political parties in their general policies for regional and urban development, and also the emphasis on particular policy measures has varied during any party's term in office. The latter usually reflects both changes in the theoretical approaches to problem solving and the modifications necessitated by experience gained from policy application. Consequently, whilst the variables used in attempting to quantify the socio-economic problems of regions are usually well defined, their levels of importance in the eyes of government planners and decision makers are under constant review.

There are difficulties and disagreements associated with the precise spatial determination of problem areas (see Chapter 12), but there is general agreement about the variables which can be used as problem indicators. Among them would be:

1. level and persistence of unemployment;
2. level and growth rate of GDP (national income) per head;

Table 8.1 Indices of regional variation in GDP per head and unemployment (UK = 100)

		GDP per head					Unemployment				
		1971	1975	1979	1983	1986	1971	1975	1979	1983	1987
'Core'	South East	114	113	115	115	116	59	69	61	68	72
	East Anglia	94	93	94	100	101	91	84	75	78	81
	East Midlands	97	96	96	98	96	85	89	72	93	94
'Periphery' Inner	South West	95	90	93	96	96	95	114	98	84	90
	West Midlands	103	100	96	90	91	85	100	98	123	112
	Yorks/Humberside	93	94	93	94	93	112	94	104	112	115
Outer	North West	96	96	97	95	94	113	128	124	125	117
	North	87	94	91	94	92	163	138	161	149	137
	Wales	88	89	88	88	86	128	133	133	130	122
	Scotland	93	97	96	99	94	170	124	141	123	123
	N. Ireland	74	80	76	75	70	221	178	186	153	168

Sources: Prestwich & Griffiths (1989, 357, (rounded)). Central Statistical Office (1987, 110 & 123; 1989, 357, - (rounded))

Employment, redistribution, subsidisation and retraining measures

3. population characteristics (growth/decline, migration, ageing, education, etc.);
4. industrial structure (types and range of industry, speed and direction of manufacturing change);
5. condition of infrastructure (social and industrial).

The variables most likely to galvanise a government into some policy action have been high and persistent unemployment, low levels of income, slow economic growth rates and population out-migration. Table 8.1 gives some indication of the regional disparities with reference to aspects of the first two criteria.

Efforts are sometimes made to group regions in a country according to common economic characteristics. The terms 'core' and 'periphery' are often used, with regions in the core generally exhibiting more gains and fewer problems with respect to recent economic change than regions in the periphery. It is clear from Table 8.1 that regional disparities do exist in the UK, with the core regions of the South East, East Anglia, the South West and the East Midlands having below-national-average unemployment figures compared with more peripheral regions, although there is not such a simple distinction when GDP/head figures are compared (Prestwich and Griffiths, 1989, 357). Whether or not these disparities constitute a 'problem', requiring government intervention, depends upon one's view of the economic system, as we discussed in Chapter 5.

In an attempt to determine the empirical effects of regional and urban policies since the 1920s, we can identify and examine their impact relative to major policy objectives. The objective of alleviating high unemployment in Assisted Areas will be discussed in this chapter, and those of other policies in the succeeding chapter. The overall aim of these policies has been to help 'poorer' regions climb towards the national 'wealth' average: in other words, to reverse any regional divergence falling below the national mean, and thereby achieve convergence – even when this meant denying 'excessive' divergence upwards by growth regions, and redistributing the gains of such regions to those in need of assistance.

8.1 Unemployment

Levels of unemployment, both in terms of the numbers of people (voters!) involved and of their persistence over time, have been the prime mover of government policy. Indeed, the spatial administration of government assistance has been mapped out on the basis of Employment Exchange (Job Centre) areas since the determination of Special Areas in 1934. Attempts by government to reduce the numbers unemployed in any problem area have taken several forms:

1. encouraging people to move out of the area and find jobs elsewhere (workers to the work);
2. encouraging firms to move to or locate new factories or offices in the area, therefore creating employment (work to the workers);
3. encouraging firms in the area to retain their workforce (i.e. to avoid

redundancies), or even to employ more, by granting them a payroll subsidy;
4. improving the employability of people by providing retraining schemes, which should also make the area more attractive to new investment.

8.1.1 Workers to the work

The movement of people from one part of the country to another in order to find jobs has been a feature of Britain's space economy ever since the early days of industrialisation. The vast majority of migrants move either because of the 'pull' of actual or perceived better opportunities elsewhere or because of the 'push' of too few opportunities or high unemployment in their home area, or for a combination of these two main reasons. The *laissez-faire* approach to national economic development, characteristic of the British government until the 1920s, meant that migration of workers from one area to another was as free as their individual circumstances permitted, and was neither encouraged nor discouraged by government. Following the establishment of the Industrial Transference Board in 1928, government assistance became available for people (especially coal-miners) who wished to leave their home areas and seek employment in more prosperous regions. As we noted in Chapter 6 (p. 115), probably one third of all those who migrated from upland to lowland Britain between 1919 and 1940 received some government assistance, usually in the form of travel allowances and family removal expenses. The emphasis on trying to move workers to areas where work could be found continued throughout the inter-war period, although in 1934 the government recognised the impracticality of wholesale population movements as a method of solving regional problems.

Migration of workers seeking work continued after the Second World War, with the South East and the West Midlands the main destinations, and Scotland, Wales, Northern Ireland, the North, North West and Yorkshire-Humberside the main regions of origin. In addition, many people left the United Kingdom altogether (over 3 million, 1964–84), seeking employment opportunities in Canada, the USA, Australia, New Zealand, South Africa and the EEC. These movements largely involved younger, better qualified (more educated) or more highly skilled people, with evidence of a high positive correlation between regional unemployment levels and net out-migration rates. Within the UK, what became known as 'the drift to the South' characterised population redistribution patterns in the post-war decades, continuing the inter-war trends which, in turn, had reversed the nineteenth-century trends. By far the largest proportion of this movement comprised individuals, and in some cases their families, making the decision to move. In those instances where an individual moved to a specific job, his or her removing/resettling expenses were often paid by the employer.

Government assistance for people moving to jobs has been available principally through the *Employment Transfer Scheme* (ETS – administered by the Manpower Services Commission) and the *Job Search Scheme*. These schemes provide financial help in the shape of grants for travel, rehousing and 'settling in' for unemployed workers who wish to move to other areas to find jobs. The numbers involved in the ETS rose from 6,000–8,000 per year in the early 1970s to over 26,000 per year in the late 1970s (Johnson and Salt, 1978), and about two-thirds of those involved migrated out of their region, with the predominant direction of movement being North to South. Many of these government-assisted migrants returned home after a short time, so that it is difficult to say whether or not the scheme has been 'successful', but certainly it has eased the financial burden of migration for several tens of thousands of people and has helped to reduce pressure on the jobs available in AAs. This particular scheme has been slightly at odds with the rest of regional policy, however, since it has encouraged workers to move to the work, whilst in almost all other schemes the government has endeavoured to move work to the workers. In addition to the ETS, there is also the government-sponsored *Key Workers Scheme* (KWS), which specifically relates to migration *into* AAs. In this scheme workers who are prepared to move to particular locations within AAs in order to take key manufacturing jobs with expanding firms are provided with council housing and financial aid for their removal. Outside the AAs similar assistance has been available for migrants to the New Towns.

Of the total number of people who have migrated within the UK for reasons of employment since the Industrial Transference Board was established in 1928, a minor but significant proportion has been supported in some way by government. The net migration figures are shown in Table 8.2. During the inter-war period, probably as high a proportion as 40 per cent of the 1.2 million interregional migrants were assisted in some way by the government, but of the 0.9 million who moved during the War and post-War years of the 1940s it is difficult to ascertain the proportion assisted. Over the three decades since 1951 the number of people leaving the northern regions and Wales has declined from 720,000 in 1951–61 to 665,000 in 1961–71 and 493,000 in 1971–81. To these figures of interregional migration must be added the dramatic losses from Greater London of 611,000, 974,000 and

Table 8.2 United Kingdom population net migration regional, gains and losses 1921–81

Regions	1921–51	1951–61	1961–71	1971–81
'The North'				
Scotland	− 675,000	−282,000	−364,000	−130,000
N. Ireland	− 100,000(e)	− 89,000	− 65,000	−105,000
North		− 80,000	− 81,000	− 65,000
Yorks/Humberside	− 912,000	− 96,000	− 65,000	− 38,000
North West		−124,000	− 94,000	−211,000
Wales	− 434,000	− 49,000	+ 5,000	+ 57,000
'The Midlands'				
E. Midlands	+ 500,000(e)	+ 39,000	+ 74,000	+104,000
W. Midlands		+ 47,000	+ 35,000	−103,000
'The South'				
South East	+1,200,000	+438,000	− 36,000	−475,000
East Anglia	?	+ 27,000	+135,000	+159,000
South West	+ 420,000	+ 99,000	+224,000	+281,000

(e) estimate   + net gain   −net loss
Source: Lawton (1982, 113)

834,000 for the same three decades respectively (Lawton, 1982, 113). Financial help from the government for the 1.9 million 'northerners' moving south during the 1950s and 1960s was very limited, but by the 1970s the ETS and the KWS were aiding between one-third and one-half of the migrants. Assistance for the Londoners moving out of the metropolis depended upon whether or not they were part of the GLC's overspill scheme, i.e. moving to New or Expanding Towns (Chapter 9).

Referring again to Table 8.2, it is worth noting that not all migration concerns people looking for work. There are also those who have finished their working lives and are looking for a pleasant place in which to spend their retirement, the numbers involved boosting the in-migration figures, and therefore the growth rates of the South West, East Anglia and Wales, especially after 1961 (see Fig. 2.11).

In total terms, however, assistance to workers wishing to take work in other parts of the country was a relatively minor part of government policy, was not well-integrated with regional policy, and was overshadowed by the scale of programmes to move work to the workers.

8.1.2 Work to the workers

Since the passage of the *Special Areas Act* (1934) successive governments have sought to encourage industrialists to locate factories in AAs. Whether these were completely new firms, branches of existing firms headquartered elsewhere, or firms willing to move part or all of their operations to AAs from more prosperous areas, the intention has been to create employment and thereby improve the levels of wealth in, and reduce population out-migration from, Assisted Areas. From the end of the Second World War, and especially during the 1960s and 1970s, it was believed that control over the location of new manufacturing capacity was the key to successful regional policy (Regional Studies Association, 1983, 3). The contributions of regional policy to AA job creation have mainly taken the form of 'pull' factors or 'carrots' (i.e. attractive financial and other inducements intended to persuade firms to build branch plants in, or to migrate to, AAs), and 'push' factors or 'sticks' (i.e. measures designed to restrict further development in already prosperous regions). The 'carrots', of course, were the RDGs, RSA, Advance Factories, REP and so forth, which we identified in Chapters 6 and 7, while the 'sticks' were principally the IDCs and, to a lesser extent, the ODPs. We will discuss the effects of the REP on AA job creation and retention in Section 8.1.3, and the impact of IDCs and ODPs on jobs in the South in Section 9.1.1, but first we should examine the effects of the major 'carrots' and 'sticks' on job creation in AAs.

'Pull' factors ('carrots')
Regional Development Grants (RDGs) were introduced into the policy package of financial inducements in 1963 and were the major instrument of regional policy until 1988. Regional Selective Assistance (RSA) was introduced in 1972 in support of the RDG. Government support for factory building (Advance Factories) and land development (industrial estates, etc.) started in 1935 and continues to the present day as part of both regional policy and the Development Commission's activities in rural areas.

As we noted in Chapters 6 and 7, the strength of *Regional Development Grant* assistance has varied considerably throughout its 25 years as a policy instrument. It is very difficult to separate the effects of RDGs on the migration of firms to AAs, and any associated job creation, from investment incentives as a whole and from the effects of all the other 'pull' and 'push' factors. It has been argued (Moore and Rhodes, 1976b) that 10–15 firms would have moved to the AAs of their own volition during the mid-1960s to mid-1970s period, given the economic conditions of the time, but that all the other moves were catalysed by regional policy. RDGs were by far the most important element in the investment incentive 'package', so it is probably fair to attribute the bulk of the effects to them.

Moore *et al.* (1986, 40–43) found that over the period 1963 to 1981, *investment incentives* on average generated 44 moves per annum into AAs, which created 72,000 *net* jobs (i.e. jobs surviving at the end of the period). Investment incentives also have an impact on firms within the AAs (the 'indigenous' sector, as opposed to the 'immigrant' sector – firms moving in from other areas), and the same authors estimate that between 180,000 and 208,000 manufacturing jobs were created by RDGs in the indigenous sectors of Scotland, Northern Ireland, Wales and the North during the period studied. There are, of course, jobs created by internal regional developments in addition to those which are policy-induced. Some of them could hardly have occurred elsewhere, for example the oil-related industrial boom in Scotland which generated over 65,000 jobs between 1972 and 1976, but where the firms concerned were in receipt of regionally differentiated government assistance, their figures are included in the above totals. For the UK as a whole, regionally differentiated investment incentives were *the* most important policy instrument, generating 307,000 net jobs (235,000 indigenous and 72,000 immigrant) and thus accounting for over 68 per cent of the total number of jobs created, 1963–81 (see Table 8.5). Hence, the AAs benefited considerably from the government expenditure of £1,163 million on investment incentives over those two decades (Table 8.3).

Since RSA started only in 1972, its budget and impact by 1981 were both somewhat lower than those of RDGs. Its direct Exchequer costs were £170 million and it generated 42,000 net jobs by 1981 in the indigenous sectors of AAs – just over 9 per cent of the total jobs created 1963–81, but almost 30 per cent of those created 1972–81 (a fairer judgement of its effect given its starting date). (See Table 8.5.) Expenditure on RSA started at about £30 million per year in the early 1970s, rose to almost £70 million in the late 1970s, averaged £80 million to £90 million in the 1980s, and is budgeted at £254 million for 1990/91. The latter figure is over 50 per cent of total regional policy expenditure, a dramatic increase from the 7 per cent of the mid-1970s and the 10–11 per cent of the late 1970s to mid-1980s, which reflects the demise of RDGs in the 1988 policy change. In part, that policy change was in turn triggered by the government's perception of RSA's *effectiveness* as a policy instrument, a point to which we shall return in Chapter 11.

Government building of *Advance Factories* and *Trading Estates* has a much longer pedigree as a policy instrument than either RDGs or RSA. During the 1930s, the government spent about £0.5 million on factory sites (Trading Estates) and buildings (Advance Factories), the Treasury loaned £1.2 million and the Bank of England provided loan capital of about £0.75

Table 8.3 United Kingdom government expenditure on regional policy, 1960/1 to 1985/6 the direct Exchequer costs of regional policy at current and constant prices, £ million)

Type of Incentive	1961/2 to 1963/4*	1964/5 to 1971/2*	1972/3 to 1975/6*	1976/7 to 1979/80*	1980/1	1981/2	1982/3	1983/4	1984/5	1985/6
Investment incentives:										
1. Investment grants, RDGs and regionally differentiated free depreciation*	—	71	193	408	491	617	690	440	410	320
2. Regional Selective Assistance	—	—	32	67	71	76	90	82	80	79
3. Local Employment Acts										
a. Government factory building/land†	8	12	17	84	141	161‡	137‡	105‡	100	101
b. Other loans/grants	12	35	34	—	—					
Labour subsidies:										
4. Regional Employment Premium	—	57	143	44	—	—				
5. Other labour subsidies	—	9	8	8	8					
6. Other assistance	1	3	6	21						
Total expenditure at current (outturn) prices	21	187	433	626	732	854‡	917‡	627‡	590	500
Constant 1975 prices	55	383	578	407	361	389	394	255	227	175

Average expenditure per financial year
* From June 1979 to 9th November 1982, there was a four month deferment of payment of grant on approved applications. This reduced the 1979/80 figure by about £110 million and raised the 1982/3 figure up to £150 million.
† Includes expenditure by Scottish and Welsh Development Agencies on land and factories.
‡ Includes land reclamation.
Sources: Moore et al., (1986b, 23) GDP deflator used to obtain constant prices; Central Statistical Office (1987, 138) for 1984/5 and 1985/6.

million through the Special Areas Reconstruction Association (Lee, 1980, 37). Additional finance was available from private investors. The hope was to attract companies into AAs by providing basic facilities and some operational subsidies. The main recipients of this money were the Trading Estates in the Special Areas and by the outbreak of War about 12,000 workers were employed in new factories, chiefly on the three estates of Team Valley (North East), Treforest (South Wales) and Hillington (Scotland). This was a minor dent in the 300,000 still unemployed in the Special Areas in 1938, however, and the numbers of factories being established in these areas remained very small: only 12 (minus 10 which closed) in 1936, 23 (minus 6 closed) in 1937 and 61 (minus 13 closed) in 1938, compared with national net totals of 942, 522 and 414 respectively (McCrone, 1969, 101).

The proportion of new factory building in the enlarged AAs during the immediate post-war years increased dramatically to over half the national total, but fell almost equally dramatically when the building of these Advance Factories was suspended in 1947. Nevertheless, over the period 1945–51, 30 per cent of the 4,700 new factories completed nationally were in the AAs and of these 600 were government-financed. Of the 933 manufacturing moves between sub-regions in this period, 463 went to AAs, creating 41,000 jobs per year, and 64 per cent of the jobs that were created by these migrating firms still existed in 1966 (Howard, 1968, 23).

The Advance Factory programme restarted in 1959 and, after a lull in 1961, picked up substantially in the 1960s (350 being built 1960–65), and peaked in the mid-1970s (thanks to substantial ERDF money from 1975). Usually Advance Factory units were fairly small in employment terms (e.g. only 12 persons on average in the Wales Standard Region: (Slowe, 1981, 222), and consequently their contribution to job creation in AAs was modest. Between 1945 and 1960 over 1,000 of these general purpose, low rent, immediately available units were built in AAs and together with other units on Trading Estates 'created' over 200,000 jobs (Lee, 1980, 54). It must be remembered, however, that this job total relates not only to immigrant firms but also to indigenous firms, since the facilities were available to both. The new programme of Advance Factory building which commenced in 1959 has largely continued to the present time, and while expenditure on the programme averaged less than £2 million per year in the 1960s, it increased to £10 million per year during the 1970s and continued to rise in the 1980s (Table 8.3). In fact, about 13 per cent of total regional assistance spending went to this programme in the 1970s, but by the 1980s the proportion had risen to 20 per cent. From the mid-1970s, spending on factory and workshop construction in Rural Development Areas also began to increase, from £4 million in 1974/5 to £13 million by 1978/9 and £17 million by 1983/4. Over the same time period, the number of units completed annually rose from 5 to 85 to 241. Firms locating in these factories have probably created over 13,000 jobs to date, with 1,200–1,500 jobs being created each year, and although minor in the context or national unemployment figures, they are of considerable significance in relation to the needs of rural areas (Chisholm, 1986).

Two points emerge from analyses of employment creation during the post-War period up to the mid-1960s: *firstly*, that in both AAs and non-AAs four out of five new firms were established by people resident in the area and were direct outgrowths of the founder's particular industrial experience (Gudgin, 1978, 109–13); and *secondly*, that indigenous growth accounted for more actual job creation than did immigrant growth in both non-AAs and AAs. For example, in non-AAs Lewis (1971) found that between 1945 and 1966 indigenous growth in the western Home Counties (London area) represented 53 per cent of the net employment increase in manufacturing jobs, while Gudgin (1978) similarly notes that such growth in the East Midlands between 1948 and 1967 accounted for 89% of net job increase. In AAs, Hoare (1983, 90) identifies intra-regional growth in Wales as having generated 71 per cent of the manufacturing employment 1945–65, and in Northern Ireland the proportion was 79 per cent.

The strengthening of regional policy measures from 1964 to the mid-1970s means that the difficulty of separating net job gains resulting from indigenous development from those of immigrant firms increases. However, Law (1980, 98) estimates that during the period 1960 to 1971, between 72 per cent and 84 per cent of the manufacturing jobs created in the five main AA regions (Northern Ireland, Scotland, Wales, North, North West) were created by firms moving in from other regions. The difference of 16 per cent to 28 per cent of the new jobs is assumed to have resulted from indigenous growth. This suggests that the various policy instruments were temporarily more successful during the 1960s at generating job growth in AAs from the immigrant sector than from the indigenous sector, but the greater importance of the latter was re-established in the 1970s, as we noted above (p. 176). From the mid-1970s, the rate of closure of established factories exceeded the rate of openings, and few firms were able to expand in the recessionary conditions that prevailed until the mid-1980s. Consequently, the dominant feature of regional economic performance and associated employment prospects became one of decline rather than expansion.

So, the creation of jobs in any region is a function partially of existing local firms expanding and new ones starting, and partially of firms moving in from another region or country. The latter may be influenced in their decision by the investment and other incentives available in a 'distressed' region – the 'carrots', but they may also be influenced by the government restrictions placed on their development in the more prosperous regions – the 'sticks'.

'Push' factors ('sticks')

The introduction of *Industrial Development Certificate* (IDC) controls in 1948 enabled the government to divert employment away from more prosperous southern Britain and into the distressed AAs of northern and western Britain. The impact of IDCs was rather limited in the late 1940s, however, as the economic upturn reduced unemployment levels and, consequently, the perceived need for intervention. Similarly, during the 1950s the Conservative Government adopted largely non-interventionist regional policies, so that it was not until after the *Distribution of Industry Act (1958)* that IDCs really began to have a marked impact on the regional redistribution of jobs. This is readily apparent in Keeble's calculations of the annual interregional movement rates per thousand UK manufacturing plants between 1945 and 1971: the rate was 1.44 for 1946–51, the post-war reconstruction and expansion phase; it fell to 0.74 in 1952–59, the non-intervention period; it rose dramatically to 1.56 in 1960–65, and it reached 2.08 in 1966–71, the periods of active intervention (Keeble, 1976, 133).

In grand total, the 20 years from 1945 to 1965 witnessed 2,756 recorded manufacturing firm moves between *sub-regions* (mainly counties) in the UK, 'creating' 762,000 jobs (gross) in destination regions by the end of 1966 (Townroe, 1979, 20). Since 1,521 of these moves were between Standard Regions i.e. *interregional* moves), creating 439,000 jobs (Hoare, 1985, 89). then 1,235 moves creating 323,000 jobs must have been within Standard Regions (i.e. *intra-regional* moves). During the 1966–78 period a national total of 8,947 firm moves were recorded, and about half of them crossed county boundaries, but the gross number of jobs created by these moves is not readily available. Nevertheless, the known figures do give some idea of the overall magnitude of movements of firms within the country, and in particular indicate the dramatic increase in numbers of manufacturing firms moving during the active policy period of the mid-1960s to late-1970s. However, only one in eight of these firms was 'persuaded' to move by government policy.

We must remember that these figures reflect manufacturing firm movements between *all* the Standard Regions and not just from prosperous to distressed regions, and also that not all firms survived their 'transplantation' – about 25 per cent failed – so that the net gain for AA regions was far lower than the numbers suggest. Indeed, if we focus just on the AA regions, then the 1945–65 period saw a *net* gain of 987 firms creating 390,000 jobs, while the 1966–78 period saw a gain of 1,098 firms creating 200,000 jobs (Moore *et al.*, 1986, 55–9). Any firm and job *gains* in AA regions which are derived from elsewhere within the country must mean that the regions of origin suffered *losses* of firms and jobs. (Naturally enough, foreign firms establishing branch plants in the UK add to net job creation – as long as more British firms are not emigrating! – and 258 foreign firms did so in the 1945–65 period, creating 108,500 jobs: Townroe, 1979, 20.) Domestically, the source regions for firms moving to AAs in the post-war years have been the South East and the Midlands, and the whole purpose of IDC controls was to instigate or encourage such regional redistribution of employment opportunities. (For a visual impression of these redistributive flows of manufacturing firms, see the maps in Sant (1975, 116) for 1945–65; Keeble (1976, 148) for 1966–71; Humphrys (1982, 327) for 1972–77; and Watts (1987, 163) for 1976–80.)

The effects of IDC controls on employment growth in AAs are probably impossible to calculate with any precision, partly because they have to be separated from those of all the other regional policy instruments, and partly because the stringency of IDC application varied considerably throughout their period of use (Chapters 6 and 7). In the early 1950s, IDC policy was applied quite vigorously, it was relaxed in the mid-1950s, strengthened somewhat from 1958 to 1961, then became very stringent until 1968, after which it was gradually relaxed during the 1970s, virtually went into abeyance from 1979 and ceased altogether in 1982. It has been estimated that IDC controls generated an annual average number of moves into British AAs (excluding Northern Ireland) of 38 in the period 1960–65, 41 in 1966–71, 17 in 1972–77, and 6 in 1978–81, which translates as a net gain of 75,000 jobs in the 1960–71 period but of only 8,000 jobs in the 1971–81 decade (Moore *et al*, 1986, 42).

On a regional basis, the DAs gained the following proportions of policy-induced movements of factories/jobs during the 1960–78 period: Wales 34.0 per cent/29.5 per cent; Scotland 22.6 per cent/19.5 per cent; North 22.1 per cent/32.5 per cent; South West 13.9 per cent/12.0 per cent; Northern Ireland 4.1 per cent/3.5 per cent; Merseyside 3.3 per cent/3.0 per cent *(ibid.*, 59). Thus, Wales was the major beneficiary of factory moves from the South East and Midlands, but the North gained the highest proportion of jobs associated with such movement. Interestingly, the South West was far more attractive to immigrant firms than either Northern Ireland or Merseyside.

There are two sides of the IDC 'coin': its *negative* effects in non-AAs and its *positive* effects in AAs. The main purpose of IDCs was to restrict 'excessive' growth in the Midlands and the South East, and this can be partially gauged by examining the refusal rates of certificates for industrial development in the non-AA regions (to be further discussed in Chapter 9). Throughout the 1950s, the refusal rate averaged 5 per cent of the total number of IDC applications, soared to 20–30 per cent during the 1960s, and then declined fairly steadily until cessation in 1981. IDC controls were especially used to restrict major labour-using projects in non-AAs, consequently their stringency in the 1960s meant that the Midlands and South East were denied at least 20–30 per cent of their potential employment growth because the Board of Trade refused IDCs for new manufacturing capacity. What proportion of the firms denied permission to build new capacity in the South actually opted to build instead in the AAs is not known. However, Moore *et al.* (1986, 43) estimate that, in total, IDC-induced moves of new capacity directed to all AAs (including Northern Ireland, North West and South West) created 89,000 *net* jobs in the period 1960–71 (half the total of all regional policy instruments). However, the employment gains in the 1971–81 decade were more than offset by losses in firms which had already located in AAs by 1971, so that only 74,000 IDC-induced jobs remained in 1981 (16% of the total number of jobs created in AAs by all regional policy instruments, 1960–81). (See Table 8.5)

While the IDC controls endeavoured to redistribute *manufacturing* employment from non-AA to AA regions, the *Office Development Permits* (ODPs) aimed to decentralise *office* employment away from London, and to a lesser extent Birmingham, although not necessarily as far away as the AA regions! The *Control of Office and Industry Act 1965* introduced the requirements of the ODP for any firm wishing to build new office space in the non-AAs. The scheme was administered by the *Location of Offices Bureau* (LOB – established 1963) and ran until 1979. During its 14 years of operation considerable numbers of office jobs (*c.* 50,000) were relocated away from southern England, although not all of them moved to AA regions. Precedents for the dispersal of offices away from London were established by the government during wartime when, for example, part of the Admiralty (Ships Division) relocated in Bath, the National Savings office in Lytham St Annes and the Ministry of Pensions and National Insurance in Newcastle-upon-Tyne. After the War, the government continued to 'set an example' of office dispersal from the capital, but this time more specifically to AA regions. Hence, Swansea gained the Vehicle Licensing Centre, Newport the Business Statistics Office, Bootle the Post Office Giro Centre, Manchester part of the Inland Revenue, and Durham and Glasgow the National Savings Bank (Townroe, 1979, 99). However, several major departments relocated elsewhere within the South (see p. 197 below).

Private offices also moved out of London but not many went to AAs. The figures for the 1963–77 period show that of the 145,000 known jobs which were decentralised only 12,000 went to the major AA regions (although including Barclays Bank to Knutsford (Cheshire) and the Midland Bank to Sheffield), but that over 5,000 went to the Midlands (2,000 to Derby), 5,500 to East Anglia, 11,600 to the South West and over 110,000 to the rest of the South East (Marquand, 1979). A further 116,000 office jobs may have also decentralised but since they were not reported to the LOB their pattern of relocation cannot be determined (Manners *et al.*, 1980, 81). Whereas the AAs benefited considerably from the inflow of government office jobs, probably receiving 29,000–32,000 of the 50,000 jobs that were moved, they were hardly touched by private firms, receiving just over 8 per cent of the total. On this level, therefore, the ODP scheme can hardly be seen as great success. However, given the necessity for so much office work to be conducted over the telephone or on a face-to-face basis, especially among financial institutions, it is not too surprising that the 56 km long-distance telephone call radius proved to be a significant threshold for relocation. This distance also meant that offices could be less than a one-hour road or rail journey from the City but still far enough out of central London to be able to take advantage of lower rents, rates and salaries. Indeed, of the 110,000 jobs that relocated from the City to the rest of the South East, almost 49,000 simply involved moves 'down the road' to other parts of Greater London. It would seem that physical distance is a major barrier to firm relocation, even when assisted by government policy.

As the figures emerged towards the end of the LOB's first decade, the 1974 Labour Government observed that the AAs were not receiving sufficient numbers of office jobs from London. It was decided in 1976 that at least the government could help by raising the proportion of its own jobs scheduled for relocation to AAs from the planned 40 per cent to about 87 per cent (from 12,000 to 27,000 jobs). Almost immediately, however, cutbacks in government spending from 1977 meant that the new target was unlikely to be achieved, and in 1979 the Conservatives reviewed the plans, reduced the posts to be relocated in AAs from 27,000 to 5,000, and abandoned the LOB itself. Scotland did benefit from one of the major surviving moves, Glasgow gaining 1,400 Ministry of Defence jobs, and Yorkshire benefited from the other, Sheffield gaining 1,500 Manpower Services Agency jobs (Law, 1980, 197–9). Annual reductions in the wages bill of the Civil Service since 1979 have meant that large numbers of staff have been made redundant, and by 1990 about 18,000 government jobs will have been lost in the AAs – a figure equivalent to 62 per cent of the jobs decentralised from London to AAs in the 16 years of the LOB's existence.

8.1.3 Payroll subsidies

A significant measure adopted by government to alleviate high unemployment in AAs has been to subsidise the labour costs of firms. In response to the perceived need for government to help the older, more labour-intensive industries in the AAs (which, after all, had the highest numbers of 'surplus' labour), as well as the newer, more capital-intensive firms (already supported through RDGs and RSA), the *Selective Employment Payments Act* was passed in 1966. This provided all manufacturers in the AAs with a diret labour subsidy, the *Regional Employment Premium* the (REP), which aimed to encourage employers to retain their existing labour force and to create new jobs. The amount of money made available under the REP scheme started at £35 million (gross) in 1967/8, rose to just over £100 million per year from 1968/9 to 1973/4, was doubled in 1974 to compensate for inflation, peaked at £239 million in 1975/6 and then declined to £213 million in the scheme's final year, 1976/7 (Moore and Rhodes, 1979, 20).

. Firms migrating into AAs do not appear to have benefited a great deal from the REP, since it reduced their labour costs by only 2 per cent compared with the 11 per cent reduction in capital costs afforded by other forms of government assistance (Mackay, 1976). Nevertheless, on average it represented 7 per cent of the wages of male manual workers, and many firms already operating in AAs found that the REP was critical to their profitability – without it they would have been 'in the red'! Hence, many jobs would have been lost without the REP subsidy and where companies were involved in plant rationalisation it undoubtedly helped to tip the scales in favour of branch plant retention in the AA (Massey, 1979). There is no question that removal of the REP in 1977 resulted directly in the contraction or collapse of a number of recipient firms, probably causing the loss of 28,000–55,000 jobs between 1976 and 1980, but precisely how many firms and how many jobs were lost because of the cessation of REP payments is difficult to ascertain given the national recessionary characteristics of the time (Townroe, 1979, 127). The REP scheme was criticised by the unions, who were afraid that it would be used to lower a firm's wage levels and thereby increase its profits, with the shareholders being the principal beneficiaries, whilst the companies were afraid that labour would demand the subsidy in its pay packets, thereby increasing labour costs in the AAs and making them less competitive with the more prosperous regions. As inflation eroded the value of the REP subsidy in the 1970s, however, employers and unions alike became less interested in its supposed benefits.

The REP was a flat-rate subsidy paid for all employees in manufacturing industry in AAs. It was preceded by two other means of subsidising the labour costs of employers, the *Selective Employment Tax* (SET) and the *Selective Employment Premium* (SEP), both introduced in 1966. Initially, both were available nationwide, but in 1968 they were abolished in non-AAs and so became regionally differentiated subsidies supporting the REP. The SET enabled an employer to reclaim from the Inland Revenue the full value of tax paid per employee, while the SEP paid each employer a premium of $37\frac{1}{2}$p per week for each man employed in manufacturing. Both subsidies were paid in addition to REP until they were discontinued in 1970 in order to provide funds for the newly created Intermediate Areas (see pp. 143–4). These two schemes ran for such a short period of time that it is virtually impossible to assess their effects on job creation or retention in AAs. Moore *et al.* (1986, 42–3) subsume the SET/SEP effects under those of the REP, and conclude that together these policy instruments generated an average of 40 moves per year 1966–71 and 30 moves per year 1972 to 1976 (when REP ended) of firms into AAs (excluding Northern Ireland where REP ended in

1978). The *net* number of jobs created by these immigrant firms in all the AA regions amounted to 23,000 in the first period, and in addition REP enabled a further 40,000 jobs to be created by indigenous firms. In the second period, however, the REP's effects were much reduced and almost all the jobs created in the indigenous sector had disappeared by 1981, thanks to the recession following REP's demise in 1976. The latter economic conditions also had a negative impact on the creation of jobs by immigrant firms, only 4,000 additional ones remaining in 1981 beyond the 23,000 of 1971. So, the overall impact of the REP/SEP schemes was 63,000 net jobs remaining in 1971, but only 27,000 net jobs remaining in 1981, i.e. a recession-induced loss of 36,000 jobs, predominantly from the indigenous sector. (See Table 8.5.)

More readily measurable in terms of its impact upon employment was the *Temporary Employment Subsidy* (TES), which was funded from 1975 until 1979. The intention of the TES was to encourage firms to delay redundancies, hence acting as a subsidy to preserve marginal employment but not to allow companies which would have otherwise gone out of business to survive. Initially the TES was available just in the AAs, but was quickly extended to the rest of the country as redundancies became a national rather than mainly an AA region phenomenon. However, this scheme was very effective in 'exporting' unemployment to the EEC, especially in the textile, clothing and footwear industries, so the EEC insisted it be withdrawn, which it was in 1979. In terms of jobs 'saved', the TES was credited with 130,000 within its first year, most of them in the North West and Midlands (Lee, 1980, 99). The gross cost to the Exchequer of the TES was £104 million, but it did not have a net cost, since more money flowed back to the Treasury (because fewer unemployment benefits were being paid and more tax revenues collected) than was being paid out in subsidies to firms (Metcalf and Richardson, 1982, 265).

Before proceeding further with our review of the effects of various government measures on employment in AAs, we should pause to consolidate the information that we now have about **the impact of the major 'carrots'** *and* **'sticks'**. Regional policy reached its greatest intensity in the 15-year period 1964–79. The direct Exchequer costs per year of investment incentives and labour subsidies (in constant 1975 prices) rose from £55 million in the early 1960s to £383 million from the mid-1960s to the early 1970s, and £578 million in the mid-1970s before beginning to decline, especially after 1982/3 (Table 8.3). At the same time that expenditures increased, the IDC thresholds were lowered and extended to cover offices as well as manufacturing, so that the number of firms, and their associated jobs, moving to AAs increased dramatically. The precise impact of regional policy measures on job creation within the AAs is difficult to assess, but both government and academic researchers have suggested 'order of magnitude' figures using linear trend, shift-share and multiple regression analysis.

In particular, the works of Gudgin *et al.* (1982) and Moore *et al.* (1986) have provided detailed estimates of the 1950–81 job impact of policy in the four main DA regions (i.e. Northern Ireland, Scotland, Wales and the North, but excluding DAs in the North West and the South West, and IAs in the North West, South West and Yorkshire/Humberside – see below, p. 190). Figure 8.1 shows 'actual' and 'expected' employment in manufacturing in the four main DA regions. Given the industrial structure of each

184

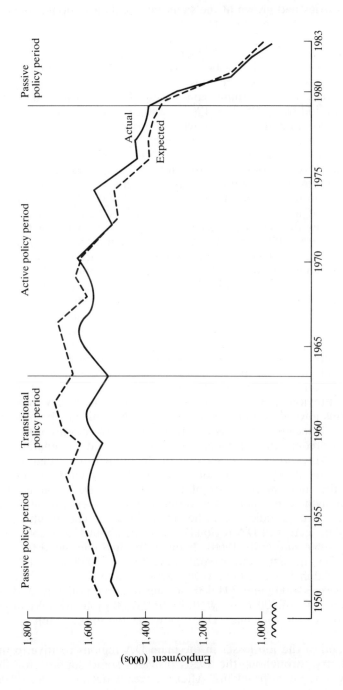

Figure 8.1 **United Kingdom: 'actual' and 'expected' manufacturing employment in the four main Development Area regions (Scotland, Northern Ireland, Wales and the North), 1950–83.**
Source: based on Moore *et al.* (1986a, 32)

DA, the maximum employment which each region could have 'expected' to create *if* its industries had grown at the same rate as their national counterparts is plotted as the broken line. The 'actual' manufacturing employment is plotted as the solid line. A comparison between the 'actual' and 'expected' curves gives us some idea of the effect of regional policy on jobs. During the passive policy period of the 1950s, the actual amount of manufacturing employment in the four main DA regions was consistently below what might have been expected, all other things considered. This gap widened during the transitional period from 1958/9 to 1963/4, and to some extent the realisation of this deterioration in the employment prospects of the traditional industrial areas prompted increased vigour in policy measures.

The active policy period from 1963/4 to 1979/80 witnessed a notable 'turnaround' for the DA regions, because although the overall trend of manufacturing employment was downwards, the 'actual' employment curve closed with and even rose above the 'expected' employment curve. In other words, the apparent impact of regional policy in this period was to slow down quite markedly the actual job decline compared with what might have been expected. There was a time-lagged beneficial impact of policy in the less active period after 1979 which lasted until 1981, but since then the actual employment figures have again fallen below the level of what might have been expected, *ceteris paribus*. Hence, the DA regions were again 'experiencing a relatively greater loss of manufacturing jobs than the nation, even after allowing for their distinctive industrial structure' (Moore *et al.*, 1986, 31).

A criticism of this method of determining the effects of regional policy is that the passive policy base-period of the 1950s may not be appropriate for gauging the effects in the 1960s, possibly underestimating the impact of stronger policy in the latter period. Also, the positive effect of policy measures in one period may be counterbalanced by the closures of plants established in a previous period – thus, in *gross* terms the policy may still be attracting firms into AAs, but in *net* terms the job gains may be minimal (or even negative) because previously attracted firms are closing down. In an attempt to overcome this problem, Moore *et al.* tried to separate the *indigenous* from the *immigrant* sectors of manufacturing. Figure 8.2 demonstrates the linear extrapolation of the 1950–63 manufacturing employment trend in the indigenous sector of the four main DA regions. The time-scale is subdivided into periods of differing policy strengths, although these should be taken as indicative rather than absolute. The graph shows that the indigenous sectors of DA regions were losing about 12,000 jobs each year during the 1950s and early 1960s. If this trend had continued through the 1960s and 1970s, the expectation would have been a 500,000 job shortfall in 1971 and 625,000 in 1981. In fact, as the 'actual' curve shows, the respective shortfalls were 384,000 and 394,000, so that regional policy is credited with the 'creation' of 116,000 jobs by 1971 and 231,000 jobs by 1981 in the indigenous sectors of the four main DA regions, as the lower graph of Fig. 8.2 illustrates.

The linear trend of the job losses in the main DA regions relative to the rest of the country throughout the 1950s provides some support for the 'divergent' view of regional problems. After the steady decline of the 1950s, the most striking feature of the 'actual' curve is its levelling off in the 1960s, followed by a rise in the 1970s, which covers the active policy period and

Figure 8.2 United Kingdom: actual (A) minus expected (E) manufacturing employment in the indigenous sectors of the four main Development Area regions.*
Source: After Moore *et al.* (1986a, 35)

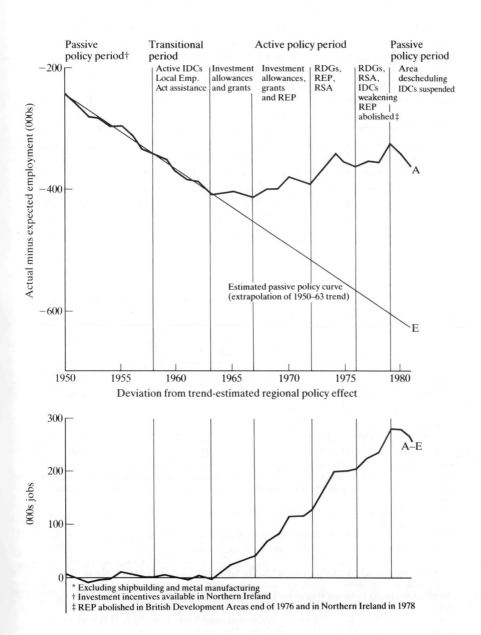

* Excluding shipbuilding and metal manufacturing
† Investment incentives available in Northern Ireland
‡ REP abolished in British Development Areas end of 1976 and in Northern Ireland in 1978

provides us with evidence indicative of some contribution of regional policy to *convergence* in the national economy. The linear trends shown in both Figs 8.1 and 8.2 suggest, however, that after about 1981 *divergence* may have reasserted itself as the dominant mode of regional economic 'development'.

The principal aim of regional policy has been to redistribute jobs from the more prosperous regions to the distressed regions and to encourage and facilitate job creation within the latter. The total numbers of manufacturing jobs created in all the AAs in the country during the period 1960–81 are summarised in Table 8.4. The *net* jobs are those jobs created by policy which have survived to the end of the period studied. Hence, policy measures created 604,000 *gross* jobs overall 1960–81, but because of contractions and closures resulting in losses of 154,000 jobs, the *net* total gain in the DAs was 450,000. As Moore *et al*. (1986, 9) comment, this was '. . . a real and substantial achievement'. But this is not all, of course, since manufacturing jobs have a beneficial 'knock on' impact on any community, generating a range of supportive employment in the service sector – the *multiplier effect*. If a medium-term multiplier of 1.4 is used (i.e. 40 new jobs in services for every 100 new jobs in manufacturing), then the 450,000 manufacturing jobs would have generated a further 180,000 service jobs. Therefore, the grand total of jobs created directly and indirectly by regional policy in DAs between 1960 and 1981 amounted to 630,000 which were still surviving in 1981. Of the net manufacturing jobs created, two-thirds (309,000) occurred in the 1960–71 period, the decade of most intense regional policy. But, as Table 8.4 shows,

Table 8.4 United Kingdom: manufacturing jobs created by regional policy in all the Developmental Areas[a]

	Immigrant firms		Indigenous firms		All firms	
	Net	Gross	Net	Gross	Net	Gross
1. Jobs created 1960–1971	170[b]	197[d]	139[e]	139	309	336
2. Jobs created 1960–1971 but lost between 1971 and 1981	−45[c]		−35		−80	
3. Jobs created 1971–1981	48	56	173[f]	212	221	268
4. Jobs created 1960–1981	173	253	277	351	450	604

[a] These estimates cover the four main Development Areas of Scotland, Wales, the Northern region and Northern Ireland plus the smaller Merseyside and South West Development Areas.
[b] Made up of 144,000 jobs in all British Development Areas plus an estimate of 26,000 for Northern Ireland.
[c] Estimated closures of 35,000 jobs in the four main Development Areas plus estimates for closures in Merseyside and South West Development Areas.
[d] Estimates of closures of policy-induced moves 1960–71 which had taken place by 1971 amount to 27,000 jobs. These jobs losses are added to net employment of 170,000 jobs to give gross employment of 197,000.
[e] Regression results from the four main Development Areas above plus estimates for Merseyside and South West Development Areas.
[f] Regression results of 115,000 jobs plus Merseyside and South West, plus 35,000 jobs lost between 1971 and 1981 which had been created by regional policy, 1960–71.
This table allows for the estimated impact of North Sea oil.
Source: Moore *et al*. (1986b, 38)

80,000 of these jobs were lost during the 1970s, so that by 1981 the contributions of the two decades to net job creation were virtually even. Qualifying these figures, however, Fothergill and Gudgin (1982, 147) argue that 90,000 of the new jobs 'created' in AAs between 1960 and 1979 were there because of the urban–rural shift of manufacturing, so they should not be included as part of the regional policy effect.

Additional to the number of jobs created by regional policy measures are those jobs 'safeguarded', in other words, jobs which would have turned into 'redundancies' were it not for government assistance. Moore and Rhodes (1979) estimated that the number of jobs 'saved' in the main DA regions up to 1980 amounted to 120,000, and these manufacturing job retentions would also have had a beneficial impact on service sector employment. So, while the regional policy measures may not have solved the employment problems of the DA regions, they certainly mitigated the speed and magnitude of regional industrial decline by a substantial margin. Many of those gains, however, may turn out to have been more temporary than permanent once we have been able to analyse the full impact of the 1980s recession on the UK's regional economies.

Given these total figures of policy-induced job gains in DA regions between 1960 and 1981, what can be said about the effects of the individual regional policy instruments discussed above? Table 8.5 summarises the effects of IDCs, investment incentives (mainly RDGs), REP and RSA. The RDGs were by far the most significant policy instrument, accounting for over 68 per cent of the total number of new jobs, while IDCs were in second place but only contributing 16 per cent. REP and RSA had relatively minor effects, especially REP after 1971. Table 8.5 clearly shows that net job creation slowed down substantially in the 1970s, with a gain of 141,000 over the 309,000 of the 1960–71 period. Moore *et al.* (1986, 43) observe that this decline in the impact of regional policy in the 1970s compared with the 1960s reflects both a weakening of policy itself and also 'a "plateau" effect as plant closures of previous policy-induced moves begin to offset new openings'. In addition, three significantly different macro-economic circumstances must be borne in mind when trying to assess regional policy effects in the 1970s relative to the 1960s:

Table 8.5 United Kingdom: the effects of individual instruments of regional policy for all Development Areas (including Northern Ireland) 1960–81

Policy instrument	Indigenous		Immigrant		Total	
	by 1971	by 1981	by 1971	by 1981	by 1971	by 1981
IDCs	—	—	89	74	89	74
Investment incentives	99	235	58	72	157	307
REP	40	—	23	27	63	27
RSA	—	42	—	—	—	42
Total	139	277	170	173	309	450

Source: Moore *et al.* (1986b, 43)

1. '. . . the stagnation of manufacturing output, employment and investment in the 1970s could also have reduced the effectiveness of regional policy. In conditions of low investment, there are fewer potentially mobile projects generated within the UK.'
2. '. . . a lower rate of investment reduces the pressure on manufacturing industry to leave the big conurbations in the non-DAs. This diminishes the number of mobile projects that could be induced by regional policy to move to DAs.'
3. 'The economic stagnation in many other industrialised countries will also tend to diminish the number of internationally mobile projects that could be attracted to DAs and increase the intensity of competition for such projects from other countries.' (*idem*)

Furthermore, 'falling demand and declining profitability' may have encouraged firms 'to use their regional investment incentives to rationalise their production', and it is not clear whether such firms 'revert towards non-DA locations' or whether they 'concentrate production around the newer plants established in AAs as a result of policy' (*idem*).

Ironically, strengthened government assistance to the 'other' AAs, the *Intermediate Areas*, during the 1970s may have reduced the impact of assistance in Development Areas. During the 1971–78 period the annual number of firm moves to IAs averaged 41, whereas it had only been 22 during the 1960s, and it is reasonable to assume that a good proportion of the increase was at the expense of the DAs. Accepting that the difficulties of calculating the job impact of regional policy on IAs are even greater than those for the main AAs, not least because they were dominated by the textile industries which were in receipt of national job subsidies, Moore *et al.* do offer some estimates. They suggest that regional policy caused the transfer of about 20,000 jobs from the IAs to the other AAs between 1959 and 1972 because of the more attractive incentives available in the latter. A further 14,000 jobs would have been lost in this way without IA status between 1972 and 1981. However, the granting of IA status meant that about 32,000 manufacturing jobs were attracted into the IAs from non-AAs, while another 25,000 jobs were 'stopped' from moving to other AAs. The *net* gain of manufacturing jobs for the IAs, therefore is estimated to be about 23,000, to which could be added a service sector multiplier of 9,000 jobs.

8.1.4 Retraining and training provisions

The desirability of retraining the unemployed in order to give them the skills appropriate to new, expanding industries is as old as regional policy itself, having started with the *Industrial Transference Board* in 1928. Workers in the AAs who had been 'laid off' from their jobs in the traditional industries were offered the opportunity of attending retraining courses prior to moving to other regions for work. Of the 277,000 workers who were assisted in their job searches during the 1929–38 decade, approximately 150,000 remained in their new areas, and of the total a substantial minority took retraining courses before moving (Lee, 1980, 32). So it could be argued that the retraining was of job-finding benefit in both the new areas and the areas of origin, although the precise details are unavailable.

Provision of retraining facilities continued to be an element of policy after the War, being included in the 1944 *White Paper on Employment Policy* and again in the 1950 *Distribution of Industry Act*, but the scale of the assistance was relatively minor. As with so many regional policy measures, it was the coming to power of the Labour Party in 1964 that wrought major changes.

The *Industrial Training Act 1964* was specifically aimed at increasing the numbers and improving the quality of people wishing to get jobs in industry. Although workers who had lost their jobs in one branch of industry could be retrained under this scheme, the primary aim of the Act was to provide vocational training at the post-school/apprentice level. It was expected that as the AAs improved their economic performance there would be an increasing demand for skilled labour, and the only opportunities then provided were those in the apprenticeship schemes of large companies. The government intended that such training should be more widely available and therefore established *Government Training Centres* (17 between 1968 and 1970, 11 of them in AAs) which reduced the training costs of firms, thereby theoretically enabling them to be more competitive. The scheme was administered by 27 Industrial Training Boards (ITBs), which in total covered almost two-thirds of the country's working population.

Funding for the industrial training scheme commenced at £0.5 million in 1965/6, doubled to £1.0 million in 1966/7 and 1967/8 and doubled again, to £2 million, in 1968/9. The latter increase reflected the new grant scheme, introduced at the end of 1967, which aimed at encouraging craft and technical training in AAs. (See Lee, 1980, 73–4.) Under the 1966 *Industrial Development Act*, the Ministry of Labour provided its own instructors to train workers at the Government Training Centres (GTCs) and also trained the instructors nominated by firms taking part in the scheme without charge. The cost to the Exchequer of industrial training assistance rose to £3 million in 1969/70 and the next year reached £4 million, primarily because of the extension of this aid to the Intermediate Areas (created by the *Local Employment Act* of 1970). Funding levels remained between £3 million and £4 million in 1971/2 and 1972/3, but then doubled to £8 million for the next two years. The reason for this dramatic increase was the *Training Opportunities Scheme* (TOPS).

The Conservative Government introduced TOPS in 1972 and hoped to expand the number of places at GTCs from 18,400 in 1971 to 60,000 or 70,000 by 1975. This commitment to expansion of training facilities was contained in the 1972 *Industry Act*, which anticipated spending about £100 million on Centres and allowances over the years 1972–76. Grants to firms in AAs which added trainees to their workforce were raised, and new funds were made available for firms that retrained those members of their labour force who would otherwise have been made redundant (Lee, 1980, 90). Following such training or retraining, it was hoped that the newly skilled worker would find employment either in his/her home area or in another region and, if the latter, further assistance was available in the shape of rehousing grants (see above, pp. 173–4). However the deepening recession of the mid-1970s meant that cutbacks in government spending were inevitable, and this was quickly revealed in the reduction of training assistance to £5 million in 1975/6 from the £8 million of 1974/5. As redundancies increased, the government did try to strengthen the Training Services Agency and the training programmes of industry, in a bid to improve retraining opportunities for the unemployed and to help workers willing to move to new jobs, but this was overshadowed by the TES programme (p. 184 above) and the Job Creation Programme (JCP).

Quite radical changes to the national system were introduced with the *Employment and Training Act* of 1981. The ITBs were reduced in number from 27 to 7 on the grounds that training for industry could be more effectively met, and more cheaply, on a voluntary basis, and the two-year Youth Training Scheme (YTS) was established to replace the one-year Youth Opportunities Programme. The YTS provides an integrated programme of training, work experience and relevant education for school-leavers and catered for 362,000 in 1987–88 (71 per cent of them in AA regions) at a cost of over £1,000 million. The main concern about the scheme is the possibility that only those 16–17 year olds on YTS have much chance of being offered employment in manufacturing, while the other 65% of school-leavers have to fend for themselves, primarily in the service sector. The 1981 Act subsequently introduced grants to employers to provide vocational preparation, reformed the arrangements for training in craft, technician and professional skills and increased the emphasis on training and retraining adults. The principal employment scheme in the late 1980s is the *Community Programme*, which involves temporary work in the community for long-term unemployed and catered for 245,000 in 1987–88. This scheme accounted for 80 per cent of the Manpower Services Commission's 1987/8 budget of £1,391 million (excluding administrative costs) and a similar proportion of the budgets for 1988/9 (£1,430 million) and 1989/90 (£1,467 million). However, while helping to reduce unemployment figures, the Community Programme is hardly addressing the fundamental national and regional economic issues raised by an inadequately and inappropriately trained workforce, a point to which we shall return in Chapter 10 (pp. 224–5).

9 The effects of policy II: congestion, industrial structure, locational and environmental measures

In the previous chapter we discussed the effects of government policy measures aimed at alleviation of high unemployment problems in Assisted Areas. In this chapter we turn to the effects of other policies which have aimed to improve the prospects of regional convergence, both directly and indirectly. The objectives of these policies have been: to ease congestion in growth areas (especially the South East) and redistribute the benefits to AAs; to improve the structure of industry in AAs and inner cities; to increase the locational accessibility of the more peripheral regions, and to improve the physical environment of AAs and inner cities.

Not all the policy measures aimed at reducing unemployment have been limited in their application to the AAs. This was especially so after 1980, when the emphasis switched from the regions to inner city areas, and when central government's concern was simply with job creation *anywhere* in the country, even in the more traditionally prosperous regions. Until 1980, however, the latter regions had been the focus of one side of policy, the 'stick', while the AA regions had been the focus of the 'carrots'. The reasoning behind the 'stick' policies reflected a belief that the more prosperous regions were growing too quickly and becoming congested. The first major policy measures which aimed to reduce such congestion were introduced shortly after the second World War.

9.1 Congestion

As we saw in Chapter 6, the Barlow Commission accepted Commissioner Stewart's suggestion of 1936 that industrial expansion around London especially should be limited, and added that in order to relieve 'overcrowdedness' both industry and population should be decentralised to trading estates, garden cities and expanded rural towns. The Commission's recommendation came to fruition in two ways: by the IDC system of control over industrial developments in non-AA regions (later assisted by ODP controls), and by the building of New Towns and Expanded Towns outside the green belts of London and other large cities.

9.1.1 Industrial Development Certificates and Office Development Permits

We discussed the impact of IDCs and ODPs on employment creation in the AAs in the previous chapter, but what of their effect on the city regions of origin, especially London? Greater London's peak year for numbers employed in manufacturing was 1961, when 1.4 million held such jobs. This was at the end of a period (1945–61) which had witnessed a *net* gain of 6,600 manufacturing jobs *per year*: 427,000 jobs had left the capital, but these had been more than replaced by new job creation. From 1961 onwards, however, a decline set in which was to result in the *net* loss of 800,000 manufacturing jobs by the end of 1985, well over half the peak figure. The rate of loss per year was 12,000 from 1960 to 1966, rose to 50,000 per year for 1966–73, and then ranged between 31,000 and 37,000 per year 1973–85 (Fothergill *et al.*, 1985, 7). The highest annual rate of job loss in manufacturing, therefore, occurred from the mid-1960s to the early 1970s, the period when IDC controls were at their strongest.

If the bulk of the jobs leaving London had gone to AAs, then it would be reasonable to assume that the IDC measures were achieving their objective. However, only 34 per cent of the 1945–61 moves went to less prosperous regions, and just over half of those went in the period 1945–51 (Howard, 1968). Between 1961 and 1971 approximately 400,000 jobs were 'lost' from London, and at the same time 89,000 jobs were 'created' in AAs because of stronger IDC policy (see Table 8.5), but the former figure includes jobs lost to bankruptcies as well as moves, whilst the latter figure incorporates moves from all the prosperous regions, not just London. During the 1960–65 period the annual average out-migration rate of London's manufacturing plants was 4.0 per 1,000 factories, whereas in 1966–71 it was 4.7 (Keeble, 1976, 134). This is indicative of some policy effect, but Dennis (1978) has shown that only 9 per cent of the moves went to AAs. In fact, Dennis examined the years 1966–74, when 390,000 net jobs were lost to Greater London, and found that 44 per cent were attributable to straightforward factory closures, 29 per cent to plants laying off workers and 27 per cent to moves (11 per cent unplanned – mainly to other parts of London, 9 per cent to AAs and 7 per cent to New Towns and Expanded Towns). Keeble's own research for the shorter period of 1966–71 showed that Greater London generated factory moves resulting in 53,000 jobs migrating to other sub-regions (mainly counties), whilst the outer metropolitan area of London yielded a further 20,500 jobs and the West Midlands 13,000 jobs (i.e. altogether 57 per cent of total UK-generated moves). Of the total moves out of London, over 62,000 jobs (41 per cent) went to non-AAs: 28,500 to the rest of the South East; 9,500 to the South West; 9,000 to the East Midlands; 8,200 to East Anglia, and 7,000 to the West Midlands (derived from Keeble, 1976, 135–7). The principal contributors to these moves were the large multi-plant companies, which transferred production capacity out of London and in doing so accounted for about 40 per cent of the capital's job losses to out-migration.

The movement out of London therefore comprised two major elements – a short distance 'overspill' into contiguous regions and a longer distance migration to the AA regions. The role of IDCs in the whole process is difficult to determine with any precision, but it must have been considerable during the 1960s when their stringency increased. In 1960–61 the Board of Trade refused permission for industrial developments in the South and the Midlands to 17 per cent of the applications, a proportion which rose to 26 per cent in 1964–65, then fell to 16 per cent in 1969–70, to 12 per cent by

1975–76 and to just 2 per cent by 1979–80 (Cambridge Economics Policy Group, 1980, 1). What is not known, of course, is the number of firms which never asked for permission to build new capacity in the non-AAs, simply assuming that they would be refused if they did. IDC controls were not evenly imposed throughout the non-AAs, however, and some locations received sympathetic treatment because of particular circumstances, e.g. in Portsmouth, to help reduce dependence on the naval dockyard, in Ashford, Brighton and Lancing, to cushion railway works closures, and in the New Towns and Expanded Towns, to stimulate industrial developments (Hoare, 1983, 103).

In answer to the question, 'What caused you to consider opening a new plant in a new location?', asked in 1973 as part of a government survey, 12 per cent of the 531 firms covered replied that it was the refusal or expected refusal of an IDC (Department of Trade and Industry, 1973, 532). The percentage of firms quoting IDC controls on *in situ* expansion as being the major impetus to change location varied regionally, however, with only 8 per cent of Greater London firms citing this reason compared with 16 per cent in the rest of the South East, but 42 per cent in the West Midlands conurbation and 35 per cent in the rest of the Midlands (Townroe, 1979, 75). After London, the Birmingham area was a significant source of migrant firms, and up to 1971 had contributed 139,000 jobs to other regions: 45,000 to the North West, 33,000 to Wales, and 10,000 each to Scotland, the East Midlands and Yorkshire-Humberside. Such movements continued in the early to mid-1970s, a total of 4,400 jobs going mainly to Scotland (1,600), Wales (1,200) and the North West (800) between 1972 and 1975, but the rate was slowing down as the recession deepened and IDC controls were eased in the latter half of the decade. So, while being a significant influence on the 'decision to move' taken by firms in the Midlands and the South, the IDC was not the single most important factor. All-in-all, however, from its inception in 1948 to its demise in 1981, the IDC programme probably influenced some 230,000 of the 400,000 jobs that 'migrated' from the non-AA to the AA regions.

From 1965 until 1979 the IDC scheme was supplemented by the ODP, the latter specifically designed to reduce the congestion of offices in London (see above, Section 8.1.2). The growth of service industry employment in London was an almost constant feature during the 1950s (45,000 jobs per year) and continued until the mid-1970s, when it peaked at 2.9 million jobs, representing 79 per cent of total employment (cf. manufacturing, with about 0.8 million at the same time). 'Basic' services (insurance, banking, professional and scientific services, public administration) continued to grow into the 1970s, but 'non-basic' services (retailing, health, education) declined. Not all the office workers in London actually lived in the city, of course, about 0.54 million commuting in every day, half of them to the centre. In turn, the commuters were partially to blame for the perceived congestion problems in the 1960s. The fear was expressed that the enormous rush-hour pressure on the public transport system and the road network would soon become intolerable, while the demand for office space was causing rises in rents. The latter was having consequential effects on the rents charged for other land uses, especially retailing, manufacturing and residential, and was also causing major speculative office building programmes, which added to

195

the congestion. The LOB aimed to encourage inter-regional decentralisation of offices from London to ease the pressures on the capital, although by restricting office building the Bureau actually contributed towards a shortage of office space, which caused even more dramatic rent increases (e.g. from £32 to £205 per m^2 in the City, 1964–74) (Keeble, 1980, 134).

Evidence was later to emerge that office employment in central London had slowed almost to a stop by the early 1960s, but the LOB started to encourage offices to move out from 1963. Initially, moves were very short-distance, particularly southwards to Croydon and westwards to Hounslow, Ealing and Richmond. Following the introduction of ODPs in 1965, decentralisation on a more regional basis started, with firms moving outside Greater London, but company preference was to stay within easy 'striking' distance of the City (Croydon, for example, received 79 per cent of the offices and 60 per cent of the office jobs (=10,000) decentralised from London, 1963–68: Daniels, 1969). Overall, between 1967 and 1976 offfice floorspace in outer London increased by 94 per cent, compared with only a 27 per cent increase in central London, albeit on a larger base (Keeble, 1980, 135). During the lifetime of the LOB some 2,000 firms moved out of central London, involving 145,000 jobs. However, as we saw in Section 8.1.2, the majority moved elsewhere in the South East, especially to towns like Reading, Basingstoke, Maidenhead and Southend, and to the New Towns, with less than 1 in 10 of the jobs going to AAs. Probably as many firms and jobs again moved out of central London over the same time period that were not reported to the LOB, but the distribution pattern would appear to have been similar to the reported moves. Within the AAs, these offices clustered in or near the largest urban centres, thus creating a pattern of concentrated decentralisation. (See the LOB map in Manners *et. al.*, 1980, 80.)

The destination pattern of office moves from central London into the South has been summarised as follows by Townroe (1979, 79–80):

(a) *Outer zone commuter towns*, with a manufacturing base but with a large pool of office-type occupations among the daily out-commuters. Many of these commuters would be only too happy to work locally and so they form a very significant locational 'pull'. These towns include Guildford, Horsham, East Grinstead, Reading, High Wycombe, Chelmsford and Tonbridge.

(b) *Seaside towns*, which overlap with the previous group but are more distant, with a different environmental attraction. This group includes Southend (the largest single concentration of these intra-regional moves), Folkestone, Brighton and Worthing; and Southampton and Portsmouth, Poole and Bournemouth.

(c) *New Towns and Expanded Towns* seeking to diversify their manufacturing base. The principal destinations have been Harlow, Basildon and Hemel Hempstead in the London 'ring' of New Towns; and Basingstoke, Swindon, Ashford, Aylesbury, King's Lynn and Bury St Edmunds of the London-sponsored town expansion schemes.

(d) More distant but *high amenity sub-regional centres*, all with good transportation links with central London. This group includes Chichester, Bath, Cheltenham, Oxford, Northampton and Peterborough (both designated New Towns in the 1960s), Colchester, Ipswich and Norwich. (Ipswich started to attract insurance companies in the LOB period and has continued to do so. By 1988 it had benefited from the in-migration of Willis, General Accident, Commercial Union, Guardian Royal Exchange and Sun Life.)

Over the period 1960–80, London experienced a net 'loss' of approximately 300,000 office jobs in addition to the net loss of over 650,000 manufacturing jobs, a total of close to 1 million. To some extent this is reflected in the 1.3 million population loss of Greater London over the two decades. Government policy was instrumental in directing probably more than half the total number to other regions, thus redistributing jobs around the country on a substantial scale. Under the LOB scheme, about 60 per cent of the relocated government office jobs went to AA regions, but several government departments simply moved to other parts of the South, complementing the moves of private sector offices (see above, pp. 181–2). For example, the Civil Service Department went to Basingstoke, the Stationery Office to Norwich, the Ordnance Survey to Southampton, Customs and Excise to Southend and the Inland Revenue to Worthing. Under the IDC scheme, about one-third of the 650,000 'lost' manufacturing jobs *may* have been directed to AAs, but the remainder were redistributed in the outer metropolitan area of London, the rest of the South East and just across the boundaries into the other more prosperous regions. In particular, major beneficiaries of the London job outflow were the New Towns and Expanded Towns.

9.1.2 New Towns and Expanded Towns (NETS)

The desire to restrict the spatial growth of large cities, expounded by the Barlow Commission in 1940 (see above, pp. 119–20), had resulted in the creation of green belts. These were designed to stop further ribbon and piecemeal estate developments around the urban fringes as they existed in the late 1940s. To cater for the expanding populations of major cities, and to rehouse those from slum areas, the New Towns were built and existing towns expanded outside the green belt. These NETs were major recipients of the overspill population from all major British cities, particularly London and Birmingham, and therefore featured in attempts both to relieve inner city congestion and to redistribute employment in manufacturing and services.

The history of New Town development was discussed in Chapter 3, but it is worth reiterating here that from the inception of 'garden cities' at Letchworth in 1903 New Town planning has been concerned with the provision of jobs in concert with housing. During both the first wave of NET building in the 1940s and the second wave in the 1960s, planners endeavoured to ensure that the employment created, especially in manufacturing, was better balanced than in older urban centres and was orientated towards growth industries (e.g. light engineering, electrical equipment). In addition, during the second wave particularly, NETs sought to diversify their employment structure by encouraging office developments that were decentralising, mainly from London. Where NETs were located in AAs, e.g. Cwmbran in Wales, Glenrothes in Scotland, Aycliff and Peterlee in the North East, they automatically qualified for all the regional incentives. It could also be argued that they benefited their own AA both by relieving overcrowding in the associated conurbation and by bringing in newer industries or providing room for the expansion of existing industries. In terms of numbers of people and firms moving into NETs, however, the migration out of London has been the most significant by far, and this was of little benefit to the AAs since the majority moved into London's outer metropolitan ring or into East Anglia.

Initially, as we saw in Chapter 6, industrial developments in NETs were restricted because of the difficulties of applying IDC exemptions outside the AAs, but once the administrative problems were solved, manufacturing firms were able to locate in NETs with preferential IDC treatment. The effects have been quite striking. Over 70% of New Town firms originated in London (Hoare, 1983, 105) and most of the moves were spatially sectoral, with south London firms going to Crawley, east London firms to Basildon, west London firms to Bracknell and north London firms to Stevenage, Harlow, Hemel Hempstead, Hatfield and Welwyn Garden City. By 1977 these eight New Towns had constructed 919 factories employing 109,000, while the 24 Expanded Towns, which also enjoyed preferential IDC treatment, had constructed almost 2,000 factories employing over 80,000 (many in East Anglia, thus contributing to the region's growth in manufacturing employment). Similarly, in the West Midlands, the New Towns of Telford and Redditch had constructed more than 580 factories employing over 15,300 (Townroe, 1979, 82). Nationally, by 1979 the 28 New Towns had generated 314,000 industrial jobs in over 3,900 factories, plus 60,000 office jobs in 1,350 firms, while 1,600 factories were occupied in the Expanded Towns. Of the total number of jobs 'created' in NETs between 1960 and 1978, about 125,000 were diverted into them by NET policy (Fothergill *et al.*, 1983 and 1985).

The NET programme was proving almost too successful even by the mid-1970s, however, and in January 1976 the GLC ended its policy of dispersing population and industry away from the capital. NETs were popular among companies because they offered IDCs (particularly significant for those London firms not wishing to leave the South East but wanting to decentralise from the capital), other assistance from local authorities, good amenities and pleasant environments. In addition, the London area NETs were well located with respect to the largest single market in the country, had excellent transport linkages and were close enough to London for migrant firms to maintain contact with other firms near their original site.

A significant effect of the policy of directing conurbation overspill to NETs was to create towns with industrial populations biased towards skilled employment, especially in growth sectors of industry. This in turn meant that skilled manual workers and their families were being 'selected' to move out of the congested older cities, leaving an unskilled workforce behind them in inner city areas. This out-migration accelerated the population decline of inner cities at a time when falling birth rates had already reduced the national rate of population increase, and this coincided with public expenditure cuts and the switch in emphasis of government policy towards inner city rehabilitation schemes. Couple these aspects with the claim of London in particular that the NETs acted as 'economic and social bloodsuckers' (Hoare, 1983, 105), while the AAs saw them as absorbing London firms otherwise destined for the less prosperous regions, and it is not very surpris-

Standard Planning Region and New Towns (with designation date and dissolution date of Development Corporation)	New Towns Population (000s)			Overspill Agreements		Dwellings (000s)			Overspill population 1968–81 (000s)
	Original	Planned	1985	Towns	No. of schemes	To be built	Completed 31 Dec 73		
LONDON and SOUTH EAST: TOTAL	356.5	1,366.4	942.3	Greater London	32	93.0	50.9		181
First wave									
Stevenage (1946–80)									
Crawley (1947–62)									
Harlow (1947–80)									
Hemel Hempstead									
Hatfield (1947–62)	98.5	668.5	523.7						
Welwyn (1948–66)									
Garden City (1948–66)									
Basildon (1949–85)									
Bracknell (1949–82)									
Second wave									
Milton Keynes (1970–89)									
Peterborough (1967–89)	258.0	697.6	418.6						
Northampton (1968–85)									
MIDLANDS and SOUTH WEST: TOTAL	117.7	423.0	227.9	TOTAL	23	27.8	17.1		
First wave									
Corby (1950–80)	15.7	83.0	48.0	Birmingham	15	21.0	10.3		48
Second wave									
Redditch (1964–85)	102.0	340.0	179.9	Wolverhampton	4	4.5	4.5		—
Telford (1968–89)				Bristol	4	2.3	2.3		—

Table 9.1 (Continued)

Standard Planning Region and New Towns (with designation date and dissolution date of Development Corporation)	New Towns Population (000s)			Overspill Agreements		Dwellings (000s)		
	Original	Planned	1985	Towns	No. of schemes	To be built	Completed 31 Dec 73	Overspill population 1968–81 (000s)
NORTH WEST: TOTAL	413.2	809.0	506.0	TOTAL	9	31.5	11.9	66
Second wave								
Skelmersdale (1961–85)								
Runcorn (1964–89)	413.2	809.0	506.0	Liverpool	4	18.5	6.0	41
Warrington (1968–89)				Manchester	4	8.5	1.4	25
Central Lancs. (1970–85)				Salford	1	4.5	4.5	—
NORTH: TOTAL	20.3	155.0	107.8					
First wave								
Aycliffe (1947–88)								
Peterlee (1948–88)	0.3	75.0	49.1					
Second wave								
Washington (1964–85)	20.0	80.0	58.7	Newcastle	2	2.6	10.5	21
WALES TOTAL	17.5	68.0	55.6					
First wave								
Cwmbran (1949–87)	12.0	55.0	46.1					

New Town								
Second wave								
Newtown (1967–)	5.5	13.0	9.5					
Llantrisant (1972, discontinued 1974)								
SCOTLAND: TOTAL	54.2	565.0	260.2					
First wave								
East Kilbride (1947–)								
Glenrothes (1948–)	6.5	275.0	157.9					
Cumbernauld (1955–)				Glasgow	66	23.3	9.6	—
Second wave								
Livingston (1961–)	40.7	220.0	97.0					
Irvine (1966–)	7.0	70.0	5.3					
Stonehouse (1972, discontinued 1976)								
TOTAL GB	979.3	3,386.4	2,094.6	TOTAL GB	132	186.1	92.1	
NORTHERN IRELAND		320.0	—					
*Second wave**								
Craigavon (1965–73)	—	108.0[a]	—					Merged into local govt. units, 1973
Antrim–Ballymena (1966–73)	—	120.0	—					
Londonderry (1969–73)	—	100.0[b]	—					

Data on overspill population targets are incomplete

* Under *Planning Order (N Ireland) 1973*, Development Commissions were dissolved and Ulster New Towns incorporated into local government structure

[a] by 2001

[b] by 1995

Source: Based on Lawton (1982, 196–7) and Balchin and Bull (1987, 80)

201

ing that the GLC sought to reduce target populations of existing agreements and determined not to enter into any new agreements with Expanded Towns (Lawton, 1982, 195).

The first wave of New Towns were generally located between 40 and 50 km from the central city with the result that some people continued to work in the city and joined the commuter flows, whereas some workers living in the city were able to find jobs in the New Towns and therefore commuted in the opposite direction. This was not seen to be very helpful in reducing the conurbation congestion, so the second wave of New Towns and the Expanded Town ('overspill' designations were focused on towns with substantial initial populations further out from the central city. Another change occurred in the planned occupational structure of second wave NETs, which also affected the first wave, and that was to broaden the economic base of these communities from an emphasis on manufacturing to one of diversification into research establishments, service industries and offices. (See above, Section 8.2.1.) This process resulted in Bracknell receiving the Meteorological Office, Harlow the administrative and research offices of BP, Hemel Hempstead the processing laboratories of Kodak and Basildon those of Ilford, while Milton Keynes was planned from the outset to receive office and service functions as well as manufacturing. However, not all NETs were as successful in attracting such employment opportunities.

As the decade of the 1970s drew to a close with a deepening recession, the NET programme of decentralising people and jobs from congested major cities essentially ground to a halt. The Development Corporations were wound down in the early 1980s (with some notable exceptions – Table 9.1) and policy emphasis shifted to trying to encourage firms to move back into inner cities, especially through the Enterprise Zone scheme. The occupational structure of the NETs, however, has meant that they have not been as badly affected by the recession as many of the older industrial towns. They continued to expand their factory space until 1982 and were successful in attracting new investment (e.g. micro-electronics in Scotland) or developing 'science parks' (e.g. Warrington). Job losses have occurred even in those industries previously seen as 'growth' sectors and well represented in NETs, especially electrical goods and scientific instruments, motor vehicles, some chemicals and synthetic fibres, and mechanical engineering. These losses have not been as great in proportionate terms, however, as those in the rest of the nation and they are much less than those of the major inner cities. The employment sectors that have helped most of the NETs to weather the recession have been precisely those which were encouraged to migrate from the older central cities in the 1960s and 1970s – the office and service sectors – and it was these moves in turn that exacerbated the inner city problems.

The diversion of government funds from NETs and the AAs into the inner cities was recognition of these problems, but little likelihood remains that such encouragement will again be given to inner city residents or firms to move out. The NETs are now very much 'on their own' in seeking to convince any mobile industry or office function to locate in them. (See Table 9.1 for New Town Development Corporation dissolution dates.) The era of trying to solve the congestion problems of conurbations by moving people and jobs out to new sites probably ended about 1980, some 50 years after the idea was first mooted, and 35 years since that idea became policy. The old central cities have experienced decongestion to the point where they are severely under-provided for in terms of employment opportunities, social services and environmental fabric, so that attempts are now under way to improve these features in much the same way as in the AAs. (See Chapters 7 and 10.)

9.2 Industrial structure, locational accessibility and environmental improvement

These three policy areas, each of which has had regional implications have existed since AAs were first identified. The emphasis placed upon each has varied, both through time and spatially, with inner cities receiving proportionately more assistance in recent years.

9.2.1 Industrial structure

One of the major problems of the places designated as AAs, even as early as the 1930s, was their apparent over-dependence upon traditional (declining) industries. This was reflected in policy measures to encourage 'newer', growing types of industry to locate in AAs, thus diversifying the area's industrial structure. Such broadening of the industrial base would, it was hoped, reduce the impact of any future downturn in the trade cycle because a smaller proportion of the workforce would be employed in susceptible industries. The building of Trading Estates and Advance Factories by the government made some contribution towards modifying the industrial structure of AAs. However, as we saw above (Section 8.1.2), many of the new firms occupying these factories were created by people resident in the area and were based on the individual's industrial experience, so that diversification from the existing structure of industry was not necessarily occurring. Other government policy instruments were more effective at such diversification, especially investment incentives together with IDC controls, since the immigrant firms were predominantly of different industrial types to those already operating in AAs. The Regional Studies Association (1983, 7) has argued that regional policy appears to have been quite successful in diverting a wide range of industries into AAs. This is illustrated by the fact that the share of Scotland, Wales and the North in UK manufacturing investment rose from 23 per cent per annum 1951–58 to 30 per cent per annum 1975–77, meaning that some structural improvements probably did help to compensate for job losses in the traditional industries.

Improving the industrial structure of an AA has always been one of the longer-term objectives of regional policy, the intention being to develop a more resilient economic base in each area. Although policy has not actively encouraged specific types of manufacturing to move in order to improve the AAs structurally, there has been a natural filtering process at work, with *export* and *national* market-orientated firms dominating the inflows, in contrast to the *local* market-orientation of most indigenous developments. Unfortunately, the recession of the mid-1970s to the mid-1980s was international as well as national, so firms suffered whether their markets were

Table 9.2 Standard Industrial Classification (SIC) of Advance Factory occupants in Scotland, Wales and the North, 1963–75

SIC		%
VIII	Mechanical engineering (especially valves, pumps and compressors; heating, ventilating, air-conditioning and refrigeration equipment; office equipment)	20
IX	Electrical engineering (especially electrical machinery; capacitors, resistors and semi-conductors)	11
XV	Clothing and footwear	10
XIII	Textiles (especially household textiles of synthetic fibres)	9
VIII	Instrument engineering (especially scientific and industrial instruments and systems)	6
XI	Vehicles (especially motor vehicles)	5
XII	Metal goods (especially engineers' small tools and gauges)	5
III	Food, drink and tobacco	4
V	Chemicals and allied products	4
XVII	Timber, furniture, etc.	4
XVIII	Paper, printing and publishing	4
XIX	Other manufacturing (especially plastic products not elsewhere classified)	10
Other uses		8
		100

Source: Slowe (1981, 138–41)

domestic or overseas, but structural diversification has probably helped to mitigate the recessionary impact a little. Details of changes to the industrial structure of AAs brought about by immigrant firms are not readily available, but some idea of the probable impact can be gained from the contribution to diversification made by Advance Factory occupants (although remembering that many such occupants were indigenous and not immigrant).

In a study of the North, Scotland and Wales over the period 1963 to 1975, Slowe (1981, 138–41) found that of 318 occupants of Advance Factories, the sectoral breakdown was as shown in Table 9.2. All the SIC sectors noted in Table 9.2 exhibited growth that was greater than the national average in 1963–75, and 51 per cent of the Advance Factory occupants were in the five fastest growing categories (SIC VIII, V, IX, XIX and VII). As far as diversification was concerned, there was considerable variation between the three Standard Regions surveyed, with Scotland gaining 91 firms in under-represented sectors (mainly instrument engineering and children's clothing), the North 42 firms (mainly electronics and plastics) and Wales 19 firms (mainly textiles and clothing). These regions also gained occupants in sectors that were already over-represented (especially derived from indigenous developments), hence Scotland 19, the North 17 and Wales 23. Therefore the *net* improvements in diversification of the industrial structure were rather less than the previous figures might suggest, but they were still notable in Scotland (Wales had already diversified its industry by 1963 compared with the inter-war years). One other noteworthy feature of Slowe's findings was that the occupants of Advance Factories employed far higher proportions of female labour (30 per cent on average) than existing firms in the regions, thus contributing to an important socio-economic change. (See Henwood and Wyatt, 1986.)

On balance, then, it would seem that the Advance Factory programme made a positive contribution to increasing the range of manufacturing types found in AAs. What of the other government policy instruments? There is ample empirical evidence to demonstrate that the over-specialisation in particular nineteenth-century industries of most of the AA regions has been progressively diminishing during the twentieth century, as older sectors developed new branches and as new technology appeared. There is also no doubt, however, that diversification of the industrial structure occurred at different rates in different regions, with the northern and western regions lagging behind the southern and eastern ones. Since the First World War the manufacturing profiles of Britain's regions have moved away from heavy dependence on a few industrial types and converged towards the more diversified national norm. Hoare (1983, 77) has shown how, since 1921, the manufacturing of most regions has moved away from over-specialisation in one or two industries towards much greater diversification, i.e. a more even spread across the whole range of manufacturing types. One region that maintained its high distinctiveness, and therefore its low diversity, is the West Midlands, and this feature of its industrial structure undoubtedly contributed to its serious problems of contraction from the late 1970s. Other regions show dramatic improvements in their manufacturing diversity, especially the North West, the North, and even the South East and East Anglia. The greatest improvement in industrial structure in almost all regions occurred in the 1960–75 period. Since this was also the time of the most intensive regional policy, the question arises as to the impact of policy measures on structural improvements compared with all other influential variables.

The principal method of determining the effect of industrial structure on regional growth or decline in manufacturing employment is 'shift-share' analysis. Shift-share asks how much change would occur in a region's employment if all its industries grew or declined at the national rate, and then compares this with what actually happened. (See Hoare, 1983, 85–9.) Shift-share disaggregates total employment change into three components (Fothergill and Gudgin, 1982, 33):

A *national component*, which is the change that would have occurred if total manufacturing employment in an area had grown at the same rate as total manufacturing employment in the country as a whole.

A *structural component*, which is the change relative to the country as a whole that can be attributed to an area's particular mix (structure) of industry. This is calculated as the change which would have occurred if each industry in the area had grown at the national rate for that industry, less the national component.

A *differential shift*, which is the difference between the expected change (i.e. the sum of the national and structural components) and the actual change in that area.'

There has been criticism of shift-share analysis, primarily regarding the effect upon results caused by choice of base year and the level of disaggregation used, but in Britain's case the results appear to be valid (Fothergill and Gudgin, 1979; Lever, 1981).

Analysis of the manufacturing employment change by region between 1952 and 1979 revealed that the *structural component* had a significant negative influence in some regions (especially the textile areas), a positive influence in others (especially the electrical engineering and vehicle areas), but little impact on other regions (e.g. five growing regions – East Anglia, South West, Wales, East Midlands and the North – did not have particularly favourable industrial structures) (Fothergill and Gudgin, 1982, 33–50). In fact, it was the *differential*, or locational, *shift* (principally the urban–rural shift), that proved to be the dominant influence, although this was an averaged trend and showed variation throughout the 27 years studied (page pp. 184–90 above).

Until 1966, industrial structure was a major influence on the rate of a region's growth, but after then its impact declined to such an extent that by 1979 it could no longer be considered a major factor in the explanation of regional growth or decline. Even if the mix of industries in each region is held constant throughout the study period the same pattern emerges. What must have happened is that changes in the national employment trends of individual industries resulted in the decreasing importance of industrial structure. While the national economy grew and employment rose up to 1966, regional disparities in growth did reflect their industrial structures. However, after the recession began in the later 1960s, industrial growth rates *converged downwards* and regional disparities consequently decreased as the regions' industrial structures became more similar. At the sub-regional level, the shift away from specialisation and towards diversification of manufacturing was already found to be quite marked by the decade of the 1960s, thus indicating a weakening of the earlier twentieth-century relationship between a region's 'traditional' industrial structure and its location *vis-à-vis* coalfields (Keeble, 1976, 45 and 98–101).

There is ample evidence to show that Britain's regions have become structurally more similar over the last two or three decades, although the remaining structural defects inherited from the past do adversely affect a region's growth rate and prospects. As we noted above, the manufacturing industry mix has improved in all the regions containing AAs, but how much of this diversification is directly attributable to regional policy instruments is difficult to ascertain precisely. Nevertheless, there is little doubt that the mobile firms which moved from more prosperous regions into the Advance Factories in AAs helped to widen the industrial base, and that the majority of other firms persuaded to move to AAs introduced new manufacturing sectors or expanded previously small sectors.

Before 1979, the hardest-hit industries in the recession were mainly those of traditional heritage (textiles, coal mining, shipbuilding, iron and steel). Consequently, because of the close relationship historically between location and industrial structure, the northern and western regions suffered proportionately more job losses than did the South and Midlands (see Chapter 2). It was possible for such a structurally imbalanced region as the West Midlands, heavily dependent upon over-represented sectors like metals and motor vehicles, to survive reasonably well because these sectors were post-War growth areas. But, as the recession deepened after 1979 it affected almost all manufacturing industry and thus became national, so that regional disparities dramatically decreased as unemployment climbed even in such previously prosperous regions as the West Midlands. While firms in 'growth industries' which were encouraged to locate in AAs by regional policy, might have mitigated the recession during the 1960s and early 1970s, they were as susceptible to cutbacks or closure as traditional industries by the late 1970s. When they did close (especially the case with a number of branch plants between 1978 and 1982), their impact was striking (e.g. British Leyland on Merseyside, 4,600 jobs lost; Talbot (UK) in Strathclyde, 9,000 jobs lost; Hoover in South Wales, 2,200 jobs lost), although these were still not on the scale of more traditional industries (e.g. British Steel job losses: Wales, 30,000; the North, 19,000). (See Townsend, 1983.)

In addition to the increased mix of manufacturing industry types that has taken place in AAs since the 1930s, some of it the result of regional policies, there has been a general restructuring of employment at the national scale. Britain has experienced a steady growth of service occupations (tertiary and quaternary) at the expense of both agricultural and manufacturing occupations (see Fig. 2.10). The change has varied regionally, but the growth of services has certainly helped to make the decline in manufacturing easier to bear, and the decentralisation of offices from London and Birmingham contributed to this process (Section 8.2.1 and 9.1.1 above). The regional shifts in employment structure between 1921 and 1976 from the primary and secondary sectors to the tertiary sector are shown in Figure 9.1.

During the recession of the late 1970s/mid-1980s those regions which were already well-structured in terms of their secondary to tertiary/quaternary occupational ratios, did not suffer a labour 'shake-out' of the same proportions as those regions heavily dependent upon traditional manufacturing. This is brought out in Table 9.3. Redundancy rates per 1,000 manufacturing employees peaked in the 1979–82 period (used to rank the Regions in the table) and then eased somewhat over the next three years, 1983–85, the national figure falling from 49 to 31. Table 9.3 also shows the occupational shift from manufacturing to services between 1979 and 1986. In 1979 there were 23.2 million people employed in the UK, 31.4 per cent of them with jobs in manufacturing and 58.6 per cent with jobs in services; by 1986 there were 21.5 million employed, 24.3 per cent in manufacturing and 67.0 per cent in services. This shift in occupational structure is reflected in every region, continuing the trend characteristic of the Third and Fourth Kondratieff Long Waves (Figs 2.10 and 9.1). The manufacturing employment declines of the traditional-industry regions of the North and West are particularly striking, as are their well-above-average redundancy rates. The regions of the South benefited from their more broadly-based industrial structure, as well as their 'better' mix of newer, non-traditional types of manufacturing, and therefore did not experience such high redundancy rates.

207

Figure 9.1   United Kingdom: changes in regional employment structure, 1921 and 1976.
Source: Law (1980)

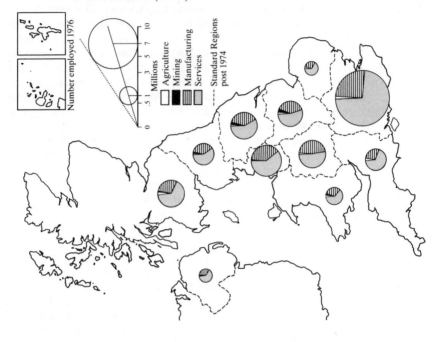

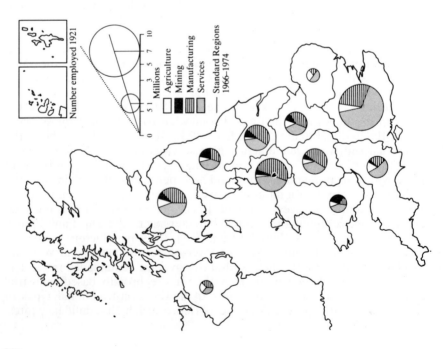

Table 9.3 United Kingdom: manufacturing and service employment, 1979 and 1986, and manufacturing redundancies, 1979–82 and 1983–85, per Standard Planning Region

	Percentage employed in manufacturing		Manufacturing redundancies per 1000 employees		Percentage employed in services	
	1979	1986	1979–82	1983–85	1979	1986
Wales	30.5	23.9	84	40	55.3	63.8
Scotland	28.8	27.7	69	46	58.2	60.6
Northern Ireland	27.9	21.3	n.a.	n.a.	61.2	70.1
North West	36.3	28.2	65	42	55.6	63.9
North	32.9	24.4	64	62	53.2	63.6
Yorkshire/Humberside	35.2	26.0	62	37	52.0	62.3
West Midlands	44.0	34.9	48	36	47.8	57.1
East Midlands	39.0	32.2	43	29	48.4	56.9
South West	27.6	23.9	42	32	62.3	67.9
East Anglia	29.4	25.7	31	11	57.2	63.8
South East	25.1	19.2	28	15	67.5	74.6
	1979	1986 UK	1979–82	1983–85 GB	1979	1986 UK
UK	31.4	24.3	GB 49	31	58.6	67.0

n.a. = not available
Sources: Martin (1986, 263); Central Statistical Office (1987, 100–1 and 106)

209

However, had it not been for the occupational restructuring of the previous several decades, the overall impact of the recession on employment in AA regions could well have been much worse.

As both manufacturing and service firms decentralised from the major towns and cities towards the urban fringe, rural areas and AA regions, they contributed to the diversification of employment in their destination areas. The loss of firms from urban areas, especially from inner cities, had significant repercussions on national policy, with the emphasis shifting from regional to urban assistance after the Labour Government published its White Paper on *Policy for the Inner Cities* in 1977 (see Section 10.2.2). As manufacturing and warehousing companies quit the conurbations for 'greener pastures', either to take advantage of government assistance or purely for their own business reasons, they left behind derelict land, deserted buildings and high unemployment – precisely the characteristics of so many AAs. The decade following Labour's White Paper saw a number of urban policy measures designed to mitigate some aspects of the growing divergence between cities and their regions, especially the Conservatives' *Local Government, Planning and Land Act* of 1980 (Section 10.2.3 below). The 'flight' of industry, and therefore employment, to the suburbs and beyond has been a feature of the constant spatial redistribution of industry since the turn of the last century, whether government-instigated or not. This process partially reflects the 'push' of inner cities: their congestion, lack of expansion space, deteriorating physical environment, high-wage unionised male labour, and high local authority rates; and partially the 'pull' of attractive and spacious accommodation, low rates, and low-wage non-unionised female labour in easily accessible locations in urban fringe or rural areas.

Ease of access is critical to the urban–rural shift of industry, both enabling and encouraging the relocation of firms and the consequent regional convergence towards diversified industrial structures. The history of technological revolutions propounded by Kondratieff (Table 1.1) not only concerns production technology improvements, but also transportation technology improvements. The transport 'revolutions' have dramatically increased the accessibility of labour, supplies and markets for industry. Coupled with the energy revolution, as measured by the 'ubiquity' of electricity supplies, this has enabled almost all types of industry to become far more 'footloose': they can locate virtually anywhere, and still have reliable, speedy, competitive access to raw materials and markets. While many of these transport improvements have occurred in response to the demands of industry and commerce, there are some which have been embarked upon by governments with the intention of facilitating other aspects of industrial policy. Such has been the case with Britain's motorway system and other infrastructural developments, which have been specifically intended to provide interregional connectivity and thus increase locational accessibility, especially of more peripheral regions in the North and West. At the same time, of course, the associated intra-regional improvements have made possible the expansion of industry and of commuter residences outside the old nodes of the transport system, the major industrial cities. So, while regional policy has *directly* encouraged industry to move from the more prosperous core regions of the South to the less prosperous peripheral regions of the North and West by government expenditure on investment incentives and the operation of IDC controls, 'infrastructural policy' expenditure has *indirectly* encouraged such moves by enhancing their feasibility and making them more attractive propositions for industry's decision makers.

9.2.2 Locational accessibility

Accepting that the bulk of goods move around Britain by road, one of the aims of government transport policy has been to improve the relative locations of peripheral areas *vis-à-vis* national economic space. This has been achieved principally through expenditure on the building of a motorway system and on the improvement (dualling, straightening, widening, resurfacing, etc.) of trunk and other major roads. The 1960s and 1970s especially saw a burst of investment in road transportation that in some ways paralleled that of the mid-nineteenth century in the railways, dramatically improving the capacity and speed of the system for the carriage of both goods and people. Indeed, the proportion of goods traffic carried on roads increased from just 60 per cent in 1960 to 80 per cent by the early 1980s, while the proportion of people travelling by private road transport over the same period increased from 56 per cent to 82 per cent (Fullerton, 1982, 359).

When the first motorway construction programme started in 1957, the depressed areas of the inter-war years were beginning to re-emerge as islands of unemployment, and this prompted acceleration of road schemes to and within the AAs. The Barlow Report (pp 119–21 above) had noted the necessity of improving the total infrastructure of any part of the country designated as an AA. It was not until the 1945 *Distribution of Industry Act*, however, that specific mention was made of the need for government policy to make provision for transport development in and to AAs in order to help make them more attractive to prospective industrialists. Until 1954, expenditure on major improvements to, and new construction of, trunk roads remained modest, with no particular emphasis on AAs. After that year government expenditure began to increase, and especially so after the national motorway plan was announced in 1957. This plan envisaged 1600 km of motorway and an additional 1600 km of dual carriageways being built by the early 1970s, with the prime purpose of linking the major industrial areas by the shortest possible network. Until 1963, however, regional policy largely ignored infrastructural development in AAs.

The National Economic Development Council published a report in 1963, entitled *Conditions Favourable to Foster Growth*, which recommended that spending on infrastructure in AAs, especially in support of growth centre development, should be increased in order to improve accessibility. This point was reiterated in the two White Papers of 1963, one for North East England and the other for Central Scotland (Section 6.1.3). Government expenditure on roads increased dramatically across the 1960s, from £32 million in 1958 to £417 million in 1973–4, and when the capital spending cuts were made in the late 1960s the AAs were exempted since their road schemes were seen as alleviating unemployment by helping to concentrate investment within them. In fact, until 1979, when public expenditure cuts in regional aid and transport really began in earnest, almost every government Act or White Paper relating to regional development stressed the need for continuing improvement in the road accessibility of AAs.

The roads built in the AAs during the 1960s were planned on the basis of generalized traffic flow information and on the belief that road construction is beneficial from the standpoint of industrial development. More sophisticated methods of assessing the need for, and the benefit-cost of, such road building were developed in the 1960s and influenced the programme after the middle of the decade. A comprehensive national strategic network of roads was proposed in 1969 and 1970. The intention was to eliminate congestion around conurbations, and to make a major contribution to industrial and regional development planning by 1982, with the construction of 3200 km of motorway and 2400 km of dual carriageway so that every town in the country of over 80,000 population would be within 16 km of such roads (Fullerton, 1982, 370). The urgency of these plans proved unfounded in the 1970s as population growth rate fell, national income declined and the price of fuel increased by five times. Consequently, the high-capacity road building programme had its share of total national transport investment cut from almost half in the early 1970s to about one-third by the mid-1970s and to less than one-fifth by the mid-1980s. The national strategic concept of such roads was abandoned in the late 1970s.

Between 1958 and 1985, some 2,850 km of trunk motorway were built (cf. 11,700 km of railway line built over a 25-year period, 1830–55), and over 5,000 km of dual carriageway and local authority motorway were constructed or improved. By 1985, therefore, only Aberdeen and Norwich of the major industrial cities remained more than 16 km from such roads. Certainly as far as AAs were concerned, their locational accessibility improved dramatically over the period 1958–85, except for their more remote rural parts. So, the construction of the motorway system has improved market access for the more peripheral areas at the national scale, and has widened the labour catchment areas of industries locating near the system at the more local scale. From the industrialist's viewpoint, the question is whether the improved accessibility of factory sites within AAs has lowered transport costs and thereby increased competitiveness, or indeed whether transport costs from periphery to core (and EEC) markets are particularly significant in total production costs anyway.

Government transport infrastructure investment discriminated in favour of AAs during the 1960s, and there is evidence to suggest that the resultant improved accessibility was a major factor (second only to government grants) influencing the decision of firms to locate in such peripheral areas (Keeble, 1976, 82). Without this government discrimination, there is no doubt that economic forces would have encouraged the concentration of such investment in the central regions along the axis from London to Birmingham, within the London – Leeds – Manchester – Bristol quadrilateral. In many respects this happened anyway, with government policy emphasis largely ensuring that the traditional AAs in the periphery were linked into this central 'box' system. The high accessibility within the central regions afforded by the transport network has enhanced their manufacturing innovation rates by facilitating frequent inter-personal contacts, thus contributing to external economies of agglomeration. This central box zone contains only one-third of the land area of England and Wales but two-thirds of the total connectivity of the high-capacity road network, national accessibility advantage seconded by the centrality of the railway system and the central zone supporting functions of seaports and airports.

It would seem that as long as the AAs are at least *linked* to the trunk road transport network, then transport costs are not likely to be a major deterrent to industrialists willing to locate in them. British Leyland did argue in 1973 that by operating in AAs rather than in more central areas over the period 1966–71 they had incurred additional transport costs of £2.4 million (Lee, 1980, 14). However, most of the industry that has been attracted to AAs has been of the smaller, footloose, high-value-added type, whose transport costs usually account for less than 2 per cent of total production costs and less than 1 per cent of sales value (Slowe, 1981, 80–81). Figures such as these help to explain why manufacturing industry was able to expand rapidly in fairly remote, relatively inaccessible, rural areas of Scotland, East Anglia and the South West during the 1960s and 1970s, while massive investment in new roads in such highly accessible urban areas as Central Scotland and North East England was unable to achieve the same objective (Fothergill *et al.*, 1985, 14). Obviously, factors other than just transport costs and accessibility must be responsible for such a dichotomy, particularly type of industry and labour availability and cost. Nevertheless, improved transportation has certainly contributed to the decentralisation of industry from older urban centres.

Transport improvements continue to enhance the potential for new manufacturing developments in the core regions relative to peripheral regions by facilitating personal contacts, improving innovation possibilities and further increasing national and international accessibility, a good example of Myrdal's 'circular and cumulative causation' (Keeble, 1976, 59). (See pp 96–7 above). With the cutbacks in public expenditure from the mid-1970s, and especially in the early 1980s, the motoway programme slowed substantially, and priority was given to completion of the M25 orbital motorway in order to ease congestion in London. The South East, therefore, received the lion's share of national transport infrastructure expenditure during the 1980s. The European Regional Development Fund continued to be biased in favour of peripheral regions, however, with Scotland receiving 21 per cent, Wales 17 per cent, the North 16 per cent and the North West 12 per cent of the £2.1 billion made available for infrastructural projects (predominantly transport, but including other types of infrastructure) between 1975 and 1988. No aid was provided by the ERDF for the South East and East Anglia, and very little for the South West.

Major road construction programmes in particular remain tangible examples of central government concern for regional development in the periphery, and specific projects have on occasion had rather obvious association with political objectives, e.g. approval of the Humber Bridge in 1966 on the eve of crucial by-elections in Humberside (Hoare, 1983, 84). In general, of course, improvements in transport technology, coupled with advances in telecommunications, have been continually occurring this century and have contributed to substantial changes in the relative locations of places, some positively and some negatively. Such change occurs irrespective of government regional policy, and some AAs would have declined as their resource base shrank regardless of their level of accessibility. Nevertheless, government policy with respect to transport provision in AAs has meant that the paucity of such facilities could never be identified as having resulted in

213

an area's lack of growth or absolute decline – the 'transport stimulates industry' argument was at least tried in practice!

9.2.3 Environmental improvement

During the nineteenth and early twentieth centuries very little concern was expressed by either industry or government about the deleterious impact of industrialisation on the environment. Such environmental degradation was to be seen in a wide variety of guises, from old mine workings and spoil heaps to cramped and unsanitary homes and factories, and in the pollution of ground, air and water. In the early years of regional policy, funds were not made available directly for environmental improvements but rather indirectly, via the job creation that such schemes as water and sewerage services, derelict site clearance, slag heap removal and park construction afforded. Indeed, of the £21 million spent or committed to AAs by 1938, 60 per cent had been directed toward improving such physical and social amenities (Lee, 1980, 35). Little employment was created by these measures, but some improvement took place in the physical environment of AAs. The War brought a halt to such programmes and the reclamation and improvement of derelict land in particular had to wait until the 1945 *Distribution of Industry Act* before it appeared as a policy aim.

The intention of the 1945 Act was to make AAs more attractive to prospective industrialists and at the same time improve the amenities, and therefore the public morale, of such areas. The power to improve social services and reclaim derelict land rested with the Board of Trade and this power was increased by the *Local Employment Act* of 1960. During the 1960s it was considered by government that environmental improvement was one means of encouraging industrial growth, and in the *Industrial Development Act* of 1966 local authorities were allowed grants covering 85 per cent of the cost of derelict land clearance. The scale of the problem was enormous, with over 34,000 ha of land defined as derelict in the mid-1960s, almost 71 per cent of which was located in the less prosperous northern regions (Manners, 1980, 35) (see Figs. 9.2 and 9.3). The *Hunt Report* (1969) identified the improvement of a decayed or inadequate environment as of positive benefit to an AA seeking to attract new industry, and in that year local authorities were allowed 75 per cent of the capital costs of clearing derelict land for industrial development. Funding for such schemes was derived by removing the 37.5 p SEP premium payable in DAs for each man per week (Lee, 1980, 83) (see p. 144 above).

Experience gained through identifying and funding derelict land clearance areas during the 1960s, and the fact that not all areas of dereliction were located in AAs, prompted a reappraisal in 1970. The key change was the creation of *Derelict Land Clearance Areas* (DLCAs). The majority of these Areas were in AA regions. In addition to the capital grant available for reclamation projects, the DLCAs outside AAs were made eligible for the 20 per cent buildings grant for a two-year period following the *Industry Act* of 1972. Shortly after this Act, surveys of derelict land showed that over 43,000 ha could be so classified in England, over 18,500 ha in Scotland and 14,000 ha in Wales, with at least as much again classifiable as 'despoiled'. Between the 1972 Act and the return of a Conservative government in 1979,

Figure 9.2   Assisted Areas and Derelict Land Clearance Areas in England, 1984.
Source: Department of the Environment (1986, 38)

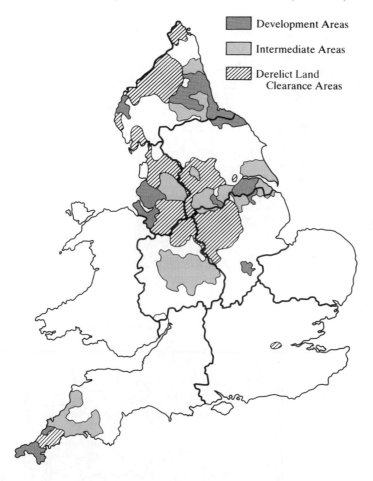

some 15,000 ha had been restored in England, 5,000 ha in Scotland and 2,300 ha in Wales, mostly of spoil heaps and surface excavation sites (Hanna, 1982, 272–3; see also Moss, 1981). Priority began to switch from old mining and industrial areas towards inner city area restoration during the 1970s. The latter included clearance of urban blight and creation of sites for housing, industry and public open space, and also programmes of steam-cleaning public buildings (town halls, parish churches, libraries, etc.) to improve the visual, aesthetic attractiveness of town centres. All this was in recognition of the fact that urban blight and despoiled countryside are con-ducive neither to a reduction in the numbers of firms and people moving away from an area, nor to an increase in the number of firms moving in. The general view was that an area's economic development prospects should be enhanced by the creation of an attractive physical environment. (See Chapman, 1980; Burgess, 1982.)

215

Figure 9.3   Distribution of derelict land in England per county, 1982.
Source: Department of the Environment (1986, 10)

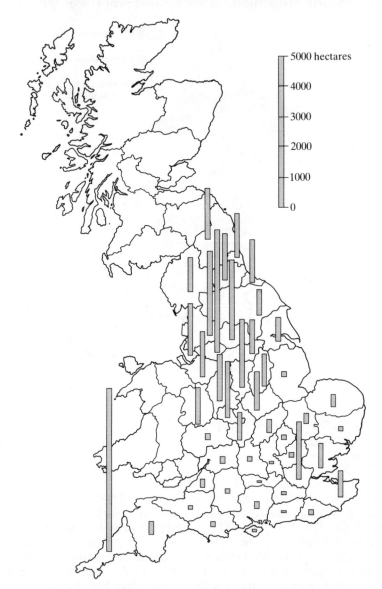

Central government has continued to support the reclamation of derelict
land and general environmental improvements in the 1980s. The crucial
piece of legislation was the *Derelict Land Act* of 1982. Within the AAs and
the DCLAs in England (Fig. 9.2), local authorities and the English Industrial
Estates Corporation are eligible for 100 per cent grants to cover approved
costs, while individuals, companies, public utilities and nationalised industries (e.g. the National Coal Board) qualify for 80 per cent grants. These

grants also apply to Scotland and Wales, where they are administered by the respective Development Agencies, directly in the former case and through local authorities in the latter (Department of Trade and Industry, 1983, 13). Outside the designated areas the grant rate is 50 per cent, except that in national parks and Areas of Outstanding Natural Beauty (Fig. 4.1) local authorities are eligible for 75 per cent grants.

One of the procedures associated with the Derelict Land Act was a survey of the derelict land in England in 1982, and its classification into five categories. The distribution of derelict land of a county basis is shown in Fig. 9.3, where there is a striking visual correlation between the thousands of derelict hectares in a county and that county's industrial heritage. Hence, the counties of the North and the Midlands, plus Cornwall, have the largest areas of dereliction, thanks primarily to old mineral workings and spoil heaps but also to deserted gas works, power stations and factories in urban areas, an overall pattern that would be repeated in Scotland and Wales. The derelict hectares in Greater London, Essex and Kent are mainly sand and gravel workings and, especially in London, urban blight. The different types of dereliction are identified in Table 9.4.

The total amount of derelict land in England in 1982 was 45,683 ha, half of it in the three northernmost regions – North, North West, Yorkshire/Humberside – with the North West alone accounting for 22 per cent of England's total (Department of the Environment, 1986, 11). In 1974 the total amount of derelict land was 43,273 ha. The 1982 total therefore indicates a 'dereliction gain' of 2,410 ha, but this is a net figure since 17,000 ha were restored between 1974 and 1982. Consequently, 'new' dereliction was growing at a faster rate (2,425 ha per year) than restoration (2,125 ha per year)! Since the 1982 Act, only 1,300 ha of derelict land have been restored annually, at a cost per hectare of £30,000 in 1984/5 but of over £50,000 in 1987/8. Although the total budgetary allocation for derelict land restoration in England rose from £74 million in 1984/5 to £83 million in 1986/7 and £81 million in 1987/8, it is not enough even to keep pace with 'new' dereliction, let alone clear all the 'eyesores' of our industrial past! Such central government expenditure was of the same order of magnitude, however, as Regional Selective Assistance up to April 1988. Spatially, it has focused predominantly on AAs and DLCAs in northern and western regions, because of their environmental legacy of coal mining, stone quarrying, and iron and steel smelting, not to mention cotton and woollen mills, shipyards and railways. Its effects are certainly regionally selective, but they are not as readily measurable as those of RSA spending.

In the last two chapters, we have discussed in some detail the known and measurable effects of regional and urban policies, in so far as they are separable from other economic factors affecting the fortunes of an area. The various original studies that we have used as source material have all added to our knowledge of the direct impact of policies, and many of them have probably influenced policy advisers at government level. Analyses of policy effects which are currently underway will no doubt similarly influence the thinking about appropriate shifts in emphases in the 1990s. In particular, of course, there is considerable interest in the effects of the policy changes introduced early in 1988, which in turn were influenced by research on policy

Table 9.4 The distribution of different categories of derelict land in England, 1982

Region	Spoil heaps	Excavation and pits	Military etc. dereliction	Derelict railway land	Other forms of dereliction*	Total
North	1,872	1,043	168	1,375	2,849	7,307
North West	2,012	1,381	398	1,648	4,603	10,042
Yorkshire/Humberside	1,070	1,433	385	1,428	1,115	5,431
West Midlands	2,174	917	330	875	1,491	5,787
East Midlands	1,225	1,258	644	1,339	732	5,198
East Anglia	15	305	251	170	63	804
South West	4,870	420	208	820	317	6,635
South East (ex. G.L.)	57	1,439	268	374	387	2,525
Greater London	45	382	364	181	982	1,954
Total for England	13,340	8,578	3,016	8,210	12,539	45,683

* e.g. disused gas works, factories, etc.
Source: Department of the Environment (1986, 11)

costs and effects covering the late 1970s/early 1980s. It will be several years before such studies appear in print. In the meantime, interest continues in not only the *effects* of previous policies, but also in their *effectiveness* – given the policy effects of factories and jobs created, moved or saved, what has been the cost to the Exchequer (and, therefore, to the taxpayer) of the different policy instruments used to achieve these ends? As a nation, is the UK getting 'value for money' in terms of central government expenditure on regional and urban policy: economically, are the benefits matching or exceeding the costs; if not, then are 'excessive' costs at least warranted by any social benefits in AAs and inner cities? The answers to such questions are open to political as much as socio-economic interpretation, but attempts have been made to determine policy effectiveness from an economic standpoint, and these we will discuss in the next chapter.

10 Policy effectiveness

In the first part of this book we looked at the historical background to regional and urban problems in the United Kingdom and endeavoured to place the sequence of events within the time framework of Kondratieff's Long Waves of economic development. In the second part of the book we have presented in considerable detail the actual policies adopted by successive governments in attempting to find solutions to the spatial problems wrought by industrial change, and we have identified the major effects that such policies have had, principally in terms of employment. The question that remains concerns the *effectiveness* of policies, and although it is a question that should be addressed by any government before embarking on new or modified policies, until recently relatively little information was available about the costs and benefits of policy instruments. As a consequence, governments have tended to identify what are believed to be the key factors in regional or urban 'distress' in the circumstances of the time and have then formulated expedient policies accordingly (Sant, 1982, 10).

10.1 Effectiveness of regional policy

While there may be political 'mileage' to be gained from the creation of jobs in Assisted Areas, at the end of the day a government needs to know the *net cost* of such jobs in monetary terms if budgetary limits are to be observed. The cost to the Exchequer is therefore one of the prime determinants of policy effectiveness, but it is also one that is very difficult to measure with any accuracy, especially since the objectives of regional policy have never been quantified. Regional policy facts and figures might give the impresssion of precision, but in reality they are approximations, usually expressed within quite a wide range of values. For example, whilst each new job created by regional policy in AAs cost the Exchequer £40,000 on average (1960–81 period, at 1982 prices), the range between industries was from £367,000 per job in metal manufacture to £10,000 per job in the clothing industry in the decade 1966–76 (Moore et al., 1986, 10–11). Interestingly, in the mid-1980s the Nissan car assembly plant in North East England received £100 million in RDGs which averaged out at £40,000 per job created.

Attempts to estimate the performance of regional policy have tended to examine both effects and effectiveness, with more emphasis upon the former, largely because they are more objectively measurable, but also because the latter involves the subjectivity of political interpretation. (See Parsons, 1986, 171–81.) Until the mid-1970s, however, few attempts were made to evaluate regional policies, least of all by those government departments actually administering them. In fact, in 1974 the Expenditure

220

Committee of the House of Commons published a report which was critical of the lack of monitoring procedures to determine policy practice and effectiveness. The Committee concluded: 'Much has been spent and much may well have been wasted. Regional policy has been empiricism run mad, a game of hit-and-miss, played with more enthusiasm than success . . . . We regret that . . . efforts have not been better sustained by the proper evaluation of the costs and benefits of the policies pursued' (House of Commons, 1974, Ch. 12, Para 170). Since 1974 much research has been completed in efforts to evaluate properly policy costs and benefits. Most of it covered the period of more active policy from the early 1960s to the middle 1970s and was concerned primarily with trying to measure the impact of policy on manufacturing employment, manufacturing investment and industrial movement. These detailed studies, many of which we have drawn upon in the previous four chapters, benefited from the substantial improvement in the availability of regional statistics from the mid-1970s onwards.

Assessing the effectiveness of regional policy has been of considerable significance since 1979, when the Conservatives took office, because since then government spending on regional aid has been cut and some policy instruments phased out. Indeed, 1979 has been seen as marking the end of the Keynesian era of major central government intervention at the regional level (see p. 92 above). Given the perceived necessity to reduce government spending levels, there has been a desire to know just how cost-effective regional policy was, since this would help determine modifications to the policy instruments. Criticism of these instruments, therefore, is part of an evaluation procedure, especially when it identifies their cost-effectiveness on a job creation basis, but there are a number of other economic factors that affect the overall effectiveness of regional policy. In Section 10.1.1 we will evaluate the policy instruments and in Section 10.1.2 consider these other factors.

10.1.1 An evaluation of policy instruments

Investment incentives (RDGs, etc)
Financial assistance to firms in, and those willing to move into, AAs has been a main feature of regional policy since 1934. Such assistance has taken the form of grants and tax allowances towards the expenses of buildings and of plant and machinery. However, *Regional Development Grants*, the most important policy instrument, have been criticised on a number of grounds, particularly that:

1. They have treated all types of industry in similar fashion, disregarding the growth prospects of specific industries in certain regions.
2. They have been biased towards capital-intensive industries, which has meant that few jobs were created and many of those that were comprised low-paid assembly work for women.
3. They were paid automatically in blanket fashion, rather than on a discretionary basis linked to specific projects, so that firms within AAs qualified as well as those moving in from more prosperous areas – in fact, indigenous firms received more aid in total than did in-migrating firms.
4. They did not differentiate between recipients on the basis of job creation (see point 2. above), but rather assumed that *any* 'new' jobs were

221

beneficial to AAs, regardless of whether they were genuinely 'new' and thus available to the local unemployment, or simply relocated from other regions (if the latter, of course, there was no net *national* gain in employment).

5. They did not differentiate between firms that were closely tied to the local AA economy and those that had greater linkage with headquarters or other firms in more prosperous areas, so that there was inevitable 'leakage' of government aid to non-AA regions (this was especially so with production branch plants of firms in AAs whose headquarters were in London or the South East).

6. They were modified so frequently by both Labour and Conservative governments that industrialists became frustrated and found long-term planning very difficult.

With such a list of criticisms, it is perhaps not too surprising that RDGs were ended as a policy instrument in March 1988!

The question of relating investment incentives to job creation was more directly addressed by the *Regional Selective Assistance* programme, introduced in 1972. Between 1960 and 1981 RDGs created over 300,000 jobs in the AAs, about two-thirds of the total number of net jobs, while between 1972 and 1981 RSA generated over 40,000 jobs. Largely because of the blanket coverage of RDG assistance, its gross Exchequer cost per job (1981) amounted of £25,000, whereas RSA incentives, at £17,000 per job, were much more cost-effective (Moore *et al.*, 1986, 43). Since RSA was made available to firms in a variety of ways it is very difficult to identify which elements of the incentives were most effective. Indeed, the emphasis on particular elements of RSA changed from year to year, as is shown in Table 10.1.

Table 10.1 United Kingdom: expenditure on Regional Selective Assistance at current prices, selected years 1973/4 to 1981/2.

Financial year	Loans equity (%)	Capital expenditure grants (%)	Interest relief grants (%)	Office and service industry grants (%)	Removal grants (%)	Training grants (%)
1973/4	90.2	0	8.8	0	1.0	0
1975/6	64.7	6.6	24.7	1.6	2.4	0
1978/9	6.8	1.1	87.5	3.0	1.6	0
1981/2	0	46.0	46.8	5.3	0.6	1.3

Source: Calculated from Table 3.3 in Moore *et al.* (1986b, 27)

In 1984 the separate *Office and Service Industry Scheme* (OSIS) was merged with the loans and grants element. During its lifetime (1973–83), OSIS accounted for less than 7% of all regional financial assistance, but did provide aid for job creation in service industries (about 40,000 jobs in the commercial, distributive and professional sectors) ranging from £2,500 per job in IAs to £8,000 per job in SDAs. In SDAs, OSIS assistance was 5.8

per cent of the total financial assistance and this generated 5.2 per cent of the total number of new jobs; in DAs the figures were 11.3 per cent of the aid and 7.2 per cent of the jobs; in IAs they were 7.6 per cent and 8.5 per cent (Daniels, 1986, 315). The interest in, and knowledge about, this scheme was rather limited, however, and its effectiveness is difficult to gauge.

The overall cost effectiveness of RSA, once demonstrated, began to in- fluence regional policy emphasis, especially following the Conservative Government's 1983 reappraisal of policy measures and the stated desire to see 'better value for money' from spending on regional assistance. During the·1970s RSA expenditure only accounted for 7 per cent of total annual regional spending; it increased to 10 per cent in the early 1980s, to 16 per cent in 1985/6 (see Table 8.3, p. 177) and to 44 per cent following the policy change in 1988. However, RSA's increasing proportion of regional expenditure occurred at the same time as regional policy decreased in its importance as a public spending priority – its proportion of GDP exceeded 0.5 per cent in 1970, but fell to 0.25 per cent in the early 1980s, and to only about 0.12 per cent by 1984 (Armstrong and Taylor, 1985). Balchin and Bull (1987, 58) comment that, 'Although in the 1960s regional policy was intended as a means of stimulating national economic growth, by the mid-1980s it was ful- filling little more than a residual role'. Indeed, they argue that the 'residualization of regional policy' was 'very probably a cause' of increased divergence of regional economies, especially that of the West Midlands, and point to regional GDP, unemployment and redundancy figures in the early 1980s as evidence (see Tables 8.1, p. 171 and 9.3, p. 209).

The reduction of automatic RDG payments after the 1983 review, and their demise altogether in 1988, occurred partly because the Conservative Government wished to reduce general spending on regional assistance (espe- cially where this appeared to involve subsidies to capital-intensive industry) and partly because such automatic payments had been demonstrated to be much less cost-effective than selective assistance. The cost per job diverted to AAs in the late 1970s to early 1980s amounted to £40,000 according to Gudgin *et al.* (1983) and they estimated that a 'cost-per-job limit' on RDGs would release £200 million annually for other types of programme. The Government believed that RDGs had been too capital-intensive in their ap- plication and had not been adequately linked to job creation, hence the cost-per-job ceiling introduced in 1984. (See Section 7.1.4) There was particular concern over the excessive costs of policy-created jobs in some industries (e.g. £367,000 per job in metal manufacturing, 1966–76 (Moore *et al.*, 1986, 65) and over grants to projects which would have occurred in specific AAs anyway (e.g. oil-related construction projects in Scotland). Regional policy emphasis therefore switched from an RDG-bias to an RSA-bias in 1984, despite the fact that half the companies in AAs claimed that RDGs were critical to their investment decisions (Rhodes, 1986, 166). The switch-over to RSA and other investment incentives was completed in 1988 (see p. 157 above), but clearly it will be some time before we are able to estimate the effectiveness of the 1988 change in regional policy emphasis.

Labour subsidies
Introduced in 1966 (the *Selective Employment Premium* – SEP) and 1967 (the *Regional Employment Premium* – REP), these subsidies were paid at a

flat rate for all employees (Section 8.1.3 above). Initially, reactions to the REP, in particular, were favourable, since it helped to compensate for lower productivity in AAs and had the effect of making labour cheaper there than in non-AAs, but criticisms soon emerged. In 1974 the REP rates were doubled in order to take account of inflation. This made the programme so expensive that it soaked up 33 per cent of the total direct Exchequer costs of regional policy (cf. 45 per cent on investment grants and RDGs) and it was therefore phased out in 1976/7 (1977/8 in Northern Ireland). The net employment creation of the REP over the period 1966 to 1981 was about 30,000 jobs, at a gross Exchequer cost per job (1981 prices) of £73,000, making it the least cost-effective of the policy instruments so far discussed. Other criticisms of the REP were that it was available to all manufacturing establishments in the AAs (as with RDGs) 'whether new or old, expanding or contracting, progressive or asleep' (Moore and Rhodes, 1976a, 218), and that it possibly encouraged firms to retain a higher labour/capital ratio than economic efficiency would dictate, thereby subsidising inefficient firms when other policy measures were encouraging higher capital/labour ratios.

Employment subsidies supported the industrial *status quo*: they did not address fundamental questions concerning the appropriateness of *labour quality* for emerging types of industrial development. The 'appropriate' ratio of labour to capital in manufacturing industry is constantly in a state of flux, varying from one type of industry to another at a point in time, and similarly varying within any one industry through time. A major feature of manufacturing industries in general, over the last couple of decades and currently, has been that of a 'de-skilling' process – capital has tended to increase at labour's expense (via the application of advanced manufacturing technology to the production process). This has been especially so in traditional industries, so the demand for traditional skills has declined. (See Beacham, 1984) 'New, industries, and updated 'old' ones, require fewer people to produce a given output. This helps to increase productivity, but the jobs previously done by skilled workers can now be done by machines tended by semi-skilled or unskilled workers, hence a 'de-skilling' of the workforce. Regionally within the UK this process is of considerable significance, since almost all the traditional manufacturing industries are located in northern and western regions. The workforce in these regions, therefore, has had disproportionate adjustment problems compared with southern regions. However, the labour quality issue, which is critical to the assessment of any labour subsidy programme's effectiveness, has national implications.

The demand is increasing for people who are technical specialists, both at the research and development (R&D) level and at the problem-solving ('trouble-shooting') level in the production process. Such individuals require particular skills, and the UK is lagging behind other industrial countries in the appropriate *education and training* (Section 8.1.4 above). Of British leavers in the mid 1980s, 25 per cent finish school without any qualifications, compared with 14 per cent in the USA and just 4 per cent in Japan. Beyond school, only 31 per cent of the 16–24-year old age group in the UK are in full-time education and training, whereas the proportions are 45 per cent in West Germany, 54 per cent in Japan and 73 per cent in the USA. In the UK, the number of manufacturing apprenticeships declined from 155,000 in 1979 to 73,000 in 1985, and the number of trainees of all kinds fell from 266,300 in 1979 to 112,400 in 1985. This is reflected in the limited amount of money spent on training by British companies, especially engineering, when compared with the international competition – less than 0.15 per cent of their annual turnover in the mid-1980s, as against an average of 2.0 per cent in the EEC and 3.0 per cent in the USA. Unfortunately, the paucity of training opportunities within Britain's engineering industry is not compensated by a wealth of recruits from universities and polytechnics, since the UK has been producing only 207 engineer graduates annually per 1 million population during the 1980s, while the USA has been turning out 350 and Japan 630.

There is little doubt that Britain's lack of trained technologists has been a factor of major significance in the country's precipitous economic decline. Sadly, compounding this poor training record has been the unwillingness of British industry to spend on *R&D* at appropriate levels, which in turn has limited the demand for more highly trained scientists and technologists. Apart from a slight increase in the late 1970s to early 1980s, the UK has committed only about 1.5 per cent of its GNP to non-defence R & D per year since 1970; between 1978–80 and 1985–87 the other major industrial nations improved their commitment considerably – France from 1.4 per cent to 1.9 per cent; the USA from 1.6 per cent to 1.9 per cent; West Germany from 2.0 per cent to 2.6 per cent, and Japan from 2.0 per cent to 2.8 per cent (National Science Foundation, 1988). The resultant states of the respective national economies speak for themselves. There are regional differences in training and R&D expenditures, as any issue of *Regional Trends* (Central Statistical Office) will attest, but any perceived problems are approached nationally rather than regionally in policy terms, and their effectiveness probably cannot be determined in the short run.

Infrastructural investments

In addition to the £18 billion (at 1982 prices) spent on investment incentives and labour subsidies within the framework of regional policy between 1960 and 1981, national governments spent a further £3 billion on Advance Factory building and Trading Estates, road construction, derelict land clearance and so on. In the early 1970s, the *Advance Factory* programme accounted for 13 per cent of total regional assistance, but by the early 1980s the proportion had increased to almost 20 per cent, reflecting the anticipated demand for numerous small factory units (Section 8.1.2 above). The net cost to the Exchequer of such factory building is quite low, however, because of the receipts from renting out the units. Indeed, in a survey of the Wales Standard Planning Region, Slowe (1981, 222) found that the capital cost per job was about £15,000 but that annual rentals of 22.7 per cent of the capital cost returned to the Exchequer, so that an Advance Factory paid for itself over $5\frac{1}{2}$ years, while a further year's rental covered administrative costs and the opportunity cost of capital investment. Hence the cost per job was zero, which would make this programme *the* most cost-effective of all forms of regional assistance! It is difficult to criticise a scheme which 'creates' jobs at no apparent cost to the national purse, but it could be argued that there is room for improvement in co-ordinating the Advance Factory programme with other elements of regional assistance, and in building more quickly in AAs of greater demand.

The question of co-ordination between infrastructural programmes and

AA investment incentive schemes is more critical with respect to the *road building and improvement* programmes (Section 9.2.2 above). In particular, government spending on these programmes in the past did not differentiate between relative levels of regional need, and the co-ordination of infrastructural spending with other policy instruments was not as comprehensive as it could have been. In general, therefore, there has been an imbalance of timing and magnitude between the support given to firms moving into AAs (which it was hoped would both create employment *and* alter the industrial structure of a region, thus improving its competitiveness) and the amount spent on infrastructural improvements (which should help solve some of a region's problems of locational and environmental disadvantage and increase its comparative advantage, at least domestically). Achievement of a high level of co-ordination between different government departments with different budgetary structures and constraints is probably unrealistic, since a radical re-organisation of the way in which central government deals with national expenditure would be required in order to place public spending largely within a regionally defined framework of the national economy. However, public spending cuts in the 1980s have meant a reduction in the planned regional development of the infrastructure, an unfortunately short-sighted policy, if indeed such development is critical to the success of private enterprise, especially in the more peripheral regions (Balchin and Bull, 1987, 53).

The cost-effectiveness of the policy instruments noted above is only providing us with one side of regional policy evaluation, however, since no consideration has been given to the effect of negative controls in the more prosperous areas.

Industrial Development Certificates
In operation between 1948 and 1982, the IDC scheme varied in the stringency of its application according to government policy at the time (Section 8.1.2 above). In order to appreciate more fully the effectiveness of policies *encouraging* firms to move into AAs, it is essential to assess the role played by policies *discouraging* firms from building or expanding in more prosperous areas. The Exchequer cost of IDCs was minimal, since they were simple to operate and only involved minor administrative expense, so that the scheme was apparently the most *cost-effective instrument of regional policy* (excluding Advance Factories), although there were other real costs.

The effectiveness of IDCs has to be evaluated on the basis of the number of jobs *not* created in the more prosperous regions (the South East and the Midlands) because of the refusal there of a Certificate. Overall, such refusals appear to have had the effect of directly stopping job growth in the non-assisted regions by 13,600 per year 1950–80 (*i.e.* over 400,000 total), and of indirectly discouraging many other firms from even applying for IDCs (assuming they would be refused), with a consequent further job 'loss' in growth regions. In theory, it was envisaged that firms refused IDCs in non-AAs would build their new capacity in AAs. In practice, there was no guarantee that this would happen, since projects for expansion could be shelved, delayed or moved abroad, especially if the company refused permission to build was a multinational. These alternative responses represented a real cost to the national economy in terms of investment, jobs and industrial capacity, but it has been argued that the deterrent effect of IDC controls was overestimated (Balchin and Bull, 1987, 51). On a positive note, IDCs had generated 74,000 manufacturing jobs in AAs by 1981, compared with the 307,000 of RDGs, the 42,000 of RSA and the 27,000 of REP (see Table 8.5, p. 189 above).

The intensity of IDC refusals, expressed as a percentage of refusals plus approvals, varied considerably throughout the three decades of operation, as we noted above (Section 8.1.2). Generally speaking, in times of national economic growth, the IDC control would seem to be fairly effective in redistributing some employment between regions. During recessions, however, when every region becomes desperate for investment and jobs, the risk of slowing down investment or causing it to be transferred overseas becomes too great, and IDCs are therefore a liability.

While it is very tempting to place considerable emphasis on the apparent cost-effectiveness of each regional policy instrument, it is well to remember that investment incentives on the one hand and industrial development controls on the other hand actually reinforce each other and are not totally independent variables. As a consequence, any attempt to assess the 'precise' *effect* and *effectiveness* of any individual policy measure can only really be expressed as an order of magnitude and not as a set of absolute facts and figures. Furthermore, in addition to the interrelatedness of the various policy instruments, their individual and combined impact on the national space economy is much influenced by a variety of other factors and conditions.

10.1.2 Other influences upon regional policy effectiveness

In our earlier discussion of the sequence of policy measures and of their effects (Chapters 6 to 9), an underlying theme was that the range of policies, their intensity of use and their cost to the Exchequer varied both between different governments and even within the period of office of any one political party. Since one of the principal aims of government policy is to send 'signals' to the business community which are indicative of the direction in which a government wishes to steer the national economy, the clearer and simpler the signals, the better! However, regional policy in the UK has been characterised by frequent changes in the types, values and geographical spread of various incentives and controls, and a failure by successive governments to specify goals clearly, with the result that we have seen only limited time periods of any consistent application of policy (Section 10.1.1 above). This has all been disconcerting to the decision maker in business, causing uncertainty and hindering development planning, especially over the longer term. (See Burgess, 1982; Green, 1977; Hoare, 1981)

The situation was particularly complex during the period 1966–77, when labour subsidies were being paid to encourage firms in AAs to hold on to their workforce whilst at the same time capital subsidies were being paid to encourage firms to improve their capital/labour ratio, and consequently their productivity and competitiveness, by modernising equipment. In more general terms, every industrialist is well aware of the fact that regional policy will almost certainly undergo major transformation just before and just after an election, even if the same political party is returned for a further period in office, so that forward planning cannot place too much reliance upon the availability or not of government subsidies. In fact, recent research indicates that prior to its demise in 1988 the RDG was perceived by industrialists as the most predictable capital subsidy in terms of the amount of grant available and its operational simplicity, and consequently it had greater influence than other forms of assistance on companies throughout their decision making process about new investment (Allen *et al.*, 1985).

The effectiveness of regional policy depends to a considerable extent upon the range, amount and spatial availability of assistance which, in turn, reflect the political philosophy of the party in power. However, the range and intensity of policy measures are also influenced by the prevailing economic conditions of the nation at the time. (See Parsons, 1986) All governments endeavour to act 'in the national interest' and regional policy is but one element in a wide range of policies affecting the nation's economy. Unfortunately, as we noted in Chapters 6 and 7, regional and sub-regional problems tend to show themselves most forcibly at times of national economic distress – the areas which are structurally and/or locationally disadvantaged have been the first into a recession and the last out. It is during times of economic stringency, therefore, that governments wish to be seen 'doing something' to help the poorer regions, for socio-political rather than purely economic reasons, but it is difficult to raise the necessary cash and to convince industrialists of the need to move and/or expand at such times. During times of prosperity, when the Treasury's coffers are fuller and industrialists' profit margins are wider and they are thinking of expansion, the gap between the poorer and better-off regions does not seem so great, consequently, the problems not so acute and their solutions so vote-catching, so at a time when the nation can perhaps best afford to tackle the root causes of regional imbalance there is little incentive to do so. As the Expenditure Committee Report concluded in 1973, '. . . governments should pursue regional policies with the greatest intensity precisely when growth of the economy makes disparities less obvious' (quoted in Lee, 1980, 119).

It is also worth noting at this juncture that national government is not alone in trying to aid companies or industries in difficulty, and in trying to attract firms into particular areas – so are local authorities, both inside and outside AAs. For example, when mid-Wales lost its grant aid status in 1984, central government assistance was replaced by a virtually identical local package: rent-free periods of up to two years on most new factory units; a small firms wages subsidy that provided 30 per cent of basic pay for six months for all jobs created, and discretionary cash grants for 'attractive' projects. As in the national situation, however, during times of economic growth, the influence of local authority assistance on the location decisions of business is probably limited, but during slow growth, stagnation or decline, every local authority is as anxious as the next to attempt at least to preserve its own industrial (and ratable) base. Where the local authorities are within designated AAs, then any assistance they can offer will be additional to nationally funded regional aid. Where they are outside AAs, then unless their actions are restricted by central government they can act relatively independently, even in contradiction to government policy. Over time, therefore, and especially during periods of 'passive' regional policy, *local* authorities 'can' act in a manner detrimental to the effectiveness of *national* regional policy.

10.1.3 Cost-benefit approach to regional policy evaluation

There is one fundamental issue which underlies any attempt to evaluate the effectiveness of regional policy. It can be expressed simply as the question, 'Would the money spent on *regional* aid have yielded greater benefits had it been spent at the national scale?' Of course, the 'benefits' are not of a purely economic nature; in reality they form part of an economic-political-social complex. Nevertheless, the question of whether the nation has achieved a net economic 'benefit' from the 'cost' of public money expenditure must be asked. The answer can be sought at two scales, the regional and the national.

At the *regional* scale, economists have not yet developed a sufficiently detailed and sophisticated analysis of all the necessary data over a long enough time period to allow accurate cost-benefit analysis. In general terms, however, the evidence of much higher numbers of people in work in the assisted regions compared with what would probably have been the case without regional assistance, as we discussed in Chapter 8, could be indicative of a positive benefit-cost ratio. At the *national* scale there is sufficient information now available to indicate the macro-economic impact of employment diversion from one region to another. Similarly, more is known of the income effects of regional policy instruments raising the demand for labour in AAs: firms reduce prices or employ more labour and thus raise total wages, although some of the extra demand will occur in non-AAs. Such additional employment in AAs, and the associated increases in output and income, are the principal benefits of regional policy measures. Indeed, if successful, regional policy should make possible tax reductions, meaning that all tax-payers in the country would see an increase in their disposable income because the labour-diversion effect was greater than the income effect in the more prosperous regions. This is complicated, however, by the effects of labour migration (usually from AAs to non-AAs in search of work) and by the effects of the balance of payments (usually because the increased output has not been able to secure adequate export growth, as has been the case since 1974). It is only where regional policy measures are capable of relaxing any balance of payments constraints that benefits of aggregate demand-expansion and labour-utilisation increases can accrue to the economy as a whole.

An evaluation of the costs and benefits of regional policy at the national scale also needs to know the extent to which labour productivity is affected. Two points can be made: firstly, that as long as any additional employment has a productivity greater than zero, it must represent an addition to the national Gross Domestic Product (GDP) but, secondly, that when regional policy simply shifts employment from wealthier areas to AAs without a national employment increase, then unless there is a marked improvement in AA labour productivity the GDP could actually decline. The latter point raises the question of productivity differences between regions but the available evidence suggests that these are minor and tended to converge over the last two decades of active policy (Moore and Rhodes, 1979, 38).

To conclude this section, we can summarise the major benefits and costs of regional policy.

The *benefits* are mainly threefold:

1. the *number of jobs* (and the associated income) created by regional policy in AAs, although probably one-third of these were national employment gains;
2. the *transfer payments* associated with policy subsidies, particularly higher wages, higher profits (dividends) and reduced prices;
3. the *psychological benefits* resulting from reductions in unemployment and, therefore, in the number of potential out-migrants (not readily expressed in monetary terms) (ibid, 39–41).

The *costs* of regional policy are also threefold:

1. *The Exchequer cost*. This is not simply the gross cost to the Exchequer, but rather the initial expenditure minus any increase in government revenue. Hence the *net* cost to the Exchequer is really the initial outlay on industrial incentives modified over time by:
   (a) loan repayments and other recoverable expenses;
   (b) changes in tax receipts when general tax rates are used to maintain the overall pressure of demand or a balance of payments position; and
   (c) changes in tax revenue/government expenditure resulting from increased employment (reduced unemployment benefits and increased tax revenue), increased output and higher profits generated by policy.
2. *The tax cost*. This is 'the value of additional revenue to be raised from higher taxation in order to restore the balance of payments position to where it would have been in the absence of policy'.
3. *The resource cost*. Sometimes referred to as the *opportunity cost* of policy, this is 'the amount of real output which has to be sacrificed in order to have the benefits of policy and to preserve the balance of payments position'. If there was no policy and national output was higher, the resource cost of the policy would be negative. It can also be argued that other types of policy to those adopted could have been used and provided greater benefit. If so, the opportunity cost of the policy measures actually used is the loss of output that would have been derived from an alternative policy (idem.).

Overall, the macro-economic impact of the regional policies being followed until 1974 was one of increased GDP, but since then balance of payments problems have been a major constraint. Therefore, the only cost item on the cost-benefit balance sheet has been the tax cost. (See Moore and Rhodes, 1979, 42–9, for a fuller orthodox economic treatment of this.) In an earlier paper covering the policy period up to 1974, the same authors (1973) argued that the annual net cost of regional development spending was zero, because government expenditure was balanced by the income derived from extra direct and indirect taxes, plus the positive effect of reduced unemployment and supplementary benefit payments. In the final analysis, whilst economists may be able to present evaluations of past regional policies in some detail, and suggest modifications to future policies in order to achieve certain objectives, the actual decision making with respect to the precise form and intensity of regional policy rests with the politicians. But which policy instruments seem most worthy of consideration for inclusion in a package of regional incentives, if indeed the latter prove necessary?

230

10.1.4 Regional aid forever?

The ultimate aim of regional and urban policy is to solve the problems of *divergence* that necessitated the policy in the first place – once the problems are solved there will be no further need of government assistance since *convergence* will have been achieved! Unfortunately, regional and urban disequilibria are economically and spatially endemic in the economic development process, as we described in our review of Britain's economic history (Chapter 2). Hence, while problems may be alleviated or even solved in one location, the forces of spatially unequal economic growth and decline will always mean that other areas will emerge with similar problems. There is fairly general agreement among regional and urban economists and planners that some form of financial or regulatory assistance from government to areas defined as having 'problems' is a fact of life. Recognition of the fact that spatial disequilibrium is a constant condition of the national economy means that, for a variety of economic, social and political reasons, attempts will always have to be made by central government to adopt some scheme of national financial redistribution in order to 'ease the pain' of regional and urban adjustments to changing economic conditions.

In 1983 the Conservative Government undertook a major review of regional and urban policy in the UK, which invited comment from the academic and business communities and formed the basis of policy until 1988. A major input came from the Regional Studies Association, a professional body representing the views of regional economists and economic geographers. (See also the comment by Chisholm, 1984b) The Association found that after 1973 the UK's deteriorating economic situation had three major consequences for regional policy:

1. In order to slow down national industrial decline, policy emphasis was shifted from a regional to an industrial sector basis, but many of the industries selected for assistance were located in the South East and West Midlands so that policy could be seen to be discriminating against assisted regions.
2. Traditional regional policy was no longer viewed as a 'useful arm of demand management' and its significance declined as policy moved away from attempts to maintain 'full' employment towards reducing both inflation and public spending.
3. The perceived national need for improving industrial efficiency by rationalising production and reducing labour costs ran counter to regional policy that had used capital subsidies and IDCs as means of generating and spatially directing employment. (Regional Studies Association, 1983, 8–9.)

The shift in emphasis of regional policy during the 1970s, coupled with the determination of the Conservative Government to reduce regional expenditure substantially in the 1980s, meant that the 'value for money' (i.e. effectiveness) of each policy instrument became the key to its survival. The concern of central government was no longer with large-scale aid to 'propel' AAs into convergence (or at least to stop them diverging more); rather, it was to identify and use those instruments which had the best 'track record' of promoting the job-creating potential of small firm expansion and service sector growth.

Investment incentives emerged as the single most important regional policy instrument during the 1970s, especially as IDC controls weakened. In theory, capital subsidies should have helped to modernise and restructure an AA's industrial base by enabling new products and processes to enhance its competitiveness, increase its exports and thus generate jobs. In practice, the RDGs facilitated capital substitution in some manufacturing industries, so that substantial amounts of public money were given to some industries which created very few new jobs (e.g. in Northern Ireland, Coca Cola received a grant of £600,000 and created just 14 new jobs; in the Shetlands, the Sullom Voe oil terminal project received £100 million in grants – £130,000 per job, each of which would have been created there with or without regional aid). The recession, with its falling demand and profitability, almost certainly encouraged some firms to use their regional investment incentives to help rationalise their production, especially by shedding labour. Indeed, two industries (textiles and chemicals) were probably able to shed labour thanks to capital subsidies, and in the case of chemicals it has been estimated that £1.4 billion in such subsidies resulted in a loss of 28,000 jobs in the four main DAs (Moore *et al.*, 1986, 64).

Blanket subsidies such as RDGs were, as we noted earlier, considerably more influential on company investment decision making than selective subsidies such as Regional Selective Assistance, so that the Government's introduction in 1984 of a ceiling on the grant payable for each job created appeared to be a logical way forward. Whether or not selective subsidies were more effective than blanket subsidies, however, remained a vexed question. Again, theoretically, selective assistance should enable public funds to be directed very specifically into those industries of greatest benefit to the region concerned, but in practical terms the criteria necessary to enable us to select appropriate industries have not yet been developed. Research into identifying such criteria continues, and Moore *et al.* (1986, 69) suggest that, since there are such dramatic variations between different industries in terms of their receipts of assistance and their employment creation (or destruction), and therefore their cost per job to the Exchequer, a financial mechanism should be developed whereby regional policy assistance could be applied more selectively within the manufacturing industry.

If the principal aim of regional policy is to reduce unemployment in AAs, are programmes directed at *labour-intensive* industries and at labour retention likely to be more effective than the capital subsidy approach? Although the main industries responding to regional assistance with job creation have been the kinds of industry already biased towards labour intensity, some capital-intensive industries have also responded very well. Policy bias towards labour-intensive industries is not necessarily wise, therefore, but again we need more information about all industrial groups in order to make appropriate judgements. *Labour retention* programmes, in the shape of labour subsidies (REP/SEP), are probably even less effective as policy instruments. Many firms seem to have treated such subsidies as a 'windfall', which had no calculable impact on their behaviour but rather leaked into wages and profits, and where the firm so subsidised had other plants outside the AAs the subsidy could be spatially re-allocated with little regard for regional

policy. So, in the short term, government support for job-creating programmes may have obvious social and political benefits, but in the longer term
investment in equipment (capital) can be of greater value. This is the
'structuralist' argument (Section 9.2.1 above): in order to strengthen a
region's economy, policy must ensure that industry and commerce are competitive, and this can be achieved more readily by concentrating on
equipment rather than on job creation (thus improving the capital/labour ratio).
Once competitive, the region should no longer require financial support and,
by definition, it will have a 'better' industrial structure than before. In addition, policymakers should 'introduce measures to stimulate industries
producing goods, the demand for which is income-elastic outside the region'
(Richardson, 1984, 30), since this will help to increase the growth rate of
the region's exports and thereby add to its economic strength. Such policies
will be far more effective over a longer time period than subsidies aimed
simply at labour retention or job creation.

The *criticisms of traditional regional policy* in general, and of certain
policy instruments in particular, are fourfold, and they address both the
effects and effectiveness of policy (see also Section 10.1.1 above):

1. 'Policy emphasis on subsidies for capital investment led to a lack of direct
   correlation between the level of aid to firms and the amount of employment generated.' The best response to regional aid regarding job creation
   in AAs was in electrical engineering and clothing, neither of which
   received much assistance. Chemicals and metal manufacturing, however,
   received the largest amounts of aid but generated very few jobs and in
   the case of chemicals, even shed substantial numbers (p. 232). The problem of a weak relationship between assistance and job creation grew
   as new investment aimed at improving efficiency levels rather than at
   increasing output by adding labour.
2. Regional policy concentrated on manufacturing, with a bias towards capital grants, especially for equipment used in the production process.
   Incentives for the service industry did not appear until 1973, which was
   too late to have any real impact, and in any case the AAs may have been
   too peripheral with respect to office dispersal from London. 'Services as
   a whole would appear to be a sector of lost opportunities for regional
   policy.'
3. Within manufacturing, regional policy led to the building of many branch
   plants in AAs, with a consequent increase in 'external ownership and control of manufacturing in the depressed regions'. Many such plants were
   of routine assembly-type production, competing directly with 'lower
   labour cost locations overseas', and they were 'only weakly integrated
   into the local or regional economy', so that their multiplier effect was
   limited. Policy had little effect on the South East, which remained the
   financial, business and administrative centre of the country.
4. Policy emphasis on employment generation in AAs did not include any
   attempt to improve their structural balance, nor 'to create conditions for
   "self-reliant" regional growth', and little success was evident of helping
   AAs develop 'new products and enterprises' for themselves which would
   form the basis of diversified long-term regional economic development.
   (Regional Studies Association, 1983, 11–12.)

Criticisms such as these had considerable influence on the Conservative Government's reassessment of regional policy in 1983/4 and the subsequent policy changes (see Section 7.1.4 above). The reservations that the Government had about blanket subsidies continued after 1984, and the apparent superiority of selective assistance over such subsidies in terms of their effectiveness (low cost to the Exchequer per job created) resulted in the suspension of RDGs in 1988 and the 'elevation' of RSA to be the principal instrument of regional policy. Current policy, therefore, emphasises selective regional assistance and the development of new firm potential in AAs and inner cities, with the result that the range of incentives now available is virtually the same for both regional Assisted Areas and Urban Programme Areas. This is not to say, however, that these incentives are being administered in a manner consistent with any spatial logic (namely, urban regions) associated with the locations of problem areas, a point to which we shall return in the final chapter.

10.2 Effectiveness of urban policy

The effectiveness of urban policy is difficult to measure. Clearly those who formulate urban policy do it to achieve certain aims, but it is also possible that there will be unexpected side-effects, some of which may be extremely damaging. Despite this, the introduction of new policy is often surrounded by an ethos of confidence in its success when in fact it is a leap in the dark. Such is the situation with much urban policy.

It has already been established from the discussion in earlier chapters that the major plank of urban policy since the Second World War has been decentralisation. This has been seen by some (Glass, 1955) as deliberate anti-urban policy. It has nevertheless been effective in reducing the population size of major conubations, slowing down, if not eradicating, the tentacle-like growth of urban areas into the countryside, and forcing on cities a more economical use of land through higher residential densities and in-filling.

It has also been an effective policy in bringing protection to large acreages of land (through green belt legislation), in generating the growth of commuter or metropolitan villages and in providing a new living experience for those inner city dwellers who found homes in the New Towns which were built to absorb the overspill population from the conurbations.

The New Towns policy, an integral part of decentralisation, was one brave experiment in building a new world after the Second World War, which gave new opportunities and improved living conditions to people who had previously largely been denied them. In its aims the policy has been effective and it has also succeeded in taking some of the population pressure off the cities. What would the urban problems of today have been like if the New Towns had not been built? Nevertheless, before euphoria over decentralisation becomes too firmly established, any objective assessment of policy must not lose sight of the externality effects, in which 'the activity of any one element in an urban system may generate certain unpriced and perhaps non-monetary effects upon other elements in the system' (Harvey, 1972).

The externality effects of urban decentralisation policy can go beyond that of pressure reduction upon urban resources, to the point where they can result in serious damage to the city which they were designed to relieve. These negative or destructive externality effects were presented in an important article written by David Eversley, the Chief Strategic Planner for Greater London in 1972. He pointed to the fact that 'from Abercrombie to the authors of the reports and plan of 1969 (Greater London Development Plan), London had been at the centre of a concentrated effort to limit its population and economic growth in the interests of an improved environment'. Population between 1939 and 1971 fell by almost 2 million and control over industrial and office space resulted in a fall in total employment – two features held in common with other large cities like Liverpool, Manchester and Birmingham. Yet the improved environment for living had not been achieved for significant areas of these cities.

It has already been pointed out how disastrous many post-war housing schemes have been, but Eversley (1972) widened the problem to consider why decentralisation was injuring the cities, and London in particular. He suggested that the problem was one of the contrast between rising costs and falling urban incomes. The rising costs resulted from:

1. Rising land prices.
2. Accelerating obsolescence. As a result of the building boom of the late nineteenth century an increasing number of private houses and public buildings, such as schools and hospitals, were reaching or had reached the end of their useful life and needed replacing.
3. Higher construction costs, which are largely met by authorities borrowing money often at high rates of interest over long periods.
4. The difficulties of carrying out public works in old congested centres. The complexity of the 'underground city' of London, for example, was underlined by the Chief Planner of the City of London. Commenting on the lack of trees in the Barbican scheme, he said that if he was given a tree costing £1.50 it would require £100 to plant it – such is the difficulty of providing soakaways under the City.
5. The increasing dependence of the urban system on public services. These include the police, education, welfare and planning, in which rises in productivity are unlikely and therefore if a better service is to be provided the cost of provision is almost certain to rise faster than in manufacturing or commercial sectors of the economy. The economic position will be further worsened if as a result of decentralisation the young and more affluent leave the cities and the old and unskilled remain, for these latter groups make greater demands on public services.

If the city is in a healthy economic state then the rising costs involved in maintaining the built and social fabrics of the city can be met. 'All things being equal a population with larger personal incomes can maintain the fabric better than a population with a smaller income' (Eversley, 1972). Unfortunately, in a situation of population and employment decentralisation it is unlikely that a healthy urban economy can be maintained. The fall in population leads to less economic activity and the community's total income will fall. If the people leaving the city are largely drawn from the middle and upper income groups, the city's per capita incomes will either fall absolutely or rise more slowly than in surrounding areas.

For the local authorities who depend for a significant proportion of their income upon the local rates, this is 'bad news'. A poorer population lives in dwellings of low rateable value, so the rate return from the residential population will decline if the more affluent leave. The population with considerable spending power will spend more in the local shops than a poor one. As the rates shops pay are roughly proportional to volume of sales and profitability then the return to local authorities will vary according to the character of the population. In a period of differential decentralisation it is likely to fall.

The urban economy will be further eroded if a policy of employment decentralisation is underway, for not only do firms pay wages and so influence the level of personal incomes, they also pay rates and add to the revenue available to the local authority.

In summary, the cost of running cities is increasing, but the resource base to meet these costs is falling because the decentralisation of people and employment goes beyond the confines of the city and their economic provision is lost. The policy of decentralisation in reducing population pressure on cities has been effective, but its very effectiveness has made it almost impossible for urban governments to resolve the increasing inner city and now outer city deprivation. To do this requires action from central government which positively descriminates in favour of urban areas and particularly those where the physical and social conditions are bad. For it is not enough merely to expand the rate support grant or introduce some form of community tax to increase resources available to local authorities. What is needed are new initiatives and new policies.

This has been the challenge for governments, which they have attempted to meet through a succession of legislative initiatives which can be considered as part of a three-stage process with, first, a period of piecemeal policies; second, the development of partnership between government and the local authorities; and third, a fostering of close co-operation between government and the private sector.

10.2.1 Period of piecemeal policies

The post-war period saw many areas of our cities transformed as large-scale redevelopment schemes mapped the destruction of industrial zones and working class housing areas. Between 1955 and 1975 3 million people were relocated from old urban areas in the UK into new housing, either in the high-rise or 'slab' estates of the inner city, or into suburban locations well away from their original homes. Government saw the major problem as a lack of housing and proceeded to build at great speed with little thought for the desires of those who were to be rehoused. Hansen and Hillier (1982/3) pointed out that such developments were designed on the assumption that the undesirable features of old communities could be planned away, and that life would be better in an environment consisting only of adequate housing, together with (eventually) a few essential shops.

If this was progress, it was achieved at heavy social cost to individuals, and to the areas they left behind. 'The demolition of a neighbourhood is not

just the destruction of buildings but also that of a functioning social system
. . . and "slum clearance" ignored the fact that most social problems found
in slums were directly related to their physical structure' (Freeman, 1987).

It was not until the 1960s that any real attention was paid to the problems
of people living in the inner city. This came initially through the setting up
by government of three committees to examine the London housing system,
primary schooling and social service provision in deprived areas. It was a
piecemeal approach to a complex problem, but at least it was a start.

The *Milner-Holland Report*, published in 1965, examined the housing conditions in London, drawing particular attention to the parlous state of private
landlordism. They were concerned with the absence of any financial institu-
tion which catered for the requirements of private investment in rented
property, and the lack of control over rents, 'a haphazard and unpredictable
process which depends upon the behaviour of individual tenants, exposing
their successors to rent increases without regard to their needs or resources,
and tending in areas of great shortage to encourage abuses and bad relations
between landlord and tenant'.

The abuses which this report exposed influenced the thinking of the
Labour Government of the day, who introduced the *Rent Act of 1965*, which
was designed to 'lay the foundation for a better relationship between the
landlord and the tenant of rented property, by introducing a new and flexible
system of rent regulation', or 'fair' rents, as we now know it.

The *Plowden Report* (Department of Education and Science, 1967) was a
landmark in educational history. It noted a relationship between family and
social deprivation on the one hand, and poor educational attainment on the
other. To break the cycle of parental poverty, poor educational attainment
and the possession of low job skills by successive generations, Plowden
stressed the need to develop a national policy of 'positive discrimination' in
order to make primary schools in the most deprived areas as good as the
best in the country. In response to this report the government set up five
Educational Priority Areas (EPAs) in 1968 in Deptford, Sparkbrook, Conis-
borough, Liverpool 8 and Dundee, financed by the Department of
Education and Science and the Social Science Research Council. This gave
preferential treatment to schools in need by slowing down staff turnover
through higher salaries and by providing building grants. If the idea was fine,
its limited nature and low resourcing did little for inner city education, but
the experience and the resulting research did expose the deprived state of a
significant proportion of poorer working class families.

The terms of reference of the *Seebohn Report (1968)* were to 'review the
organisation and responsibilities of local authority personal social services in
England and Wales, and to consider what changes are desirable to secure
an effective family service'. In doing this they recommended the need for
'social planning' and for the setting up of areas of special need which should
be accorded priority in the allocation of resources: 'We are convinced that
designated areas of special need should receive extra resources comprehensively planned in co-operation with services both central and local,
concerned with health, education, housing and other social needs.'

Milner-Holland, Plowden and Seebohn were as one in recognising the
deepening problems of the inner city, but even taken together their work
was insufficient to enable the legislators to formulate policy which could be

seen as a clearly defined and comprehensive approach to inner city deprivation. To do this would depend upon a deeper understanding of the
dimensions of the problem, which could only be achieved through more
widely framed studies of inner city areas. These came in 1972 with the setting
up of three inner city study teams for Liverpool (Areas D), Birmingham
(Small Heath) and Lambeth, by the Department of the Environment. They
were instructed to explore the problems, and possible solutions in
these areas. Their work was invaluable in bringing to light the plight of these
areas, and acting as a catalyst to more concerted government action.

Peter Hall (1977) suggested that 'politicians tend to rediscover the urban
poor every half decade of so'. If this period of piecemeal activity achieved
anything it was to reawaken politicians' interest in the inner city. Knowledge
of the conditions in these areas and their deep-seated problems were at least
brought to light, but government reaction was uncertain and the legislation
lacked a coherent structure, for it only nibbled at individual areas of concern
such as education and the provision of social services without focusing on
the fundamental need to revitalise the economy. To do this would be a Herculean task requiring insight into how new confidence could be injected into
these areas at a time when the national economy was going into deepening
depression.

Nevertheless, one foundation stone was laid during this period which was
to become a constant though changing feature of successive governments.
This was the Urban Programme which fostered the idea of greater co-operation between central government and those local authorities where
deprivation was more acute.

Under the *Local Government (Social Need) Act of 1969* urban aid was
made available 'to raise the level of social services in areas of acute social
need, and thus help to provide an equal opportunity for all citizens'. These
areas of 'special social need' were not defined in the Act, but government
circulars referred to 'localised districts within urban areas which contained
marks of multiple deprivation, including old, overcrowded houses without
plumbing and sanitation; persistent unemployment; above average family
sizes; and a high proportion of children in trouble or in need of care; or a
combination of some or all of these'.

The Urban Programme was widened in its scope under the Labour administration in 1977 to cover industrial, environmental and recreational
provision. Its expenditure was increased and the co-ordinating responsibility
for the programme passed from the Home Office to the Department of the
Environment. Its role was further expanded and sharpened under the Conservative Government and is today still part of their policy initiatives.

10.2.2 Development of partnership between government and the local authorities

The incoming Labour Government in 1974 presented a strong commitment
to local government by seeking to work in partnership with it over the
problems besetting the large conurbations and their inner areas. This
partnership was facilitated by the fact that most of these local authorities
were Labour controlled and viewed the regeneration of run-down areas in
similar ways. Regeneration, it seemed, meant restoring an economic base

which would provide work for the local working people, and an improved housing and recreational environment.

This form of approach was to be seen in the working of the Joint Dockland Committee in the London Docks, which was set up in 1974 by the Department of the Environment based on a collaborative venture between the Government, the Greater London Council and the London boroughs of Newham, Tower Hamlets, Southwark, Lewisham and Greenwich. The Committee largely adopted a 'bottom up' approach by involving local people in the planning process as a means of discovering an acceptable way forward.

The concept of partnership was fundamental to the government approach to planning, as was made clear in the White Paper 'Policy for the Inner Cities' published in June 1977, which formed the basis for the *Inner Urban Areas Act* of July *1978*. This Act, along with a major memorandum from the Department of the Environment, gave 'additional powers to local authorities with severe inner area problems so that they may participate more effectively in the economic development of their areas'. Included in these powers was the ability to make grants and loans for industrial building and to declare Improvement Areas. These were to be run-down areas of industrial or of mixed industrial and commercial use which required revitalisation. In all, 48 areas were designated under the Act, with either formal or informal partnership arrangements. The original designations were:

Districts containing 'Special Areas' (partnership areas)

Birmingham	Islington
Greenwich	Lambeth
Lewisham	Liverpool
Newham	Manchester
Southwark	Salford
Tower Hamlets	Newcastle upon Tyne
Hackney	Gateshead

Districts containing Inner Area Programmes (Programme Authority Areas)

These have no formal partnership arrangement, but are invited to draw up inner area programmes.

Bolton	Nottingham
Bradford	Oldham
Hammersmith	Sheffield
Kingston upon Hull	South Tyneside
Leeds	Sunderland
Leicester	Wirral
Middlesbrough	Wolverhampton
North Tyneside	

Other districts

These are designated districts which can make use of the powers under the Act.

England

Barnsley	Rochdale

Blackburn	Rotherham
Brent	St Helens
Doncaster	Sandwell
Ealing	Sefton
Haringey	Wandsworth
Hartlepool	Wigan

Wales

Blaenau Gwent	Rhondda
Cardiff	Swansea
Newport	

To fund the new inner city programme Peter Shore, the Secretary of State for the Department of the Environment, diverted funds from the New Towns and Expanded Towns (NETs) programmes as part of a radical rethink about the decentralisation policies which had been followed since the end of the Second World War. The NETs programme was conceived at a time when demographers were forecasting a population of 70 million in Britain by the year 2000. In the event, it was clear by 1975 that a figure closer to 58 million was more realistic. The Labour Government therefore began the termination of state dispersal policies, which were finally laid to rest by the Conservative Government after 1979.

The attempts to revitalise the inner city areas by the Labour Government were short-lived because they lost the election in 1979. Nevertheless, some important issues were raised by the approach adopted by the Government towards the inner city. The London Dockland Joint Committee's work provided some of the firmest evidence that the way to regenerate these problem areas was not by restoring an economy based largely upon manufacturing industry providing work for semi- or unskilled workers. The age when manufacturing industry had flourished in the inner parts of cities was gone; new activities and a new purpose for these areas would have to be found. The 'bottom up' approach of the Joint Committee brought some improvement to Dockland but it did not resolve the underlying economic problem of generating new employment.

To a degree the Labour Government was trapped because an important segment of its voting base lay in these areas, and so any radical new proposals to alter them fundamentally would not have been met with favour. Much Labour thinking, particularly at local level, was locked into the past, and understandably they could not accept policies which did not directly favour them.

On the positive side the widening of the Urban Programme, the 1977 White Paper, and the designation of Partnership schemes maintained and enhanced the growing commitment of successive governments to the inner city.

10.2.3 Closer co-operation between central government and the private sector

At an early stage in the life of the Conservative Government of 1979 a new radical approach to town planning was revealed by Michael Heseltine, the Secretary of State for the Environment. In a speech to the summer school of the Royal Town Planning Institute he was critical of the hierarchy of planning, planners and plans, which was costly to maintain and whose objectives were often obscure. Planning had become inflexible and unresponsive to an extent that it was damaging to the economic development of the country. 'The inexorable slide down the economic league table' which Britain had experienced was to some degree due to planning. What was required therefore was less planning at local authority level, but where it was necessary it should produce results quickly and efficiently, and should be an aid to economic advance, not an obstacle. In effect this was a philosophy of 'State withdrawal' or 'rolling back the frontiers of the State' in order to allow private enterprise to operate more freely.

The philosophy soon became reality with the introduction of Enterprise Zones and the two Dockland Development Corporations, for which provision was made in the *1980 Local Government, Planning and Land Act*. The Enterprise Zones are subject to simplified planning procedures in order to unlock land for industry and commerce, and within limits they have achieved this in England on some 700 hectares and at a cost of £90 million. There are 25 Enterprise Zones in the UK, which, up until the beginning of 1986, had created a net gain of 35,656 jobs. A further Enterprise Zone is planned for Inverclyde in the Strathclyde area of Scotland. Local authorities now have powers to set up 'Simplified Planning Zones', in which certain developments in designated zones will be allowed without the need for a planning application. These can be used widely in inner cities to lift barriers to investment and lessen delays. Derby and Birmingham are the first authorities to introduce these Zones.

The Development Corporations, of which there will be ten in England and one in Cardiff, are also designed to speed up the planning process and release public land for private commercial and residential developers. Their powers over land have been described by Cullingworth (1985) as 'breathtaking'. The Secretary of State can make an order authorising that land held by local authorities or other public bodies both inside and outside the Urban Development Area can be invested in the Urban Development Corporation. This can be done without any right of appeal from the bodies concerned. The land so acquired is then prepared and made available to the private sector as part of the philosophy of 'demand-led planning'.

If the successes of the Enterprise Zones have been limited in generating new employment, the record of the Dockland Corporations, particularly London, proves that they can be quite spectacular. To date over 60,000 new jobs have been provided largely within the Isle of Dogs Enterprise Zone, which lies within the Dockland designated areas. The two concepts in tandem have certainly provided a catalyst for the transformation of the whole of Dockland.

Development so rapid and spectacular is seen by the local 'Eastenders' as the outcome of a system designed for profit, not people. There is in this new landscape a stark contrast between the new private houses and flats and the high-rise and slab estates of the local authorities. The lack of gain so far experienced by the 'locals' results from the fact that the local authorities, in contrast to the Development Corporation, have had their grants from central government cut and yet they are still expected to fulfil their responsibility for public housing, education and the social services. The gap between those

241

who have and those who have not is widening as a direct result of government policies. Nevertheless, in such a large operation as dockland regeneration, which inevitably creates a new order, it is difficult to avoid problems of this kind. What is important is that lessons are learnt and future initiatives in both existing and designated Development Corporations take greater cognizance of the needs of local people.

Enterprise Zones and Development Corporations are but a part of a government package which has evolved during the last eight years 'to help cities meet the challenge of change'. The overall aim of these programmes is to regenerate the older, run-down, derelict areas of our cities not only by attracting the interest and investment of the private sector with such grant schemes as the *Urban Development Grant* or *Urban Regeneration Grant* (now known as the *City Grant*), but also by promoting joint action by government departments, local authorities, the private sector and many local agencies which have a part to play in urban regeneration. In this respect, the *Urban Programme* is an important instrument of government, intended to provide support for a wide range of projects submitted by local authorities as part of the Inner Area Programme for their districts. Much of the funding is to be used by local authorities to assist private sector projects which will aid the economic development of the inner cities. In 1987/88 £294 million is available for the Urban Programme with some £70 million of this for cleaning, landscaping and tidying up run-down industrial and commercial centres, improving inner city parks and open spaces and helping small businesses improve their premises and surrounds. The programme is also supporting nearly 90,000 inner city jobs or training places.

The Government, in 1985, set up *City Action Teams* in London, Birmingham, Liverpool, Manchester/Salford and Newcastle/Gateshead. This enabled regional directors of government departments to pool their efforts, and develop new projects and programmes which could form the basis for private sector involvement. Then in 1986 the *Inner Cities Initiative* was launched to enable joint government departmental action in areas where unemployment is particularly severe. Task forces have been now set up as laboratories for trying out new ideas and approaches.

If the aim of the Conservative Government is to 'roll back the frontiers of the State', it is extremely energetic in increasing its own power. The urban policy initiatives, which are given spatial expression in Fig. 10.1, suggest that although the local authorities have a role to play in all this activity, the Government is drawing more power in urban affairs unto itself. A centralised system is emerging in which increasing encouragement is given to private sector initiatives backed by public sector finance.

There is no doubt that the urban landscape is changing and regeneration is evident, but according to Professor Robson levels of unemployment and poverty are still 'horrendous' in spite of billions of pounds spent in urban renewal. In a lecture given to the 1988 Institute of British Geographers he cited recent evidence from a study he had carried out in deprived areas of London, Birmingham, Glasgow, Bristol and Manchester, which showed that the impact of inner city policies on jobs had been minimal. One of the reasons he gave for this failure of government policy was the confusion between different government departments and agencies in spite of the attempts to co-ordinate actions: 'In some cases, one agency gives money with one hand and a different one takes it back with the other'.

Figure 10.1 Urban policy initiatives in England, April 1987.*
Source: *The Planner* (June 1987)

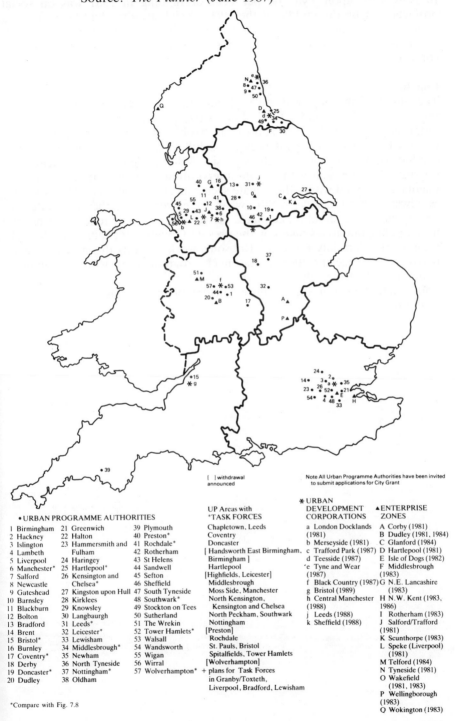

[ ] withdrawal
announced

Note All Urban Programme Authorities have been invited
to submit applications for City Grant

**✶ URBAN
DEVELOPMENT
CORPORATIONS**

UP Areas with
*TASK FORCES

Chapletown, Leeds
Coventry
Doncaster
[Handsworth East Birmingham,
Birmingham]
Hartlepool
[Highfields, Leicester]
Middlesbrough
Moss Side, Manchester
North Kensington,
Kensington and Chelsea
North Peckham, Southwark
Nottingham
[Preston]
Rochdale
St. Pauls, Bristol
Spitalfields, Tower Hamlets
[Wolverhampton]
+ plans for Task Forces
in Granby/Toxteth,
Liverpool, Bradford, Lewisham

● URBAN PROGRAMME AUTHORITIES

1 Birmingham	21 Greenwich	39 Plymouth
2 Hackney	22 Halton	40 Preston*
3 Islington	23 Hammersmith and	41 Rochdale*
4 Lambeth	Fulham	42 Rotherham
5 Liverpool	24 Haringey	43 St Helens
6 Manchester*	25 Hartlepool*	44 Sandwell
7 Salford	26 Kensington and	45 Sefton
8 Newcastle	Chelsea*	46 Sheffield
9 Gateshead	27 Kingston upon Hull	47 South Tyneside
10 Barnsley	28 Kirklees	48 Southwark*
11 Blackburn	29 Knowsley	49 Stockton on Tees
12 Bolton	30 Langbaurgh	50 Sutherland
13 Bradford	31 Leeds*	51 The Wrekin
14 Brent	32 Leicester*	52 Tower Hamlets*
15 Bristol*	33 Lewisham	53 Walsall
16 Burnley	34 Middlesbrough*	54 Wandsworth
17 Coventry*	35 Newham	55 Wigan
18 Derby	36 North Tyneside	56 Wirral
19 Doncaster*	37 Nottingham*	57 Wolverhampton*
20 Dudley	38 Oldham	

a London Docklands
(1981)
b Merseyside (1981)
c Trafford Park (1987)
d Teesside (1987)
'e Tyne and Wear
(1987)
f Black Country (1987)
g Bristol (1989)
h Central Manchester
(1988)
j Leeds (1988)
k Sheffield (1988)

**▲ENTERPRISE
ZONES**

A Corby (1981)
B Dudley (1981, 1984)
C Glanford (1984)
D Hartlepool (1981)
E Isle of Dogs (1982)
F Middlesbrough
(1983)
G N.E. Lancashire
(1983)
H N.W. Kent (1983,
1986)
I Rotherham (1983)
J Salford/Trafford
(1981)
K Scunthorpe (1983)
L Speke (Liverpool)
(1981)
M Telford (1984)
N Tyneside (1981)
O Wakefield
(1981, 1983)
P Wellingborough
(1983)
Q Wokington (1983)

*Compare with Fig. 7.8

243

Robson also pointed to the conflict between economic and social goods. In Newcastle upon Tyne 60 per cent of funding in 1981 was on social projects, but by the middle of the 1980s social spending had been reduced by half. Clearly as the efforts to attract private investment were introduced, the main goals of government policy became more economic than social in character.

Conclusion

The plight of the deprived areas of our cities has been evident for a long time, if not fully understood. Successive governments have developed programmes and policies to address the problems of these areas. Billions of pounds have been spent (at present £2 billion a year) and endless studies conducted, and yet the difficulties persist. What is clear to the present Conservative Government is that State intervention alone is insufficient and the talents and capital within the private sector must be mobilised. The problem, as always, is to decide within what framework of policies, institutions and agencies this should take place. As yet it is too early to say whether the urban policy initiatives taken by the present Government constitute the right framework. Certainly Professor Robson's work suggests this may not be so, partly at least because there is too much programme set within a confusing structure. What may therefore be required is concentration and simplification of activities to produce a more efficient means of bringing new resources to the major cities.

11 New technology

As we discussed in Chapter 1 Nikolai Kondratieff pointed out that in capitalist countries about every half century they went full circle from bust to boom time and then back again. His ideas were amplified by Joseph Schumpeter who suggested that each of these waves was based upon a new industrial revolution, and their configuration was one of a slow upward gradient of growth followed by a fairly sharp slide. Schumpeter also underlined Kondratieff's view that during the recession period of the wave there would be a considerable generation of new inventions which would be applied at the start of the next wave. This would be the period of innovation which in a short time would bring forward new processes, new products and new industries. If these ideas are considered in a time sequence, then it is suggested that they show statistical regularity with the peak of innovation occurring between 11 and 17 years before the upswing of a new wave. At present time the peak of innovation is calculated to occur in 1989 (previous peaks were 1764, 1825, 1886 and 1935 according to Gerhard Mensch in *Stalemate in Technologies,* Hall, 1981), but what form is it taking and where is it occurring?

In the previous chapters the groups of innovations and the location of their application has been described. In this chapter the Fifth Kondratieff Wave is examined and the questions posed above answered.

What form the innovations will take, is already clear. The emerging high technology industries are based upon either genetic engineering with the production of new drugs, new forms of nutrition and alternative energy resources, or on the microprocessor, which is at the centre of the microelectronics industry. They hold their original locations in common, for both are Californian and are spin-offs from fundamental research within university departments. Genetic engineering is closely associated with the University of California in San Francisco, the microprocessor with Stanford University. Both have been the basis of new industries which are now spreading throughout the western world, but it is the second of these technologies which is more relevant in the context of this book and to which further attention will be given.

11.1 Micro-electronics

Its beginnings in the Santa Clara Valley, or Silicon Valley as it has become known, resulted from the work and inspiration of one man, Frederick Terman, Professor of Electrical Engineering at Stanford University. He encouraged his graduates to set up businesses near the campus, he obtained major research grants from the US government, and then created the first science park near the gates of the University. His enthusiasm and support for new sophisticated technologies explains, to a large extent, the success in the adjacent Santa Clara Valley, where during the 1970s over 25,000 jobs were created each year, and its international fame assured. Now there are over 700 electronics-related companies, and many others support or service this high technology complex. The success of the Santa Clara Valley is the success of Terman's belief that there should be a community of interest between the University and local industry, which can be fostered by a University with a community of technical scholars. If these scholars are sensitive to the needs of local industry and a two-way flow of information and ideas is created, then there is the basis for technological advance and application. In the Santa Clara Valley this has been achieved, and in many other parts of the world their ideas have been applied with considerable success, as will be seen later when the Cambridge phenomenon is explained.

It is important to understand, in the first place, 'this most remarkable technology ever to confront mankind' (Sir Ieuan Maddock, 1978). It has a number of important properties which make its impact on the technology scene so profound:

1. Its ability to extend or even displace man's capacity for thinking, his intuition or his judgement. It has been suggested (MENSA Conference, July 1984) that electronics will replace man's mind as steam replaced man's muscle. In less than 40 years intelligent machines will be part of our everyday life.
2. Its pervasiveness. There is virtually no field in manufacturing, the utilities, the service industries or commerce, that can fail to be influenced by its advance. The new technology has already altered the factory. Cars can now be built almost entirely by robots, whilst in the office a transformation has occurred with the arrival of sophisticated word processors and computerised information storage and retrieval systems which are cost-effective.
3. Its speed of advance. Never has a powerful technology advanced so rapidly in such a short time. In 1979 for example, there were 2,000 robots in the USA. It is forecast that by 1990 this could be over 200,000.
4. The use of the silicon chip on which thousands of electronic functions can be placed has revolutionised electronics and brought about miniaturisation. The most important breakthrough came in 1952 with the concept of the integrated circuit, where a number of transistors could be put into a single package. Then in 1960 engineers created transistors in the surface of a silicon chip and miniaturisation took on a new dimension. Since that time the number of transistors on a chip has rapidly increased; in 1965 it was 30 components, in 1975 30,000, in 1978 135,000 and today over 250,000 components can be placed upon a chip the size of a first class stamp. At the time of writing the super chip is being developed, which could revolutionise still further the electronics industry and provide industry and the public with far more complex electronic aids in much smaller forms.
5. Its cheapness. The miniaturisation of computer technology has been accompanied by considerable cost reductions. Once a silicon chip is designed it can be mass produced at very low cost, which will continue

to fall as volume production rises. It is recent experience that in spite of periods of inflation the price of such electronic goods as televisions, video recorders, computers and washing machines has fallen.

6. Its reliability. One of the noticeable features about the consumer goods listed above is their increasing reliability. Rarely is it necessary to strike a blow at the television set to steady the picture or bring life to the screen. The combination of falling price and increasing reliability increases considerably the inroads that micro-electronics are making into almost every facet of life.

7. Its flexibility. Because microprocessors are programmable their performance can be changed quickly and cheaply, as distinct from all other engineering products.

All these properties add up to a potential application which appears to be endless. What is of particular concern is the ability of micro-electronics to erode away many jobs, in fact to replace humans by machines. Robots are no longer part of fantasy or science fiction – they are real, and are becoming highly sophisticated in the work that they can do. They are reprogrammable and multifunctional, enabling them to carry out such bizarre functions as those of dogs for the blind, and of nurses to assist people in wheelchairs. The speed of take-up of these micro-electronic appliances in manufacturing industries is spectacular. In 1983 there were in the British manufacturing industry 1,000 robots; by 1985 they had risen to 5,000, and between 1984 and 1987 the number of firms using robots more than doubled, while companies using computers for manufacturing rose from 42 per cent to 72 per cent.

The impact of technological change on employment has fascinated a wide range of experts, whose forecasts have shown a marked change over time. In the last decade they have moved from gloomy prognostications about enormous job losses to a growing belief that micro-electronics brings new opportunities and an improved quality of life.

The fear of job losses was based upon a view that after the 1960s, which witnessed a new range of employment in such areas as computer programming and systems analysis, the 1970s and 1980s would see technology reducing jobs as the western world entered a post-industrial age. Employment would become a luxury rather than a right and less than 10 per cent of the population of Britain would be required to produce all the goods that were needed.

Today in the United Kingdom it is difficult to determine how great the level of unemployment in manufacturing is due to new technology because a restructuring process is taking place at a time of world economic depression. For Britain this is further complicated by its relative decline as a manufacturing nation *vis-à-vis* other advanced industrial nations (USA, Germany, Japan) and a group of newly industrialising nations in the Third World (South Korea, Taiwan). Nevertheless, some indication of the impact on employment of the introduction of micro-electronics is given by Northcott and Rogers (1984). They indicate that job losses in manufacturing between 1981 and 1983 were for non-shopfloor workers 2 per cent, for the skilled workforce 12 per cent, and for routine shopfloor workers 71 per cent. It is lack of competitive edge within a wide range of traditional industries like

247

textiles, heavy engineering and shipbuilding, that has resulted in jobs disappearing – maybe for ever, with little hope of new employment within the regions of Britain where these industries are indigenous. This may be too pessimistic a view, for in Scotland at least, new electronic industries have located in what is termed the 'Silicon Glen' in the lowlands of Scotland. In 1987 40,000 people were employed in electronics, which was more than in the traditional industries of coal, shipbuilding and steel.

The decline in manufacturing employment is a characteristic of all western countries as they pass into the post-industrial age, but it is the intensity and steepness of decline which sets the UK apart and has led to the suggestion that long term de-industrialisation is in operation. If this is so, then rather than fear new technology it should be welcomed as a means of 'stopping the rot' and of providing a platform upon which to build a new manufacturing sector, a point discussed in Chapter 2.

A feature of the post-industrial age is the growth in importance of the service industries, and an increase in employment in the quaternary sectors. In other words, more people will work in white collar jobs within the mushrooming office blocks which have been a feature in most of our cities within the last two decades. Until quite recently it was possible to observe that offices contained the technology of the nineteenth century. The typewriter and the telephone were the main technological aids to a system that relied heavily upon human labour. Today the technology of the office has been revolutionised with the introduction of microprocessors. A large section of the workforce is engaged in producing and processing data rather than handling and processing raw material. Investment per office worker amounted to less than US$2,000 compared with US$25,000 per factory worker in USA in the late 1970s, but this 'investment gap' closed in the 1980s as the office has filled with more advanced word processors, new equipment and techniques to store, retrieve and transmit data on microfilm, and electronic postal networks. Furthermore, the innovations in telecommunications enable offices to plug into national and international networks, with the result that information is now sent and received more rapidly than ever before. As an example, the Facsimile (or Fax) transmits text and/or graphics at very high speed, and at low cost compared with the telex and postal services. A copy of a letter or report on A4 paper can be sent to the USA in under a minute. The Fax machine converts the document into a series of electrical pulses, which are then sent down a telephone line. At the other end the image is reconstructed by a printer which responds to the electrical impulses and prints out the image in tiny dots. If, as is likely, the cost of these machines falls, it is possible that they could find their way into not only an increasing number of offices but also into the home. The home could become the office of the future. In 1988 there were nearly half a million terminals in operation in Britain, and the figure is doubling each year.

The competition by manufacturers of high tech products to sell to this growing market has brought smaller, more sophisticated hardware at a price which even small companies can meet. Sir Clive Sinclair paved the way with his cheap computers, but more recently Amstrad have made a quantum leap in this direction with the introduction of the PC1512. This modestly priced computer undercuts many much more expensive machines yet can rival them in the tasks it can undertake.

Table 11.1 Forecasts of the impact of new technology on employment

Report	Types of job affected	Number
Siemens, 1978	40% office jobs in Germany carried out by computers by 1990	2 million typing and secretarial jobs lost
Nora and Minc, May 1978	Banking and insurance jobs in France	30% reduction in jobs in next 10 years
Barron and Curnow, 1979	Secretaries, typists, clerks and managers	10–20% unemployment levels in next 15 years
Jenkins and Sherman, 1979	Information processing jobs	30% displacement by 1990
Virgo, 1979	Private sector services – clerical and administrative staff – particularly in insurance, banking and building societies	40% jobs at risk in the 1980s
	Public sector services	Up to 2/3 of all clerical and administrative jobs at risk

Source: 'Information Technology in the office: the impact on women's jobs', 1980, 3.

All this seems to indicate a serious loss of employment opportunities, particularly for women, as technology takes over the office. This pessimistic view has been supported by a number of forecasts of job losses in office employment (Table 11.1).

Evidence from a wide range of sources would suggest that the present high levels of unemployment not only in Britain, but within the EEC, are likely to grow worse. The unemployed may be reclassified as the recreational classes, and the role of educational institutions may change from providing skills and academic qualifications for a working life to developing creative skills to enable people to live fulfilled lives without work.

If such a scenario came to pass the implication for society would be extreme. Work is important to men and women to meet basic physiological and biological requirements, social activity and self-esteem (Argyle, 1972). Each person has a basic need for food, warmth and security. Food, clothing and housing are purchased with money gained from working and security by paying taxes to support armed forces and a civilian police force. At work we meet people and develop friendships. An American study found that of those who would work even if they did not need the money, 31 per cent, gave social contacts as their reason (Morse and Weiss, 1955). Self-esteem is another important human factor. It covers all kinds of individual self-satisfaction, from the sense of achievement through work, to the satisfaction of supporting oneself and having a status in society. For the unemployed the lack of self-esteem which the loss of work brings may be harder to live with than the loss of income.

Human beings require work, but the foregoing discussion on high technology suggests that this may become a privilege enjoyed by a minority. More recent investigations (Riche, 1983; Levitan and Johnson, 1984) mainly in the USA suggest that this will not be so. Riche points to the experience of the past three decades in the USA, maintaining 'that as long as the economy is growing, the introduction of innovations with tremendous potential for productivity gains can be compatible with rising employment'. During the period 1950 to 1980 when new technologies were diffused widely in industry and offices, employment increased by 77 per cent whilst output grew 177 per cent. This optimistic picture is supported by Levitan and Johnson, who, making the same assumption that a healthy rate of economic growth will be maintained, believe that aggregate demand for new goods and services will generate new employment opportunities. Although some readjustments are necessary, it seems that work is here to stay.

Readjustment is an important concept in this context, because jobs and skills are disappearing, but new ones are emerging. People must readjust by developing new skills. Management in industry and governments alike must introduce retraining schemes ahead of job loss so that unemployment is avoidable wherever possible. This increasing need for skills is part of what is termed the 'skill-twist', in which the demand for low or unskilled jobs will fall whilst the demand for higher skills, particularly in engineering, will rise.

The pace of human readjustment cannot match the speed of technological change and to varying degrees society will introduce a braking mechanism to slow this change down. Capital intensive industries already have vast investment in existing plant and machinery and cannot afford to replace existing equipment. To find new capital for this purpose when a company is already borrowing from the bank will be extremely difficult. It has been estimated that the replacement of only 5 per cent of all blue collar workers in Western industrialised nations would require investment totalling $3,000 million in each of the next 40 years (President of Unimation, Inc., largest US robot manufacturer).

The reaction of the Luddites towards the introduction of machinery into the factories of the nineteenth century is a reminder that those likely to suffer change can react strongly against it. The attitude of the unions today towards technological change is an important element, as is the attitude of society in general. In recent times the newspaper industry has witnessed this opposition by the printing workers, whose skills have largely been made redundant by new technology. In this example, the unacceptable face of technology has appeared for all to see, as the workers of Fleet Street have lost their jobs to another group of skilled workers, the electricians, who in the case of *The Times* are now employed in a new factory in East London. The introduction of new methods of working and new machinery is not always easy when there is an aversion by workers to this new order.

What seems likely, therefore, is that, rather than a revolution, there will be an evolutionary process in which the introduction of new technology will be controlled to enable society to go some way towards absorbing change without too much dislocation of employment. Furthermore, this evolutionary process will open up new opportunities, which will be to society's advantage, for improving the quality of life.

Change in technology brings changes in location of workplace. For the regional policy makers of the UK the new technology provides little hope of a rebirth of manufacturing in the older industries of the North and South Wales. Tomorrow's industries are not going to be born in yesterday's regions, according to urban policy advice given to President Carter. In Britain the signs are clearly there that the location of high technology is away from the old industrial areas, or 'smoke stack Britain', to a broad belt that runs from Oxford and Winchester through the Thames Valley and Milton Keynes to Cambridge (Hall, 1981). This southern arc of development has a partial explanation in the attractiveness of the South as a place to live, but more to do with the presence of international airports and prestigious universities.

The international airport provides one focus of activity, particularly for those firms whose parent company is abroad. The M4 corridor along the motorway leading away from Heathrow airport contains American high technology corporations, many from Silicon Valley in California, who wished to establish European beachheads close to the airport. The skills needed for these firms were to some extent already in the area, because the corridor contained a number of government research establishments particularly concerned with defence. It was, nevertheless, not based upon indigenous activity; it did not spring from the research found within our own universities.

11.2   Cambridge: a case study

To illustrate this university-based location and the development of the Silicon Valley model, one looks to such centres as Cambridge. In Cambridge a number of factors came together to create an environment which was exceptionally conducive to the creation of totally new companies in the high technology field. The stimulus came from government when in the late 1960s, as part of what was described as the red-hot technological revolution, universities were urged to increase their contact with high technology industries. A Cambridge University Committee was appointed to examine what could be done 'to lower the threshold' (Bullock, 1983) of the University to commercial interaction in order to forge some form of relationship between the world of academia and industry. The result was the recommendation, in late 1969, of a moderate expansion of science-based industry close to the city to take full advantage of the research, equipment and libraries, and to feed back information and experience into the University and other scientific organisations within the city. The visible result of the recommendation is the science park, an area of land to the north of the city owned by Trinity College.

The project began modestly on a 14-acre site in April 1970. It then proceeded by phased development to a size of 112 acres with some 63 companies now involved in a wide range of high technology or 'leading-edge technologies' concerned with the promotion of innovation. The connections between these companies and the University of Cambridge may not be so strong as those between Stanford University and the Santa Clara Valley, but they are significant. Perhaps more importantly, the science park provided the catalyst for high technology development within the Cambridge area and for the emergence of what is now described as the 'Cambridge phenomenon' (Segal Quince & Partners, 1985). This phenomenon is suggested as having a number of distinctive characteristics:

(a) The presence in and immediately around Cambridge of a large number of high technology companies, mainly in the computing hardware and software, scientific instruments and electronics industries, and increasingly also in biotechnology.
(b) Within this sector a very high proportion of young, small, independent and indigenous companies, and correspondingly a low proportion of subsidiary operations of large companies based elsewhere.
(c) A long record of high technology company formation in the area. This proceeded at a very modest rate until the 1960s when there was a slight increase in activity, followed by a further increase in the early–mid 1970s and a very substantial increase in the late 1970s which shows no sign of abating.
(d) The tendency for the high technology firms to be engaged in research-design-development activities or in small-volume, high-value production. As a corollary there is an absence of large-scale production undertaken by the firms themselves (such volume production as there is being subcontracted elsewhere).
(e) The many direct and indirect links that can be traced between these firms and the University and associated research complexes, and also between the firms themselves.

What has happened in Cambridge, began first in the USA, where it has been clearly demonstrated that innovations come directly from fundamental and applied research, so a link with a university is essential. These new industries employ scarce and very valuable researchers, who will only come if a highly innovative milieu is present and if financiers are prepared to venture capital. Such conditions were found in Cambridge where a 'skill cluster' (Hall and Preston, 1988) was established and financial institutions, in particular Barclays Bank PLC, were prepared to risk capital.

All this is bad news for governments which are seeking ways of reinvigorating the older industrial areas, where such environments are rarely present. Nevertheless, there are some grounds for optimism for the innovations have, if successful, to go into manufacture and this is unlikely to occur in this southern belt of innovation. In Cambridge, through strict planning controls, it is not allowed, so companies like Sinclair produced their computers in the Timex factory in Dundee and the ill-fated C5 car in the Hoover factory in Merthyr Tydfil. The opportunity for job creation is therefore possible, so long as Britain can compete with countries like South Korea and Taiwan in the manufacturing and assembly of products – if not, Britain's innovatory ideas will go elsewhere and the opportunities will be lost.

A pattern has emerged of growing disparity of opportunity between the South and the rest of Britain, and between urban and rural areas, since the environment of the countryside or of small towns is conducive to these high tech companies (Gould and Keeble, 1984). Something akin to the cottage industries which existed prior to the Industrial Revolution in the nineteenth century can be found in Hampshire, Berkshire and parts of East Anglia, where new technology and the emergence of the small firm go hand in hand.

11.3 Working from home

At the same time the new technological developments have great potential for revolutionising where and how people work, though not necessarily associated with the innovation companies directly. The microprocessor and optic fibres, which are central to information technology (IT), now enable certain people to work at home if they so wish. As early as 1965, the data generated from the San Francisco Bay Area Transportation Commission and analysed by Jones (1973) of Stanford University indicated that '22 per cent of the trips to work in the morning were substitutable and therefore 22 per cent of the occupations could take place in the home'.

M.J. Aldrich (1983) in a lecture on the 'Wired Community' described staying in a remote, two-hundred-year old cottage in the Yorkshire Dales in which the telephone linked him, with direct-dial capability, to over 100 countries, and the computer could be connected by telephone line to his office computer located in Sussex. This would give him all the information and communication services that existed on his office desk: in-tray, diary, messaging, mail, filing and even an electronic waste bin. He could have 'done [his] job in that remote and beautiful cottage'.

To many this position, if desired, may seem unattainable. Yet Marsh (1981) bravely forecast that around the year 2018, if present trends continue, an event will occur of startling significance for the way we run our lives. In that year there will be more computer terminals than telephones, many of which will be in the home. The Post Office suggest that by the year 2000 there will be as many residential telephones as households. Although not equivalent to a telephone in every home it does widen the possibility of more people working from home, for computer can talk to computer down a telephone line. It seems technology is increasingly undermining the need for all communication to involve physical movement.

The implications of these developments are enormous in their impact on our lives and it is worth while considering some of the advantages and disadvantages that working from home brings:
Advantages

- The responsibility of being one's own boss.
- Flexibility of time (not tied to office hours).
- Less distractions at home than in an office and therefore less time wasted.
- No travelling, bringing a saving in time and money and a reduction of pressure on road and railway.

Disadvantages
- Isolation: cross-fertilisation of ideas missing; no feedback (except via the computer screen).
- Isolation: no social contact.

253

- Work much longer than time officially employed.
- Too much contact with the family leading to tension and family rows.
- More interruptions at home from the family.
- Confidentiality is more of a problem in the home.
- Not enough space at home.

Working from home raises important issues about job satisfaction, the relationship between work and non-work, and the links between the employer and his employees if they are usually at home. Evidence so far would suggest that where firms have taken advantage of computer-based telecommunications to free professional staff from an office-bound life, the results have been more than satisfactory. A study published in November 1987, *The Telecommuters* (Kinsman, 1987), showed that provided the communications and management were properly designed, tele-working (working from home) could bring great benefits to both firms and employees.

For firms included in the survey it was an important advantage to be able to tap the skilled female labour who opt out of the conventional labour market. Competition for workers with four or more years computer experience can be fierce so the offer of home-based employment is an attractive proposition. Working from home was also advantageous to firms because it cut their overheads. In a normal business rent, rates and the rest of bureaucracy will double the pay cost of the average worker. If to this is added the evidence from the survey that the tele-worker is more productive than his full-time counterpart, then this type of working has considerable benefits for companies. But what about the worker?

There were reservations about working from home, as some employees found an emptiness and a feeling of being cut off, but generally this new form of working was welcomed. It made it possible for employees to work in whatever way fitted into the rest of their life, and they could maintain and develop their careers at speeds which suited them. Nevertheless, for tele-workers to be successful in the home environment required self-discipline, confidence and an ability to work on their own. A move to more home-based work is not without problems for firms and their employees, but large computer companies like ICL have demonstrated that home-based schemes are successful if the management systems are carefully designed and properly trained supervisors are used.

A significant step towards more home-based work has come from the recognition of its value by the Confederation of British Industry (*The Times*, 4 August 1988), whose director-general, Mr John Barham, now plans to press companies to move much more of their UK workforce out of the office and into homes linked by telecommunications: 'We are now in the midst of a telecommunication revolution which is moving so fast that there will be no need for many people to commute in the accepted sense to London, Birmingham, Manchester, Glasgow or a score of other cities.' The Confederation forecast that telephone-linked computers and Facsimile machines could allow 4 million people, or one in six of the working population to carry out their jobs and business at home by 1995. For the Confederation and for the Henley Centre for Forecasting (*The Times*, 30 August 1988), a number of important advantages would be gained from encouraging 'telecommuting':

(a) A reduction in company overheads through savings in high-cost office space and greater worker efficiency.
(b) An impact on the problem of skill shortage. New skills could be acquired from those at home because, with less time spent travelling to work, there would be more time to combine training with work.
(c) Savings in medical treatment and lost working days.
(d) A drop in commuting traffic, both road and rail. The introduction in January 1989, by British Rail of fare increases of up to double their former level, particularly for those travelling the longer distances on inter-city services, may encourage this.
(e) Changes in house prices. Pressure could be taken off the South East, for example. The flexibility of location of work place could have interesting repercussions on the national housing market.

The home itself would also change in order to absorb the joint role of home and work place. Houses would become larger with more rooms and recreational space around them, or take on a new form. Essex County Council in their new town of South Woodhams Ferrers have introduced the 'studio home', which combines a studio or office of a maximum of 100 m² with a residential unit. They have also separated the home from the work place in other dwellings by building a single-storey building at the opposite end of the garden from the house.

11.4 Conclusion

There are dangers in forecasting what might happen in the future, but it is already clear that modern technology has eliminated the ties which fix a particular industry to a particular place, and is changing the nature of manufacturing industry as smaller companies develop to apply and further this technology. In 1988 about 25 per cent of the national workforce was employed in some 1.6 million small companies. With the larger firms utilising more robots they will cease to be the major employers because robots will be cheaper than people to employ and perhaps less trouble. As increasingly more people accept the opportunity to work at home, and with it the flexibility to live where they wish, this could have radical implications for population movement in Britain, with more people seeking rural environments, possibly in areas of outstanding natural beauty such as the Yorkshire Dales or the Lake District, if the planners allow. The journey to work could be dramatically reduced but the extent to which people travel may increase if they have more leisure time and increasing affluence. All will depend upon the willingness of the British people to accept new technology, to introduce and use it, and to provide sufficient investment in research and risk capital in 'leading edge' industries to achieve and maintain a position alongside the developed nations of the world.

12 A spatial framework for regional and urban policy

Throughout Part I of this book we demonstrated that in the whole field of national economic development only one thing is constant, and that is *change*. The same can be said about regional and urban policy, as most of Part II of this book has sought to illustrate. Just as in the day-to-day world of all industrial economies nothing stays the same, and as the nation, its counties, cities and towns must change in order to cope with new economic forces and challenges, so must government policy. We saw in Chapters 6 and 7 how regional and urban *policies* have gone through a whole series of modifications since their inception in the 1920s–1930s, and how the political parties have adopted different definitions of what constitute regional and urban economic 'problems' and have developed different policy instruments to deal with them. In Chapters 8 and 9 we focused on the measurable *effects* of those policy instruments – the factories built, firms persuaded to move, jobs created in Assisted Areas, and so on. In Chapter 10 we endeavoured to give some indication of the *effectiveness* of policy instruments, primarily in terms of the net cost to the Exchequer of each job created, and of the fact that the number of 'new' jobs in a Member of Parliament's constituency has considerable political significance.

The presentation of policy facts and figures in Chapters 6 to 10 had a common underlying theme: that any discussion of regional and urban problems and policies has distinct *spatial* connotations – it takes place within a geographic context. A large number of government policies are, or appear to be, *aspatial*, in the sense that they deal with national rather than geographically differentiable problems. The 'delivery' of any associated programmes via regional or local offices is purely for administrative convenience, and does not necessarily imply that the 'problem' has any particular spatial characteristics. In the case of regional and urban policy, however, the programmes are designed and delivered on a spatial basis (e.g. DAs, IAs, UPAs, EZs). An important topic of discussion among professional and academic economists and geographers, therefore, is whether or not the geographical areas used in regional and urban policy deliberations represent the most appropriate spatial framework, regardless of the level of spending or specific policy details.

Adoption of the most appropriate spatial framework for regional and urban policy is fundamental to problem delineation and programme delivery. Therefore, the framework needs to be based on well-established geographic areas, which already possess particular economic functions, which are flexible in their capacity to respond to changing economic conditions, and which interrelate with each other in a mutually supportive manner. Policy measures administered through such a framework should be 'efficient', avoiding duplication of effort or conflicts of interest, but to date 'problems' have been identified first, then policies designed to address them, and finally an arbitrary set of geographical boundaries decided upon for programme administration purposes.

12.1   The current spatial framework: travel-to-work areas

Current regional policy remains committed to a reduction of regional imbalances in employment opportunities using a range of selective grants available in AAs within a spatial framework defined by travel-to-work areas. Although the spatial relationship between place of work and place of home is in process of change from larger industrial cities and towns to smaller rural settlements, the vast majority of people are still urban-orientated in terms of both work and home. Travel-to-work areas are usually dominated by an urban centre and as such are wholly or partly *urban regions* which, in turn, may be grouped together in a complex of conurbation regions each under the domination of a major urban centre. This fact of the spatial organisation of people and industry (manufacturing and services) has not, however, resulted in the total co-ordination of all government spending on regional and urban assistance. In reality, of course, regional assistance is virtually as town-and-city-orientated as is specific urban assistance, since most manufacturing and even a great deal of mining are located in or near urban centres. Separating the urban from the regional organisation of economic space is very largely for administrative, and therefore budgetary, convenience, since in reality both elements of this spatial arrangement are integrated and inseparable. The urban bias of regional assistance is also supplemented by the inducements to industry afforded by infrastructural developments and by the promotional activities of local urban authorities.

The schemes of incentives offered to Britain's regions and inner cities since March 1988, continue to be administered within travel-to-work areas. This is an established and convenient geographical framework, but it is not necessarily a set of functional areas which possesses the sensitivity and flexibility necessary to demonstrate changes in the spatial balance of industrial structure and the urban–rural shift in employment emphasis. In the latter respect, the finding by Fothergill and Gudgin (1982) that urban areas lost jobs in the 1970s much more quickly than did rural areas, with the resultant shift in relative employment emphasis to the latter, points to a need for job creation assistance being spatially co-ordinated in *urban–rural regions*.

Between 1960 and 1981, employment in manufacturing declined by 51 per cent in London, 43 per cent in the conurbations, 29 per cent in non-conurbation cities and 18 per cent in other large towns, but in small towns it just about held its own (down 1.4 per cent), while in rural areas it grew by over 26 per cent (Fothergill et al., 1985, 6). Over the same time period, regional policy contributed to this urban loss/rural gain trend by generating two manufacturing jobs in the rural subregions of AAs for every single manufacturing job created in their conurbations (Moore et al., 1986, 55). However, the most rapidly growing employment sector is not manufacturing but services, and since services are predominantly urban-based there is considerable logic in policy trying to take account of the employment opportunities being generated by service industries in and near towns and cities. This would need to be complemented by policy recognition of the fact that the employment potential of an urban centre *and* its rural hinterland should be treated as parts of an interrelated whole, and not dealt with as separate and distinct entities for purposes of assistance disbursement.

The functional interrelatedness of city and region is recognised in principle by central government but largely ignored in practical terms. To a large extent this is probably because of the precedents of administration that we noted in Chapter 6 – namely, the administration of regional policy by the Department of Trade and Industry (DTI) and of urban policy by the Department of the Environment (DOE). Even the methods of data collection and scales of areas considered by the two departments are different. The DTI aggregates local employment office areas into travel-to-work areas, whereas the DOE starts at the more discrete spatial scale of the census ward and then ranks urban local authorities according to the proportion of wards meeting certain socio-economic criteria before designating the areas to be assisted. According to researchers at Newcastle University's Centre for Urban and Regional Development Studies (CURDS), if unemployment rates are used as the chief criterion for determining priority areas in regional and urban policy, the results are quite similar in AAs because the problem is widespread, but they differ markedly in large cities where the more prosperous suburban wards offset the poorer inner city wards in any overall assessment, to the detriment of the latter (CURDS, 1984, 3).

12.1.1 Delimitation of regions

It is always difficult to know how best to draw boundaries around 'problem' areas (as we briefly discussed in Chapter 1) and to define and administer the most beneficial 'treatment'. To date, delimiting the spatial extent of problem areas has been based largely upon administrative convenience because this eases data acquisition – the facts and figures needed by decision makers are already being collected by some government department. The boundary lines around regions are not hard and fast, however, and can be modified in order to take account of changing circumstances (e.g. population redistribution through migration), as happened to the 1964 Standard Planning Region (SPR) boundaries in 1974 when county boundaries were redrawn (compare Fig. 7.1 with Fig. 7.4). It is well to remember that SPRs are simply collections of counties that reflect fairly broad administrative units, although they do substantially influence the way in which we perceive the spatial organisation of the country. But do such planning regions form sections of the country with which not only administrators and academics can identify, but so too can people in general?

The most crucial feature of SPRs is that they and their sub-regions (counties, travel-to-work areas, census wards) are the units of spatial classification for many government statistics. Also, they are used extensively by the media and can be identified fairly readily by the majority of the population, although the latter's 'allegiance' is often more local than regional. There is a danger, however, of thinking of SPRs as normal, natural, supremely rational divisions of national economic space. People, politicians and planners can become so imbued with the 'personification of territory' idea that, 'regions become more than mere territory but organic wholes, greater than the sum of their inhabitants, with ends of their own' (O'Sullivan, 1981, 193–4). The relationship between regional ideas and regional policy is discussed in detail by Parsons (1986, 170–202).

In essence, this reflects the basic question of an individual's identification with space, ranging in scale from the street gang's 'turf' through a person's neighbourhood, home town, county, region, nation and even international grouping (e.g. European). Identification with, or a sense of belonging to: Europe, promotes internationalism; Britain, centralised nationalism; England, Scotland, Wales or Northern Ireland, decentralised nationalism; counties or regions, provincialism. In times of economic growth and prosperity, provincialism seems to come to the fore, bolstered by a sense of economic autonomy, with clamourings for decentralisation of power from Westminster not only to Edinburgh, Cardiff and Belfast but also to Newcastle, Leeds, Manchester, Birmingham, Bristol and so on. In times of stagnation or economic decline, however, there is greater consciousness of a need for central government to 'do something' to help those parts of the country hardest hit by the recession.

12.1.2 The urban–rural spatial continuum

The fact that regions are not independent economic units has been recognised, of course, since the beginnings of regional policy, but the extent to which the regions are interrelated has not always been fully appreciated. Regional economists and planners, and perhaps even politicians, have belatedly realised that, in terms of the aims and objectives of social and economic spatial planning, the regions and the nation are inseparable. Indeed, the SPRs are relatively small in size and consequently have a high degree of openness between them, so that regional statistics are deceptively simplistic in that they do not show *inter*regional connectivity, nor do they readily indicate *intra*-regional urban–urban linkages let alone urban–rural links. However, the SPRs are large enough for their internal diversity in virtually any variable we care to measure to be much greater than any external difference between them. The smaller the area used, the more accurate the picture of disparities in the space economy. Therefore, any arithmetic average at the SPR level of aggregation is bound to give an inaccurate impression of reality. As Professor D. W. Rhind commented in a letter to *The Times* (13 August 1986), '. . . the very use of these regions [SPRs] as area units obscures the real and often dramatic differences between the various parts of Britain'.

Each region, whatever its size, contains within it both urban and rural areas, and just as they interact economically, so do all the regions at all scales, and in so doing contribute towards the total national economy. It is naive, therefore, to differentiate in policy between the 'urban' and 'rural' elements of a region, since both are integral parts of a whole; they do not function independently and cannot logically be treated independently. This is particularly so in view of the urban–rural shift in manufacturing capacity and employment over the last 20 years, as we noted above (p. 257). This shift is 'chiefly a response to agglomeration diseconomies in hitherto relatively unindustrialised and often rural areas', according to Keeble (1981, 213). In particular, manufacturing firms were looking to rationalise and restructure industry on both economic and spatial bases (Massey and Meegan, 1979) and they were encouraged to leave urban areas by:

1. the need for higher floorspace/worker ratios as capital intensity increased; and
2. the availability and lower price of land, both attainable in rural areas (Fothergill and Gudgin, 1982).

Indeed, Keeble (*idem*) argues that the manufacturing performance of the SPRs during the 1970s 'was chiefly to be explained by the precise mix of sub-regions within each region, in terms of levels of urbanisation'. It would seem, therefore, that a spatial framework of appropriately scaled urban regions and sub-regions is essential to an understanding both of the way in which the national space economy operates and of the 'best' way of organising and administering government financial assistance.

12.1.3 Value of Standard Planning Regions

How suitable then, are SPRs and their subdivisions as areal units for displaying and 'guiding' the spatial balance of the nation's economy regional assistance? Should we use the current SPRs for anything other than convenient groupings of statistical data collection and presentation? See Appendix. Are there other groupings of administrative areas which would provide a spatial framework more sensitive to problem identification and government assistance programming than those currently in use?

Regional economists have been loathe to 'grasp the nettle' of regional boundary drafting since, as Richardson (1978, 17) observes: '. . . defining regions precisely is such a nightmare that most regional economists' prefer to shy away from the task, and are relieved when they are forced to work with administrative regions on the grounds that policy considerations require it or that data are not available for any other spatial units'. Indeed, in its report responding to the government's *White Paper* of 1983 asking for reactions to its regional policy proposals, even the Regional Studies Association Panel (1983, 132) argued that, 'With all their shortcomings . . . the Standard Regions offer a manageable number of spatial units for which a regional tier of organisation of several relevant government departments is already in place.' Passing judgement on the 'where' questions of national housekeeping within an existing spatial framework may ease the strain on regional economists, but it does not necessarily yield *optimal* solutions in this respect, rather *satisfactory* ones.

12.2 Functional urban regions

Half a century ago, the Barlow Commission recommended that, in order to achieve the equable regional development of national economic growth, industrial location planning and population housing planning should both come under the roof of one government department. As we noted in Chapters 6 and 7, not only did this not happen, but no truly coherent national strategy for the British space economy emerged either; indeed, strategies developed in individual planning regions often failed to take account of proposals formulated in adjacent regions! Barlow's admonition of 1937 is still relevant today since, as research in the 1970s and 1980s has shown, when it comes to talking about the spatial context of regional planning we are not really referring to SPRs, rather we think in terms of functional urban regions. We must realise that we cannot separate the growth regions from the declining regions, the South from the North, old conurbations from New Towns, inner city from suburb, urban from rural, industrial developments from population change – all are interconnected elements of the national economic system. Are there any alternatives to the current SPRs which offer viable spatial frameworks, are fairly easy to implement and administer, and are identifiable by the population? There are many, but we will consider three, all of which concur with the suggestion of House (1982, 10) '. . . that provincial metropolis can help stabilise their hinterlands and act as the political, economic or social foci of either freshly defined or reinforced regional identities'.

12.2.1 City regions

As we saw in Chapter 3, during the nineteenth and twentieth centuries the geographical impact of the growing metropolitan centres was increasingly one of reorganising the pre-industrial rural landscape into new urban regions. The administrative significance of this emerging spatial pattern was not really recognised until the creation of the Greater London Council in 1965 and was then considered by the Royal Commission on Local Government in England, whose recommendations appeared in what is known as the *Redcliffe-Maud Report* in 1969. These recommendations resulted in some changes to local government boundaries (most of which dated from the 1890s) and in the creation of the metropolitan counties, with consequences for the SPR map in 1974, but it was only in the case of the new county of Avon, centred on Bristol, that the concept of the city region was truly taken into account. In fact, in a dissenting memorandum to the Redcliffe-Maud Report, Derek Senior, an urban geographer, suggested a quite 'radical' modification to the existing county-based spatial organisation of the country with a 42 city-region structure (see Fig. 5.1, p. 103). These city regions could be readily aggregated into SPRs of greater functional significance than those currently used.

12.2.2 'Real' regions

An attempt to delineate England's regions from an historical perspective has been made by Waites (1984, 166) with a map of eight provinces '. . . divided into real regions which have historical validity and a meaning to the people' (Fig. 12.1). A newly created region like Humberside (1974), however, with little historical identity, would take at least a generation to build new loyalties to any regional identity.

These *real* regions are based on the pre-1974 counties, are therefore readily recognisable, and their 'capitals' generally conform with established urban centres of regional significance, so that transformation of Waite's map into functional SPRs would be fairly straightforward. This slightly 'romantic'

Figure 12.1 The 'real' provinces and regions of England (cf. Figs 5.1 and 12.2). Source: Waites (1984, 166)

(A) Provinces
⊙ Provincial capitals
Numbers = Regions
● Regional capitals
Letters = cities

Key to provinces and regions

Pennines
Province (A)
1. Northumbria
2. Cumbria
3. Ouse
4. Deira
5. Elmet
6. Lancastria

Danelaw
Province (B)
7. Lindsey
8. Trent
9. Shires

Mercia
Province (C)
10. Delamere
11. Borders
12. Arden

East Anglia
Province (D)
13. Wensum
14. Orwell
15. Colne

London
Province (E)

Weald
Province (F)
17. N. Downs
18. S. Downs

Wessex
Province (G)
19. Solent
20. Stonehenge
21. Chilterns

West Country
Province (H)
22. Cotswold
23. Exe

Key to City initials

(A)
C – Carlisle
Ne – Newcastle
M – Manchester
L – Leeds
Y – York
H – Hull

(B)
D – Derby
Le – Leicester
No – Northampton
Li – Lincoln

(C)
Ch – Chester
Bi – Birmingham
He – Hereford

(D)
N – Norwich
I – Ipswich
Co – Colchester

(F)
Ca – Canterbury
Br – Brighton

(G)
O – Oxford
Sa – Salisbury
S – Southampton

(H)
B – Bristol
E – Exeter

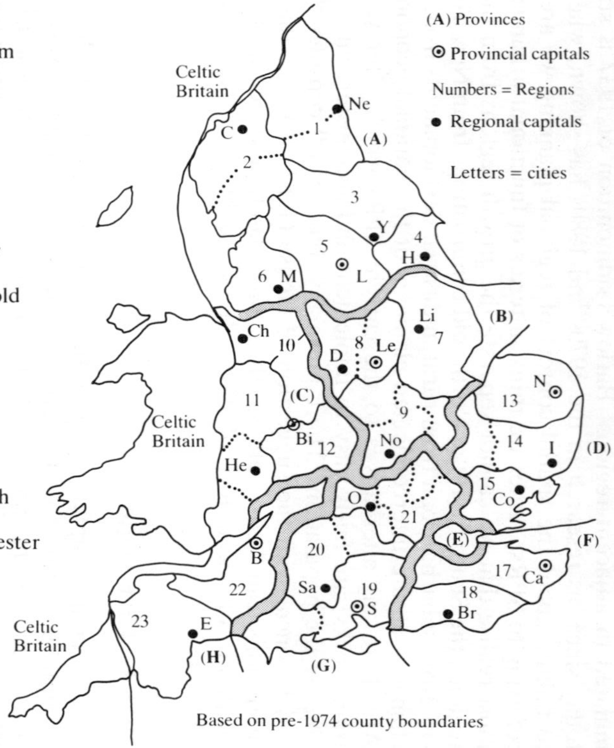

Based on pre-1974 county boundaries

yearning for provinces and regions based on historic identity of place is complemented by Waite's claim that, 'Equally important . . . is the recognition that our country must give more scope for regional consciousness not only in its everyday life but also in its political administration' (*idem*).

12.2.3 Functional regions

To some extent, the latter point has been subsumed within the CURDS attempt to break down national space into areal units based on patterns of commuting linkage to established urban centres. Hence, the *city region concept* is again used to provide a framework more suitable than local authority boundaries for data collection, analysis, presentation and forecasting (Fig. 12.2). This is the first real attempt to provide a consistent set of criteria that can be utilised for quantitative analysis countrywide, and can display data at scales ranging from local labour market areas to metropolitan regions (defined as major cities with their commuter ring).

Although at the disaggregated level the 228 functional regions make for a complex set of areal units that are too small for strategic planning purposes, such regions can be aggregated into a series of large-scale areas necessitating relatively little modification to existing SPRs. Such a redrafting of the regional map would provide us with statistically acceptable and administratively workable SPRs. Thus, we could satisfy political requirements in a truly functional spatial framework of city regions that both reflect the daily organisation of our living and working routines and allow the flexibility necessary to accommodate change. The time for such a revision of the map of regional and urban administration is now. Indeed, the process may already have started, if for other reasons, with the dismantling of the financial structure of the metropolitan counties in 1986.

12.3 City regions as an administrative framework

It has become increasingly evident to researchers examining the effectiveness of regional and urban policy that at the local 'grass-roots' level, where the assistance is actually made available to firms, there is considerable confusion. The confusion partially arises from a lack of clarity in the regulations: when it is hard to understand the rules, perception of the incentives is affected and possibly even unfavourably distorted, especially among smaller firms. Probably a greater contribution to the confusion, however, is the fact that assistance is made available via several different routes, depending upon whether the source is local, national or the EEC, and also the fact that the areal unit of disbursement may differ from the allocation unit. For example, both Derelict Land Clearance Orders and ERDGs from the EEC have been designated or allocated on the basis of Employment Office Areas, but actually disbursed on a local authority boundary basis (Buswell, 1983, 26 Regional Studies Association, 1983, 16–17).

The lack of standardisation and consistency of regional and sub-regional areas could be solved by adoption of the CURDS city region framework. Such a simplified spatial approach would also lend itself to a less complex bureaucracy that could handle all forms of assistance from whatever source.

Figure 12.2   Great Britain: functional regions and metropolitan regions. (cf. Figs 5.1 and 12.1)

Source: Centre for Urban and Regional Development Studies (1983, 2)

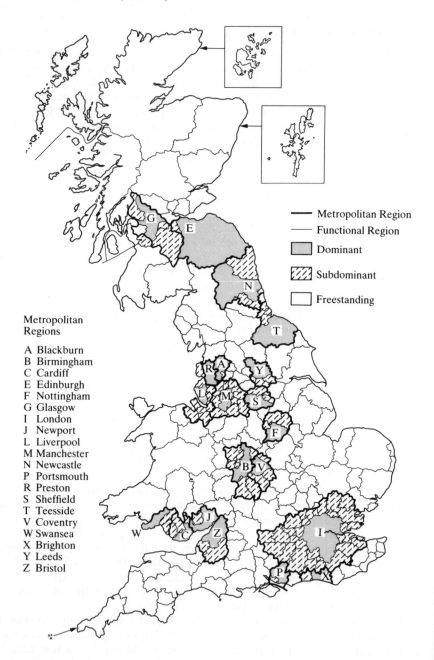

Metropolitan Region
Functional Region
Dominant
Subdominant
Freestanding

Metropolitan Regions

A Blackburn
B Birmingham
C Cardiff
E Edinburgh
F Nottingham
G Glasgow
I   London
J   Newport
L Liverpool
M Manchester
N Newcastle
P Portsmouth
R Preston
S Sheffield
T Teesside
V Coventry
W Swansea
X Brighton
Y Leeds
Z Bristol

Hence, aid for inner city schemes, Enterprise Zones, Advance Factory building and firm relocation assistance, whether derived from EEC, national or local sources, could be comprehensively managed by a single, locally-based agency under the authority of each regional administration. These forms of aid management would also need to be co-ordinated, if not integrated, with expenditure upon housing, transport and other public infrastructure provision within a total regional development strategy.

Administration of such central government expenditure on a city region basis would require the creation of new regional bodies, which could operate within a nationally determined programme aimed at economic growth. In due course, these bodies could become a new tier of government, dedicated to regionalism on the basis of popularly recognised regional identities, and associated with the necessary devolution of power from Westminster. The reasons for some form of regional devolution of power and administrative responsibility are fivefold:

1. There is a need to fill a policy vacuum between local district councils and the national level of government.
2. The traditional view of regionalism, highlighting differences and inequalities, not only illustrates but also provides a framework for a needed redistribution of national resources.
3. There is a need for better co-ordination and articulation of the existing regional administrative structure (compare Figs 12.1, 12.2 and 5.1 with Fig. 1.1).
4. There is considerable dissatisfaction with the present two-tier system of political administration at both the county and district level, which could be overcome by eliminating one (probably the county administration) and replacing it with a regional administration.
5. In order to strengthen regional identity and sense of purpose, and to provide sufficient control over the pursuit of planning goals, there is a need for some devolution of power from central to regional and local government (Moore, 1986; see also Balchin and Bull, 1987, 65–9; Regional Studies Association, 1983, 117–34.)

The question seems to be not so much whether regional devolution will take place, but the form that such a change will assume. The change itself is probably inevitable, and has numerous precedents in other EEC countries, especially France, West Germany and Italy, but there is concern as to whether it will occur incrementally or as a major upheaval, and whether any regional government or development agency will have any real support among the region's population. The latter would almost certainly be assured if the spatial framework adopted employed a combination of the CURDS scheme at the city region scale and Waites' scheme at the broader regional scale.

12.4 Economic planning regions for the Fifth Kondratieff Wave

Inadequate research has been completed into just how efficiently economic space is, or can be, organised around urban centres of different sizes, and

265

how one regional grouping compares with another. Such research is a pre-requisite for any regional definition. In practical terms, regional economists would generally argue that a population of about 3 million is desirable for regional economic planning units, whilst each basic sub-regional unit (city region) should contain not less than 250,000 people. Once defined, the growth *potentials* of these urban regions need to be explored, rather than concentrating on their *problems*, and policy goals stated clearly, over a longer term, and administered as simply as bureaucracy will allow. Given the 'footloose' nature of industrial location, its redistribution from conurbation to smaller town, the shift in employment emphasis from manufacturing to service industries, and the increasing efficiency and availability of transport and communications, it is crucial to equity in any reallocation of national wealth that the most appropriate sizes and structures of planning and administration regions are sought.

We would suggest that Standard Planning Regions, if they are to be anything other than *ad hoc* creations 'having neither administrative significance nor contemporary geographical reality' (Rhind, 1986), must bear some relation to popular spatial awareness. They should comprise sub-regions based upon urban spheres of influence ('functional regions'), and thus provide a framework for the possible identification of 'growth areas' (city regions of concentrated investment) as a means of disseminating economic growth. These could be integrated with appropriate Kondratieff Fifth Wave 'leading-edge' industries, like electronics, biotechnology, robotics, pharmaceuticals, aerospace and information technology. Any euphoria about the job prospects emerging from these sectors, however, should be tempered by the knowledge that Britain's electronics industry lost 62,000 jobs between 1978 and 1985! Nevertheless, there will be employment gains in these 'sunrise' industrial sectors over the next couple of decades, many of them associated with defence spending and most of them in the counties around the western side of London (Hall *et al.*, 1987). Indeed, procurement for the Ministry of Defence accounts for half of the output of Britain's aerospace industry and over 20 per cent of the output of the electronics industry, and of the total national defence expenditure in 1983/4 of £8 billion, 68 per cent was spent in the South; 54 per cent in the South East alone (M. Breheny, University of Reading). Regional and urban assistance pales into insignificance in comparison! Central government could contribute substantially to regional growth prospects by distributing its defence budget largesse proportionately to northern and western regions, not to mention the benefits that would also derive there from the relocation of more government offices in the less prosperous areas – something that devolution would encourage, if not demand. This will not solve the regional and urban problems of the country, however, since such problems are endemic as spatial manifestations of the whole process of economic growth, but it would ease some current inequities.

As we move out of the Fourth and into the Fifth Kondratieff Long Wave of economic development, competition between growing industries will give rise to new regional imbalances which will be complemented or exaggerated by the continuing decline of older industries. At the national scale, our growth rate to the end of the Fourth Wave (*c.* 1995) needs to be twice its current rate if unemployment is to be reduced below 1.5 million (2.16 million in late

1988, according to government figures). But, whatever the rate of economic growth, most of the employment gains (see p. 40) will undoubtedly occur in the South East which, together with parts of East Anglia and the South West, is developing into a 'super region'. Without adequate government action to redress this macro-regional economic divergence, there is a danger that socio-politically even the 'English' national identity will be strained by the growth of a southern super region which looks increasingly to Europe (to be reinforced by EC economic integration and the Channel Tunnel in 1993) and decreasingly to the rest of the nation – peripheral English, Welsh, Scottish and Northern Irish alike!

Some parts of the country are better endowed with locational advantages for industrial development than others, and within regions the same spatial unevenness of opportunity holds true. There never has been, and there never will be, total *national* spatial economic convergence. Since all forms of industry wish to minimise costs by locating as efficiently as human judgement allows with respect to factor inputs, some locations must be more attractive than others. Economically, this is not always that easy to demonstrate, but *the* all-important influence upon the 'where-to-locate' decision may well be the subjective perception of a region's business climate; hence, in a 1985 national survey of electronics firms considering relocation, 30 per cent expressed a preference for the South East and 15 per cent for the South West, (Hudson and Williams, 1986, 80). The spatial reorganisation of industry is a constant phenomenon, only its intensity and locational preferences varying through time. Consequently, growth across all regions, whatever their shape and size, is impossible. Nonetheless, central and local government decision makers can at least help to mitigate some of the resultant inequities by focusing attention on the most appropriate regional structures, by adopting simplified mechanisms for the disbursement of assistance, and by treating all aspects of urban region economies as integral parts of an indivisible whole, the *national* space economy.

Appendix

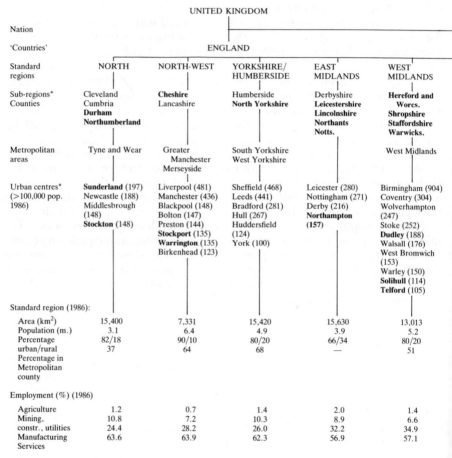

<table>
<tr><td></td><td colspan="5" align="center">UNITED KINGDOM</td></tr>
<tr><td>Nation</td><td colspan="5"></td></tr>
<tr><td>'Countries'</td><td colspan="5" align="center">ENGLAND</td></tr>
<tr><td>Standard regions</td><td>NORTH</td><td>NORTH-WEST</td><td>YORKSHIRE/
HUMBERSIDE</td><td>EAST
MIDLANDS</td><td>WEST
MIDLANDS</td></tr>
<tr><td>Sub-regions*
Counties</td><td>Cleveland
Cumbria
Durham
Northumberland</td><td>**Cheshire**
Lancashire</td><td>Humberside
North Yorkshire</td><td>Derbyshire
Leicestershire
Lincolnshire
Northants
Notts.</td><td>**Hereford and
Worcs.**
Shropshire
Staffordshire
Warwicks.</td></tr>
<tr><td>Metropolitan areas</td><td>Tyne and Wear</td><td>Greater
Manchester
Merseyside</td><td>South Yorkshire
West Yorkshire</td><td></td><td>West Midlands</td></tr>
<tr><td>Urban centres*
(>100,000 pop.
1986)</td><td>**Sunderland** (197)
Newcastle (188)
Middlesbrough
(148)
Stockton (148)</td><td>Liverpool (481)
Manchester (436)
Blackpool (148)
Bolton (147)
Preston (144)
Stockport (135)
Warrington (135)
Birkenhead (123)</td><td>Sheffield (468)
Leeds (441)
Bradford (281)
Hull (267)
Huddersfield
(124)
York (100)</td><td>Leicester (280)
Nottingham (271)
Derby (216)
Northampton
(157)</td><td>Birmingham (904)
Coventry (304)
Wolverhampton
(247)
Stoke (252)
Dudley (188)
Walsall (176)
West Bromwich
(153)
Warley (150)
Solihull (114)
Telford (105)</td></tr>
</table>

Standard region (1986):

	NORTH	NORTH-WEST	YORKSHIRE/HUMBERSIDE	EAST MIDLANDS	WEST MIDLANDS
Area (km²)	15,400	7,331	15,420	15,630	13,013
Population (m.)	3.1	6.4	4.9	3.9	5.2
Percentage urban/rural	82/18	90/10	80/20	66/34	80/20
Percentage in Metropolitan county	37	64	68	—	51

Employment (%) (1986)

	NORTH	NORTH-WEST	YORKSHIRE/HUMBERSIDE	EAST MIDLANDS	WEST MIDLANDS
Agriculture	1.2	0.7	1.4	2.0	1.4
Mining,	10.8	7.2	10.3	8.9	6.6
constr., utilities	24.4	28.2	26.0	32.2	34.9
Manufacturing	63.6	63.9	62.3	56.9	57.1
Services					

* Sub-regions and urban centres
Bold type — growing 1981–86
Roman type — declining 1981–86

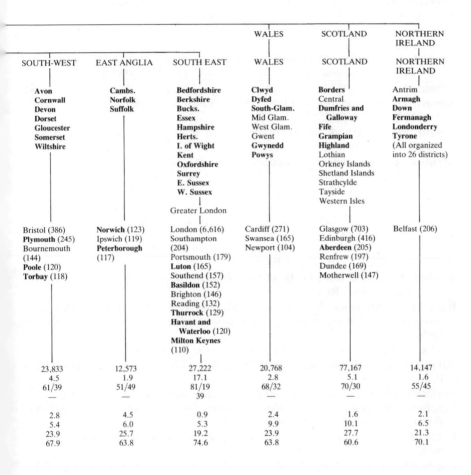

			WALES	SCOTLAND	NORTHERN IRELAND
SOUTH-WEST	EAST ANGLIA	SOUTH EAST	WALES	SCOTLAND	NORTHERN IRELAND
Avon	**Cambs.**	**Bedfordshire**	**Clwyd**	**Borders**	Antrim
Cornwall	**Norfolk**	**Berkshire**	**Dyfed**	Central	**Armagh**
Devon	**Suffolk**	**Bucks.**	**South-Glam.**	**Dumfries and**	**Down**
Dorset		**Essex**	Mid Glam.	**Galloway**	**Fermanagh**
Gloucester		**Hampshire**	West Glam.	**Fife**	**Londonderry**
Somerset		**Herts.**	Gwent	**Grampian**	**Tyrone**
Wiltshire		**I. of Wight**	**Gwynedd**	**Highland**	(All organized
		Kent	**Powys**	Lothian	into 26 districts)
		Oxfordshire		Orkney Islands	
		Surrey		Shetland Islands	
		E. Sussex		Strathcylde	
		W. Sussex		Tayside	
				Western Isles	
		Greater London			
Bristol (386)	**Norwich** (123)	London (6,616)	Cardiff (271)	Glasgow (703)	Belfast (206)
Plymouth (245)	Ipswich (119)	Southampton (204)	Swansea (165)	Edinburgh (416)	
Bournemouth (144)	**Peterborough** (117)	Portsmouth (179)	Newport (104)	**Aberdeen** (205)	
Poole (120)		**Luton** (165)		Renfrew (197)	
Torbay (118)		Southend (157)		Dundee (169)	
		Basildon (152)		Motherwell (147)	
		Brighton (146)			
		Reading (132)			
		Thurrock (129)			
		Havant and Waterloo (120)			
		Milton Keynes (110)			
23,833	12,573	27,222	20,768	77,167	14,147
4.5	1.9	17.1	2.8	5.1	1.6
61/39	51/49	81/19	68/32	70/30	55/45
—	—	39	—	—	—
2.8	4.5	0.9	2.4	1.6	2.1
5.4	6.0	5.3	9.9	10.1	6.5
23.9	25.7	19.2	23.9	27.7	21.3
67.9	63.8	74.6	63.8	60.6	70.1

Bibliography

Abercrombie, P. (1945) *Greater London Plan 1944*. London, HMSO.

Aldrich, M. J. (1983) 'The Wired Community. A Social Perspective'. Paper given to the Council of Europe's Conference on 'Cities in Transition'. Swansea.

Allen, K., Begg, M., McDowell, S. and **Walker, G.** (1985) *Regional Incentives and the Investment Decision of Firms*. London, HMSO.

Allison, L. (1986) 'What is urban planning for?', *Town Planning Review* **57**.

Allnutt, D. and **Gelardi A.** (1980) 'Inner cities in England', *Social Trends*, 39–51. London, HMSO.

Alonso, W. (1960) 'A theory of the urban land market', *Regional Science Association Papers and Proceedings* **6**, 149–57.

Archbishop of Canterbury Commission (1985) *Faith in the City. A Call for Action by Church and Nation*. London, Church House Publishing.

Argyle, M. (1972) *The Social Psychology of Work*. Harmondsworth, Penguin.

Armstrong, H. and **Taylor, J.** (1985) *Regional Economics and Policy*. Oxford, Philip Allen.

Ashworth, W. (1954) *The Genesis of Modern British Town Planning*. London, Routledge and Kegan Paul.

Balchin, P. N. and **Bull, G. H. (1987)** *Regional and Urban Economics*. London, Harper and Row.

Ball, M., Bentivegna, V., Edwards, M. and **Folin, M.** (1985) *Land Rent, Housing and Urban Planning. A European Perspective*. London, Croom Helm.

Banks, F. R. (1957) *Sussex*. Harmondsworth, Penguin.

Barron, I. and Carnow, R. (1979) *The Future with Microelectronics*. London, Frances Pinter.

Barlow Commission *See* Report (1940) of the Royal Commission, *op. cit.*

Beacham, R. (1984) 'Economic activities: Britain's workforce, 1971–81', *Population Trends* **37** (Autumn), 6–13.

Booth, C. (1902) *Life and Labour of the People in London*. London, Macmillan.

Boudeville, J. R. (1966) *Problems of Regional Economic Planning*. Edinburgh, Edinburgh University Press.

Bourne, L. S. (1975) *Urban Systems. Strategies for Regulation*. Oxford, Oxford University Press.

Breheny, M., Cheshire, P. and **Langridge, R**. (1983) 'The anatomy of job creation? Industrial change in Britain's M4 corridor', *Built Environment*, **9**, 61–71.

Briggs, A. (1968) *Victorian Cities*. Harmondsworth, Penguin.

Briggs, A. (1983) *A Social History of England*. London, Book Club Associates.

Browett, J. G. (1977) 'Export base theory and the evolution of the south African Space economy', *South African Geographical Journal* **59**, 18–29.

Browne, L. E. (1985) 'Conflicting views of technological progress', *Economic Impact* **49**, 8–14.

Bullock, M. P. D. (1983) *Academic Enterprise, Industrial Innovation and the Development of High Technology Financing in the United States*. London, Brand Bros.

Burgess, J. A. (1982) 'Selling places: environmental images for the executive', *Regional Studies* **16**, 1–17.

Burke, G. (1971) *Towns in the Making*. London, Edward Arnold.

Buswell, R. J. (1983) *North in the Eighties. Regional Policies for a Decade of Development*. Regional Studies Association, London.

Cabinet Office (1988) *Action for Cities*. London, HMSO.

Cambridge Economics Policy Group (1980) *Economic Review* 6. Farnborough, Gower.

Cambridge Information & Research Services/CIRS (1986) *Industrial Development Guide, 1985–86*. Royston, CIRS.

Cameron, G. C. (ed.) (1980) *The Future of British Conurbations*. London, Longman.

Central Statistical Office (1987a) *Regional Trends 23*. London, HMSO

Central Statistical Office (1987b) *Social Trends*. London, HMSO.

Centre for Urban and Regional Development Studies (1983) *Functional Regions: Definitions, Applications, Advantages*. Factsheet 1. University of Newcastle, CURDS.

Centre for Urban and Regional Development Studies (1984) *Residential Unemployment Rates: Regional and Urban Policy Perspectives*. Factsheet 8. University of Newcastle, CURDS.

Champion, A. G. (1976) ' Evolving patterns of population distribution in England and Wales', *Transactions of the Institute of British Geographers* **1**, 401–20.

Chapman, K. (1980) 'Environmental policy and industrial location', *Area* **12**, 209–16.

Cherry, G. (1972) *Urban Change and Planning. A History of Urban Development in Britain since 1750*. Henley, G. T. Foulis.

Cherry, G. (1982) *The Politics of Town Planning*. London, Longman.

Chisholm, M. (1984a) 'The Development Commission's factory programme', *Regional Studies* **18**(4), 514–17.

Chisholm, M. (1984b) 'Regional policy for the late twentieth century', *Regional Studies* **18**(6), 348–52.

Chisholm, M. (1986) 'The Development Commission's employment programmes in rural England', in Healey and Ilberry (eds), *op. cit.*, 279–91.

Chote, P. (1983) 'Retooling the American work force', *Economic Impact* **41**, 29–32.

Chorley, R. J. Haggett, P. (1967) *Socio- Economic Models in Geography*. London, Methuen.

Christaller, W. (1966) *Central Places in Southern Germany* (translation of

1933 publication, by C. W. Baskin). Englewood Cliffs, New Jersey, Prentice Hall.

Colemen, A. (1985) *Utopia on Trial. Vision and Reality in Planned Housing.* London, Hilary Shipman.

Commission of the European Communities (1978) *Regional Development Programmes, United Kingdom 1978–1980.* Luxembourg, CEC.

Communication Studies and Planning Ltd (1980) *Information Technology in the Office: the Impact on Women's Jobs.* London, CSP.

Cook, C. and **Stevenson, J.** (1983) *Longman Handbook of Modern British History 1714–1980.* Harlow, Longman.

Cooke, P., Morgan, K. and **Jackson, D.** (1984) 'New technology and regional development in austerity Britain: the case of the semi-conductor industry', *Regional Studies* **18**. (4), 277–89

Cosgrove, I. and **Jackson, R.** (1972) *The Geography of Recreation.* London, Hutchinson.

Cullingworth, J. B. (1979) *Essays on Housing Policy. The British Scene.* London, George Allen and Unwin.

Cullingworth, J. B. (1988) *Town and Country Planning in Britain*, 10th edn. London, George Allen and Unwin.

Damesick, P. (1987) 'The changing economic context for regional development in the UK' in Damesick, P and Wood, P (eds) *Regional Problems, Problem Regions and Public Policy in the U. K.* Clarendon, Oxford pp 1–17.

Daniels, P. W. (1969) 'Office decentralization from London: policy and practice', *Regional Studies* **3**, 171–8.

Daniels, P. W. (1986) 'Producer services and the post-industrial space economy', in Martin and Rowthorn (eds), *op. cit.*, 291–321.

Darwent, D. F. (1969) 'Growth poles and growth centers in regional planning – a review', *Environment & Planning* **1**, 5–31.

Davies, J. G. (1972) *The Evangelistic Bureaucrat.* London, Tavistock.

Demko, G.(ed.) (1984) *Regional Development Problems and Policies in Eastern and Western Europe.* Beckenham, Croom Helm.

Dennis, R. (1978) 'The decline of manufacturing employment in Greater London', *Urban Studies* **15**, 63–73.

Department of Education and Science (1967) Central Advisory Council for Education (England), *Children and their Primary Schools* (Plowden Report). London, HMSO.

Department of Employment (various years) *Employment Gazette*, London, HMSO.

Department of the Environment (1974–6) *Inner Area Studies: Reports.* London, HMSO.

Department of the Environment (1977) *Recreation and Deprivation in Inner Urban Areas*, London, HMSO.

Department of the Environment (1977) *Policy for the Inner Cities.* White Paper, Cmnd 6845. London, HMSO.

Department of the Environment (1977) *Housing Policy: A Consultative Document.* Green Paper, Cmnd 6851. London, HMSO.

Department of the Environment (1985) *An Inquiry into the Condition of the Local Authority Housing Stock In England.* London, HMSO.

Department of the Environment (1986) *Transforming Our Wasteland: The Way Forward*. London, HMSO.

Department of the Environment (1987) *Housing Policy: A Consultative Document*. Green Paper, Cmnd 6851. London, HMSO.

Department of the Environment (1987) *Housing: The Government's Proposals*. White Paper, Cmnd 214. London, HMSO.

Department of Trade and Industry (1973) *Expenditure Committee (Trade & Industry Sub-Committee), Minutes of Evidence 4th July 1973*. London, HMSO.

Department of Trade and Industry (1983) *Regional Industrial Development*. White Paper, Cmnd 9111. London, HMSO.

Department of Trade and Industry (1988) *DTI – The Department of Enterprise*. London, HMSO.

Dicken, P. and **Lloyd, P.** (1981) *Modern Western Society. A Geographical Perspective on Work, Home and Well being*. London, Harper and Row.

Dower, M. (1965) *The Challenge of Leisure*. London, Civic Trust.

Dury, G. H. (1961) *The British Isles*, London, Heinemann.

English Tourist Board (1978) *Planning for Tourism*. London, ETB.

Eversley, D. (1972) 'Rising costs and static incomes: some economic consequences of regional planning in London', *Urban Studies* **9**, 347–68.

Form, W. H. (1954) 'The place of social structure in the determination of land use', *Social Forces* **32**, 317–23.

Fothergill, S. and **Gudgin, G.** (1979) 'In defence of shift-share', *Urban Studies* **16**, 309–19.

Fothergill, S. and **Gudgin, G.** (1982) *Unequal Growth: Urban and Regional Employment Change in the UK*. London, Heinemann.

Fothergill, S. and **Gudgin, G.** (1983) 'Trends in regional manufacturing employment, the main influences', in Goddard and Champion (eds). *The Urban and Regional Transformation of Britain*, London, Methuen p. 27–50.

Fothergill, S. and **Vincent, J.** (1985) *The State of the Nation*. London, Pan Books.

Fothergill, S., Kitson, M. and **Monk, S.** (1983) 'The impact of the New and Expanded Town programmes on industrial location in Britain, 1960–78', *Regional Studies* **17**, 251–60.

Fothergill, S., Kitson, M. and **Monk, S.** (1985) *Urban Industrial Change*. London, HMSO.

Freeman, H. (1987) 'Mental health and urban policy', *Cities* **4**, 106–111.

Friedmann, J. (1966) *Regional Development Policy,* Cambridge, Massachusetts, MIT Press.

Frost, M. and **Spence, N.** (1982) 'Regional policy in Great Britain', *Geoforum* **13**, 97–106.

Fullerton, B. (1982) *The Development of British Transport Networks*. Oxford, Oxford University Press.

GLC. *Research Memorandum RM 467, Recreationally Disadvantaged Areas in Greater London*. Report of an analysis of provision for sports and active recreation by M. Nicholls.

Gaffikin, F. and **Nickson, A.** (1984) *Jobs Crises and the Multinationals*. Birmingham Trade Union Group. Nottingham, Russell Press.

273

Garner, B. J. (1967) 'Models of urban geography and settlement location' in R. J. Chorley and P. Haggett (eds). *Socio-Economic Models in Geography* London, Methuen, pp. 303–60.

Glass, R. (1955) 'Anti-urbanism' in M. Stewart (ed.) *The City: Problems of Planning*, Harmondsworth, Penguin, pp. 63–71.

Goddard, J. B. and **Champion, A. G.** (eds) (1983) *The Urban and Regional Transformation of Britain*. London, Methuen.

Goldsmith, M. (1980) *Politics, Planning and the City*. London, Hutchinson.

Gould, A. and **Keeble, D.** (1984) 'New firms and rural industrialisation', *Regional Studies* **18**, 189–201.

Green, H. (1977) 'Industrialists' information levels of regional incentives', *Regional Studies* **11**, 7–18.

Griffiths, A. and **Wall, S.** (eds) (1989) *Applied Economics*, 3rd edn. Harlow, Longman.

Griffiths, P. (1975) Homes Fit For Heroes: A Shelter Report on Housing. London, Shelter

Gudgin, G. (1978) *Industrial Location Processes and Regional Employment Growth*. Farnborough, Saxon House.

Gudgin, G., Moore, R. and **Rhodes, J.** (1982) 'Employment problems in the cities and regions of the UK: prospects for the 1980s', *Cambridge Economic Policy Review* **8**, 1–81.

Gudgin, G., Moore, R. and **Rhodes, J.** (1983) 'The great divide', *Sunday Times*, 16 January.

HM Government (1978) *Inner Urban Areas Act*. London, HMSO.

HM Treasury (1987) (2) *Government's Expenditure Plans 1987–88 to 1989–90*. London HMSO.

Haggett, P. (1965) *Locational Analysis in Human Geography*. London, Edward Arnold.

Haggett, P. (1975) *Geography: a Modern Synthesis*. London, Harper.

Hall, P. (1966) *World Cities*. London, Weidenfeld and Nicolson.

Hall, P. (1977) 'The inner cities dilemma'. *New Society* **39**, 223–5.

Hall, P. (1981) 'The geography of the Fifth Kondratieff Cycle', *New Society* **5** (958), 535–7.

Hall, P. and **Preston, P.** (1988) *The Carrier Wave, New Information Technology and the Geography of Innovation 1846–2003*. London, Unwin Hyman.

Hall, P., Breheny, M., McQuaid, R. and **Hart, D.** (1987) *Western Sunrise: the Genesis and Growth of Britain's Major High Tech Corridor*. London, Allen and Unwin.

Hall, P., Thomas, R., Gracey, H. and **Drewett, R.** (1973) *The Containment of Urban England*, 2 vols. London, George Allen and Unwin.

Hamnett, C. and **Randolph, W.** (1982) 'The changing population distribution of England and Wales 1961–81, clean break or consistent progression', *Built Environment* **8**, 270–80.

Hanna, L. W. (1982) 'Environment and landuse', in The UK Space: resources environment and the future. J. W. House (ed.), *op. cit.* 204–81

Hansen, J. and **Hillier, W. E. G.** (1982/3) 'The architecture of community', *Architecture and Behaviour*, **2**, 5–25.

Harrison, F. (1983) 'U. K. land policies and the political parties', *Land Use Policy*, **1**, 25–33.

Harrison, P. (1983) *Inside the Inner City*. Harmondsworth, Penguin.

Harvey, D. (1972) 'Social processes, spatial form and the redistribution of real income in an urban system', in M. Stewart (ed.) *The City: Problems of Planning*, Harmondsworth, Penguin Education, pp. 296–37.

Healey, M. J. and **Ilberry, B. W.** (eds) (1986) *The Industrialisation of the Countryside*. Norwich, Geo Books.

Henwood, F. and **Wyatt, S.** (1986) 'Women's work, technological change and shifts in the employment structure', in Martin and Rowthorn (eds), *op. cit.* 106–37.

Herbert, D. T. (1982) 'The changing face of the city', in Johnston and Doornkamp (eds), *op. cit.*, ch. 10.

Herbert, D. T. and **Smith, D. M.** (1979) *Social Problems and the City: Geographical Perspectives*. Oxford, Oxford University Press.

Hirscham, A. (1958) *The Strategy of Economic Development*. New Haven, Connecticut, Yale University Press.

Hoare, A. G. (1981) 'Why they go where they go: the political imagery of industrial location', *Transactions, Institute of British Geographers* **6**, 152–75.

Hoare, A. G. (1983) *The Location of Industry in Britain*. Cambridge, Cambridge University Press.

Hoare, A. G. (1986) 'What do they make, where, and does it matter any more? Regional industrial structure in Britain since the Great War. *Geography* **71**, 289–304.

Holland, S. (1976) *The Regional Problem*. London, Macmillan.

Holland, S. (1978) *Beyond Capitalist Planning*. Oxford, Blackwell.

House, J. W. (ed.) (1982) *The UK Space: resources, environment and the future*, 3rd edn. London, Weidenfeld & Nicolson.

House, J. W. (1982) 'The regional perspective', *in ibid*, 1–87.

House of Commons (1974) Report of the Expenditure Committee, Session 1973–74, *Regional Development Incentives*. London, HMSO.

House of Lords Select Committee (1973) *First Report on Sport and Leisure*. London, HMSO.

Howard, E. (1898) *Tomorrow: a Peaceful Path to Real Reform*. Re-issued as *Garden Cities of Tomorrow* (1902). London, Faber.

Howard, R. S. (1968) *The Movement of Manufacturing Industry in the UK 1945–65*. Board of Trade. London, HMSO.

Howenstine, E. J. (1986) 'The consumer housing subsidy approach versus producer housing subsidies. International experience', *Cities* **3**, 24–40.

Hudson, R. and **Williams, A.** (1986) *Western Europe Economic and Social Studies: The United Kingdom*. London, Harper & Row.

Humphrys, G. (1982) 'Power and the industrial structure', in House (ed.), *op. cit.*, 282–353.

Humphrys, G. (1984) 'Trends in textiles', *Geography* **69** (2), 150–3.

Hunt, H. A. and **Hunt, T. L.** (1985) 'Human resource implications of robotics', *Economic Impact* **49**, 22–30.

Hurd, R. M. (1903) *Principles of City Land Values*. New York, The Record and Guide.

Institute of Family and Environmental Research (1981) *Leisure Provision and People's Needs*. Dartington Amenity Research Trust. London, HMSO.

Institute for Manpower Studies/Occupations Study Group (1986) *UK*

Occupation and Employment Trends to 1990. London, Butterworths.

Jenkins, C and **Sherman, B.** (1979) *The Collapse of Work*. Eyre. London, Methuen.

Johnston, R. J. and **Doornkamp, J. C.** (eds) (1982) *The Changing Geography of the United Kingdom*. London, Methuen.

Johnson, R and **Salt, J.** (1978) Employment Transfer Policies in Great Britain. *The Three Banks Review* 126, p 18–39.

Jones Jnr., D. W. (1973) *Must We Travel? The Potential of Communication as a Substitute for Urban Travel*. California, Institute for Communication Research, Stanford University.

Jones, E. (1966) *Towns and Cities*. Oxford, Oxford University Press.

Jones, G. P. and **Pool, A. G.** (1940) *A Hundred Years of Economic Development in Great Britain (1840–1940)*. London, Duckworth.

Jones, M. E. F. (1984) 'The economic history of the regional problem in Britain, 1920–38', *Journal of Historical Geography* **10**(4), 385–95.

Keeble, D. E. (1976) *Industrial Location and Planning in the UK*. London, Methuen.

Keeble, D. E. (1980) 'The South East, East Anglia and the East Midlands', in Manners *et al.* (eds), *op. cit.*, 101–99.

Keeble, D. E. (1981) 'Manufacturing dispersion and government policy in a declining industrial system: the UK case, 1971–76', in Rees *et al.* (eds), *op. cit.*, 197–215.

Keeble, D. E. (1984a) 'The Changing Spatial Structure of Economic Activity and Metropolitan Decline in the UK'. Paper presented at a Conference on *The Future of the Metropolis*, Technical University, West Berlin, October.

Keeble, D. E. (1984b) 'Industrial location and regional development', in Short and Kirby (eds), *op. cit.*, 40–51.

Kellett, J. R. (1969) *The Impact of Railways on Victorian Cities*. London, Routledge and Kegan Paul.

Kinsman, F. (1987) *The Telecommuters*. Chichester, Wiley.

Kirby, A. (1978) *The Inner City – Causes and Effects*. Corbridge, Retail and Planning Associates.

Kondratiev, N, (1925) 'The major economic cycles', English translation in *Lloyds Bank Review* **129**, 41–60.

Lavery, P (ed.) (1974) *Recreational Geography*. Newton Abbot, David and Charles.

Law, C. M. (1980) *British Regional Development Since World War I*. Newton Abbot, David and Charles.

Lawton, R. (1982) 'People and work', in House (ed.), *op. cit.*, 103–203.

Le Corbusier (1971) *The City of Tomorrow and its Planning*. London, The Architectural Press.

Lee, D. (1980) *Regional Planning and Location of Industry*, 3rd edn. London, Heinemann.

Leigh, R and **North, D.** (1978) 'Regional aspects of acquisition activity in British manufacturing industry', *Regional Studies* **12**, 227–45.

Lever, W. F. (1981) 'The inner city employment problem in Great Britain, 1952–76: a shift-share approach', in Rees *et al.* (eds), *op. cit.*, 171–96.

Lever, W. F. (1987) *Industrial Change in the United Kingdom*. Harlow, Longman.

Levitan, S. A. and **Johnson, C. M.** (1984) 'The future of work', *Economic Impact* **45**, 33–39.

Lewis, E. W. (1971) *The Location of Manufacturing Industry in the Western Home Counties.* Unpublished MPhil thesis, University of London.

Ley, D. (1983) *A Social Geography of the City.* London, Harper and Row.

Lowry, I. (1965) 'A short course in model design', *Journal of the American Institute of Planners* **31**, 158–66.

McCallum, J. D. (1979) 'The development of British regional policy', in Maclennan and Parr (eds), *op. cit.*, 3–41.

McCrone, G. (1969) *Regional Policy in Britain.* London, Allen and Unwin.

Mackay, R. (1976) 'The impact of Regional Employment Premium' in A. Whiting (ed) *op. cit.*, The Economics of Industrial Subsidies London, HMSO.

Mackintosh, J. P. (1968) *The Devolution of Power.* Harmondsworth, Penguin.

McLaughlin, D. B. (1985) 'The impact of micro-electronics on office jobs', *Economic Impact* **49**, 31–36.

Maclennan, D. and **Parr, J. B.** (eds) (1979) *Regional Policy: Past Experience and New Directions.* Oxford, Martin Robertson..

Maddock, I. (1978) *Technology, Choice and the Future of Work.* London, British Association for the Advancement of Science.

Marsh, P. (1981) *Silicon Chip Book.* London, Abacus.

Mandel, E. (1975) *Late Capitalism.* London, New Left Books.

Manners, G., Keeble, D., Rodgers, B. and **Warren, K**. (eds) (1980) *Regional Development in Britain*, 2nd edn. Chichester, Wiley.

Marquand, J. (1979) *The service sector and regional policy in the UK.* Research Series 29. London, Centre for Environmental Studies.

Marquand, J. (1980) *Measuring the Effects and Costs of Regional Incentives.* Government Economic Service Working Paper 32. London, Department of Industry.

Marshall, M. (1987) *Long Waves of Regional Development.* Basingstoke, Macmillan.

Martin, R. (1986) 'Thatcherism and Britain's industrial landscape', in Martin and Rowthorn (eds), *op. cit.*, 238–90.

Martin, R. and **Rowthorn, B.** (eds) (1986) *The Geography of De-Industrialisation.* Basingstoke, Macmillan.

Massey, D. B. (1979) 'In what sense a regional policy?', *Regional Studies* **13**, 233–43.

Massey, D. B. (1986) 'The legacy lingers on: the impact of Britain's international role on its internal geography', in Martin and Rowthorn (eds.) *op. cit.*, 31–53.

Massey, D. B. and **Meegan, R. A.** (1979) 'The geography of industrial reorganisation: the spatial effects of the restructuring of the electrical engineering sector under the Industrial Re-organisation Corporation', *Progress in Planning* **10**(3), 155–237.

Mensch, G. (1979) *Stalemate in Technology: Innovations Overcome the Depression.* Cambridge Massachusetts, Ballinger.

Ministry of Town and Country Planning (1945) *National Parks in England and Wales* (Dower Report). Cmnd 6628. London, HMSO.

Moore, B. C. (1986) 'Regional Development Proposals'. Paper presented to the Royal Town Planning Institute Conference, St Catharine's College, University of Cambridge.

Moore, B. C. and **Rhodes, J.** (1973) 'Evaluating the effects of British regional economic policy', *Economic Journal* **83**(329), 87–110.

Moore, B. C. and **Rhodes, J.** (1976a) 'A quantitative analysis of the effects of the Regional Employment Premium and other regional policy instruments', in A. Whiting (ed.), *op. cit.*, 191–219.

Moore, B. C. and **Rhodes, J.** (1976b) 'Regional economic policy and the movement of manufacturing firms', *Economica* **43**, 17–31.

Moore, B. C. and **Rhodes, J.** (1979) *The Impact of Regional Policy*. Unit 7, Course D323 Political Economy and Taxation. Milton Keynes, Open University Press.

Moore, B., Rhodes, J. and **Tyler, P.** (1986a) *Actual and expected manufacturing employment in the four main development area regions*. HMSO.

Moore, B., Rhodes, J. and **Tyler, P.** (1986b) *The Effects of Government Regional Economic Policy*. London, HMSO.

Morgan, K. (1986) 'Re-industrialisation in peripheral Britain: state policy, the space economy and industrial innovation', in Martin and Rowthorn (eds), *op. cit.*, 322–59.

Morris, C. (1949) *Journeys of Celia Fiennes*. London, Cresset Library.

Morse, N. C. and **Weiss, R. R.** (1955) 'The function and meaning of work and the job', *American Sociological Review* **20**, 191–8.

Moss, G. (1981) *Britain's Wasting Acres: Land Use in a Changing Society*. London, Architectural Press.

Myrdal, G. (1957) *Economic Theory and Underdeveloped Regions*. London, Duckworth.

National Science Foundation (1988) 'A widening gap', *The Wall Street Journal Report*, 14 November, R21.

National Trust (1985) *An Introduction*. London, National Trust.

National Trust (1986) *Annual Report*. London, National Trust.

Newton K. (1986) 'The death of the industrial city and the urban fiscal crisis', *Cities*, **3**, 213–18.

Nora, S. and **Minc, A.** (1978) *L'informatisation de la Société*. Documentation Francais, Paris.

North, D. C. (1955) 'Location theory and regional economic growth', *Journal of Political Economy* **63**, 243–58.

Northcott, J. and **Rogers, P.** (1984) *Microelectronics in Industry*. London, Policy Studies Institute.

Office of Population Censuses and Surveys (1986) *General Household Survey*. London. HMSO.

Office of Technology Assessment (1985) 'The emergence of computerised manufacturing', *Economic Impact* **49**, 15–21.

O'Keefe, P. (1984) *Regional Restructuring Under Advanced Capitalism*. Beckenham, Croom Helm.

Opie, I, and **Opie, P.** (1969) *Children's Games in Street and Playground*. Oxford, Oxford University Press.

Ordnance Survey (1982) *The Ordnance Survey Atlas of Great Britain*. London, Book Club Associates.

O'Sullivan, P. (1981) *Geographical Economics*. Harmondsworth, Penguin.

Pahl, R. E. (1969) 'Urban social theory and research', *Environment and Planning* **1**, 143–53.

Pahl, R. E. (1979) 'Socio-political factors in resource allocation', in. Herbert and D. M. Smith *Social Problems in the City*. Oxford, Oxford University Press, pp. 33–46

Parsons, D. W. (1986) *The Political Economy of British Regional Policy*. Beckenham, Croom Helm.

Patmore, J. A. (1970) *Land and Leisure*. Harmondsworth, Penguin.

Patmore, J. A. (1983) *Recreation and Resources, Leisure Patterns and Leisure Places*. Oxford, Basil Blackwell.

Perroux, F. (1950) 'Economic space, theory and applications.' *Quarterly Journal of Economics* LXIV, 89–104

Perroux F. (1955) 'Note sur la notion de "pole de croissance", *Economie Appliqúe* **8** 307–20

Pigram, J. (1983) *Outdoor Recreation and Resource Management*. London, Croom Helm.

Planner, The (June 1987) 'The action for cities – the government programme in England', 16–17.

Pred, A. (1977) *City Systems in Advanced Economies*. London, Hutchinson.

Prestwich, R. and **Griffiths, A.** (1989) ' Regional and urban policy', in Griffiths and Wall(eds), *op. cit.*, 354–74.

Rapoport, R. and **Rapoport, R. N.** (1975) *Leisure and the Family Life Cycle*. London, Routledge and Kegan Paul.

Ratcliffe, J. (1981) *An Introduction to Town and Country Planning*, 2nd edn. London, Hutchinson.

Rees, J., Hewings, G. J. D. and **Stafford, H. A**. (eds) (1981) *Industrial Location and Regional Systems*. Beckenham, Croom Helm.

Regional Studies Association (1983) *Report of an Inquiry into Regional Problems in the United Kingdom*. Norwich, Geo Books.

Report (1918) of the Committee on *Questions of Building Construction in Connection with the Provision of Dwellings for the Working Class* (Tudor Walters Report). Cmnd 9191. London, HMSO.

Report (1940) of Royal Commission on the *Geographical Distribution of the Industrial Population* (Barlow Report). Cmnd 6153. London, HMSO.

Report (1942) of the Committee on *Land Utilization in Rural Areas* (Scott Report). Cmnd 6378. London, HMSO.

Report (1942) of the Expert Committee on *Compensation and Betterment* (Uthwatt Report). Cmnd 6386. London, HMSO.

Report (1965) of the Committee on *Housing in Greater London* (Milner-Holland Report). Cmnd 2605. London, HMSO.

Report (1968) of the Committee on *Local Authority and Allied Personal Social Services* (Seebohn Committee). Cmnd, 3703. London, HMSO.

Rhind, D. W. (1986) 'Unreality in a regional frame', letter to the Editor, *The Times*, 13 Aug.

Rhodes, J. (1986) 'Regional dimensions of industrial decline', in Martin and Rowthorn (eds), *op. cit.*, 138–68.

Richardson, H. W. (1973) *Regional Growth Theory*. London, Macmillan.

Richardson, H. W. (1984) *Regional and Urban Economics*. Harmondsworth, Penguin.

Richardson, H. W. (1984) 'Approaches to regional development theory in Western-market economies', in Demko (ed.), *op. cit.*, 4–33.

Riche, R. W. (1983) 'The impact of technological change', *Economic Impact* **41**, 13–18.

Rivers, P. (1974) *Politics by Pressure*. London, Harrap.

Rodgers, H. B. (1969) 'Leisure and Recreation', *Urban Studies* **6**, 368–84.

Rosenberg, N. and **Frischtak, C. R.** (1983) 'Long Waves and economic growth: a critical appraisal', *The American Economic Review* **73**(2), 146–57.

Rostow, W. W. (1955) *An American Policy in Asia*. New York ch. 7

Rostow, W. W. (1960) *The Process of Economic Growth*, 2nd edn. Oxford, Clarendon Press.

Rostow, W. W. (1964) *The Stages of Economic Growth*. Cambridge, Cambridge University Press.

Rostow, W. W. (1983) 'Technology and unemployment in the Western World', *Challenge* **26** (1), 3–17.

Rowntree-York, (1902)

Rowthorn, B. (1986) 'De-industrialisation in Britain', in Martin and Rowthorn (eds), *op. cit.*, 1–30.

Sant, M. E. C. (1975) *Industrial Movement and Regional Development*. London, Pergamon.

Sant, M. E. C. (1982) *Regional Disparities*, 2nd edn. London, Macmillan.

Schumpeter, J. (1939) *Business Cycles*. New York, McGraw-Hill.

Segal Quince & Partners (1985) *The Cambridge Phenomenon, The Growth of High Technology Industry in a University Town*. Cambridge, Segal Quince and Partners.

Senior, D. (1965) 'The city region as an administrative unit', *Political Quarterly (London)* **36**, 82–91.

Short, J. R. (1984) *An Introduction to Urban Geography*. London, Routledge and Kegan Paul.

Short, J. R. and **Kirby, A.** (1984) *The Human Geography of Contemporary Britain*. London, Macmillan.

Siemens (1978) Internal report on 'Impact of Office Technology in Federal Rep. of Germany'. Discussed in Dangelmayer 'The Job Killers of Germany'., *New Scientist*, 8 June, 1978.

Simmie, J. and **James, N.** (1986) 'Will science parks generate the Fifth Wave?', *Planning Outlook*, **29**, 54–57.

Simmons, J. (1986) *The Railway in Towns and Country 1830–1914*. Newton Abbott, David and Charles.

Slowe, P. M. (1981) *The Advance Factory and Regional Development*. Aldershot, Gower.

Smith, D. M. (1971) *Industrial Location*. New York, Wiley.

The Sunday Times Book of the Countryside (1980). London, Times Newspapers Ltd.

Susman, P. H. (1984) 'Capital restructuring and the changing regional environment', in O'Keefe (ed.), *op. cit.*, 91–107.

Thirlwall, A. P. (1980) 'Deindustrialisation in the UK', *Lloyds Bank Review*, **144**, P22–37

Townroe, P. M. (1976) *Planning Industrial Location*. London, Leonard Hill.

Townroe, P. M. (1979) *Industrial Movement: Experience in the US and the UK*. Farnborough, Saxon House.

Townsend, A. R. (1983) *The Impact of Recession*. Beckenham, Croom Helm.

Trevelyan, G. M. (1964) *Illustrated English Social History: 4.* Harmondsworth, Penguin.

University of Cambridge (1980a) *UK Economic Policy and its International Context. Cambridge Economic Policy Review,* **6**, No. 1. Aldershot, Gower.

University of Cambridge (1980b) *Urban and regional Policy 1966–78. (Cambridge Economic Policy Review,* **6**, No. 2.) Aldershot, Gower.

Vedder, R. K. (1983) 'Robotics and the economy', *Economic Impact* **41**, 19–27.

Vining Jnr, D. R. and **Kontuly, K.** (1978) 'Population dispersal from major metropolitan regions: an international camparison', *International Regional Science Review,* **3**, 49–73.

Virgo, P. (1979) *Cashing in on the Chips.* London, Conservative Political Centre.

Waites, B. (1984) 'The search for Britain's regions', *Ecologist* **14**(4), 161–6.

Watts, H. D. (1987) *Industrial Geography.* Harlow, Longman.

Whiting, A. (ed.) (1976) *The Economics of Industrial Subsidies.* London, HMSO.

Wingo Jnr, L. (1961) *Transportation and Urban Land.* Washington, Resources for the Future, Inc., Johns Hopkins Press.

Zuboff, S. (1983) 'Computer-mediated work: a new world', *Economic Impact,* **41**, 33–38.

Index

Plowden Report, 237
polarisation effect, 97
Policy for the Inner Cities, White Paper
  (1977), 210
Poor Law, 112, 113, 115
population densities, 14, 15, 28, 42
Port Sunlight, 131
Preston, 133
primary activities, 13, 19, 27, 31, 33, 35, 155
prosperity sharing, 132
provincialism, 259
Public Health Act (1848), 133
Public Health Act (1875), 134

quaternary activities, 13, 19, 27, 31, 37,
  155, 207
quality of life, 57, 62, 72, 101
Queens Park Rangers, 72

railways, 22, 28, 35, 45, 46–7, 71, 72
Reading, 60
'real' regions, 261–2
recession, 27, 125, 149, 155, 158, 184, 191,
  206–7
Redcliffe-Maud Report (1969), 261
redundancy, 191, 207, 209
Reform Act (1867), 134
region, 1, 258ff
Regional Development Grants (RGGs),
  150, 153, 157, 175–6, 189, 221–3, 228, 232
regional development theories, 90
Regional Economic Planning Board,
  138–140, 142
Regional Economic Planning Council,
  138–140, 142, 150
regional economists, 89, 266
Regional Employment Premium, 142–3,
  145, 149, 183–4, 189, 223–4, 232
Regional Industrial Development (White
  Paper 1983), 109, 153
regional inequalities, 42, 91, 172, 228
regional multiplier, 95–6, 188
regional policy
active, 120–1, 184ff
criticisms, 233–4
passive, 120–1, 186ff
Regional Selective Assistance (RSA), 150,
  153, 157, 176, 189, 217, 221–3, 232
Regional Studies Association, 109, 153,
  231, 233, 260
rehabilitation, 162
relative location, 213
Rent Act (1965), 65, *164*, 237
repair grants, 65
Research and Development, 40, 224–5
resource base, 11
Restriction of Ribbon Development Act
  (1935), 136
retraining, 190
Rhind, D., 259, 266
Rhodes, J., 230

ribbon development, 51
Richardson, J. G., 131
Ridley, N., *164–5*
'right to buy' legislation, *164*
roads, 35, 211
Robson, B., 242
Rochford Council, *167*
Ronan Point, 63, *160*
Rostow, W., 93–4
Royal Commission on the Geographical
  Distribution of the Industrial Population
  – *see* Barlow Commission
Royal Commission on Local Government in
  England – *see* Redcliff-Maud Report
Royal Commission on the State of Towns
  (1844–5), 131, 133
Royal Town Planning Institute, 241
rural depopulation, 33, 42
Rural Development Areas, 178
Russell, R., 68

Salford, 242
Saltaire, 131
Salt, T., 131
San Francisco, 245
San Francisco Bay Area Transportation
  Commission, 253
Santa Clara Valley, 245–6, 251, 252
Scarborough, 69, 71
School leavers, 149, 192, 224
Schumpeter, J., 5, 245
science parks, 202
Scotland, 15, 33, 61, 62, 76, 109, 204–5,
  214–5, 223
Scott Report, 55, 74, 75
seaside towns, 196
secondary activities, 13, 19, 2k7, 31, 35, 37,
  155, 207
Secretary of State for Scotland, 76
Seebohn Report, 237
Select Committee on the Health of Towns
  (1840), 133
Selective Employment Payments Act
  (1966), 142, 183–4
Selective Employment Premium, 142, 144,
  183, 214, 223–4, 232
Selective Employment Tax, 142, 144, 183
Selective Financial Assistance, *see* also
  Regional Selective Assistance) 145
Senior, D., 102–3, 261
service jobs, 37, 39, 207ff, 257, 266
Shaftesbury, Lord, 132, 133
Shaw, B., 84
Sheffield, 153, 155
Shift-share analysis, 205
Shore, P., 60, 240
simplified planning zones, 241
Sinclair, Sir C., 248, 252
Slowe, P., 204, 205
social engineering, 135, 136
Social Science Research Council, 237

Wheatley Act (1924), 53
White Paper on Central Scotland (1963), 129, 211
White Paper on Control of Land Use, 74
White Paper on Employment Policy (1944), 120–1, 191
White Paper on Investment Incentives, 70, 144
White Paper on North East England (1963), 129, 211
White Paper on Policy for the Inner Cities (1977), 210
White Paper on Regional Industrial Development (1983), 109, 153, 260
White Paper, DTI – The Department of Enterprise (1988), 157

Wigston Magna, 43
Wilmslow, 60
Wingo, L., 102
Winchester, 45, 251
Wolverton, 46
Women, 28, 205, 210
Worker midgration, 173
Worthing, 70

Youth Employment Subsidy, 149
Youth Opportunities Programme (YOP), 192
Youth Training Scheme (YTS), 192
Yorkshire, 57, 61, 62
Yorkshire Dales, *168*, 253, 255